THE WOMEN OF ROYAUMONT

THE WOMEN OF ROYAUMONT

A Scottish Women's Hospital on the Western Front

Eileen Crofton

TUCKWELL PRESS

First published in 1997 by
Tuckwell Press Ltd
The Mill House
Phantassie
East Linton
East Lothian EH40 3DG
Scotland
Copyright © Eileen Crofton 1996
All rights reserved
ISBN 1 898410 86 0
British Library Cataloguing-in-Publication Data
A Catalogue record for this book
is available on request from the
British Library

The right of Eileen Crofton to be identified
as the author of this work has been asserted
by her in accordance with the Copyright, Design and Patent Act 1988

The publishers acknowledge subsidy from

THE SCOTTISH ARTS COUNCIL

towards the publication of this volume

Typeset by Falcon Oast, East Hoathly, East Sussex
Printed and bound by Cromwell Press
Melksham, Wiltshire

To Miss Helen Lowe MBE, who has done so much, and still battles to keep alive the memory of Dr Elsie Inglis. Without Elsie Inglis there would have been no Women of Royaumont and no story to tell.

Also to John who has shared 50 years with me, and to our children, Richard, Patricia, Pamela, Alison and Ian, who have contributed greatly to my education.

CONTENTS

Foreword

It is a privilege and honour to commend this book to all who are interested in the changing and important role of women in our society. *The Women of Royaumont: A Scottish Women's Hospital on the Western Front* began from a chance encounter but clearly it became a labour of love and scholarly research as the story unfolded. This is a tale of achievement that is worthy of remembrance and admiration. It is based on records and well-preserved correspondence as well as upon the vivid memories of survivors. 'These quiet women ... were the true pioneers. They did not call upon the world to listen to what women might, could or should do under quite different conditions; they simply did – under the existing conditions – first the thing that needed to be done, then and there.'

The tranquility and beauty of the thirteenth-century Cistercian Abbey, open-air treatment in the cloisters, professional excellence, appetising food and a happy atmosphere engendered by leadership of the highest calibre were therapeutic, but physical conditions were daunting. The bitterly cold winters, large draughty rooms, shortages of fuel, mediaeval plumbing and cooking facilities, no lifts and back-breaking tasks of carrying hot water and stretchers up long stone stairways, preparation of wards, operating theatres, makeshift x-ray rooms and a pathology laboratory in a dusty and long uninhabited monastery called for fortitude, determination, ingenuity and the courage to endure things which could not be altered.

In spite of these handicaps, the hospital remained open from January 1915 until March 1919. It became in the end the largest continuously operating voluntary hospital in France with 600 beds. The Commandant, Miss Frances Ivens, was asked to open an ancillary casualty clearing station and also a canteen to meet the needs of French soldiers in transit for whom social amenities, even bare necessities, were woefully deficient. The unit became an example for its orderliness, efficiency and clinical services. It was one of the few centres chosen by the Pasteur Institute in Paris for pilot studies of anti-gas gangrene serum.

Being near the front line, the hospital and its outlying unit were designated as casualty clearing stations. Such establishments were described in the British History of Army Medical Services as 'the pivot on which the system of collecting and evacuating the sick and wounded turned'. Periods of intense activity when the working hours of the doctors exceeded those in the British Army hospitals alternated with periods of inactivity as lines of battle changed. Both situations demanded courage, discipline and endurance, not only from those in the hospitals but also from the ambulance drivers maintaining vehicles and ferrying seriously injured men through dangerously unsafe roads.

In all, 10,861 patients were admitted to Royaumont and the ancillary hospital at Villers-Cotterets. 8,752 were soldiers, mainly from the French and French Colonial Armies, with a few British and American men and German prisoners of war. The death rate among the injured servicemen was 1.82%, a tribute to the surgical and nursing skills of the staff, especially when one takes into account the number of very serious injuries. The higher death rate of 4.37% amongst the 527 civilian inpatients who were admitted in quiescent intervals probably reflected the different age groupings and hardships of civilians. In addition, 1537 civilians attended as outpatients.

The *esprit de corps* of all categories of staff was a remarkable feature of this group. The sense of community included the patients, the local villagers and notable helpers including the fearless Curé and Chaplain to the hospital, M. L'Abbé Rousselle. This bond of unity was to last beyond World War Two in the Royaumont Association. Much is owed to the personality and wisdom of Miss Ivens, who led by example, and recognised that each member of staff had a vital role to play. She had the support of a sensible Committee at home. Her task was not easy. The demands of the surgical work and administration were pressing and not all her colleagues were easy-going and adaptable. It is fitting that the book includes short biographies of these splendid women and their helpers. It also takes account of the entertainments, ceremonial parades when staff and patients were decorated by France, and the humour that lightened the atmosphere.

Much has changed since 1915. Women now have the vote, women doctors are no longer a relatively rare species, often viewed with distrust, although the prejudice against women surgeons has not completely disappeared. They are now commissioned in the Royal Army Medical Corps, whereas their services had been rejected in World War One. The chauffeuses of Royaumont demonstrated that they were able mechanics and drivers. The organisation of smooth and speedy transport of the injured is recognised as a priority. Meticulous débridement of injuries remains essential, but the repeated and daily dressing of wounds is no longer practised, thanks to antibiotics and the seminal work of the late Professor Joseph Trueta, the surgical hero of the Spanish Civil War.

Some things are unchanging in times of crisis, such as the need for courage, compassion and the rare gifts of common sense and humour. This book pays tribute to these qualities, shown so eminently by the women of Royaumont, and will ensure that their memory remains a green and pleasant one.

Ruth E. M. Bowden
OBE, DSc, FRCS
Emeritus Professor of Anatomy (RFHSM, University of London), Former President of Medical Women's Federation, currently Hon. Archivist, Royal Free Hospital School of Medicine

Preface

This book arose quite by chance – a perfect example of serendipity.

A last-minute decision to attend a conference of the European Medical Association on Smoking and Health in 1990 led me to a totally unexpected sequel: some years of growing discovery and excitement, numerous interesting contacts and some valued friendships as the story gradually unravelled.

The conference was held in the beautiful Cistercian Abbey of Royaumont about 30 miles north of Paris, now a delightful cultural centre and an important tourist attraction. Arriving in thick mist on a dark November day, its beauty was not immediately apparent, but on succeeding days a conducted tour in better weather revealed the glorious architecture of the thirteenth-century building in its lovely setting among trees still resplendent in their autumn colours and the surrounding canals and waterways in the grounds. We were told the story of the Abbey – and, as an aside to me, and because I came from Scotland – our guide pointed out the plaque in a dark corner which commemorated the fact that the abbey had been a military hospital during the First World War, and was a 'Scottish Women's Hospital'. This, however, was not considered sufficiently important to be conveyed to the rest of the international group.

I was so intrigued by this that on my return home I began to make enquiries and to read the early accounts published in 1917 and 1919,[1] from which I learned the names of a few of the women who served there, and some basic facts although seen through slightly suspect rose-coloured spectacles.

As a medical woman – and proud of what medical women have contributed to medicine – my first intention was to concentrate on this particular aspect of the story of the hospital. I had not gone far, however, when I discovered that the part played by women doctors – of crucial importance as it was – was only a part of the story. I became more and more involved with all the women who were engaged in a unique and extraordinarily successful enterprise. I decided then that it was the story of this community as it evolved over the years of war that was the story I wanted to tell. It also became clear to me that the story had been forgotten. In the abbey itself, only the bare fact of its existence seems to be known. To most people in this country, if they have heard of the Scottish Women's Hospitals at all they recall the tremendous retreat from Serbia over the mountains in 1915, the gallantry of Dr Elsie Inglis and her tragic death on landing in England in 1917 after the retreat of her hospital from Russia. This story has now been told,[2] but the story of Royaumont is a fascinating one on its own and deserves a fuller study. I have tried to do justice to it. It begins by focusing on the events in the hospital throughout the war, as well as the almost insuperable difficulties faced by the pioneers in setting up their hospital and the problems arising from an unexpected increase in the numbers of patients as the French authorities were discovering how inadequate their own medical service was to cope with the numbers requiring treatment. The increasing competence of this woman-staffed hospital throughout 1915 prepared them for their remarkable achievements during the 1916 Battle of the Somme. Although 1917 proved a relatively quiet period in spite of the desperate fighting further north, they expanded their activities by opening a canteen in war-damaged Soissons and, at the request of the French, set up a hospital at Villers-Cotterets near the front line as a casualty clearing station. The rapid German advances in 1918 led to an enormous volume of work in the parent hospital at Royaumont, the evacuation of Villers-Cotterets, and a subsequent period of tremendous stress which bore comparison with the work of British front-line casualty clearing stations though without the reserves which the Army could provide.

The book goes on to discuss the personalities and careers of some of the very interesting women involved, both medical and non-medical. It concludes with an account of the adventures of a few of the now much older Royaumontites caught up in events in France in May and June, 1940.

As is often the case in wartime conditions, there were periods of intense pressure and periods of comparative quiet and inactivity. These two aspects of life called for adaptability and qualities of character in those who participated.

One of the outstanding features of this story is the gradual emergence of a strong and unique sense of community which lasted not only throughout the period of active service, but which persisted for many years afterwards through their formal links by means of the Royaumont and Villers-Cotterets Association and their friendships, often lifelong. It must be almost unique that a wartime association should persist as theirs did, with regular newsletters and meetings until as recently as 1973.

The strong sense of community – not always to be seen in an all-woman setting – was remarkable. It must have owed much to the quality of their 'Chief', Miss Ivens. It must also owe something to the fact that they knew, and were proud, that they were doing a well-worthwhile job, one that was recognised and highly valued by the French authorities and in all the villages around who benefited by the presence of 'Les Dames Anglaises'. To be a 'Royaumontite', to be the recipient of the medal of the Scottish Women's Hospitals, and, for some of them also, medals from the French Government, was a distinction and source of pride in their later lives.

The hospital was what they made it. Its success – and it *was* a success – was theirs and belonged to them all. They were dependent on their own resources and could not summon outside help in times of crisis. The success of the hospital depended on all the different departments. Efficiency in the kitchen and the clerical department was no less important than in the departments concerned with the direct care of the patients. There was mutual respect, which existed despite occasional misunderstandings, some of which are recorded in the story. That there should also be some misunderstandings with the Committee at home is not surprising, but it was a tribute to the members of the Committee who visited from time to time that a fuller appreciation of the difficulties faced by the Unit working in what was in fact a totally unsuitable building led in most cases to their resolution.

The history of these women illustrates the changing role of women in the early part of the twentieth century and, in particular, the impact of the war. For many, probably all of them, their experiences at Royaumont formed a watershed in their personal lives. For some it opened new windows of opportunity; for others their return to civilian life brought less change than they might have expected and perhaps hoped for.

---

1. Antonio de Navarro *The Scottish Women's Hospital at the French Abbey of Royaumont* (Geo Allen and Unwin, 1917) and Mrs Eva Shaw MacLaren, *A History of the Scottish Women's Hospitals* (Hodder and Stoughton, 1919).
2. Dr Leah Leneman, *In the Service of Life: The Story of Dr Elsie Inglis and the Scottish Women's Hospitals* (Mercat Press, 1994).

Acknowledgements

I am sometimes overwhelmed by the number of people who have helped me in the writing of this book. I am grateful to all of them and only hope that I have not betrayed their trust in me.

I owe a big debt of gratitude to Miss Helen Lowe who generously placed at my disposal her Register of the Royaumont staff, her collection of Newsletters of the Royaumont and Villers-Cotterets Association and other material and whose unfailing interest has greatly encouraged me.

Dr Leah Leneman shared with me much material arising from her own researches on the Scottish Women's Hospitals which was relevant to Royaumont. Although we shared information, I am conscious that the debt was very much on my side.

I would also like to thank Dr Harold Swan, Hon. Archivist of the University of Sheffield, for his continuing interest and listening ear, and Professor Alexander Fenton, Director of the European Ethnological Research Centre, for reading my text, encouraging me, and making many useful suggestions.

I acknowledge with gratitude the enormous help of my publisher, John Tuckwell, who has shown unending patience in guiding a tyro through the mysteries of publishing. Any deficiencies that remain are mine, certainly not his.

Finally I am grateful to Professor Ruth Bowden for much useful advice, and am honoured that she has written an introduction to the book.

Among the individuals I acknowledge the help of: Mrs Audrey Acland, daughter of Orderly Starr; M. l'Abbé Bigo, Presbytère de Viarmes; Mrs Mona Calder, daughter of Orderly Watt; Dr Hilda Cantrell and Dr James Carmichael for memories of Miss Ivens and Miss Nicholson; Mr Samuel Courtauld, great-nephew of Dr Courtauld; Dr Betty Cowan, for information on Dr Guest at Christian Medical College, Ludhiana; Mrs M. Crowther, daughter of Dr Hamilton; Mr Tam Dalyell, Mr Wm Dalyell and Dr Martin Davey for information on Dr Elsie Dalyell; Mme Marie-Christine Daudy, daughter of M. Henri Gouin, and granddaughter of M. Edouard Gouin for a tour of the Abbey and making it possible to examine the Visitors' Book; Sir Alastair Denny, for information on Orderly Denny; Mr Harold Francis FRCS and the late Professor Sir Norman Jeffcoate for information on Miss Ivens; Mrs Morag Fairlie, niece of Chauffeur Smeal; Mr Wm Garrett, son of Dr Lillie; Mr James Gray and Mrs Gray, formerly Cook Simpson; Dr Jean Guy for information on Edith Stoney; Miss Rachel Hedderwick, daughter of Cook Littlejohn; Mrs M. Kappagoda, for information on Dr Hendrick; Miss Heather Mackay, niece of Auxiliary Nurse Chapman; The late Dr Grace Macrae, formerly Orderly Summerhayes; Mrs Amy Maddox and Mrs Sue Morris, nieces of the three Inglis sisters; Mlle Maloum-Gerzo, of the Abbey of Royaumont; Mrs Anne Murdoch, daughter of Dr Henry; Mrs Margaret Nisbet, daughter of Orderly Manson; Mrs Margaret Oddy, daughter of Sister Dunderdale; Mr David Proctor, nephew of Orderly Proctor; Miss Mary Pym for information on Miss Ivens; Dr Elizabeth Rees, for information on Miss Ivens and Miss Nicholson; Ms Margaret Randall, niece of Orderly Davidson; Mr G. D. Richardson for information on the Dalyell family; Mrs Catriona Reynolds, niece of Orderly Nielson-Gray; Dr Ann Shepherd, niece of Dr MacDougall; Mrs Ailsa Tanner, granddaughter of Mrs Robertson; Dr J. F. Tessier for advice on French writing on the First World War; Dr Christopher Silver, for a photograph of Miss Ivens; Dr I. Simmonds, son of Chauffeur Banks; and Miss M. P. Simms, niece of Orderly Simms.

I acknowledge also the help of many institutions, libraries and museums: Mr Adrian Allen, Assistant Archivist, University of Liverpool; Mr Michael Barfoot, Edinburgh Medical Archives Centre, University of Edinburgh; Mme Thérèse Blondet-Busch, Musée d'Histoire Contemporaine, Photothèque de l'Hotel National des Invalides, Paris; Mr Peter Carnell, Library Archivist, University of Sheffield; Mr D. M. Cook, Librarian, Liverpool Medical Institute; Mr David Dougan, Librarian, Fawcett Library, London Guildhall University; Miss Joan Ferguson, former Librarian and Mr Ian Mills, Librarian, and his staff, Royal College of Physicians of Edinburgh; Miss A. Fletcher, Medical Librarian, Royal Free Hospital School of Medicine; Dr Leslie Hall and Miss S. M. Dixon, Contemporary Medical Archives Centre and Mr Wm Schupbach of the Iconographic Collection, Wellcome Institute for the History of Medicine; Mr Graham Hopper, Dumbarton District Library; Dr Elizabeth van Houts, Archivist, Newnham College, Cambridge; Mr Peter Liddle, Keeper of the Liddle Collection of First World War Archive Material, Leeds University; Mr Colin McLaren, Head of Special Collections, University Archivist, Aberdeen University; Mme Annick Perrot, Conservateur du Musée Pasteur, Paris; Mrs Kate Perry, Archivist, Girton College, Cambridge; Mr Simon Roberts, Department of Documents and Mrs Hilary Roberts, Department of Photographs, Imperial War Museum; Ms Margaret Robins, Archivist, Women's College Hospital, Toronto; Mr M. A. M. Smallman, Sub-Librarian, Queen's University, Belfast; Mr K. E. Smith, Archivist, University of Sydney; Mr Robert Smith, Keeper of Muniments, University of St Andrews; Mr Alastair Tough, Archivist, Greater Glasgow Health Board, University of Glasgow; Dr Ian White, Hon. Archivist, St John's Hospital for Diseases of the Skin, St Thomas's Hospital, London; Miss Hazel Wright and her staff, Department of Rare Books and Manuscripts, Mitchell Library, Glasgow; and to the staff at the National Library of Scotland, the Edinburgh Central Library and the French Institute, Edinburgh.

Abbreviations

ADF	Association des Dames de France
CC	*Common Cause*. Journal of the NUWSS, 1914–1919
IWM	Imperial War Museum, London. Collection of Documents. SWH Collection
L (RFH) SMW	London (Royal Free Hospital) School of Medicine for Women
ML	Mitchell Library, Glasgow. Department of Rare Books and Manuscripts. SWH Collection. Held in numbered tins and boxes, approximately in date order, but not further catalogued
MWF	Medical Women's Federation
NL	Newsletters of the Royaumont and Villers-Cotterets Association, 1923–1973. Held in Liddle Archive of First World War, University of Leeds SWH Collection. Box Miss Miller
NUWSS	National Union of Women's Suffrage Societies
RTO	Railway Transport Officer
SWH	Scottish Women's Hospital(s)
VAD	Voluntary Aid Detachment

Illustrations

PART ONE

The Hospital

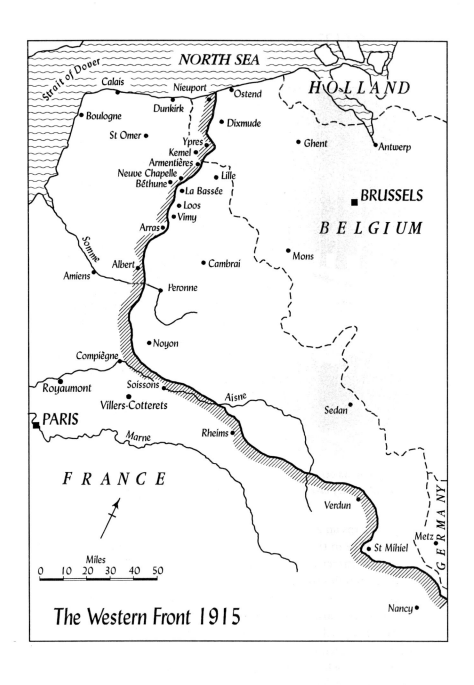

NORTH SEA

Strait of Dover

Calais

Nieuport

Ostend

HOLLAND

Boulogne

Dunkirk

Dixmude

St Omer

Ypres

Ghent

Antwerp

Kemel

Armentières

Neuve Chapelle

Lille

Béthune

La Bassée

BRUSSELS

Loos

Vimy

BELGIUM

Arras

Somme

Albert

Cambrai

Mons

Amiens

Peronne

Noyon

Compiègne

Royaumont

Soissons

Aisne

Villers-Cotterets

Sedan

PARIS

Marne

Rheims

FRANCE

Verdun

Metz

St Mihiel

GERMANY

Miles

0   10   20   30   40   50

Nancy

The Western Front 1915

CHAPTER ONE

THE STORY BEGINS

The Abbey of Royaumont in winter. Beautiful at all times of the year, it has changed little externally over the years. (By courtesy of Miss Heather Mackay).

This story concerns an abbey, a hospital, some women and the war.

It all took place in the Abbey of Royaumont, one of the most beautiful of all the lovely Cistercian abbeys of France. Set in gently rolling wooded country some 30 miles to the north of Paris, in the Département of Seine-et-Oise, it is still in relatively unspoilt country. The continual expansion of Paris, drawing ever closer since the First World War, has not yet engulfed it, though the nearby villages are gradually losing their local character. The roads are now of a quality that would have aroused the envy of those women ambulance drivers who, dodging potholes, tried to protect their wounded passengers from the jolts and bumps of the 12-mile journey on atrocious roads from the railhead at Creil.

The train service nowadays is perhaps not very much better than the one they knew. But for those travelling to and from Paris in the First World War it must have been a very much more beautiful journey than it is now, especially in Spring when the orchards were in flower.

The journey from England now is, however, very different. A rapid and comfortable flight to Charles de Gaulle airport, bears no comparison with the crowded cross-Channel steamers with the ever-present danger of submarines, and the slow, and often devious, journeys by train to Paris and on to Viarmes.

Today the air traveller can look down on a cross roads, where he can see, clearly visible, the Royaumont Monument, marking the limit of the German offensive in 1914 and commemorating those who died in the hospital. And if he is quick enough he might also catch a glimpse of the Abbey of Royaumont itself, among its trees and its landmark *flèche*.

The forests where the women loved to wander and picnic are still there, but the trenches they sometimes explored are gone. There are possibly fewer of the wild flowers that so delighted them. Did they, perhaps, gather too many of the lilies-of-the-valley? We know that the *poilus* (the French private soldiers) were allowed to do so, and that they delighted in offering great bunches to the sisters and orderlies. The beauty of the unspoilt countryside in those days made an unforgettable impression. In Spring and Summer they remembered:

> The fields blue with cornflowers and scarlet with poppies – the woods carpeted with cowslips, lilies of the valley, dwarf daffodils, and all made gayer and more exciting by gorgeous butterflies, dragon flies and moths.[1]

And in November:

> I have no words to tell of the beauty of that Autumn forest [the forest of Beaumont]. The hush of St Luke's peace was over all the forest, that dream beauty which comes with a still November, a kind of hushed period of farewell when the tattered banners of scarlet and gold hang on the edge of the winds. A perfect sunset lit the forest aisles with subtle light ... and the misty blue distances between the tree vistas had the spell of moonlight on them. The names too of these forest alleys were a perpetual delight to me – imagine such a light shining along the 'Route de la Pierre Turquoise'. In these woods Blanche de Castille used to ride on her white palfrey. When we emerged from the wood a new beauty awaited us, a great copper moon rising on the loops of the Oise – Seen through the straight poplars it was like a Japanese painting ... That ride home through the little village of Beaumont and by the Oise in the last lingering purple twilight and glorious moonlight was unforgettable.[2]

THE SCOTTISH WOMEN'S HOSPITAL FOR FRANCE.

The Scottish contingent leaving Waverley Station, Edinburgh, on December 2 1914.
Miss Mair, President of the Scottish Federation of the National Union of Women's
Suffrage Societies sees them off. (In centre, in hat).
Published in Edinburgh Evening News March 12 1914.

The trees in front of the Abbey, in their Spring or Autumn foliage, shrouded in snow, or sparkling with frost, are the same ones they saw nearly 80 years ago; and the canals and waterways around the Abbey buildings, where convalescent *poilus* so hopefully went fishing, are there still.

The buildings themselves struck every newcomer then as they still do today with their beauty. The cloister court is unchanged, though the rose garden has disappeared. In imagination the visitor can picture the cloister court filled with beds, and patients lying there experiencing the healing power of the sunshine and the lovely surroundings and the nights of peace and quiet. 'On moonlit evenings', Navarro tells us, 'the scene was one of indescribable beauty. The old grey masonry, assuming then a ghostly pallor, shone like marble in the dark, shimmering sky.'[3] The terrace above the cloisters, where they used to sit and rest and chat, has now been removed – it had been a nineteenth-century addition. Behind the present buildings there is a field where a crater remains from a shell which landed in 1918.

The interior of the buildings is now much changed. The entrance hall, so large and impressive in the hospital era, has been divided, but happily concessions to modern ideas of comfort have not gone so far as to install a lift. The visitor must still climb 71 steps to the second floor, and is thankful not to be burdened with a heavy patient on a stretcher. Nor, with modern heating and plumbing, must fuel and water be carried up all those stairs.

The hospital wards are recognisable from their beautiful vaulting and ornamental pillars. How impossible it must have been to black out those tall Gothic windows when the Zeppelins and Gothas were overhead.

The well-heated bedrooms with their ensuite bathrooms are a far cry from the primitive conditions of wartime, and would have seemed an unbelievable luxury to the women who strove to keep themselves warm and clean in those early days. Perhaps also they might have envied the sanitary arrangements enjoyed by the monks of the thirteenth century who were provided, in what is now known as the *Maison des Latrines*, with no fewer than 60 seats placed back to back and draining into a canal. A generous allowance, it would seem, for 180 monks! How useful these would have been for the patients. Sanitary arrangements were pretty primitive and the graceful lectern in the refectory was later used as a convenient depository for bedpans![4]

All those coal-burning stoves seen in the old photographs, with the flues finding their way out through the old stone walls, are gone without a trace. Gone also is the monstrous stove in the kitchen on which Michelet, the renowned chef, used to dance, and gone also is the sink. Instead there are priceless mediaeval tapestries, and a superb fifteenth-century statue of the Virgin and Child.

Standing in the great Refectory, or perhaps enjoying one of the concerts that frequently take place there, the visitor requires a keen imagination to picture it when it was a ward of wounded, often desperately wounded, men; beds on each side and a row down the middle – 100 in all: brilliant scarlet bed covers against the soft grey of the old stone and Gothic pillars and a giant Canadian flag reminding us that this was the 'Canada ward'. It must have looked even more colourful at Christmas time when it was decorated with great branches and bunches of mistletoe, and how beautiful it must have been when the old Curé celebrated Mass in the candlelight.

One visitor, who was herself a part of that wartime community, tells us what it was like to be a part of that great endeavour:

> I dreamed dreams of a grey, dusty austere Royaumont, where eager grey, blue and white figures hurried about, intent and tight-lipped, or enthusiastic and laughing; rows of red-blanketed beds in the quiet nights and the soft pad of feet and the long shadows moving on the high stone walls; of a purpose and unity of mind; of life and of death and of memories too deep for words ... something of which nobody left in the whole building knows.

On his tour of the Abbey the observant visitor might notice a rather worn and inconspicuous plaque, the plaque which first roused my interest in the Abbey:

Ici de 1915 à 1919 Miss Frances Ivens CBE MS Lond étant Médicin-Chef

du Scottish Women's Hospital établi dans l'Abbaye de Royaumont par la
bonne grace de son propriétaire M. Edouard Gouin et la generosité de
donateurs Britaniques et Alliés.

Dix mille huit cents soixante et un soldats français blessés reçurent
d'un personnel exclusivement feminin les bienfaits d'un dévouement sans
limite.

What was this hospital? And who were these women?

The History of the Abbey[6]

The Abbey was founded by Louis IX of France (later known as Saint Louis) in
1229. His father, Louis VIII, had the ambition to endow a monastery. When
he died, his 12-year-old son lost no time in carrying out his wishes, with the
help of his redoubtable mother, Blanche de Castille.

The little boy took his duties seriously. The Abbey was to be under the
Cistercian order that called for simplicity as a reaction to the Cluniac foundations which had become over-elaborate and decorative. However, as this
was to be a royal foundation, simplicity was somewhat modified. It was to be
known as Royaumont, or Mons Regalis (though there is little evidence of a
mount). It was well-endowed – in fact its subsequent history showed that it
was too well-endowed.

It is told that the boy king would ride over to the Abbey from his nearby
castle at Asnières, mingle with the labourers (lay brothers) and encourage
them to greater efforts. He would himself push a wheelbarrow loaded with
stones (as the orderlies at the hospital had to manhandle heavy stones when
they were struggling to prepare their hospital). He would rebuke those who
made too much noise, or rested from their labours. 'Monks keep silence, and
you should be silent', he told them; and 'Monks don't rest, you ought not
to rest'.

With or without this encouragement the Abbey church was ready for
dedication on Sunday 19 October 1235 (an event which the hospital staff
commemorated almost 700 years later in 1915). It was dedicated to the
Holy Cross, Our Lady and All the Saints. King Louis donated a piece of
the True Cross, a fragment of the Crown of Thorns, some relics of St
Thomas of Canterbury, and some relics of St Agnes. It is interesting in
view of the later history of the Abbey that there was a female input into
its dedication.

Many stories are told of Louis' piety. He took part in the Cistercian custom
of washing the feet of the poor (in a later chapter Orderly Starr records how
she washed the feet of the wounded *poilus*). Louis, in an excess of zeal, wanted
to go further to demonstrate his humility by washing the feet of the monks.
He was restrained, however, by the Abbot, who suggested some people might

speak ill of it – in other words he might be accused of showing off.

Louis used to visit the infirmary, and with his own hands prepare food and place it carefully in the mouth of a leper, removing any grains of salt which might cause pain. (One will be reminded later of Starr's special patient with the wounded mouth whom she fed so patiently and carefully – fortunately with more success than St Louis with his leper.) Like the orderlies 700 years later, St Louis swept the floors, and at mealtimes carried his plates to the *guichet* (hatch) into the kitchen – the very same *guichet* through which meals passed when the monks' refectory was used as the staff dining area before it was transformed into the large Canada ward during the Somme offensives. Sometimes St Louis would read to the monks from the pulpit where later the orderly Don, a trained opera singer, delighted her listeners on Christmas Eve 1917.

King Louis died at Tunis on the Second Crusade, but his endowments to the Abbey were continued and even increased. Unfortunately its wealth attracted attention, and the initial period of devotion and austerity gave way to laxity and a falling away from its lofty ideals.

During the Hundred Years' War the Abbey underwent a hard time, and in 1240 was even occupied by the English for a short period – the last British occupation before that of the Scottish Women's Hospital from 1914 to 1919.

In 1516 the King gained the right to appoint 'Commendators'. These appointments, being highly profitable, were much sought after, and were a useful source of patronage for the king. Religious duties were not required, and commendators could be responsible for the worldly affairs of a number of abbeys. Some of the commendators surrounded themselves with 'une agrèable et joyeuse societé'. Cardinal Mazarin, already abbot-commendator of a number of abbeys, added Royaumont to his list. For reasons best known to himself he handed Royaumont over to the ten-year-old Prince of Lorraine in whose family it remained when it became a beautifully furnished *maison de plaisance*. A later abbot was not content with the abbey as it stood and built a palace (later known as the 'Chateau') alongside. However, he was not to enjoy this. The French Revolution broke out. He fled to Austria where he was reported to have died in misery.

In 1790, when there were only 10 monks remaining, the National Assembly decreed the destruction of the Abbey Church. This was duly carried out in 1792 – only the north-east tower was too strong for them and still stands today as the *flèche*, the emblem of Royaumont.

The Abbey was sold, its contents scattered, and a cotton mill installed. Later, in the nineteenth century, pavilions in the grounds were popular holiday resorts for fashionable Parisians. In 1864 the Abbey was sold to the Oblate Fathers, and then in 1869 to the Sisters of the Holy Family. It was a religious building once more. Much preparatory work was done after the damage caused by the industrial installations but the return to a religious use was not to last. In 1905 a law was passed against religious orders and the Sisters had to leave for Belgium. The property was bought by M. Jules Gouin (who already owned the Chateau). It lay empty until the outbreak of war. By this time it was the property of M. Edouard Gouin, his son, and it was he who offered it to the French Red Cross which led to the 'occupation' of the Scottish Women's Hospital for the next four-and-a-half years.

The Origins of the Scottish Women's Hospitals

The Scottish Women's Hospitals of the First World War were the inspiration of one remarkable woman. On the outbreak of war Dr Elsie Inglis conceived the idea of setting up hospitals that would be run exclusively by women, and offering them for service in the war effort. She carried through her project until her own tragic death in 1917, but she had laid such firm foundations that Scottish Women's Hospitals continued in active service up to and beyond the end of the war.

It was a magnificent achievement, especially in the face of society's attitudes towards women, and particularly medical women, in the early years of the twentieth century.

The nineteenth century had seen many struggles by women to raise their standards of education, to widen the opportunities for women in employment, and to correct at least some of the injustices they suffered regarding property and other rights. By the end of the century women had gained access to universities. After a long, and sometimes bitter struggle, they were able to qualify in medicine and, by having their names on the Medical Register, be legally entitled to practise medicine. When Elizabeth Garrett Anderson gained admission to the Medical Register in 1865, she was only the second woman to do so. The medical profession were perturbed, they closed ranks, and denied women access for the next twelve years. But others were pressing hard on the closed door and Elsie Inglis was one of the early pioneers to do so.

In Edinburgh Sophia Jex-Blake, having won her own personal battle for registration in 1877, was battling with the Edinburgh medical establishment to get instruction, practical experience and access to examinations for women students. Elsie Inglis was one of her students. At an early age Elsie showed the stuff of which she was made when she, with others of her fellow-students, rebelled against Jex-Blake's autocratic ways and, with outside help, set up a rival, successful, Medical College for Women in Edinburgh. She herself qualified in 1892, and set up practice. She was successful and did much social and medical pioneering work for poor women in the slums of Edinburgh.

She soon became involved in the campaign for votes for women, and in due course became the Honorary Secretary of the Scottish Federation of Women's

Suffrage Societies whose President was Miss Mair, a granddaughter of Sarah Siddsons, the unquestioned queen of the stage from the late eighteenth century until her death in 1831. Miss Mair had played a notable part in the campaign for women's education in Scotland. The Scottish Federation was allied to the National Union of Women's Suffrage Societies (NUWSS), whose President was Mrs Millicent Fawcett, a younger sister of the pioneer Dr Elizabeth Garrett Anderson. The policy of both these organisations was to pursue their aims through peaceful and constitutional means. These were the 'suffragists'. For some women these methods were too slow. Mrs Emmeline Pankhurst and her daughters founded the Women's Social and Political Union (WSPU) which adopted militant tactics and became known as the 'militant suffragettes'. These women became increasingly active in the years before the war, and gained considerable notoriety. They actively sought imprisonment and caused the government of the day more than a little embarrassment through their policy of going on hunger-strike when they were imprisoned.

On the outbreak of war, however, both these groups, militant and non-militant, caught up in the general outburst of patriotic feeling, resolved to lay aside their campaigns for the vote, and devote themselves to the war effort. (There were, however, some among them who remained totally opposed to the war.) To Dr Elsie Inglis this seemed a golden opportunity not only to further the war effort (which she supported), but also to demonstrate what women could achieve, particularly in a field of medicine where they might have an opportunity to show their skills in areas other than the traditional ones of caring for women and children. Dr Anderson had no doubts either. She was an old lady of 80 on the outbreak of war but she told the volunteers, 'My dears, if you are successful over this work you will have carried women's profession forward by a hundred years'.[7]

Elsie Inglis was an achiever. She had determination, and she knew how to be ruthless when she thought it necessary. She had a remarkable gift of persuading others to do what she wanted, she could gain support from influential people, and she could attract devoted followers. In addition she never spared herself.

Even before the war she was involved in the training of young women for Voluntary Aid Detachments, but on the outbreak of war she envisaged something much more ambitious.

In Edinburgh, on August 12th 1914, at a meeting of the Scottish Federation, the scheme began modestly enough with a proposal from Dr Inglis 'that the Federation should give organised help to Red Cross work'. Miss Mair, the President, then proposed that the empty St George's School in Melville Street (the school for girls which she had helped to found, and which had moved to new premises) should be applied for and equipped as a hospital. One can almost feel Dr Inglis' mind leaping ahead as she then proposed 'that Melville Street should be equipped as a hospital staffed entirely by women – and if not required at home should be sent abroad'.[8]

Finding that the school building in Edinburgh was not available, she then proposed, with the backing of the Committee, to offer the proposed unit of 100 beds to the War Office or to the Red Cross. Both offers were summarily turned down ('Go home and sit still' was the oft-quoted phrase). There was no interest in a hospital staffed by women.

She decided, again with her Committee, to offer units to France and to Serbia – her plans were growing day by day.

On 15th October she wrote to the French Ambassador in London:

> I am directed by the Executive of the Scottish Federation of Women's Suffrage Societies to ask Your Excellency's consideration of our scheme for organising medical aid for the help of our Allies in the field.

> The Federation proposes to send out hospital units, officered by women doctors, and staffed by fully trained nurses and properly qualified dressers. The Units will be sent out fully equipped to nurse 100 beds. Should Your Excellency's Government desire such aid as we are proud to offer, it will be very willingly placed at the service of the French Red Cross. Our Units will be prepared to move from place to place as the exigencies of war may require, and to utilise such buildings as may be placed at our disposal.[9]

A similar letter went to the Serbian authorities. Both offers were accepted. In both countries it was recognised that their medical services were very inadequate. The Serbian story is a fascinating one, but is not the subject of the present book.[10] Dr Inglis now had the enthusiastic support of the NUWSS, and they agreed on an appeal for 'Scottish Women's Hospitals for Foreign Service'. Meetings were arranged, including a very large one in London on October 20th, where she outlined her plans to a big audience.

Back in Scotland a specially convened Committee, the Scottish Women's Hospitals Committee, was organised to receive donations and offers from volunteers. Sub-committees were set up to deal with hospitals, personnel, equipment, uniforms and cars. Premises were obtained in St Andrew's Square, Edinburgh, gifted by the Prudential Insurance Society.

Excitement was mounting – money was flowing in; by October 30th Common Cause (the journal of the NUWSS) announced: 'Dr Inglis has got her first £1000! One hospital is secure and will go to Serbia'. There were plenty of volunteers – 'surgeons, nurses, medical students and members of Voluntary Aid Detachments ... there is no doubt of success in this way ... but many more are needed'.

The press work in the NUWSS offices in London was co-ordinated and master-minded by V.C.C. Collum, who was to play a major role in the subsequent history of Royaumont.

By November 6th £2,800 had been collected; they were now aiming at three hospital units (the figures seen very small to us; they were estimating £1000, later £1500, to equip each 100-bed unit). By November 13th two units were ready.

By November 20th Common Cause reported that Madame de la Panouse, President of the French Red Cross, was actively seeking a building which would accommodate the unit of these 'Dames très sérieuses', and by November 27th the decision had been taken that it should go to the Abbey of Royaumont. With £5,500 in hand they felt confident that they would be able to make a beginning, though aware that fundraising would be a continuing and demanding task.

So, by the end of November, the links between the Abbey and the Scottish Women's Hospital were firmly in place, and the foundation had been laid for its distinguished future which was to last longer than anyone conceived at the time.

The War

It is now time to examine the military situation in Northern France from the outbreak of war in August 1914 until the arrival of the hospital and the reception of the first patients in January 1915.

This was one of the most dramatic periods of the war. It was in essence a war of movement, not to be repeated until the German onslaughts of 1918 and their subsequent repulse.

After the declaration of war on Germany on August 4th by Britain and Belgium the so-called 'Battle of the Frontiers' began on August 14th. The Germans advanced rapidly, sweeping all before them. Amiens, Soissons, Laon and Reims fell; British and French forces were in retreat and Paris itself was threatened. What had seemed to be an inexorable advance was, however, halted by what has been described as 'a combination of misjudgements of the German High Command and a piece of brilliant opportunism on the part of General Gallieni, the Governor of Paris'. He launched the successful 'Battle of the Marne', checked the German advance, and saved Paris. This 'Miracle of the Marne' signalled the end of the war of movement and initiated the horrors of trench warfare. In the first five months it was reckoned that the French lost 300,000 men killed, including 5,000 officers, and 600,000 men were captured, wounded or missing.

In September the Germans made a great effort to reduce Antwerp (in which they succeeded in October), and destroy the Belgian Army. The German cavalry, the Uhlans, swept across to the Belgian coast. With the Allies in full retreat the Uhlans ranged at will over North-West France. It must have been at this time that they bivouacked in the Abbey — and left behind quantities of straw and other debris for the first orderlies to clear.

The German advance had in fact drawn very close to Royaumont. On September 4th 1914 they reached the crossroads only a mile from the Abbey. This is recorded on the Scottish Women's Hospital Monument erected here after the war:

> Le quatre septembre 1914 l'ennemi est venu jusqu'ici. La victoire de la
> Marne l'empêche d'aller plus loin'.

It was here also that, in the absence of the Mayor of Asnières who had fled, the dearly loved Curé had stood for several days ready, if it should prove necessary, to plead with the German commanders for the safety of his village. He knew what had happened to the mayor of Senlis. (See Chapter 9).

By the end of 1914 stalemate had been reached; both sides were beginning to dig in, and it was not until February 1915 that fighting was renewed. By this time Royaumont was just beginning to get organised.

The story of the Abbey, the hospital, the women and the war had begun.

References

1. NL 1973, p. 7, Mrs Falconer (née Manson).

2. Mrs Robertson. Letter 10 Nov 1916, by kind permission of Mrs Ailsa Tanner.

3. Navarro, *The Scottish Women's Hospital at the French Abbey of Royaumont*, p. 171.

4. Personal communication, Dr Grace Macrae (née Summerhayes).

5. NL 1950, p. 3. Mrs Haydon (née Richmond).

6. Information drawn from Henri Gouin and Claude-Jacques Damme, *Royaumont. Mons Regalis*. Editions Valhermeil 1990.

7. Royal Free Hospital Press Cuttings, Book 5 p. 86.

8. McLaren, *A History of the Scottish Women's Hospitals*, pp. 4–7.

9. ML Tin 49, Inglis to French Ambassador, 15.10.14.

10. Leneman, *In the Service of Life*.

CHAPTER TWO

The Hospital That Went to France

The recruitment of volunteers destined for the Royaumont Unit proceeded apace and by mid-November selection was complete.

In the first instance the Unit was to consist of seven doctors, ten nurses, seven orderlies, two cooks, a clerk, an administrator, two maids and four chauffeurs. Two of these chauffeurs were men, as there was some doubt whether the French authorities would permit women to drive in the war zone. (Later all the chauffeurs were women.)

The great experiment began.

On December 2nd the Edinburgh *Evening News* published a photograph of the Scottish contingent leaving Waverley Station, Edinburgh for London. Six nursing sisters, three orderlies and two cooks were seen off under the benevolent eye of Miss Mair, President of the Scottish Federation of the National Union of Women's Suffrage Societies. In their long skirts, sensible shoes, hip-length cloaks with velvet collars and tartan facings, and their broad-brimmed hats, they looked both determined and doubtful. Perhaps some of the doubtful expressions arose from the uncertainty as to how precisely they should position their hats. Miss Mair clearly had no hesitation as to how hers should be worn (p.5).

What were the motives that led them to volunteer? It could be adventure, an opportunity for a more varied experience than life had so far offered them, a response to the wave of patriotism that was sweeping the country, or because they were strong supporters of women's suffrage. Dorothy Littlejohn, a highly trained cook from the Edinburgh College of Domestic Science, was certainly no supporter of women's suffrage. She was actively opposed to the idea. Moreover she did not approve of women doctors. This was strange as her father was the great Sir Henry Littlejohn, the first Medical Officer of Health for Edinburgh and one of the most distinguished Medical Officers of Health at the time. After initial hesitation about female doctors he had become a strong supporter of Sophia Jex-Blake in her prolonged and traumatic campaign to obtain medical education for women. His daughter clearly had very different ideas. Indeed Dorothy Littlejohn's daughter relates how furious her mother was that on arrival in London the party was 'paraded' before Mrs Millicent Fawcett in the offices of the NUWSS. She wanted no part of that.[1]

The Doctors

Who were these seven doctors who were pioneering the entry of women into totally new fields of activity? Fields that they had probably never even imagined a few short months before?

The appointment of Miss Francis Ivens[1] as Chief Medical Officer (Médecin-Chef) was almost certainly the most crucial one in effecting the transformation of a small medical unit into a hospital of 600 beds which was later described as 'the crack hospital of the war'. At the age of 44 she had an established position as consultant obstetrician and gynaecologist in Liverpool. She had been a brilliant student at the London School of Medicine for Women and a Gold Medallist of London University. In addition she was only the third woman in the UK to obtain the degree of Master of Surgery. She had been keenly interested in the suffrage movement (the non-militant wing) for a number of years and on the outbreak of war had volunteered her services to the Women's Unit in Belgium under the leadership of Mrs Stobart. However, the German advance had led to the withdrawal of the Unit before Miss Ivens could join it. She was then free to volunteer for the Royaumont Unit.

Miss Ruth Nicholson, a graduate of Durham University, had worked in the mission field in Palestine where she had gained wide surgical experience. She later became second-in-command at Royaumont and served continuously until 1919 when the hospital closed.

Dr Agnes Savill, one of Glasgow University's most distinguished women graduates, was a consultant in London with a high reputation in Dermatology and Electro-therapeutics. This involved radiological work, and it was in that capacity that her expertise was so valuable in Royaumont. Her connection with Royaumont was maintained throughout the war, though not on a continuous basis. Her credentials in the women's suffrage movement were impeccable, as she had been one of three (the other two being distinguished male surgeons), who, in 1912, conducted an enquiry into the appalling treatment of women hunger-strikers in prison.

Dr Winifred Ross had been resident surgeon in Paisley Parochial Hospital after her graduation from Glasgow University. Her surgical experience included the treatment of male patients, an area which some regarded at that time as too indelicate for women! Dr Berry (née Augusta Lewin) had been a fellow-student of Miss Ivens and had public health experience. She served right through to the summer of 1918. Dr Hancock had been Resident Medical Officer at the Hospice in Edinburgh. This had been founded by Dr Elsie Inglis as a surgical and gynaecological service for women, and a centre for district midwifery. It was in an area of appalling

---

1. I have used the title 'Miss' for the chief surgeons (Ivens and Nicholson) in accordance with British custom. All others are referred to as 'Dr'.

poverty and overcrowding. She would have known Dr Inglis well. Dr Heyworth had only recently qualified and it was intended she would work in a junior capacity as a 'dresser'.

Such was the initial medical team; most of them will become familiar as the story unfolds.

Departure

The Edinburgh contingent joined up with members coming from other parts of the country and proceeded to Folkestone accompanied by Dr Inglis herself who had come to see them off. (She herself followed a few days later.) There was, on that Friday, a terrific gale blowing. The Army decided that it was too rough to embark the troops, but Dr Inglis was insistent that her women would sail, come what may. She was not one with whom new recruits were prepared to argue, so on they went. Hatches were battened down and the wise ones took their seasick pills. After a 'simply terrible crossing' lasting three hours longer than scheduled, they landed at Boulogne and began the struggle with Customs and red tape. Littlejohn was in better shape than most (she had taken her 'Mothersill'), and also spoke some French, so it was left to her to negotiate with the authorities. This done, they proceeded to Paris.[2]

Dorothy Littlejohn was not exaggerating the severity of that storm. The following morning Sister Martha Aitken in Boulogne (who had no connection with the SWH) wrote in her diary:

> All night long it has blown a gale and the big windows in the casino shook very much. Every minute I expected to see them blown in. Rain, thunder and lightning accompanied the wind. The sea is lashed into a white fury and below the casino one can see the spray dashing the sea wall. The hospital ship had taken refuge in Boulogne Harbour. During a flash of lightning one can see the white cliffs of Dover. Towards morning we hear several guns being fired and two rockets sent up. I expect it is some poor ship in distress. Poor souls on a night like this.[3]

Cicely Hamilton, travelling a few days earlier than the main Unit to take up her duties as Clerk, also had a rough crossing. Looking back in 1946, she remembered:

> the tumbling steamer as it neared the harbour, making wide circles to avoid the mines. The unfamiliar faces of Indian soldiers looking down from a familiar Boulogne quay, the slow devious journey to Paris – devious because mainline bridges had been blown. And finally Royaumont – picturesque, impressive and most abominably chilly.[4]

Meanwhile in Paris, Miss Ivens and a few others who had travelled with her had learned that their equipment had not arrived; that its whereabouts were

unknown; that M. Gouin, the owner of the Abbey, had accommodated Cicely
Hamilton, the Clerk, and Mrs Owen, the Administrator, in his own part of
the Abbey as a temporary measure, but that he could offer no further
accommodation; and that he strongly urged them not to come. This was not
in accordance with the ideas of Miss Ivens who elected to proceed regardless
of the warnings. She was as determined as Dr Inglis herself to get on with the
tasks ahead and it was no part of her plan to idle in Paris while work was
waiting to be done. If there were no beds for her staff, she could buy mattresses, stuff them with straw, carry them by train, and lay them on the floor.
So this is exactly what they did.

Early Experiences

This early experience in the Abbey was not what they expected.

On December 11th Littlejohn was writing home to her fiancé:

> This Abbaye is 1½ miles from Viarmes, such a nice little country town,
> with quite good shops. The Abbaye itself is charming with lovely old
> cloisters and a real old-fashioned garden with a little fountain in the
> middle. The inside rather appals one at first, it's so very large and so
> many odd staircases etc; in fact it is very eerie, especially as there is no
> light anywhere at the moment, and, as you know, a candle doesn't give
> much. ... The room I had felt very musty and in the morning my dress
> felt so damp I was afraid to get into it so what the uninhabited portion
> will be like I dread to think.[5]

They had set out from home under the impression that the Abbaye de
Royaumont was 'a fine house with ample accommodation, good drainage and
water supply, and electric lighting'.[6] There was no Trades Description Act in
those days, and they found the facts far otherwise. It was correct in only one
respect. It did have ample accommodation.

Apart from the deficiencies of water, heating and lighting, the Abbey was
in a deplorable condition with the accumulated dirt of years. Debris in the
vast rooms of the building included masses of heavy masonry on the ground
floor and straw and rubbish left behind by the Uhlans who had bivouacked
there during the Battle of the Marne.

On December 17th Cicely Hamilton reported:

> Those first few days at Royaumont I shall always look back on as an
> experience worth having. In surroundings of mediaeval grandeur – amid
> vaulted corridors, gothic refectories and cloisters – we proceeded to camp
> out with what we carried. The Abbey, in all its magnificence, was ours;
> but during those first few days it did not offer us very much more besides
> magnificence and shelter. It had not been lived in for years and its water

supply had been practically cut off when the nuns left for Belgium. Hence we carried water in buckets up imposing staircases and along equally imposing corridors. Our only available stove – a mighty erection in the kitchen which had not been lit for a decade – was naturally short-tempered at first, and the supply of hot water was very limited. So, in consequence, was our first washing; at times very limited indeed. Our equipment, after the fashion of baggage in these times of war, was in no great hurry to arrive; until it arrived we did without sheets and blankets, wrapped ourselves in rugs and overcoats at night, and did not do much undressing.[7]

And Littlejohn, working as cook in the kitchen, confirms:

I had an awful morning trying to get food ready, with a plumber every now and then putting my fire out. We have got a huge chef's range, in fact some of the parts are so heavy it is quite difficult for women to shift them. You see, in this place, there is really nothing to work with until our things arrive from Edinburgh, so, for 25 people, we are cooking with two small pans, some rather wee bowls of the country, a kettle and that's all. The dishes are equally scarce, so it's a case of eternally washing up and also double meals and really by the time we have cooked and fed all that lot we are almost past food, but don't think I am grumbling; it will be better later on. ... This kitchen is a huge place with lovely arches and a nice door into the garden. At present we have nothing but candles, so it looks very gloomy, but they are going to put in a certain amount of electric light and also putting in a kind of hot water system which will be a comfort as at present every drop of hot water has to be specially boiled and also the kitchen is the only place you can get any at all.[8]

Cicely Hamilton had more to say about the difficulties:

We borrowed teacups from the village ironmonger, and passed the one knife around at meals for everyone to have a chop with it. We are as short of lamps as we are of knives – shorter; and we wandered about our majestic pile with candle-ends, stuck in bottles; little twinkling candle-ends that struggled with the shadows under the groined roofs ... we are getting electric light in now, and already I find it in my heart to regret those bottled candles with their Rembrandtesque effects. Two of them, faintly dispersing the gloom at one end of the vaulted kitchen – while the pillars climbed to lose themselves in the blackness ... I try to console myself for their loss by reflecting that the staring electric bulbs are more practicable for hospital purposes. But I am glad that I saw the kitchen before the bulbs were put in.
    We did not easily get our staring electric bulbs; nor did we easily get

our water laid on, our drains attended to, or broken windows mended. We live, you see, in the land of compulsory military service – where the plumber, the glazier, the electrician can only attend to your wants when he has not been ordered to the colours ... Our preparations have been slow – but if they have been slow they have been sure. Drains, water, heating, lighting – everything in spite of the difficulties, is finally getting itself done. A few days ago our equipment condescended to arrive – and now we have knives all round and blankets and towels.[9]

Looking back in 1955 Mackay (clerk 25.1.15 to 14.7.17) remembers 'when we scrubbed the floors by candlelight, the candle moving along as the scrubbers progressed'.[10]

This was the situation with which Miss Ivens, who had the ultimate responsibility, had to cope. Some of this emerges in her regular reports to the Scottish Women's Hospital Committee in Edinburgh. With her characteristic understatement she reported on 6th December that Royaumont looked lovely but was 'rather uncomfortable owing to lack of household implements'.[11]

She had much to do. She made a tour of inspection with M. Gouin, the owner, and his architect, M. Pichon (who became a very good friend to the hospital). They discussed the best way to heat such an impossibly large and draughty building.

Anthracite stoves were to be installed and a hot water system was planned

The doctors in 1915 in the Abbey cloisters. Sitting, Miss Ivens. Standing, from left to right, Dr Savill, Dr Nicholson, Dr (Mrs) Berry, Dr Ross and Dr Hancock. (By permission of the Imperial War Museum).

with top priority for the operating theatre. Sanitary arrangements were reviewed. The discovery of a bye-law whereby no sewage could be discharged into the river was a near disaster (M. Gouin himself was unaware of this) and threatened the very existence of the hospital. A second and more welcome discovery that there were cesspits underneath the Abbey averted this, and arrangements were made to adapt the plumbing accordingly. Sanitary facilities were never more than barely adequate at Royaumont. At one point Miss Ivens was even contemplating military-style earth closets, but this desperate measure seems to have been avoided. It was all a far cry from the original arrangements of 60 seats for the 180 monks in the thirteenth century.

Miss Ivens visited nearby hospitals to see how a French hospital was run. She had to negotiate a written legal agreement with M. Gouin. It was settled amicably that they could have the use of the Abbey for a year or 'as long as the war lasts'. (No one expected this would be another four-and-a-half years.)

She learnt that permits would be required from Army authorities before they could collect patients from the railhead at Creil, and there were doubts whether women drivers would be acceptable. She found that doctors had to provide evidence that they were properly qualified. This would have been easy if they had known beforehand, but Paris had to be searched to find a copy of the British Medical Register.[12]

On December 11th the missing equipment – such as it was – arrived, but not surprisingly there were gaps. The Committee had done its best, but they had a formidable task and no model to follow. The staff became skilled at improvising:

> Until a fire shovel appears Miss Hamilton replenishes it [the stove] with morsels of slack (stolen from the kitchen) with an ancient soup ladle.[13]

When the x-ray room was fitted up a fish kettle served as a cistern for the development of the films. The developing was done at first in a cupboard where a forgotten cold water tap was discovered.[14]

Dr Inglis visited the hospital and did her best to speed up the supply of certain items, particularly cars, for which she had left instructions before she left Edinburgh. She scolded the Committee for the delay: 'There is a perfectly magnificent opportunity before us if we can seize it ... we have made a really good start ... Royaumont is *perfect* and if we can get enough motors it will be one of the finest hospitals in France'.[15]

Miss Ivens had to decide the allocation of the various rooms. There was plenty of scope for choice as, in the first instance, they were only planning 100 beds. However, a thirteenth-century abbey did provide problems with dampness, dirt, general decrepitude and an extremely complex layout.

She selected rooms on the dry upper floors and one room on the first floor which, between them, could accommodate 100 beds. These were fitted with stoves, electric light and primitive bathrooms (though they did not actually contain baths). They were scrubbed, scrubbed and scrubbed again. When the equipment arrived it was carried up the stairs by the women. They were proud of their work and what they had achieved in such a short time. The wards, they thought, looked most welcoming with the scarlet coverlets on the beds, bedside tables, dressing trolleys and screens in place.

A Setback

The hospital had to be inspected by the Service de Santé of the French Red Cross before it could be passed to receive patients. This inspection took place on December 24th. To the great disappointment of all who had worked so hard, it was not successful. Only the ward on the first floor, Blanche de Castille (named after the mother of St Louis) was passed. The Inspectors from the Sanitary Department of the Military Government of Paris couched their report in no uncertain terms. They wrote that apart from the beds in the wards, the installation was incomplete. The bottles in the pharmacy were still lying on the floor. The fittings of lavatories and bathrooms were rudimentary; the x-ray apparatus was still to be fixed up. They criticised the reception arrangements as too far from the entrance. The second-floor wards, aired and lit by skylights, and with sloping roofs, provided insufficient air for patients. They called them the 'cowsheds'. Other smaller rooms designed for isolation were quite unacceptable. Nothing could have been more definite – 'This floor is not favourable for hygiene or health'. 'It is a pity', they went on, 'that by too much haste in the very praiseworthy intention of rapidly forming an auxiliary hospital the organisers did not think of grouping the rooms and to keep them close to the service rooms.' They disliked the slow-combustion stoves – 'most troublesome from the point of view of health, dangerous and should be forbidden'. They wanted porcelain wood burning stoves and porcelain sanitary fittings.[16]

It was a bitter blow. Littlejohn, from her kitchen, wrote home indignantly:

> The top wards we considered ideal were condemned. Simply disgusting, after all the hard work the nurses have had with them, and stoves and electric light put in and bathrooms made – one ward passed and now they have to make some very large and damp rooms on the ground floor turned into wards.[17]

The feminist Collum was more outspoken: 'Brass-hatted inspectordom', she fumed, and 'Blame the women.[18]

Miss Ivens herself, while not accepting every point, realised there was some sense in the Inspector's report. It was disappointing but 'we are not taking official snubs too much to heart', she wrote to Dr Inglis on January

2nd ... 'I am determined to carry the thing through against all obstacles'. She was big enough to admit that she had made a mistake in her initial allocation of rooms and regretted that 'the change to downstairs was not done at once'.[19]

Not surprisingly there was a slump in morale. They were all extremely tired and personality problems arose. For instance:

> Both Miss Swanston and I [Littlejohn] feel utterly disgusted with it all
> and that we are being of no use but to feed a lot of quarrelling women ...
> If we don't get wounded soon Miss S and I think we might look for
> something else ... I wouldn't mind slaving away all day if the place were
> full of soldiers, but these women, no![20]

In spite of her grumbles Littlejohn was much appreciated by the orderlies and when she left to get married after the expiry of her six-month contract the orderlies presented her with a travelling clock inscribed 'To the hand that fed us, Orderlies, Royaumont 1915'. This remains a treasured possession in her family.[21]

The cooks were cheered by a gift of mistletoe from a grocer woman (the trees around the Abbey are full of mistletoe), decorated with flags and ribbons.

At this point the magnificent leadership qualities of Cicely Hamilton and Miss Ivens revealed themselves. The Unit was to have the most superb Christmas festivities that could possibly be organised, and the disgruntled cooks rose to the occasion and excelled themselves with traditional Christmas fare. Cicely Hamilton brought all her experience of acting, play-writing and producing to design a Pageant of the History of the Abbey through the ages.

It was a turning point. When it was over the Unit was more able to face the tremendous task the Inspectors had left them of preparing the ground-floor wards. All the clearing, cleaning and scrubbing was still to be done.

Two large rooms to the left of the entrance were now prepared to be the 'Marguerite d'Ecosse' and 'Jeanne d'Arc' wards, and a smaller room sepa-rated off from the entrance by a red curtain was for the reception of the patients. Beyond were the rather primitive bathrooms. The entrance hall was designed to impress visitors with the beauty of the inside of the build-ing. The Gouins sent some of their beautiful furniture and they planned in due course to include potted palms as decoration. Altogether there were now 96 beds.

Things were now moving in the right direction. The operating theatre, sterilising room, dispensary and x-ray room were complete and the second inspection was awaited with some anxiety. On December 31st Miss Ivens wrote that the workmen were finishing, but there was still no coal, anthracite or wood, and washing was 'a problem'.[22] Littlejohn could confirm this:

The great excitement today (20.12.14) was I had a bath for the first time for a fortnight ... I managed my canvas bath ... I have set a fashion, everybody is clamouring for a loan of my bathroom.[23]

And again on December 26th:

Yes, I have to use my canvas bath and find it very nice indeed, it's nearly always out on loan as I and one of the doctors are the only ones to have baths.[24]

Sister Jeffrey spoke later of 'the monthly bath in Paris'.[25]

Miss Ivens and Dr Savill took their difficulties to Dr Robinson, President of the British Red Cross in Paris. He explained there was constant antagonism between the civil and the military authorities: 'Dr Savill and I are both quite jolly for we realise we are not the only sufferers'.[26]

On January 7th M. and Mme. Gouin made their final inspection and declared themselves highly delighted. Mme. Gouin was reported to have said, 'You English are so practical', and M. Gouin found the sterilisers for the instruments 'le dernier cri'. Miss Ivens herself felt 'the despised bathrooms were much cleaner already'.[27]

Things were looking up. Coal arrived, and on January 6th the second inspection took place, this time without a hitch – 'how nice he was, such a contrast to General Février – delighted with everything'.[28] Formal permission to admit patients arrived on January 10th. They could now call themselves Hôpital Auxiliare 301 (HA 301).

They had to face yet another inspection – this time from Dr Coussergues, the head doctor from the *gare régulatrice* (distributing station) at Creil, who would be responsible for the allocation of patients to them. The Director – or *'gestionnaire'* – at Royaumont (the official appointed by the French Red Cross to look after military documentation etc.) had advised Miss Ivens, 'It is more important to be on good terms with this man than the President of the French Republic'. Fortunately when he came, 'the stoves did not smoke and the x-rays worked beautifully'. Dr Coussergues was fully satisfied with all he saw and was specially delighted with the x-ray installation which was the only one in the neighbourhood.[29]

Meanwhile Miss Ivens and the *gestionnaire* travelled round the neighbouring villages in the Gouins' pony-carriage. They visited the mayors and the curés, introducing the hospital. Miss Ivens was well-received and was touched when she was presented with one franc from a French workman – the first French donation.

Miss Ivens also visited the evacuating hospital in Creil where patients were held until a decision was made as to their destination. 'Very rough and ready', was her verdict. There were a lot of sick, but some of the hospitals in the area were refusing to take them. 'Isn't it horrible of them?' she wrote. Later she

The hard-working ambulances were well cared for but do not give the impression of great comfort for the wounded. This may have been one converted from a private car. Later they were purpose built.
(By permission of the Imperial War Museum).

visited another French hospital and watched some operations: 'Their methods do not appeal to me'. Another hospital – this time at Senlis – was 'appalling'. Royaumont was looked upon as a 'palace' in comparison.[30]

Miss Ivens had a heavy responsibility. Other members of the Unit – nurses, orderlies, doctors and cooks – had the hard physical work. There were no great comforts for the staff. The kitchen floor was awash with water from the sink which tended to drain on to the floor. Clogs brought in from the village solved that particular problem until more definitive arrangements could be made. On the domestic front two old women were employed to wash clothes and linen in the river. They were known as Mesdames Frotter as they used the time-honoured method of rubbing the clothes to clean them. Later local enterprise in the village provided a more effective service. Water remained a problem. Even some months later members of the Unit 'were requested to avoid all waste of water: it is not suggested that they should cease to wash, but they must wash with discretion and economy'.[31] Drainage was a particular worry for Dr Berry with her background in public health. She was remembered afterwards for cleaning out the drains herself – she was always ready to turn her hand to any task that needed doing.

In January a new orderly (unidentified) was writing home:

> Such a lovely old place, but Mon Dieu, the cold. We three sleep in an
> enormous room with a window at one end ... Last night we slept with all
> our worldly goods on top of us ... our mattresses are made of straw and
> smell of the stable ... the cooks, Miss Swanston and Miss Littlejohn make
> their orderlies work like slaves.[32]

And Littlejohn complained they had to give up the help of a French woman
in the kitchen when the new orderlies arrived – 'most willing and know nothing so it's been a hard week for us'.[33]

In the early days – and indeed for a long time afterwards – staff recall using
the same enamel plate for meat and pudding, and responding to the calls for
help in washing up – which was a greasy and a not very salubrious business.
Doctors, nurses and orderlies, with much ingenuity, 'furnished' their respec-
tive sitting rooms and sleeping quarters. Packing cases were much in demand
and valuable bits and pieces were 'acquired' from some rooms containing
household junk discarded from the neighbouring chateau.

The accounts were the responsibility of Cicely Hamilton who proved to
have a flair for bookkeeping, a surprising talent for one who had made her
reputation in acting and playwriting. One of her very enjoyable duties was
her monthly trip into Paris to have her accounts audited.

Fuel was a major problem. The Germans were occupying France's coalmin-
ing areas and it was a cold winter. Some hospitals in Paris were even closing
down as a result. Coal had to be brought from England, and transport was
difficult until a motor lorry was acquired, and the chauffeurs had to add this
to their long list of heavy duties. In one 'crise de charbon' the chauffeurs
loaded 1-cwt sacks of coal (15 sacks to the lorry) – unloaded it – and returned
to the depot for more until 20 to 40 tons had been carried, and the emergency
– for a while – overcome.[34]

This lorry was the result of a campaign by the chauffeurs who objected
strongly – and very reasonably – to carrying heavy goods in their ambulances
when 'these cars had been bought with our hardly saved money and personal
sacrifice for the beloved *poilu*'. These personally-owned cars were converted
into ambulances each to carry four stretchers. Later purpose-built ambulances
were provided which were the property of the SWH. One chauffeur, Prance,
tells the story of how they persuaded their Médecin-Chef to write to the
Committee and request a lorry:

> An ambulance was ordered to take Miss Ivens to Clichy Hospital, go on
> to the vegetable market while she was at the operations, and pick her up
> on the way home. That vile road, all cobbles and pot-holes ... The chauf-
> feur [it was Prance herself] bent down to the clock on the dashboard, put
> it forward ten minutes, and smeared its face with an oily rag. With a

cheery 'Good morning' the Chief took her uneasy seat on the unsprung, thinly cushioned board next to the driver. Pleasant conversation beguiled the way along the Paris road till the turn was reached down that shocking street through Clichy, a 2-mile martyrdom, 'How are we for time?' Hastily polishing the clock face with a driving glove – 'Good gracious! – We shall be late – I mustn't on any account keep those doctors waiting – AS FAST AS YOU CAN!' Followed a furious drive, at express speed, twisting this way and that in a vain endeavour to avoid potholes, but succeeding only in plunging into the worst ones, to right and left we swung. Our poor Chief was hurled against the wooden side, flung up to the roof, hell for leather we went, and presently arrived bruised and breathless at the hospital. The Chief straightened her hat and entered the hospital … The chauffeur put the clock back. … On the return journey, the Chief – 'I don't think we should drive so fast now, there is no hurry really'. Then, as we turned into the Royaumont road: 'I see what you chauffeurs mean, this road is terrible, we must not use ambulances for this work (the marketing) – a lorry is a necessity – I shall go in to Creil with one of you anyhow and cable straight away for a LORRY!'[35]

The chauffeurs (they preferred this term to 'chauffeuses') were in a way a breed apart. They were required to be at least 24 years of age (Prance was almost 40). They were recruited from a class well-enough off to be accustomed to driving; many of them had their own cars. The British War Office refused Dr Inglis's offer of a hospital as is well-known, but they also refused passes to the women to drive their own vehicles in the French Military Zone. Yes, they could *ride* in their own cars, but men must drive them. As Collum reported – 'Dr Inglis only grinned! "It will be alright" she assured them, and it was'.[36] Once in France, the owner-drivers were able to snap their fingers at London. These independent-minded women were also able to hold their own with the French military authorities. Marjorie Young (chauffeur 5.10.15 to 1.7.17 and 3.11.18 to 23.3.19) was instructed by a French soldier that it was not possible for her to go along a certain road. 'Pour moi tout est possible', she said, as she let in her gear and drove off.[37] Their independence was fostered by the fact that, at least for most of the time, they had their own quarters in the Abbey stables. They had their own timetable as casualties usually arrived at the railway station at Creil, 12 miles away, late at night or in the early hours, and patients who were to be evacuated left in the early evening. So meals were eaten separately, and there was little mixing with other members of staff.

Some of the orderlies, perhaps brought up with rather traditional views, looked a little askance at these women. One was seen smoking a pipe. 'Could they be suffragettes?' they wondered.[38] They were accomplished drivers and were also responsible for the maintenance of their vehicles and minor repairs.

It was because of the uncertainties regarding the use of women as drivers that the all-woman principle was waived and two men were employed as chauffeur-mechanics. Later these became an embarrassment to Miss Ivens. The women had proved their worth and she felt they could do anything the men could do to keep the cars on the road. She made her views clear to the Committee in August 1915:

> It places me in a very awkward position to have useless men hanging about when we have any of the French authorities here if they are of military age, for there is a distinct feeling that England is not doing its utmost and it is most humiliating – not only that, but it does not look well to pose as a woman's hospital and yet have men here ... it exposes us to criticism.[39]

The Uniform Controversy

Perhaps it is not surprising that the choice of uniforms was one that aroused many grumbles, considerable controversy, opposing viewpoints, offended sensibilities and general dissatisfaction and ill-feeling between those in the field and the Committee at home. After all they were volunteers, they were not under military discipline and had very different perspectives on dress.

The uniform which was selected by the Committee, and which was to be made by Edinburgh tailors, consisted, for the doctors, of a formal grey coat and skirt with facings of Gordon tartan. This was one bone of contention as Miss Ivens herself registered a personal objection to wearing tartan.

One of the first complaints passed back to the Committee was by Dr Inglis herself:

> I want a decision about the uniform. The stuff is shoddy and the sewing coming undone. Not a single collar fits – in fact – as Dr Ivens has said "It is a mercy Royaumont is in the country – for we could not go out of doors in Paris". ... We were told that we were paying 5/- a yard for that stuff – which I have no doubt we were, but that it was worth 5/- a yard is simply not the case. Imagine coats and skirts that are not fit to be seen after a month's wear.[40]

And Miss Ivens to Dr Inglis on December 31st 1914:

> I think if the doctors had a well-cut grey tunic each nearly tight to the throat, with a belt, it would add to their comfort very much, for one is really ashamed to appear before the outside world in our present garments ... I don't think there is much wrong with the nurses. The chauffeurs have had to get hold of khaki overcoats. [This was a

requirement of the military authorities.][41]

Later the chauffeurs also had to get rubber boots and heavy goatskin overcoats to protect them from the cold during their night work in freezing winters. And in 1918 when they were driving under bombardment they were issued with steel hats.

Miss Ivens, always elegantly dressed herself, was still unforgiving about the Committee's choice of uniform when she responded to Dr Henry's apology for reporting on her arrival in July 1917 wearing mufti. Dr Henry explained that she had felt self-conscious in the drab cotton uniform issued in London. Miss Ivens reassured her:

> I'm glad you did. I have told the Edinburgh Committee that we are too
> near Paris to be dressed like nannies! Tomorrow Nicol in Paris will take
> your measurements.

The result, Dr Henry reported, was a 'coat and skirt of light grey twill with red velvet *caducées* [a recognised medical emblem including serpents and wings] in the lapel and a heavy dark blue for winter.[42]

When they learned about it, this blue uniform greatly displeased the Committee. Grey was authorised, blue was not:

> The Uniform Committee were unanimously of the opinion that the doc-
> tors should not be allowed to wear this uniform.

A telegram was sent – 'Blue uniform unauthorised we are sending out grey material'. Miss Ivens responded that the doctors were already wearing blue. The Uniform Committee said they would not pay. The Hospital Committee then stepped into the fray – the Uniform Committee gave in and the doctors were satisfied and continued to wear their blue uniforms.[43]

There was worse to come, however, from the Committee in London in 1916:

> I have just seen in all its horrible details the uniform in which we send
> out our hospital nursing staff. It made me almost cry with rage and
> shame – shame for the poor girls who have to wear it, shame that mem-
> bers of our hospital should be seen in it, shame that foreigners should
> think such a rigout is the Englishwoman's idea of working and workman-
> like clothes, and rage that Edinburgh after more than two years' practical
> experience should be sending out something so ill-cut and ill-made, so
> unsuitable to the occasion.[44]

And this was at the height of the Somme battles! It seems that those who had to wear it had more urgent tasks to do – at least there is no record of the nurses having such violent views.

However, Armstrong, who was a clerk in 1917, thought:

Perhaps the Committee chose the design with a view to our protection among the licentious soldiery. [It seems that it was the outdoor uniform which made the hackles rise.] It was lucky, wasn't it, that our indoor uniforms were a lovely shade of blue.[45]

In September 1915, Miss Loudon, the Administrator, was writing back to Miss Mair:

Please don't send out hats. We can get grey hats in Paris to match our costumes. We will have them very simple. The memory of the first doctor's hats is still green.[46]

French visitors were more tolerant:

Les médecins ont un uniforme: c'est une costume tailleur très simple d'un gris très doux à l'oeil et que la doctoresse-en-chef porte avec grâce, sans aucun signe spéciale; elles revets aussi la grande blouse classique. Toutes les doctoresses ont, comme insigne, la caducée des médecins-majors, mais en argent, sur velour gris. 'Sisters' et 'Orderlies' sont vêtues de gris bleu, les unes avec la coiffe traditionelle, les autres coiffées d'une gentille petite charlotte [Mob-cap. Charlotte named after Charlotte Corday famous for the murder of Marat during the French Revolution] de la même couleur de la robe (ou blanche pour les cuisinières) qui encadre gracieusement leur mine éveilée.[47]

We leave the last word on uniforms with an orderly, Starr, going on leave and donning her mufti:

One gets thoroughly sick of going about like a Scotswoman in those hideous grey coats, so I feel like a lady again.[48]

The Language

What did they make of the task on which they had so blithely embarked? To undertake total care of hundreds of foreigners – very few of whom would have any knowledge of English? How many of them could converse in French? How many of them had even a rudimentary knowledge of the language? The French Service de Santé wanted all the doctors and nurses to make a declaration that they could speak French. This was a little idealistic, and the requirement does not seem to have been taken very seriously.

Possibly the weakest group in terms of language proficiency was the sisters. Some of them had literally no knowledge of French when they arrived but they were successful, in varying degrees, in communicating with their patients. When Madame Fox, a local French lady, came to live in the hospital in 1917 after the death of her husband, Miss Ivens welcomed this for a variety of reasons, not least that the sisters would have an opportunity to improve their French.

The story is told of one sister – newly arrived – who was very puzzled and upset by the great distress of a patient on his return from the theatre: 'I'm sure I said nothing to upset him'. She had only one French word, and that was 'oui'. The patient's distress was explained by the man in the next bed – 'Mon camarade a demandé à la sistaire: "Est-ce que je vais mourir?" She used her complete vocabulary in her reply 'Oui, oui'.[49]

Yvonne Barclay (orderly 25.5.16 to 28.5.17) recalled a sister dressing a boy's foot. 'An' noo, c'est fini, bonnie laddie'. 'Qu'est ce que "bonnie laddie", Sistaire?'. 'Och. C'est le Scotch for Antret' (his name). They understood each other.

The sisters carried on gallantly and many of them devised their own system of communication. Sister McGregor (Jessie Leslie McGregor 28.7.16 to 18.11.17 and 2.3.18 to 30.12.18) apparently had her own inimitable way: 'Conversation was always carried on in a series of staccato monosyllables, half French, half English; yet every man understood what she meant'.[50]

Sister Williams (Janet Williams 25.11.15 to 25.11.16) was remarkable. She had charge of the Senegalese ward. They knew very little French and no English at all. Sister knew even less French than they did. In spite of that they developed an extraordinary amount of understanding. She even discovered a great deal of their family history and the number of their wives.[51]

The orderlies came from privileged family backgrounds. Many had had a good education and knew a certain amount of French. Nevertheless Miss Ivens was critical and said she had no idea that the majority of girls were so badly educated.[52] Littlejohn was able from the beginning to deal with the local tradespeople, and there were others who could manage quite well. A few took lessons in the village though their accent did not always improve as much as it might. There always remained some mistakes which they enjoyed looking back upon in later years. One of these was told of an orderly receiving a telephone call from the Army authorities in Creil during the hectic summer of 1918. 'Combien de lits disponibles?' She could not say as they were already required to collect from 'une caniche toute pleine de blessés' (*Une caniche* is a bitch). For weeks afterwards every passing officer was enquiring tenderly about the caniche and the fate of her large family.[53]

Simms (Florence Beatrice Simms, orderly, 1.12.17 to 28.8.18), writing to her old governess, bemoaned the fact that 'I'm afraid I shall never learn to speak properly, however hard I try. You see, I never know what people are talking about, they talk at such a terrific rate'.[54] Her friend, Summerhayes, (Grace Summerhayes, orderly, 13.12.17 to 16.8.18) was much more confident. She reckoned she had two kinds of French – her correct schoolgirl French, and the French the *poilus* spoke: 'My French in the end was either very up or very down'.[55] Figgis was probably not the only one who 'spoke French rather correctly but slowly, conceding nothing to Gallic vivacity'.[56]

One of the greatest successes of the early appointments was that of Cicely Hamilton who went as a clerk but rapidly became more and more indispensable to the smooth running of the whole organisation. She was of enormous value to Miss Ivens in the early days with her facility in French, both written and spoken. Miss Ivens relied on her greatly to assist her in all the delicate negotiations with the French authorities. Miss Ivens herself, though she was completely fluent in French as the war progressed, had some difficulty in the early days. Her standard question to a newly admitted *poilu* was 'Etes vous blessé ou malade, Monsieur?' It became complicated for her to follow when the man replied that he was both and went on with a wealth of detail.[57] But, as with everything she undertook, including a thorough knowledge of military surgery after a career in obstetrics and gynaecology, she set herself to learn. She told one story against herself (which contradicts the assertion that she lacked a sense of humour) that after a ward concert she rose and made her little speech, only to realise later that she had thanked 'ourselves for giving the men such a delightful concert'.[58]

Some of the doctors probably had more knowledge of German than of French. A number who had qualified in the early years of the century had pursued postgraduate education in German-speaking centres, Vienna, Freiburg, Zürich and others. This was, of course, due to the difficulties put in the way of women who wanted to advance in their chosen specialties. Their proficiency in French was probably no greater than when they left school. The outstanding exception to this was Dr Wilson who arrived in November 1915 and remained until her tragic early death from appendicitis in 1917 while she was on leave in the South of France. She was the most fluent speaker of them all and was a noted linguist also in German, Arabic, Greek, Latin and Hebrew.

Not all the doctors learned French as competently as Miss Ivens. Dr Courtauld, for instance (who could have held her own in German), never became confident enough to travel by herself in France. After the war she was anxious to explore those parts of Brittany from which her Huguenot ancestors had come to England. She persuaded Cicely Hamilton to accompany her to help her along. Nevertheless when work beckoned she did not hesitate to volunteer after the war to work in the devastated villages of Northern France. Miss Ivens kept up extensive friendships with French colleagues and friends right up to the Second World War, and until her marriage in 1930 spent her holidays in France, often with members of her former unit. She was then completely fluent. There was probably a general raising of the standard of French speaking, as in the last Christmas celebrated at Royaumont, Christmas 1918, the Unit produced a splendid pantomime – 'Cinderella' – all in fluent French including the songs which they composed.

From the other side of the linguistic barrier some of the patients made some effort to learn English. One said goodnight to his sister every evening by singing 'Sleep, my little one, Dream my pretty one'[59] and they all became proficient in singing Tipperary, 'in excellent English and most tunefully'.[60]

In comparison with the difficulties which the other SWH units must have experienced in Serbia, Rumania, Greece and Russia, the Royaumont Unit had an easy time.

One way or another, with mutual aid, determination and sheer necessity, the question of language was no insuperable barrier to communication or good relations in general or to the maintenance of discipline.

References

1. Personal communication from Miss Rachel Hedderwick, daughter of Dorothy Littlejohn.
2. IWM. Letters of Dorothy Littlejohn to her fiancé, H.J. Hedderwick, 11.12.14.
3. Mrs Withell's Diary, 1914–1915, unpublished, p. 39, kindly communicated by Mr Charles Clark.
4. NL 1946.
5. IWM, *loc. cit.*
6. *CC*, Cicely Hamilton, 11.12.14, p. 599.
7. *CC*, CH, 24.12.14, p. 622.
8. IWM, *loc. cit.*
9. *CC*, CH *loc. cit.*
10. NL 1955, p. 8.
11. ML. Tin 12, Loose leaf file, F. Ivens to Committee, 14.12.14.
12. ML. Tin 12, FI to E. Inglis 31.12.14.
13. ML. Tin 12 FI to Compton, 3.1.15.
14. MHF Ivens *Brit. Med. J.*, Aug. 18 1917, p. 203.
15. ML. Tin 13, EI to Compton, 26.12.14.
16. ML. Tin 12, Report of Sanitary Department of Military Government of Paris, 24.12.14.
17. IWM. DL 26.12.14.
18. 'Skia' (V.C.C. Collum) *Blackwood's Magazine*, November 1918, p. 614.
19. ML. Tin 12, FI to EI, 2.1.15.
20. IWM. DL, *loc. cit.*
21. Miss Rachel Hedderwick. Personal Communication.
22. ML. Tin 12, FI to EI, 31.12.14.
23. IWM. DL, 20.12.14.
24. IWM. DL, 26.12.14.
25. *Auntie Mabel's War: an account of her part in the hostilities, 1914–1918*, p. 31.
26. ML. Tin 12, FI to EI, 2.1.15.
27. ML. Tin 12, FI to EI, 7.1.15.
28. ML. Tin 12, FI to Crompton, 6.1.15.
29. ML. Tin 12, FI to EI, 10.1.15.
30. ML. Tin 12, FI to EI, 15.1.15.

31. FL. Box 304/2, Loudon 1.7.15.

32. NL 1961, p. 5, extracts from orderlies' letters home.

33. IWM. DL 7.1.15.

34. 'Skia', *op. cit.*, p. 620.

35. NL 1936, p. 11, E. Prance, 'Education of a Well-loved Chief'.

36. NL 1941, p. 37.

37. NL 1966, p. 2.

38. IWM. Diary of M.L. Starr, 18.10.15.

39. ML. Tin 12, FI to Laurie, 1.8.15.

40. ML. Tin 13, EI to Crompton, 26.12.14.

41. ML. Tin 49, FI to EI, 31.12.14.

42. Dr Leila Henry. Reminiscences, kindly made available by Miss Helen Lowe.

43. ML. Uniform Committee Minutes, 4.12.17.

44. FL. Box 304/3, Kinnel to Gosse, 28.7.16.

45. NL 1968, p. 6.

46. ML. Tin 2, Loudon to Mair, Sept. 1915.

47. *Livre d'Or des Oeuvres de Guerre 1915*, by Lucie Berillon, 'Une Visite à l'Hôpital de Royaumont', pp. 4–5.

48. IWM. Starr Diary, 7.12.15.

49. NL 1964, p. 9.

50. NL 1939, p. 8.

51. Mrs A.M. Robertson, letters transcribed by her granddaughter, Mrs Ailsa Tanner and kindly made available.

52. ML. Tin 12, FI to EI, 6.4.15.

53. NL 1966, p. 6.

54. F.B. Simms, letter to her governess 1.9.18, kindly supplied by her niece Miss M.P. Simms.

55. Dr Grace MacRae, née Summerhayes. Personal communication 12.7.93.

56. NL 1968, p. 6.

57. NL 1937, p. 9.

58. ML. Tin 12, FI to Russell, 12.3.16.

59. IWM. Starr Diary, 18.10.15.

60. ML. Tin 42, Loudon to Maris, 26.9.15.

CHAPTER THREE

The First Year

Royaumont received its first patients in January 1915. To appreciate the work of the hospital during its first year it is useful to examine briefly the main facts of the military situation.

The Military Situation in 1915

By the end of 1914 stalemate had been reached; both sides were digging in, and it was not until February 1915 that fighting was renewed.

At the beginning of 1915 the approximate line of the German Front ran from Verdun in the East, westwards through Reims, Soissons and Noyon. It then turned northwards to Albert, Vimy Ridge, Loos, Neuve-Chapelle, Armentières, Ypres and to the coast south of Ostend.

Throughout 1915 much of the Allied war effort on the Western front was concentrated on the eastern end where the Germans were straining to capture Verdun. However, in February and March the French made repeated attacks in Champagne, trying to penetrate the German defences. French losses were appalling – 50,000 men in these two months alone. Then in April they lost 64,000 men in a disastrous attack on St Mihiel, further to the east, towards Verdun.

Between May 9th and June 18th the French were attacking further north between Lens and Arras – losing 102,000 men in the process. Between May 15th and May 27th the British were engaged in attacks on Festubert, south of Neuve-Chapelle.

This enormous loss of life produced little change in the military situation. Some relaxation of effort followed until September 15th when the French renewed their attacks in Champagne, and the French and British together attacked in Artois. Losses in these September attacks amounted to 242,000 (nearly twice the German losses of 141,000).

In the later months of 1915 there was again stalemate and, thanks to the onset of winter, a period of relief for the soldiers in the trenches and the hard-pressed hospitals behind the lines.

The Position of Royaumont

Royaumont was particularly well-suited to take casualties from the Reims, Soissons, Noyon sector. All these areas fed by rail into the *gare régulatrice* at

Creil, 12 miles from the hospital. It was at Creil that patients were distributed to the various hospitals in that particular war zone; one of these was Royaumont. Apart from a short period in 1918 when the rapid German advance put Creil temporarily out of action, it remained a critically important centre throughout the war. It was convenient for the military authorities to have Royaumont where it was, but for Royaumont, 12 miles from Creil on bad roads, it was a heavy burden for the hard-pressed chauffeurs, particularly during the 'rushes'.

Nevertheless, as Collum commented: 'Chance or destiny flung our little emergency Unit of women into the one spot in the whole of France where it could prove of greatest value'.[1] Activity at Royaumont followed the course of the fighting with periods of intense activity and quieter periods in between. Their greatest 'rushes', or 'flaps' as they called them, came in April, May and September.

The Patients Arrive

On January 10th 1915 the hospital was recognised as a military hospital and was to be known as Hôpital Auxiliaire 301 (HA 301).[2]

On January 11th the first six patients arrived – all sick. The authorities were not yet ready to trust them with wounded soldiers. These patients were brought in by Army ambulances which had taken four hours to cover the 12 miles from Creil. They were completely exhausted. After this example of gross inefficiency Miss Ivens was able to obtain permission for her women drivers to collect the patients in future. The Unit was delighted to have patients at last – they were beginning the work for which they had volunteered.[3]

By the end of the month they were getting a few wounded cases, and by February 5th they had 55 patients, half sick, half wounded. By the end of February the hospital was almost full – with 95 of the beds occupied.

They were being closely watched by the medical authorities. Miss Ivens reported that she had to do a number of abdominal operations under their critical supervision – 'fortunately all went well'.[4] It was not surprising that the French were anxious – they had no experience of women working as doctors in hospitals, let alone as surgeons – if a woman doctor worked in a hospital it had to be as a nurse! Could these women really cope? was the unspoken question. It must have encouraged them when Cicely Hamilton overheard the men saying to a visiting colonel that they had a 'marked preference for the service of women doctors'.[5]

Towards the end of February, in view of a typhoid epidemic in the neighbourhood, Miss Ivens was invited to staff a hospital at Mont-à-Terre, near Creil. Miss Ivens was never one to turn down a challenge and welcomed this as an indication that they were beginning to overcome suspicion and mistrust. Preparations were made and staff appointed to leave. However, the epidemic abated rather rapidly and the whole exercise was cancelled.[6] This may have been fortunate in the light of new demands soon to be made on the hospital.

Other marks of confidence followed. The Army authorised them to collect casualties direct from the train at Creil rather than from the Creil Hospital.[7] This saved the wounded men much unnecessary and painful movement.

They were also asked to provide another 100 beds. To accommodate these the former chapter house of the Abbey on the ground floor became the 'Millicent Fawcett' ward; the guest refectory of the monks became the 'Queen Mary', and the 'cowsheds' on the second floor became the 'Elsie Inglis' ward.

The Army was now prepared to pay 2 francs a day for each patient and to supply petrol, tyres and other necessities for the vehicles. (The Army was desperately short of vehicles at that time.) The equivalent of £1000 was provided for the new beds – the beds themselves were to be returned 'after the war'. ('Very poor quality', said Miss Ivens.)

It had been agreed with the Committee and with the French authorities that, provided the care of soldiers received top priority, any slack could be used to treat the civilian population. This was immensely popular with the local communities as there was a great scarcity of medical facilities of any kind. Miss Ivens reported on March 19th that the outpatient department was growing to an embarrassing degree. Women naturally predominated. No charge was made but a box was provided for contributions.

Patients were increasing in numbers – on March 22nd there were 137 – but – where was the equipment?

Miss Ivens was more than a little concerned:

> We are in a dire need of equipment, no beds, sheets or blankets … cutlery and utensils for patients dreadfully short. I shall have to stop taking patients today unless the equipment comes.[8]

And again she vented her anger on the Committee:

> Patients have poured in daily, and as the equipment was painfully inadequate and meagre for 100 beds it reached vanishing point with 158 patients. In addition constantly increasing staff whose requirements were entirely unprovided for. Weeks ago I wired for more sheets and pyjamas but I got no response … It is most discouraging for nurses to see their beds covered with stained, dirty sheets … soldiers wandering to and fro to the x-ray room half-clad for lack of dressing gowns and pyjamas … Dressings are practically exhausted and none have come … The loyalty of the staff has been strained to the breaking point by the unnecessary dis-

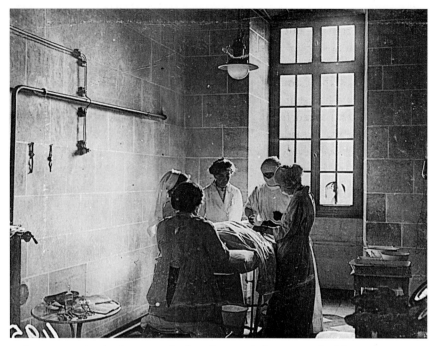

An operation in the theatre on the first floor. Note the stove on the left, smoke exiting through a hole in the wall. Electricity supply was primitive but functional. All these fitments had to be removed when the hospital closed in March 1919.
(By permission of the Imperial War Museum).

comforts ... We have had to borrow sheets and blankets from the poor of Asnières. The staff have given up their bedsteads and replaced them with borrowed horrors ... do try and get some constant supplies out. Otherwise we might just collapse.[9]

Collum tells an endearing story of Miss Ivens which goes some way to account for the love her staff had for her:

As usual the new equipment went astray and there was a raid on staff beds. It used to be uncommonly cold sleeping on the floor. If beds were not forthcoming at the first hint of their need, the Médecin-Chef had a way of giving up hers to start with. I remember passing my bed on to her the first time. She sent this also to the new ward. Meanwhile I had commandeered another. Of course I had to offer it again – we could not have our M-C sleeping on the floor. Next time I got a broken bed which I patched up. It served the purpose fairly well; but again the M-C handed over her bed, and I was on the floor once more. So, with a sigh, I took along my broken bed, which she retained, I believe, as it was too 'groggy' for a wounded man. I had now given up a bed as a bad job, and till the missing equipment had come I slept resignedly on the floor.[10]

The patients always came first with Miss Ivens. On April 6th the equipment had still not arrived – but in spite of that they had a great bed-moving day. 'All the French horrors are banished to our rooms and the patients are neatly comfortable on our nice straw mattresses.'[11]

On behalf of the Committee Dr Inglis remonstrated with Miss Ivens: 'We thought we had sent you everything you asked for, and you evidently felt that you had asked for many things that you did not get'.[12] And on March 30th to the Treasurer: 'There seems to have been a glorious muddle at Royaumont over everything just now'.[13] However, the situation was saved when large quantities of absolutely invaluable stores arrived from a hospital at Cherbourg which was closing down, and soon after that the long-awaited equipment from home arrived and order returned. The crisis was over.

Dr Inglis visited the hospital once more at the end of April on her way to Serbia to command one of the SWH Units there. She wrote a reassuring letter to Miss Mair, the President of the Scottish Federation:

> I am more than ever delighted with the place. The wards are beautiful. The operating theatre is as perfect as any I have ever seen, and the whole place is in perfect order. The patients – 178 were in today – seemed most contented, and everyone on the staff seemed well and keen. There is no doubt that the hospital is a great success, and that the credit belongs to Dr Ivens. The staff has worked splendidly. So that, in my opinion the thing to do is to support Dr Ivens in her 'plans' – of course insisting on estimates, for *that* is her weak point![14]

And to the Treasurer she wrote of 'Dr Ivens's management of the place, and her patience and persistence in the face of really extraordinary difficulties in the way of red tape etc has made our work there really something to be proud of'.[15]

Dr Inglis was also delighted to open and name the 'Elsie Inglis' wards on the second floor. These were the same that had been so roundly condemned only three months earlier.

The extra 100 beds had to be inspected again, but this time the inspection went off without a hitch. The inspector actually apologised for his previous 'boorish behaviour', measured again, and pronounced them fit for use. Miss Ivens wondered if his change of heart could be because he was 'obviously bowled over by the "petite bonnet bleu" of Miss Inglis (Etta) who is a very charming person'. Much to Miss Ivens's relief he didn't ask about the lavatories – 'the one thing that is weighing on my mind and which I see no means of improving'.[16]

Miss Ivens had certainly been very angry with the Committee over the delays in sending equipment; she had been very sensitive to the criticisms of M. Gouin (the owner) who did not like to see patients wandering around without proper clothing or to the suggestion that they were not getting enough food. It must have been humiliating for her to borrow from poor villagers even though they were pleased to help the hospital which was already doing so much for them. It was possibly for her the most unhappy period of the entire war – she had a dread of falling down on any job. Later in August of that year she wrote:

> Our experience in the Spring in trying to provide for the extra patients while we waited weeks for equipment ... would not encourage me to repeat such a *nightmare of worry and anxiety*. [My italics]

It would perhaps have been surprising if there had not been a few misjudgements in the selection of personnel. The Committee were inexperienced and were ignorant of what the work would entail or the qualities that would be needed. Some of the appointments were brilliant – or particularly fortunate. Among these were Cicely Hamilton, the first clerk (later administrator), and Vera Collum, who came as an orderly, but later became a highly skilled radiographer. The two problem appointments were, curiously enough, made by Dr Inglis herself. Mrs Owen, the first administrator, was, it seems, totally out of her depth. She spoke no French and had no idea how to handle the difficult conditions she found. It was a relief when she resigned. Her replacement was Mrs Harley – who could not understand why she (Mrs Owen) 'could not get on with Miss Ivens except that she had too difficult a task and got thoroughly worried'.[17]

Mrs Harley was a strong character. She was prominent in the suffrage movement, and was the sister of Sir John French, the Commander-in-Chief of the British Expeditionary Force. She was then in her sixties. After three months at Royaumont she transferred to the tented hospital that the SWH opened at Troyes under Dr Louise McIllroy. When that hospital in due course was sent out to Salonika Mrs Harley went with it. Her subsequent history until her death from an exploding shell in 1916 is part of the Serbian story and is told elsewhere.[18] She seems to have been a difficult and autocratic character though this was more manifest in her later career than at Royaumont. Probably her posting spared Royaumont some of the problems other units experienced.

Miss Tod, the first Matron, who took up her post in February, was elderly, already retired, and had been accustomed to traditional nursing in traditional settings in Scotland. She too found conditions at Royaumont more than she could cope with. She was also far removed psychologically from the 'modern woman' who was well represented at Royaumont. She looked askance at Cicely Hamilton. When she saw her going about in a workman's smock she was puzzled. Was it true that she had been an actress? And what could have brought her to this? Recalling the incident later, Cicely could not recall her answer but said that she might have said 'the drink' 'if she had not been so

kindly, so serious and so Scotch!'[19] Mrs Williams had come from the
Cherbourg Hospital with her two children. She was known as the 'rabiot'.
(This term is defined in the dictionary as a) surplus of food after distribution
of rations, and b) illicit profits.) She lived in the village with her children
until 1916, and her expert knowledge of French made her a very valuable
acquisition in the office. Miss Tod, however, was doubtful. Mrs Williams
took trouble with her appearance, powdered her nose and scented her bath,
and Miss Tod considered her silk underwear positively demi-mondaine.[20]
Her very traditional views seem to have extended to the suitability of
women to be doctors at all. Dr Inglis herself reported that she had said to
one orderly who was ill, 'Don't you think you should send into Paris for a
man?'[21] Miss Ivens found her 'not loyal' to women doctors – a cardinal sin
with Miss Ivens. She also considered her 'too old and unadaptable for the
hand to mouth existence we have here'.[22] Mrs Harley was quite clear that
Miss Tod was not a success. She grumbled, found fault and discouraged the
orderlies. She would have to go. It must be placed to the credit of Dr Inglis,
and a sign of her humanity that, in spite of being critical, she was at pains
to spare her from humiliation and to allow her to return home 'with honour'. 'She is too old for the post and we oughtn't to have asked her. But we
did put her in, and so we must not hurt her in getting her out ... Don't let
her know that I told you she cried. She is so proud she would hate that.'
However when she died in 1929 there were some in the Unit who remembered her with affection, 'perhaps having forgiven us all for turning out to
be adventurous ducklings so very different from the sedate chicks she had
expected to hatch'.[23]

With the increasing number of patients tasks multiplied. For Cicely
Hamilton there were the forms required by the military authorities:

> The number and docketing of French military patients is not a job to be
> trifled with. Four documents for every man entering and the same for
> leaving, and seventeen for a death. Recapitulatory reports, telling every-
> thing all over again – every five days.[24]

According to Miss Ivens it was as bad or even worse for her. She and the
French *gestionnaire* had 27 military forms to sign as soldiers arrived.

Another task that they had not foreseen was dealing with the soldiers'
clothing. This was an important part of the work of the hospital and one that
distinguished it from the work of other hospitals (together with the supply
of toothbrushes). On her arrival in February Collum described the work
vividly:

> On arrival I was confronted with seventy piles of filthy tattered clothing,
> most of it in sacks, ranged in some semblance of order round and across
> the room, each sack with a number, from one upwards, corresponding to

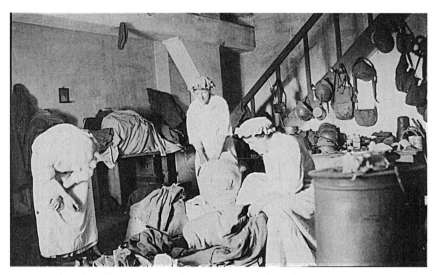

Two views of the Vêtements Department at the top of the building. Dismissed by the French inspecting authorities as 'cowsheds', and unfit for patients, it later became an almost ideal ward, named after Elsie Inglis, the founder of the Scottish Women's Hospitals. It was used for the French Colonial troops.

Sorting the filthy, bloodstained, torn clothing was an unpleasant task. The work was eased when Orderly Gemmell devised a pulley to move the heavy sacks up and down the stairs. (By courtesy of Miss Helen Lowe).

rough pencil entries in a penny notebook, giving the owner's name, and the ward he was in, and the date of his admission ... The cowsheds with their stinking, crawling burden, became a nightmare. I remember our great field day with the soiled clothes, when we had prevailed upon a village washer-woman of the pre-Marne days to get her fires and boilers going again. The pile was higher than my own head: we packed the clothes into half a dozen ticking mattress cases and took them by motor to the village: the reek of them penetrated into the inhabited wing of the hospital and brought a horrified CMO (Chief Medical Officer) to the scene, who at once acquiesced in our scheme cost what it might.[25]

The 'vêtements' department as it was called, having started in the 'cowsheds', was moved up to the very top of the building – 'One could have set a row of cottages with their back yards inside it'.[26] An enterprising orderly devised a pulley to haul up the heavy sacks, thus saving the weary orderlies at least one of their heavy chores. The French Army were not renowned for looking after the welfare of their troops. They were unable to provide replacement clothing. So, whatever the condition of clothing, it had to be repaired.

A routine was established, basically unchanged throughout the life of the hospital:

> The clothes are fumigated in great cupboards, and next day the sacks are sorted, soiled linen is sent to the wash, and outdoor clothing hung from the rafters in a good courant d'air. The mending is undertaken by a wonderful Frenchwoman, Madame Fox, the wife of an English resident in our village.[27]

Most of her helpers were volunteers, but the owner of a local factory, M. Delacoste, loaned two of his workers every afternoon:

> We ourselves tackle the uniforms with the noble assistance of Mrs Hacon, a prominent member of the Shetland Branch of the National Union of Women's Suffrage Societies, through whose ingenuity I have seen the 'veste' of an artillery man, minus half a sleeve, made into a wondrous garment with warm woollen cuffs – all because there was nothing in the world to mend it with but a pair of navy blue bedsocks – and an old scarlet sock repair a breach made by shrapnel in a pair of infantry trousers![28]

This was before the French Army were clad in 'horizon bleu', their version of khaki.

They were proud of their vêtements department. Cicely Hamilton reported that:

> rumour has it that the Royaumont men turn up at Creil depot considerably smarter than the majority of the other 'évacués' of the District, and that Mme Fox is to go to Creil one evening in order to compare the results of her handiwork with less successful efforts in the mending and cleaning line. She has been granted the honorary rank of 'directrice-adjointe du bureau de vêtements de l'hôpital auxiliaire 301 de Royaumont'. I invented the title myself and she deserves every single word of it.[29]

Hospital routines evolved by degrees for staff and patients. These included the arrangements for the arrival and departure of the wounded. Dr Henry, who arrived in 1917 when the routine was well-established, describes how the Hall Porter, having been alerted from the distributing centre in Creil, listened for the sound of the ambulances. She then blew her horn (a useful instrument before the days of hospital bleeps), and the orderlies rushed to the entrance, leaving only one on duty in charge of the ward. 'Each', she said, 'had her station as on board ship.' The orderlies unloaded the ambulance (each ambulance carried four stretchers), and they were:

> laid on the flagged floor of the inner hall. Tags attached to the uniforms were checked. These gave indication of the type of wound, whether from bullet or shrapnel. Those who had haemorrhaged or were already suffering from infection were quickly discovered by the stench. Clothing was cut off; swabs taken and sent to the laboratory … hot drinks were available to all, then they would be borne up the wide stairs to the next floor where the x-ray and operating theatres were ready for them.

Or they went straight to the wards – for those on the second floor there were 71 steps. She reminds us: 'There were no men orderlies and no elevators. The girl orderlies undertook all these heavy tasks'. In the wards Dr Henry remembered how the *poilus* greeted the newcomers. They would:

> Introduce him, sit beside him and calm his fears. I have seen such gentleness between the veterans and the young recruits. You'd hear a new patient being questioned 'Can you sing? – What kind of music do you like? – Well, we all sing here, but it's comme il faut, some verses we leave out. These are all English ladies'.[30]

Miss Ivens was quite aware that some of these verses were not fit for the ears of the young orderlies in her care. She deputed Miller, who had good French, to make sure they were not 'Pas convenables'.[31]

The chauffeurs covered that bumpy 12-mile journey from Creil each entirely on her own. One of them remembers opening the door on arrival wondering if her casualties were alive or dead.[32]

Discharges also followed a certain routine. They usually took place about 6 p.m., and they were given a good send-off by their fellow-patients, by the staff who had looked after them, and by Miss Ivens herself who made a point of being there whenever possible. Some might be going on leave, some for further treatment in another hospital, and some unfortunate ones back to the Front. Feelings were very mixed when they left but the staff tried to make it as easy as they could:

> Practically every evening and punctually at six, we, to use the French term, 'evacuate' a certain number of patients, and their departure is

usually the liveliest moment of the day. It looks, sometimes, as if everyone who is able to walk had come to cheer them on the road. Variety of costume is always charming, and the crowd round our front door, in so far as it consists of patients, is clad chiefly in pyjamas of different hues, and wears what headgear it fancies, chiefly 'kepis' and Zulu straws. Miss Ivens reads over the men's papers – a necessary precaution this, as any warrior without the correct documents is liable to be returned on our hands. We have never yet fathomed what would happen if anyone's papers were absolutely and irretrievably lost, but we imagine that in such an eventuality he would have no legal existence, and that the only way out of the difficulty would be to exterminate him and bury him secretly. The evacuated ones, having been duly identified, there is much hand shaking, much thanking of doctors and nurses. It takes some time till everyone and everyone's bundles are hoisted in and the car is off.[33]

With routines getting established and with increasing confidence, the hospital was now on the way to becoming a 'Unit'. Reference has already been made to certain disagreements and incompatibilities in the early days, but it does seem that, as the hospital settled down, and one or two misfits left, a very positive esprit-de-corps developed which was a striking feature of the hospital throughout its life, and was maintained for years after the War through the Royaumont Association. This esprit-de-corps was undoubtedly fostered by the appreciation of the *poilus*, the admiration of their village neighbours, and the increasing value set on their services by the military and medical authorities.

Dr Ross, on a visit back to headquarters in June 1915, was asked by the Committee if there was much discontent among themselves? She replied that 'it was a "perfect paradise" compared to similar institutions in this country'.[34] And in September Dr Boissières, inspecting on behalf of the French authorities, said Royaumont was 'one of the few Hôpitals Etrangères which had not given them 'unspeakable ennuis''.[35]

In May Miss Ivens began experimenting with the sun treatment of wounds. Beds were wheeled out into the cloisters, at first by day only, later by day and night. Wounds were exposed, protected by gauze soaked in saline solution. This treatment, combined with the peace and beauty of the cloisters, produced good results. Navarro wrote:

The beautiful Gothic cloisters and box-bordered court offered a habitation that for picturesque repose was unobtainable even by millionaire sanatoria: by day, a harbour of unaccustomed novelty and enchantment; and when evening was come, a night of silence and stars – the soothing babble of the fountain lulling the nerve-racked sufferers to peaceful sleep. On moonlit evenings the scene was one of indescribable beauty. The old

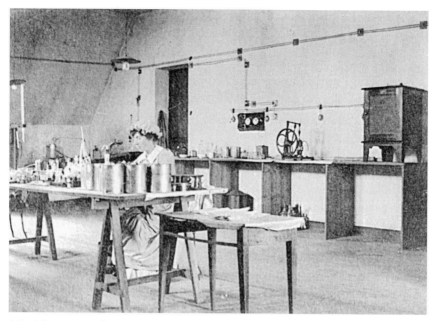

The laboratory at the top of the building. Orderly Smieton at work, a valued technician, who was later awarded the Croix de Guerre.
(By courtesy of Miss Helen Lowe).

grey masonry, assuming then a ghostly pallor, shone like marble in the dark shimmering sky.[36]

The hospital continued to develop. In May a laboratory was prepared on the top floor. This was under the direction of Dr Elizabeth Butler. Royaumont was indeed fortunate to obtain her services. She had graduated from Glasgow University with Honours in 1890. She took her MD degree with 'the highest honours the University could bestow'. In due course she was awarded a Beit Memorial Research Fellowship from the Lister Institute. (Dr Elsie Dalyell, an Australian, who worked later at Royaumont, had also been a Beit Fellow. These were two of the most eminent women scientists of the time and contributed in no small measure to the high reputation that Royaumont came to hold.)

For Dr Butler the opportunity to work at Royaumont came at a very appropriate time. She had been working on a cancer research project in Lemberg, Austria, when war broke out. She found herself a refugee. She resigned her fellowship, concealed her papers (hoping to recover them after the War), and returned home. She and her husband were then without any means of livelihood. Being fluent in French and German, she wrote to the Secretary of the Lister Institute, 'I shall be glad to help as a doctor, dresser or nurse, at home or abroad'.[37] This led to the Royaumont appointment, though it is to be hoped that she did not let Miss Ivens know of her willingness to work as a nurse. Miss Ivens was always insistent that women doctors should work as doctors and have the same conditions of service and pay as men. Anything else was letting the side down. Dr Butler brought her husband with her who worked as a chauffeur for a short time, so the Butlers' employment problems were resolved happily for the time being.

On June 25th the new laboratory was opened, and a 'deluge of generals' descended to inspect it.[38] (Whether they had any qualifications to judge its quality was a moot point, but there was still intense interest in what the women were doing, and, besides, they always enjoyed the Royaumont teas.)

The prestige of the laboratory was further increased by the interest taken by Professor Weinberg of the Pasteur Institute in Paris who was the leading expert on gas gangrene (see Chapter 10). His confidence was such that he conducted many of the trials of his new gas gangrene sera in the hospital. Lecturing in Glasgow in March 1916, he said that he had seen hundreds and hundreds (!) of military hospitals, but none the organisation of which won his admiration so completely. He was compelled to express his admiration of the manner in which cases were treated. He could not imagine any activity on the part of women that would so effectively further the cause of the women's movement as the work of the Scottish Women's Hospitals.[39]

In addition to Dr Butler other new doctors arrived in 1915. Dr Meiklejohn was a pathologist who had been a Carnegie Research Fellow, a rare distinction for a woman. Dr Wilson was an experienced missionary doctor from Palestine. Dr Hawthorne took on the supervision of the x-ray department in the absence of Dr Savill. (Dr Savill divided her time between Royaumont and her consultant work in London.) It was Dr Hawthorne who trained Collum in radiography. Collum's talent for photography had been noticed by Miss Ivens who was always on the alert to spot the potential of her orderlies. Collum later distinguished herself in the great 'rushes' resulting from the Somme battles of 1916 and again in the last desperate struggle of 1918.

With a new Administrator and a new Matron Miss Ivens was relieved of some of the work which had fallen so heavily on her shoulders. Miss Loudon (the 'Robin') probably did not fully realise the extent of the problems she was to meet in the next eighteen months, but her delightful personality and concern for the welfare of the whole Unit won her many friends, some of them literally lifelong. She fell in love with Royaumont and wrote enthusiastically of her first impressions:

> I am very happy here, and the staff are so nice and what is really delightful is they all have Royaumont first in their minds and are determined that it shall be second to none. You would be amused at the quite

friendly – but quite obvious desire to keep well ahead of Troyes! [the second SWH hospital in France]. It's like rival schools. Of course we [observe the 'we' after a fortnight] are extraordinarily fortunate in having a Chief like Miss Ivens.[40]

As the laboratory opened, the number of admissions increased – a nightly average of 28 compared to the previous 4 to 12 – mostly coming from the shelling in the Albert-Arras sector. 'Still, though the staff is distinctly pressed just now, it likes it. It likes to feel that Royaumont is known as the hospital where a man gets his full 100% of chances.'[41] The appreciation of the patients was the greatest encouragement. 'One patient badly wounded in the arm assured me that he should (sic) take away with him a very substantial souvenir of Royaumont – his arm!'[42] The surgeons took the greatest trouble to try and preserve limbs. In many hospitals amputation was resorted to very readily; it was often the easiest option.

Some slackening off in July enabled them to celebrate July 14th with a concert in the Refectory organised entirely by the patients. Cicely Hamilton described the colourful scene:

> Rows of beds with their vivid scarlet coverlets on one side, long cane chairs on the other – benches in the centre – groups of nurses, orderlies, chauffeurs and kitchen staff. Gay red of coverlets and soldiers' bed-jackets, beautiful blue of orderlies' dresses, sprinkling of military uniforms and snowy veils, with the sober grey of the little knot of doctors made a magnificent colour scheme in the old Gothic building with its stained glass windows filtering the afternoon sunlight on the parquet floor, and the stone pillars, the blankets and the uniforms.[43]

The patients were now in the throes of a veritable craze constructing 'bagues boches', carefully fashioned finger rings from pieces of aluminium from shells or other pieces of war ironmongery, for their wives, sweethearts and every nurse and orderly within sight. The search was on for unringed fingers, and great was the competition to adorn them.[44]

Athletic sports were organised in which patients, orderlies, sisters and doctors all took part – 'course aux brancards' (stretchers), 'course aux vêtements', tugs of war, potato races and so on – a novelty to the French patients who were delighted with this example of British eccentricity.[45]

In August they celebrated the founding of the Abbey by Saint Louis – not entirely appropriately – with modern music and a tombola.[46]

Domestic problems interrupted the smooth running of the hospital. £16 had to be found to improve the hot water supply. The kitchen orderlies were now too busy to wash the floors themselves, so French women were recruited. The solution was more trouble than it was worth, however, as they flooded the floor with copious buckets of water and conditions were worse than before. An SOS went back for eight or nine strong, healthy, Scotch (sic) servants.[47]

There were endless problems with coal and electricity. The dynamo for generating electricity simply ate coal; they tried coal dust but this was inadequate. Some of the underground electrical wires were damaged and the whole installation was totally insufficient for the work it was required to do. Electric light had to be limited to the theatre and the x-ray room; a dynamo was hired from Paris at considerable expense – but even with this the supply of light for the theatre could not be guaranteed. They were reduced once more to candles in bottles, and Miss Loudon found that 'penny Chinese lanterns do very well for candle-sticks'. Poor Miss Loudon was torn between the need to heat and light the hospital and the need to keep expenses down. She exclaimed:

> I have come to the conclusion that the most necessary qualification for an
> Administrator is a knowledge of plumbing and engineering, of both of
> which I am entirely ignorant.[48]

There was not enough electricity for sterilisers, and now even alcohol for spirit lamps was running short. There was a shortage of blankets – the staff were passing theirs to the patients. Miss Loudon begged the Committee for 5000 yards of gauze and 1 cwt of cotton wool every month. Couldn't we use more moss for dressings? she wondered. (Sphagnum moss, collected by volunteers in the boggy areas of Scotland and elsewhere, sterilised, dried and packed, was very useful for the copiously discharging wounds of modern warfare on account of its absorbency and softness.)

In September they were cheered by the arrival of their beautiful x-ray car, gifted by the London Society with the very latest and most perfect equipment obtainable. The car had its own dark room, an independent water supply, and facilities for developing films in transit. It was to be used for the benefit of other patients in neighbouring hospitals, none of which at that time had even the most rudimentary equipment. Patients would now be saved unnecessary and painful journeys. Madam Curie herself had advised on its equipment, and took a great interest in the adaptation of x-rays to serve the war effort and the needs of humanity. 'J'ai fait cela moi-même', she said, 'très souvent, et cela va très bien et sauve beaucoup de vies humaines ou êmpeche les infirmités.'[49] However, there was a drawback in having such a very wonderful machine, and putting it on show in London before taking it over to France. It may have encouraged contributions to the Scottish Women's Hospitals, but – it was seen by the War Office! Cicely Hamilton reported to Dr Savill in London on August 28th:

> A new and dreadful hitch to the x-ray car – The War Office comman-
> deered the engine, then they refused to release the car from the works

until Austins had delivered a specified number of cars to them. Yesterday we heard that at last our car was released and could start; but now they refuse to give Captain Humphries leave to come out [he was to help in getting it operating] and Major Barrett doesn't want to go without him ... Most satisfactory if you [Savill] would come over for a day or two and let them go through everything with you ... if possible Butt [the manufacturers] will agree to send out one of their own men ... I am so afraid that if we are not quick at getting it out of the country the War Office will think of some new hitch.[50]

Dr Savill did come out, the x-ray staff were trained. The War Office was foiled.

On September 24th the hospital was alerted, a rush was expected and they were ordered to evacuate as many patients as possible. 'I think we have evacuated every man who could crawl', Miss Loudon reported. The rush materialised over the next five days. Wounded were pouring in day and night. They were coming from the Arras and Souchez sections of the French Front and later from the heavy fighting round Hébuterne. They were all, Miss Ivens reported, 'horribly infected. I have never seen such wounds, gangrenous and offensive to a degree. We amputated three limbs, and there are several on the verge'. Even her Downs forceps were worn out with heavy use.[51] On one day they performed 22 operations, and on the following day 18.

A young Canadian orderly, newly arrived, recorded her first impressions in her diary, and her grim experiences in the rush of work which followed. Marjorie Starr arrived at the Abbey on September 6th and wrote: 'A little fountain plays perpetually ... water just tantalises me, no bath now for two weeks and none in view for another fortnight'.[52] Starr found her first flea – 'We scrub and clean so much there isn't a corner for them to live in (must have come from the trenches at Arras'). (Sister Jeffrey was asking her mother to send out flea pads – whatever they may have been.) Starr, however, was 'not tired at all, just dirty'.

She seems to have been flung into the deep end. On September 15th she wrote: '15 beds to make myself, perfect stream of bedpans, 3 horrid dressings to prepare and then bandage up and clear away – and when the other sister came back if she didn't get me to scrub lockers and I jolly well had to smile and do it'.

Cleaning feet and nails was a 'smelly job'. They were 'very particular about nails here on account of the microbes'. She saw her first operation:

all tendons and nerves mixed up – agony of dressings so great they gave him chloroform, and it took 6 of us to hold him while he was going under – got all sprinkled with blood and pus as he was very septic.

By September 18th she was 'never so tired in all my life'. They were short-staffed, there were painful dressings, the new cases were 'simply filthy'. 'Then, when they were all cleaned up, the chimney sweep arrived – there was soot everywhere even on the patients' bandages, a man came down from oper-ation, the patients' suppers had to be served – and all at once'.

On September 24th:

everyone worked to death ... in our cleansing room pipe burst and flooded ... the kitchen boiler went wrong and kitchen fires had to be put out, so no hot water ... and the electric light engine got cranky and light so dim.

On the next three days they were in the thick of the rush. 'Spent the day cleaning dirty people.'

She described the reception of the patients:

When the Hall Porter hears motors coming she blows a horn and we all flock to the entrance except one in the wards, lift stretchers and lay on floor ... if stretchers go to out-patients' room where we blanket bath ... clothes into sack. Walking cases to cleansing room – bath there behind curtains and one of not badly wounded [patients] ... bath them. Then we finish them up and get them to bed. I never saw such filth ... straight from the trenches – all gory. Still they come, the wounded. Every hour as soon as one lot is cleaned and put to bed the next ambulance arrives, and the worst of it is that in the middle of the excitement the meals for the others have to go on. Also ... in the middle of dressing a horrible wound, have to run to someone else with a bedpan.

And again, on the 28th:

How we all groan when we hear that blast [blasted] horn and then we stampede for the entrance with all the blue dresses and caps of the sisters lifting the stretchers out of the ambulance, and really today each one seems worse than the last: one arm will simply have to be amputated, he had poison gas as well, and the smell was enough to knock me down, bits of bone sticking through and all gangrene. It will be marvellous if Miss Ivens saves it, but she is going to try it appears, as it is his right arm. He went to x-ray, then to theatre, and I believe the op was rather wonderful, but I had no time to stop and see as I had to help and carry the stretchers. They come right from the trenches, with only temporary dressings, and we operate, and as soon as possible move them on. No poky little wounds now, they are all serious. I mind the smell, or should I say stink, of the wounds more than anything. I can't seem to get away from it. I get to bed about 9.30, and after a good wash (her own rubber bath had arrived by this time) sprinkle my bed with perfume so as to get it out of my nostrils as my clothes even smell of it. We have so little disinfectant, not enough to drown the odour of it all. The operating theatre is a horrible hell these days.[53]

They were fitting up a second operating theatre in one of the ward kitchens.

As all the ambulant patients had to be discharged, the orderlies no longer had their help with the chores, and to add to their heavy work in the wards they had to carry all the coal, and the stretchers themselves. 'It is the stretcher cases that wear us out, carrying heavy men up those stairs is much too heavy for girls, even four of us'.

The orderlies were getting up at 4.30 a.m.: '40 beds to be made, 30 help-less – all beds to be changed as dressings soaked through. High nervous pressure while dressings are being done 8–12.30. Everyone worn out and nerves all on edge'.

Her difficulties were increased by the sister who was supposed to be training her:

And really I never knew whether I was standing on my head or my heels, and I never seemed to get through, as she never let me finish anything in peace, always fly away to get this or that, then why wasn't it done? I suffered in silence, but I would just come up here when I was off and cry from pure wrought-up nerves.

Her stress was noticed and she was placed under a different sister – 'And now it is just heaven in comparison – she is from the Royal in Glasgow. [This was probably Sister Lindsay.] Everyone was pitying me and I evidently won Matron's favour by never complaining'.

How thankful she was later on to have this change of sister when:

It rather sent my heart to the bottom of my boots when I lifted the stretcher out and saw what I had, or rather smelt it … all his lower jaw was blown away, and it was fearfully sceptic (sic) and his clothes and body were in the last word in dirt and goriness. I am sure he had been lying sometime in mud unattended to before being picked up. [This was highly likely as at that period the collection of wounded from the battle-field was very inefficient, particularly in the French lines.]

This patient became very important to her. Her knowledge of French enabled her to help him through, and the sight of his gradual improvement, in which she played an important part, must also have helped her through her own period of stress.

Next day:

the man with the awful mouth seems a little better. I had to try and get an egg down his throat but it was no use, he couldn't swallow: his tongue seems half gone. They always have to call me to him as I seem to be the only one who can understand what he wants to say.

On October 1st she found herself in charge of a ward all alone (with a sister nearby to call if needed), supper for 16, four of whom had to be fed. 'The man with the wounded mouth was to have liquid food poured down his throat through a tube: it isn't a pleasant job but anything to help the miserable man.'

By October 4th 'my poor man with the wounded mouth is getting on. I feed him on milk every time I have a minute to spare, through a rubber tube'.

On October 8th 'my smelly friend with the mouth is doing well and he is a little more wholesome to go near'.

On October 18th, after a spell away from the wards she saw him again – 'I got a shock when I saw the man with the mouth. He had been shaved and walked into the refectory himself, he can eat soft food quite well and his mouth is nearly healed and he can talk quite well'.

And on November 4th: 'I think the man with the mouth will soon be away now, and as he is quite cured and very little disfigured and he talks quite well and eats enough to make up for lost time'.

Finally on November 28th: 'my "smelly friend" as I call him (the one with the shattered jaw) is so well that they operated to get a stray bit of shrapnel out of his neck … it was a great success and he is doing well'.

Her collection of photographs includes one of her 'smelly friend'.

She was beginning to feel the strain. There was some relief when she went on night duty – no longer getting up at 4.30 a.m., and spared the ordeal of the daily dressings. She described her new work:

> such an eerie existence in the old Abbaye at night with only a lantern,
> and I had four fires to stoke, and if they went out I jolly well had to light
> them and fish for sticks and nothing to chop them with if you do find
> any, but I managed to find the lid of a box and chopped it with a shovel.

Miss Loudon, the Administrator, arranged for her to have a few days' rest in Paris and then a month in the kitchen 'till my nerves get better':

> It will not be so interesting of course, but I am not thinking of seeing
> things now, I just want to rest my mind and get away from the horrors
> for a little. Several of the girls have given up completely under the
> strain, but I hope this change will just pull me up in time, and I
> won't mind the hard work if I have no responsibility.

Starr's experience shows that as far as the demands of the work allowed the staff did consider the needs of the young orderlies. In Starr's case they relieved her in time as her subsequent career showed. Her spirits rose and she found she was enjoying life again:

> We work in the quaintest old place, all stone arches: it must have been
> where wine was served to the monks in the old days, and then later was

the scullery of the convent. Three girls usually run it and the other two here are awfully nice and we have lots of fun over our dish slinging. You ought to see us throwing those tin plates about, they go like lightning.

She didn't however remain very long in the kitchen but began work as a store-keeper: 'I am sure I shall feel a perfect lady, no more dirt for a few days anyway'. She described the procedure on the death of a patient:

The night orderly, Miller [Miss Marjorie Miller, orderly, later Auxiliary Nurse 30.8.15 to 28.2.16 and 9.9.16 to 30.12.18], had to help carry the body to the chapel – she says it was rather a gruesome sight. Miss Duncan, the Matron [Miss Isabella Duncan, Matron, 6.15 to 15.12.16] went first down three flights of steps and through the moonlit cloisters carrying a lantern and these three girls carrying the stretcher, draped in a sheet and a piece of paper pinned on his chest with his name, age 19, and then the name of the witnesses who were there when he died, Miss Ivens, the surgeon, a sister and Richmond. [Richmond [Miss Susan Eleanor Richmond, later Mrs Haydon, orderly, 6.7.15 to 11.10.16] was an actress and subsequently had a very successful career on the London stage.]

On another occasion she witnessed a funeral at Asnières and has left this account:

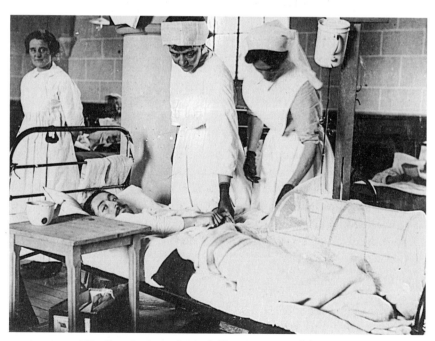

Miss Ivens on a ward round. Note irrigation of the wound.
(By permission of the Imperial War Museum).

First a line of choirboys followed by the coffin, then the priest, after that
the old mother of one and the relations of the other, then their comrades
from the wards ... Then crutches, slings and bandaged heads followed
each other two by two, then two of our lady doctors in uniform and a
band of village women all in black who go to all the funerals so that the
poor souls have plenty of mourners. It seems strange that they don't have
a military funeral still this is war in grim earnest and there is no time nor
men to be spared for show. The wounded who followed had their uniforms
on, as in the hospital they wear blue trousers and red flannel coats belonging to us, that is when there is enough to go round: now we have 204
patients so there is a variety of costumes given out, but nothing like the
variety of the French soldiers at the funeral, some were Zouaves, some even
had black faces [probably Senegalese], some in blue trousers, some in red,
but none ever so clean in all their soldier lives as they do (sic) when they
leave here with all the uniforms cleaned and disinfected and mended. [At
this time there was indeed a great variety of uniforms in the French Army.
It was only in 1916 that the Army was provided with steel helmets and
'French Blue' uniforms – not as good camouflage as the British khaki or
the German 'feldgrau' but much the same when covered in mud.]

Her interest in the medical work continued. On November 4th she reported:

There are several very bad cases of gas gangrene, which is nasty and
smelly and, of course, very dangerous. I was very glad I wasn't the poor
VAD yesterday who got a leg to burn as the theatre sisters were too busy
to attend to it. [An incinerator was provided for the disposal of limbs,
dressings and other rubbish.] It is bad enough to hold the stump for
dressings without having to handle the lifeless limb.

On November 20th she was reporting a lull – for the time being the rush was
virtually over. Back to nursing in the wards again, she was called on by the
doctor to translate a patient's story (soon to become all too common from the
fearful conditions in the trenches as the wet weather set in). The patient
described the terrible mud, and how the shells made holes in the bottom of
the trenches. With mud up to his knees it was impossible to see where the
holes were, and he fell in up to his chest. He struggled for five hours to get
out until, responding to his whistle, rescuers got ropes and hauled him out.
He was one of the lucky ones as three men had been drowned in the mud on
the same day.

    Throughout her account one can sense her pride in the hospital and her
admiration for the work of the surgeons. Of two badly wounded patients she
wrote: 'Their legs are really awful, and in a French military hospital would
have been amputated long ago, but Miss Ivens is doing her best to save the
limbs'.

Starr has given us some insight from an orderly's point of view. The sense of strain was shared by others. While she was nursing the Matron during a short illness, Starr remarked on what a difficult time the Matron had with so many squabbling sisters.

Miss Ivens herself had a problem with one of the doctors which must have caused her some annoyance.

Dr Rutherford had arrived at Royaumont in June 1915, and resigned suddenly on October 23rd. She wrote to Mrs (Dr) Russell of the Committee:

> During the greater part of the time the hospital has been established the cases have been chiefly of a light nature, but recently more serious cases have been received. Unfortunately during the past few months two patients have been trephined with grave results. On the 20th inst another cerebral case occurred in which surgical interference seemed imperative, and owing to the unfortunate result in the former cases I ventured to suggest to Miss Ivens, for her own sake and that of the hospital, the advisability of obtaining a second opinion. She received my suggestion in bad part, and afterwards, in public, asked me to leave the theatre. After the operation I reiterated to her that my suggestion was a friendly one and not in the nature of a criticism, but offered to resign immediately as she had resented my action. Accordingly I left Royaumont the following day. I regret if this slip has caused inconvenience either in the Hospital or to the Committee, but in the circumstances no other course was possible.[54]

Mrs Hunter, the Chairman of the Hospital Committee, said that she had received a number of complaints about Dr Ivens's surgery on a recent visit. The Committee also received a letter from Miss Ivens who stated that 'she had just become aware of disloyalty in the medical staff', and she wanted the Committee to recall one member. Mrs Hunter felt she could not continue in her office unless these complaints were thoroughly investigated.

Mrs Russell, who was medically qualified and was a member of the Committee, went out with the specific remit to explore the situation. (In other words the question was 'Was Miss Ivens up to it?') It was a delicate task for Mrs Russell, but she reported back after her visit that she had 'investigated thoroughly, studied the medical statistics and interviewed affected members. The French authorities were abundantly satisfied – they were still sending cases after these reports had reached them, Dr Coussergues [Médecin-Chef of the Army Zone in which Royaumont was placed, and therefore representing the highest medical authority] frequently brought visiting doctors to visit and invited Miss Ivens to inspect work at other hospitals and the hospital was thoroughly inspected at regular intervals'. Mrs Russell went on to reassure the Committee 'they had no cause for anxiety whatever, but on the contrary had cause to be proud of the work being done by Miss Ivens and her assistants'. The Committee resolved unanimously that they send a vote of confidence to Dr Ivens.[55]

Most surgeons would agree that Miss Ivens had some justification in requesting an assistant to leave the theatre if she had been criticised – publicly – for her handling of a very difficult operation. Most surgeons would also agree that in the conditions prevailing at that time there would inevitably be some cases that would go wrong. All surgeons were learning on the job how to deal with war wounds. Miss Ivens was no exception, turning her skills from gynaecology in peacetime to the far different casualties of war. She had, in her usual thorough way, taken great trouble to equip herself in her new tasks. Looking back from a knowledge of the achievements and the results obtained at Royaumont by the end of the war, it seems Mrs Russell's report was justified and no mere whitewashing exercise.

To be fair to Dr Rutherford, who had been genuinely worried when she saw a case 'going wrong', though she was not as wise as she might have been in the way she acted, it should be recorded that after leaving Royaumont she went on to serve with the RAMC in Malta and Salonika, and after the Second World War worked as a medical officer in UNRRA (United Nations Relief and Reconstruction Administration).

Dr Rutherford's departure on October 23rd must have left a problem for the remaining staff – Miss Loudon reported the week October 24th to 30th was 'rather dreadful':

> The doctors and nurses and theatre orderlies work from morning to night and from night to morning; if there is another advance I don't know what will happen. The wet weather means much mud in the trenches, and mud on wounds means dirt and that usually means poison and gas gangrene and all sorts of horrors.

She reserved a room at the hotel in Creil for the use of the chauffeurs who had to wait, often for long periods, in the cold and wet for the arrival of the hospital trains. And just then the cesspits had to be cleared out. 'You can imagine the odours', she moaned – and this was in addition to the smell of gas gangrene. And those damaged electric cables were not yet repaired.[56]

It was rather inopportune that the Queen of Serbia chose that time to visit the hospital. History does not relate how she reacted to the all-pervading smell, but on the surface everything went well. The tour of the hospital was made, the polite things were said, the statutory photographs were taken, and appropriate decorum was observed.

Starr gives us some insight into what went on behind the scenes. The Queen arrived before she was expected. The doctors were still getting into their best uniforms. An ambulance was standing at the front door collecting the dirty uniforms from the trenches to take them away for disinfecting and cleansing. In panic the hall porter flew off and found one of the doctors, who arrived just in time to receive the Queen. One of the chauffeurs was invited to drive the Queen to the Chateau nearby and was invited to stay and have lunch with Her Majesty. Starr commented:

> She was an awful swell in her new uniform and gloves. We had such a laugh, it took her an hour to get her hands presentable; she does all her repairs herself and her hands have got just like a mechanic's.

The progress and achievements of the hospital were followed with great interest by many of the leading women doctors of the time, who recognised that the reputation of women in the medical profession depended in part on their performance in difficult war conditions. If they could perform well there it would be difficult for the sceptics to maintain that women were not strong enough or able enough to be regarded as the equals of men. It was already recognised that women could give valuable service in looking after women and children and in filling unpopular but necessary positions in the local authority 'workhouse' infirmaries, but could they really be proficient in general surgery, and, even more doubtfully, in military surgery? Were they, in short, tough enough? And what if they should fail?

Miss Louisa Aldrich-Blake (later Dame Louisa, only the second women to receive that honour) had no doubts on the subject. She was herself a distinguished surgeon – she was the first woman to obtain the degree of Master of Surgery (Miss Ivens was the third). From 1914, in addition to her surgical work, she was Dean of the London (Royal Free Hospital) School of Medicine for Women (L(RFH)SMW). Her heavy workload prevented her (as she wished) from volunteering for service overseas, but she used her vacations to work at Royaumont in 1915 and again in 1916. She turned her hand to many kinds of activities, from making toast to major surgery. Orderly Starr, looking at her from afar, decided she was a 'charming person'. The patients, who referred to Miss Ivens as 'la Colonelle', decided Aldrich-Blake was 'Madame la Générale'.

It was a happy arrangement, and Miss Ivens wrote at the time of her death in 1925, referring to her 1915 visit:

> The greater part of her time was spent in the theatre, looking for elusive bullets or bits of shells in inaccessible positions. Her patience and pertinacity impressed both theatre staff and x-ray departments. I can only remember one failure, but there were many brilliant successes.

And in 1916 when 400 beds were in use:

> Cases of gas gangrene had poured in, and the work had been strenuous and exhausting. With her characteristic energy Miss Aldrich-Blake dressed in the wards, did re-amputations, or anything else that was

needed. She was much interested in the sera treatment of gas gangrene, which we were then successfully trying in some of the worst infections. ... She was most sympathetic with our difficulties, and I do not remember hearing a word of criticism though she must have noticed a great deal that could have been improved upon.[57]

Another prominent medical woman to visit Royaumont in 1915 was Dr Louisa Martindale who left her impressions of the Unit. After professional visits to a number of hospitals in Paris she proceeded to Royaumont to spend some time helping in the hospital. Travelling comfortably in her first-class carriage, she was recognised by a member of the Unit, and, taken out of her luxury, was introduced to the economical ways of the Scottish Women's Hospitals who were all, including Miss Ivens, travelling third class. She had happy memories of Dr Savill's pianola in the gallery of the refectory, and the Spanish melodies of Antonio de Navarro who was collecting material for his book on the Abbey. That was the cultured side of life at Royaumont; but then she had to adapt to some of the other realities. Her 'cell' had a bed, a chair, a packing case and a basin (still no bathroom). At mealtimes she had a single enamel plate which had to serve for two courses, and a single enamel mug which did duty for wine and coffee. (Later, the staff had to do without the wine, though for the patients it was always a part of their rations.) But the food was splendid – Michelet, the famous chef, was in the kitchen – temporarily then – though later he returned as a permanent member of the Unit, having been seconded by the Army. Knives were in very short supply, and the first thing Dr Martindale did when she got home was to send out a dozen or so for the doctors. She spent her time usefully doing dressings, operating, filling in forms, writing reports, and doing other necessary chores. She was

> Tremendously impressed ... There were no men to help carry the heavy patients. Women, some of whom had never before done any housework, worked all day at washing up in that huge, badly equipped, ancient kitchen, or helped to clean, mend and repair, each soldier's kit ready for departure. Most of all I was lost in admiration of the splendid organising and administrative powers of the CMO [Chief Medical Officer], Miss Ivens – of her endurance, courage and above all her surgical skill.[58]

Another visitor, still comparatively young when she visited and helped out at Royaumont, was Dr Mary Lucas-Keene, already on the teaching staff of the London (Royal Free Hospital) School of Medicine for Women. She later became the first woman professor of Anatomy, not only in Britain, but in the entire world. She was the first woman to examine for the Royal College of Surgeons of England.

Dr Margaret Joyce was an old friend of Miss Ivens, whom she had known since her late 'teens. It was Margaret Joyce who had pointed the young Frances towards a career in medicine. She, along with Dr Vera Foley, both prominent practitioners in Liverpool, also devoted a month's holiday to work at Royaumont.

These 'working visitors' indicate the enormous interest and pride felt by medical women in the work there. Although their commitments at home prevented them from joining the Unit, they could not resist having at least a finger in the pie.

There was another worry for the Hospital Committee at home towards the end of 1915. This was financial. It did seem to them, deliberating in Edinburgh, that Royaumont was proving very expensive. It now cost them £1000 a month in addition to the 2 francs a day per patient which they received from the French Government. (Dr Inglis had originally calculated £500 per month.) Did they really need 72 pairs of rubber gloves per month? The demands for gauze seemed to them to be exorbitant. They really must try and use less than one ton of coal a day. And did they really need a staff of 90?

Miss Kemp and Dr Russell went into this very thoroughly on their visit of inspection. They said clearly and definitely that there was 'no extravagance at Royaumont'. It would be quite impossible to work the hospital with a smaller number of staff. The size and inconvenience of the building and the serious nature of the cases necessitated keeping the staff at the present level.[59]

Right through to the end of November the hospital was particularly full – there had been an influx of bad cases since the advance at Loos.

With the slackening of the work as winter approached, Starr spent some of her spare time exploring the trenches nearby (these were never actually used but had been prepared after the Battle of the Marne). There were other new activities:

> A lot of doctors and orderlies and even some of the nurses have organised
> a hockey team, but yours truly won't join, the suffragettes would be too
> much for me ... The hockey team is getting on – I wouldn't care to play
> with them, they are a burly lot, a good many of them suffragettes. I say
> they are keeping in training for after the war, but I must say they are a
> jolly lot just the same.

On December 2nd there was a party to celebrate the opening of the hospital in 1914. Miss Ivens supplied champagne and 'gave us a spanking supper'. They put on fancy dress and danced till midnight.

On December 13th the men got up a party. They had a gramophone, and those who were able, danced. Poor Starr would 'quite like to have danced with them too, but it wouldn't do, we have to keep our dignity, or we wouldn't be able to keep order as we do and get respect from them'. (It sounds as if she were quoting from a pep talk for new orderlies.)

The year ended with a splendid Christmas party. Cicely Hamilton produced a scene from her own play, *Diana of Dobson's,* which had been such a success on the London stage. Cicely herself played the part of Diana. Not only did the Unit enjoy it, but they felt also, through Cicely, that they were at the centre of culture.

And so 1915 drew to a close. They had had their first baptism of fire. In later years Collum looked back with nostalgia to 'the more leisured days of 1915'.[60]

1916 came in, bringing new challenges when Royaumont was called upon to greater efforts and greater achievements during the 'Big Push' in the Battles of the Somme.

References

1. 'Skia' (V.C.C. Collum), *Blackwood's Magazine*, Nov. 1918, p. 615.
2. ML. Tin 12, F. Ivens to E. Inglis, 10.1.15.
3. ML. Tin 12, FI to EI, 15.1.15.
4. ML. Tin 12, FI to Mrs Laurie, 1.2.15.
5. ML. Tin 49, C. Hamilton to Crompton, 20.2.15.
6. ML. Tin 12, Harley to EI, 26.2.15.
7. ML. Tin 12, FI to EI, 11.3.15.
8. ML. Tin 12, FI to EI, 27.3.15.
9. ML. Tin 12, FI to Laurie, 26.3.15.
10. 'Skia', *op. cit.*, p. 617.
11. ML. Tin 42, FI to EI, 6.4.15.
12. ML. Tin 13, EI to FI, 30.3.15.
13. ML. Tin 13, EI to Laurie, 30.3.15.
14. ML. Tin 13, EI to Mair, 25.4.15.
15. ML. Tin 13, EI to Laurie, 25.4.15.
16. ML. Tin 12 (loose leaf file), FI to EI, 6.4.15.
17. ML. Tin 12, Mrs Harley to EI, 10.2.15.
18. Leneman, *In the Service of Life.*
19. Hamilton, *Life Errant*, p. 117.
20. NL 1931, p. 1.
21. ML. Tin 13, EI to Miss Mair, 25.4.15.
22. ML. Tin 12, FI to EI, 6.4.15.
23. NL January 1929.
24. ML. Tin 49, C. Hamilton to Miss Crompton, 20.2.15.
25. 'Skia', *op. cit.*, p. 616.
26. *Ibid.*
27. *Ibid.*
28. *Ibid.*
29. CC, C. Hamilton, July 15 1915.
30. Dr L.M. Henry. Reminiscences presented by her to Miss Helen Lowe who

kindly made them available to me.

31. NL 1970, p. 2.

32. Liddle Archive in Leeds University. Taped interview with Miss Margaret Ainslie Stewart, chauffeur, 5.5.17 to 7.11.17.

33. ML. Tin 42, C. Hamilton, 2.8.15.

34. ML. Tin 1, Report to Personnel Committee, 5.6.15.

35. ML. Tin 12, FI to Miss Marris, 17.9.15.

36. Navarro, *The Scottish Women's Hospital*, p. 171.

37. Wellcome Institute for the History of Medicine. Dr Elizabeth Butler to Secretary, Lister Institute, 31.8.14.

38. ML. Tin 12, FI to Miss Marris, June 1915.

39. ML. Tin 42, 3.3.16.

40. ML. Tin 12, Miss Loudon to Mrs Laurie, 26.6.15.

41. *CC*, July 2 1915.

42. *CC*, July 9 1915.

43. *CC*, Cicely Hamilton, July 30 1915.

44. *CC*, V. Collum, July 30 1915, p. 219.

45. *CC*, C. Hamilton, August 27 1915, p. 261.

46. *CC*, December 3 1915, p. 450.

47. ML. Tin 42, Miss Loudon to Marris, 6.8.15.

48. ML. *loc. cit.*, 29.9.15.

49. FL. Box 304/3. Quote from Mme Curie, April 1915.

50. FL. Box 304/3, C. Hamilton to Dr Savill.

51. ML. Tin 42, FI to Marris, 29.9.15.

52. IWM. Diary of Marjorie Starr (Orderly 30.8.15 to 26.2.16). Dates of entries as given in text.

53. Mabel Jeffrey (Sister 27.3.15 to 1.3.16); *Auntie Mabel's War*, p. 31.

54. ML. Tin 6, Rutherford to Russell, 23.10.15.

55. ML. Tin 41, Mrs Hunter's Report to the Hospital Committee, 27.11.15.

56. ML. Tin 42, Loudon to Marris, undated.

57. Frances Ivens. Newsletter Medical Women's Federation 1926, p. 19–20.

58. Louisa Martindale, *A Woman Surgeon*, pp. 166–8.

59. ML. Tin 41, Hospital Committee Minutes, 15.10.15.

60. NL 1937, p. 10.

CHAPTER FOUR

1916: The Year of Testing

The Military Situation

The military situation in 1916 which formed the background to the work of the hospital was influenced initially by the great struggles further east. As far as the French forces were concerned, the winter lull ended on February 21st with the German attack directed towards Verdun. On February 25th the Germans captured Fort Douaumont, one of the key strongholds which the French had left, inexplicably, virtually unmanned. Had the Germans realised it at the time, the way to Verdun was wide open, but they missed the chance, and the opportunity never recurred. Instead, an increasingly grim situation developed with repeated attacks by both sides, enormous losses, but barely any change in the front.

Then on April 9th the Germans lodged a full-scale offensive along the whole of the Verdun front on both banks of the Meuse. Fighting continued with little gained on either side through May and into June. Conditions in the trenches were appalling; there were periods of continuous rain and other periods of excessive heat. Suffering was intense.

On June 7th the second great Fort, supposedly guarding Verdun, Fort Vaux, fell to the Germans. On June 11th Pétain, who was now (although only temporarily) in charge, pressed Joffre, the Commander-in-Chief, to bring forward the relief offensive which had been planned with the British on the Somme. On June 20th the situation became even more desperate with the first use of the new gas diphosgene which paralysed the French artillery. On the 23rd the Germans made a significant advance.

The preliminary bombardment on the Somme by the British began on June 24th and was followed on July 1st by the infantry forces of both the French and British going 'over the top'. The preliminary bombardment had been tragically ineffective and the casualty rate was unbelievably high. On that one day the British lost 60,000 men of whom 20,000 were killed. The French lost as many men as they had in the previous three months' fighting, which had, itself, been on an enormous scale.

This was the terrible beginning of the 'Great Push'. It was followed by five months of pointless slaughter.

Now began the period of greatest stress that Royaumont had known so far, which was eclipsed only by its experience in the great battles of 1918. But it gave Royaumont the opportunity to prove that it was able to meet the challenge.

At Royaumont

The New Year came in quietly enough. Surveying her staff, Miss Ivens was pleased. The *bouches inutiles*, as she called them, had left, and morale was high.

As 1916 opened they felt they were beginning to get to grips with the conditions in which they were working – relations with the French authorities were becoming increasingly friendly – initial mistrust had been overcome. Dr Bossières, inspecting, had declared that Royaumont was 'one of the few *hôpitals étrangères* which had not given them unspeakable ennuis'. A visitor reported: 'Today it is known far and wide in the countryside as a refuge for the wounded under the care of the *dames écossaises*.'[1]

Royaumont did not confine itself to purely medical care when other needs arose. One day in early January, 180 men, exhausted, hungry and cold (but unwounded), arrived at the Abbey. They had been on the road for several days – victims of the French Army's lack of canteens and rest centres, and with pay a mere pittance of 20 sous a day they were in no position to help themselves. At the hospital hot meals were quickly provided, straw was laid on the floor of the great refectory, and they slept. Later, to the astonishment of the staff, the men roused themselves and gave them a concert by way of thanks.[2]

Beds were now increased to 250. Further help was requested from them as Dr Coussergues, in charge of the *gare régulatrice*, begged the loan of two of the Royaumont sisters to direct a large new surgical ward at the Creil Hospital because the level of training of their own nurses was so inadequate. Miss Ivens, with the blessing of the Committee, agreed to send two or three sisters each month in rotation, provided always that the Abbey's needs were met.[3]

Some improvements in the domestic arrangements were made. M. Pichon, the architect, 'went over the drains most carefully',[4] though the later history of the Abbey seems to suggest that, as the population increased and the years rolled on, sanitary problems were never really resolved in spite of frequent emptying of cesspits. The washing now went to a military laundry instead of being farmed out to a number of individual women in the surrounding villages.[5] A close eye was kept on the requirements of the staff, and white petticoats were definitely not acceptable.

Wine was obligatory for the *poilus* as decreed by the Army and was now to be available at army rates, but the hospital still had to cover the cost. Miss Ivens, generous to a fault where the welfare of the hospital and the patients was concerned, asked the Committee to use the £100 increase in salary they had offered her, and which she said she did not really require, to cover the cost of the *poilus'* 'pinard'.[6]

A new electrical installation was approved to run on petrol, at the cost of 12,000 francs, and by early April it had begun to 'marcher'.[7] The scullery still required a new sink and a new *marmite* (for heating and storing water), and a second lorry was becoming essential. Intense cold and snow exacerbated the transport problems and again the supply of coal was threatened. The military authorities, however, proved helpful, and supplied them with a weekly truckload from Rouen, to be fetched in their hard-working lorry. Even the six-and-a-half tons allowed was barely sufficient, and kitchen fires had to be ruthlessly cut.[8]

Royaumont experienced its first loss in the death of Sister Gray in January some days after an apparently successful operation for appendicitis. She was buried in the local churchyard with full military honours. One of her patients wrote of 'good, kind Miss Gray who has always something gently to do with us' (sic).[9] She and her sister were among the very first arrivals in November 1914, and her sister – who called herself 'Disorderly' (by all accounts a most inappropriate nickname) – gallantly returned after a short period at home. She then remained, a valued auxiliary nurse, throughout all the later tumultuous periods in the history of the hospital till the final closure in 1919.

In April the Committee sent over two of its members to make a thorough inspection. Mrs Laurie and Mrs Robertson were impressed with the organisation:

> Our impressions of the Abbaye de Royaumont are of the most pleasant, the work being carried on there appears to be excellent; the members of the staff are working most harmoniously together, there seems to be a tremendous feeling of esprit-de-corps among them all, and the patients speak in most appreciative terms of all that has been done for them by our noble women.
>
> The curés of Asnières and Viarmes as well as the municipal authorities of other little towns surrounding the hospital are all most grateful for the assistance we have been giving to the civil patients whom Dr Ivens has, – with the consent of the Committee, and, I consider, very wisely, – been taking in whilst the number of her soldier patients has been decreasing. We inspected very thoroughly the whole of the hospital, the orderlies' dormitories, Sisters' bedrooms, wards, kitchen, store and other departments. Mrs Hacon has now taken over the superintendence of the kitchen department ... an admirable arrangement as constant supervision is necessary, and this is the department where the greatest saving can take place, and where close attention to detail must be given to curtail waste as much as possible.
>
> There is no doubt that the patients are extremely well fed.[10]

Easter came, and all who could went to Mass in the village, 'hopping and jumping on crutches'.

Miss Ivens gave much thought to maintaining the morale of the patients: concerts were a regular feature, some given by staff, some by the men, and there was great rivalry between the wards. They were allowed into the woods to pick the *muguets* (lily of the valley), and they fished in the stream. The presentation of medals was an occasion for celebration for the whole hospital. Miss Ivens organised a competition for the men to write their personal *histoires de guerre*. For many this was not simply a way of passing the time, but a therapeutic measure to exorcise some of the horrors they had undergone. Every entrant (and there were 64) received a prize – a photograph of the Abbey. The best got a larger photograph, so everyone was pleased.[11]

An example of one *histoire* was written by Eugène Boutet, a farmer in civil life. He wrote of his experiences since the Battle of Loos (September 25–26, 1915):

> On the evening of the 26th, with several of my companions, we buried many of the unfortunates who had been killed on the 25th – they were all without arms or legs, or their chests torn open – it was frightful. This was my first experience of the labyrinth trenches. During the month of November we suffered many privations, bad weather (every day it poured), shells, mud and water up to our waists. At night we were frozen; it was, indeed, 'agréable'![12]

Blanche de Castille Ward on the first floor. Note draw-string bags for personal belongings. Irrigation of wound in patient by pillar on right.
(By courtesy of Mrs Anne Murdoch).

As they approached one of their peak periods of activity resulting from the Somme battles of 1916, there were some tiresome claims made of waste and extravagance which had to be met. No one knew quite who had made them but Miss Ivens took them seriously and reviewed the administration. Mrs Hacon, now kitchen superintendent, was succeeding in 'feeding staff and patients as cheaply and efficiently as possible under difficult conditions'. She pointed out that 'a well-equipped store room does not mean that stores are given out lavishly. The most expensive times are when we have to live from hand to mouth, buying in Paris from day to day'.

But as regards dressings and drugs she was adamant. She pointed out to the Committee:

> It is absolutely essential now to be ready for a heavy demand. The inspect-ing generals expect us to be prepared for all emergencies and any defi-ciency would be noted at once, and placed against us as a bad mark ... As I think I told you before, our standard has to be that of the Paris hospitals, in which zone we are placed geographically, while our preparations have to be of such a character as to enable us to meet any emergency at a moment's notice as we draw our wounded straight from the Front. To combine the two is by no means an easy task, and if I sometimes appear to make unreasonable demands let me assure you they are well-considered. I am well aware that the hospital has cost a great deal of money, but I think that it has done its best to get good value, ... 1693 soldiers and 138 civil-ian patients have been treated, with only a mortality of 17. 1898 opera-tions have been performed. Figures which I think speak for themselves.[13]

So Miss Ivens was consciously preparing for the testing time to come. The quieter times during the spring were, she explained, because the French Army's main involvement was in the battle for Verdun, and the wounded from there went to Lyons, or Paris, not to them. But, she went on, 'we all anticipate a great offensive soon'.[14]

By May 21st Miss Ivens was reporting that she had been approached by Dr Coussergues on the feasibility of increasing to 400 beds if needed. She was 'afraid we are to be in for a terrible time. All our *blessés* are to be evacuated Thursday'. She arranged a second temporary theatre in the Blanche receiving room – it had a stone floor and a good light. The organisation for the recep-tion of the wounded was reviewed and the staff prepared. Domestic arrange-ments were again overhauled:

> It is now a pleasure to go into the kitchen and see the improvements that have been made in the direction of both cleanliness and order, and to feel that every item is scrutinised so that no leakage shall take place. Mrs Hacon works in conjunction with Tollitt and Grandage, the store and linen keepers, and I feel that they are all competent and conscientious.[15]

To ensure an adequate supply of orderlies, on whom the whole Unit was crucially dependent, advertisements appeared in June – 'Ladies 24–35. Able to speak French or German fluently, and must have had some hospital experience or training in domestic science ... Lose no time in applying'.[16]

Miss Ivens was now happier with her nursing department. In April she had reported that it was 'in better control and efficiency' under Miss Duncan. She felt the selection of nurses by the Committee was much improved. 'I like your nurse [Winstanley] very much. She is, as are also a number of newcomers, a much nicer type of nurse than we had some months ago'. (Miss Ivens did not mince her words.) 'There seems to be much less disagreeableness than there was amongst them.' She informed the Committee: 'The better educated they are, the more they like being here. The more ignorant and lower class ones miss the town, and have not sufficient resources in themselves to avoid being bored in their off time'.[17]

On the medical side Ruth Nicholson was now second-in-command (as she had been unofficially since the beginning), and the major surgical work was shared between her and Miss Ivens. Dr Courtauld was principal anaesthetist. The laboratory was now under Dr Elsie Dalyell who had followed Dr Estcourt-Oswald in May. The x-ray department, under Dr Savill, now had three very well-trained radiographers, Collum, Berry and Buckley. The wards were looked after by Drs Berry, Ross and Wilson. They knew each other well by this time. It was a strong team and they worked well together. Apart from Dr Wilson who died in 1917, lifelong friendships were forged between them.

Dr Courtauld had been a fellow-student of Miss Ivens at the London School of Medicine for Women – a mature student, as she had spent six years working as a nurse before moving to medicine. She and Miss Ivens had studied and brewed cocoa together, though after graduation their paths went separate ways. Dr Courtauld had gone to a mission hospital in South India where she gained great experience as an obstetrician and anaesthetist (though she always insisted she was not a missionary). Miss Ivens herself had invited her to apply and she had joined the Unit in January 1916. Although she was the oldest member of the Unit, she stood up to the 'rushes' well – as well as the younger ones she felt. Dr Wilson came from the mission field in Palestine. Dr Dalyell who arrived in May was already distinguished in her field of bacteriology. Like Dr Butler before her she was a Beit Research Fellow of the Lister Institute in London. She was very successful in training selected orderlies to carry out the necessary laboratory procedures.

The hospital now had considerable expertise – and was so recognised after its first eighteen months. Hospital routines were by that time well established, so that when the 'Big Push' came it was probably as well prepared as it was possible to be under wartime conditions.

Dr Savill pointed out that, as well as the organisation of the hospital, 'experience of dealing with heavily infected wounds had been gradually built up throughout 1915 ... a course of action had been worked out'. Every case on admission was examined by one of the ward surgeons and smears taken from the wounds for bacteriological examination. In the minds of all was the horror of gas gangrene. It was this dread which dictated the order in which patients were sent to the theatre, as delay in operating could make the difference between life and death.

And so they waited. June passed, relatively quietly, but with growing anticipation. Miss Ivens, like the wise chief she was, tried to give everyone a period of rest.

The Big Push

Dr Savill wrote later:

> We had received warning that the offensive was to begin about the end of June, and when we heard the guns thundering by day and by night from the 25th of June we realised that our share of the labour entailed by all military operations was about to commence.... On July 2nd the anticipated rush began, and for 10 days, almost without intermission, it continued.... Royaumont is situated only 25 miles behind the firing line, and cases reached us a few hours after being wounded when sent direct from the Front, and 2–3 days later when they had been detained for 'rest' in hospitals nearer the Front.[18] [This 'rest' was later realised to be a thoroughly bad idea – prompt operative treatment was essential to limit infections and in 1917 the whole system was changed to take account of this.]

The most vivid description of 'The First Week of the First Great Push' was written by Collum, one of the radiographers. It was indeed fortunate for the Unit and for our knowledge of the history of the hospital then and subsequently that Collum had recovered sufficiently to return to work at Royaumont. She had been very seriously injured in February of that year when the Sussex, in which she was travelling, was torpedoed.

In her own words:

> On the first [July] we waited, full of tense, suppressed excitement. The Great Push had begun – how were the Allies faring? Our hospital had been evacuated almost to the last man. Our new emergency ward of 80 beds had been created in what had once been as big as an English parish church (*sic*) – [this was the refectory] – our theatre and our receiving rooms had been supplied with a huge reserve of bandages and swabs, of lint and gauze and wool; our new x-ray installation [a second machine] had been fitted up to the last connection; our ambulances were waiting ready to start at a moment's notice in the garage yard. The incessant thunder and boom of the great guns had never been silent for days. This day, at dawn, the

Patients were nursed in the cloisters during the summer months. The terrace was a nine-teenth century addition and has now been removed. It was much used, however, in the time of the hospital.
(By courtesy of Mr David Proctor).

thunder had swelled to an orgy of terrific sound that made the whole earth shiver; then, a few hours later, had ceased, and we could hear once more the isolated reports of individual cannon. Those of us who had been at the hospital through the attacks of June 1915, and the more serious push in Artois on September 25th, went early to bed. If the call came in the night we could always be summoned – meanwhile, we slept when we could. The later-comers marvelled at our lack – our apparent lack – of anticipation and excitement, and waited up long into the night. July 2nd dawned. The morning hours dragged on, placid in the hot sunshine of high Summer. Our ambulances were called out to await the first train of wounded at our clearing station. It was at noonday dinner that the telephone message came through that they were arriving shortly with very bad cases. The ward Sisters and their staffs went over their arrangements once more; the women orderlies stoked up their hot water *marmites* attached to each ward and to the operating theatre, and the Sister who presided there counted over again her reserve drums of sterilised cloths and swabs. We, in our department, once more tried our tubes to make sure they were regulated and working to a nicety, and the little group of women doctors collected by the window that opens above the entrance hall and watched for the cars to come.

Absolute readiness – and then – speed without haste. That was what we had to aim at; on that must depend the chances of many a human life. The long blast of a whistle from the entrance hall – how well we were to know it! – and almost to dread its insistent iteration during the next few days. This was the porter announcing the arrival of the first convoy from Cr [eil], sixteen stretcher cases. No sooner had the men been lifted out and carried to the various receiving rooms than the cars went back to the *gare régulatrice* for more. Trains were arriving from the Somme in one long stream. The drivers never ceased journeying backwards and forwards all that afternoon and all that night, and the three women and the man, who drove our four ambulances, carried over a hundred cases over the first 24 hours of that nightless week. They slept a little by turns, so that during the first twenty days of the great push there were always some of our cars at the clearing station, night and day, and the cases distributed to our hospital never had to wait there longer than was necessary.[19]

From her viewpoint in the x-ray rooms Collum described how, as the men were brought in more quickly than they could be dealt with, she was put in charge of the second x-ray machine which had recently been installed in another room, and then the patients could be 'put through' more quickly:

Very soon, the surgeon-in-chief was hard at work, with the anaesthetist and the assistant in the operating theatre, each ward surgeon bringing up her own cases and assisting with them. It grew dark, and still the wounded came in. By ten o'clock we had a long line of stretchers lying in the corridor outside the x-ray rooms and the theatre, – at one end wounded men waiting to be examined by us; at the other, those who had already been examined, and who were waiting their turn for operation. The two storekeepers and the kitchen orderlies, who had gone off duty, organised themselves into a stretcher squad, and kept the x-ray couches and the operating theatre supplied. Down another corridor the other assistant radiographer had arranged her developed plates to dry – dozens of them. Some time after midnight our doctor [Dr Savill] had to retire to bed. She was not a strong woman and she had to be ready for the new day's work at 8 a.m. At four o'clock the other assistant, having developed 63 photographs since two o'clock in the afternoon, followed her. We knew the surgeons had more cases waiting for them than they could possibly operate on during the night. One or two of the ward surgeons dropped off, aware that they would have to begin work early in the morning. But the theatre went on, and the other surgeons who were waiting their turn to get their most urgent cases done, filled up the time by getting on with the list that was to be examined under the x-rays.

She went on:

> Cases continued to come in all day, but as everyone was a stretcher
> case, and each car could only carry four, while the clearing station was
> 12 kilometres distant, the hospital was able to absorb them as they
> came in, so that there was little if any delay in attending to the poor
> fellows.
>
>   Their wounds were terrible ... many of these men were wounded –
> dangerously – in two, three, four and five places. That great enemy of the
> surgeon who would conserve life and limb, gas gangrene, was already at
> work in 90% of cases. Hence the urgent need for immediate operation,
> often for immediate amputation. The surgeon did not stop to search for
> shrapnel and pieces of metal: their one aim was to open up and clean out
> the wounds, or to cut off the mortifying limb before the dread gangrene
> had tracked its way into the vital parts of the body. The stench was very
> bad. Most of the poor fellows were too far gone to say much ....[20]

She remembers that they then

> had accommodation for 400, and for weeks we worked, once we were
> filled, with never a bed to spare. Our operating theatre was hardly ever
> left vacant long enough to be cleaned during the small hours and it
> became a problem how to air the x-ray rooms during the short hours of
> dawn that stretched between the ending of one day's work and the begin-
> ning of another's. We were fighting gas gangrene and time was the factor
> that counted most. We dared not stop work in the theatre until it became
> physically impossible to continue. For us who worked, and for those
> patient suffering men, lying along the corridor outside the x-ray rooms
> and the theatre, on stretchers, awaiting their turn, it was a nightmare of
> glaring lights, of appalling stenches of ether and chloroform, and violent
> sparking of tired x-ray tubes, of scores of wet negatives that were seized
> upon by their respective surgeons and taken into the hot theatre before
> they had even had time to be rinsed in the dark room. Beneath and
> beyond the anxiety of saving men's lives, there was the undercurrent of
> anxiety of the theatre staff as to whether the boiling of instruments and
> gloves could be kept level with the rapidity with which the cases were
> carried in and put on the table, as to whether the gauze and wool and
> swabs would last! – and with us it was anxiety for the life of the tubes,
> anxiety to get the gas gangrene plates developed first, to persuade them
> to dry, to keep the cases of the six surgeons separate, to see that they did
> not walk off with the wrong plates – for we had pictures that were almost
> identical, duplication of names, and such little complications. And it all
> had to be done in a tearing hurry, and at the end of a day that had already
> lasted anything from 10 to 18 hours, and no mistakes to be made. I do

not think we lost a case from delay in locating the trouble and operating in all that first terrible week of July. The losses were due to delay in reaching the hospital.[21]

Collum tells of her personal work schedule over the first few days:

July 2nd 2 p.m. till July 3rd 7 a.m.

July 3rd 11 a.m. till supper time. Rest till 10 p.m. Worked 10 p.m. till 6 a.m. on July 4th.

July 4th Slept 6 a.m. till noon. Dinner. Worked till supper. Rest till 10 p.m. Worked 10 p.m. till 4 a.m. July 5th.

July 5th Four hours sleep after 4 a.m. Worked till 11 p.m.

July 6th Sleep one hour, then wakened as a new convoy had come in and some of the cases needed immediate operation.

She describes how she felt:

I do not think I have ever felt so sleepy and tired as I did when I got downstairs – it is so much easier to carry on than to be called up, when you are nearing the end of your powers of keeping awake. We worked as in a dream. My legs and hands did not seem to belong to me, and I heard my own voice far away as if it came from somebody else. It had become impossible to work quickly, and I found it necessary to make great efforts to remember little things and do them correctly. We got to bed again before dawn.[22]

On the last day of the week our x-ray staff had an addition, the chief assistant having come back hastily from leave in England.[23]

This was Buckley, a medical student who had interrupted her training to come to Royaumont as an orderly. She had gone home to sit a medical exam. She completed her medical studies after the war and specialised in radiology in which she had a very distinguished career, including serving as a consultant radiologist in the RAMC in World War Two. It is interesting to speculate that it might have been her experience at Royaumont which led to her choice of career.

Collum again:

Thenceforward we were able to tackle the work comfortably, each getting some time off during the day, and dividing the night's work among us in shifts of two. Further, since the hospital was full, we could not be rushed by any great influx of serious cases. We settled down to steady, hard work that continued through the rest of July, August and September, varied once or twice by emergencies, such as when we admitted 80 cases in one day (after having evacuated a good number to make room for them), and before nightfall had examined 40 of them under x-rays and operated on 20.[23]

There were other vivid recollections of that first desperate week. Dr Savill snatched a few moments on the 4th of July to write home:

We have had a ghastly time of horrors since Sunday. Men badly wounded pouring in at the rate of 70 to 100 per day. We took 150 photos in x-ray rooms since Sunday noon, and many screenings and localisations in addition.... Our photos had to dry all along the wall in the gallery. You can picture the scene – surgeons demanding their photos and I chained to the x-ray room.... Miss Collum has worked singlehanded for the two nights and afternoons. Miss Berry all day long in dark room developing at post-haste, I alone in x-ray room ... When Miss Berry was not developing she undertook singlehanded one of the x-ray rooms....

Canada Ward, formerly the monks' refectory, contained 100 beds; one row on each side and two rows down the centre. Heating was provided by four stoves, smoke passing through holes in the old stone walls. The lectern was used for storage of equipment, including bedpans.
(By courtesy of Miss Helen Lowe).

Miss Ivens had operated Sunday 1.0 p.m. to 5.45 a.m. next day; then from 9 a.m. Monday to about 5 this morning (July 4th); and again from 10 a.m. to-day, and is still hard at it and likely to be so till tomorrow.[24]

Dr Dalyell, heading the bacteriological laboratory, recalled those first few days:

> – there have been simply awful days and nights. I hear the poor people in the operating theatre cleaning up madly … a swab of every wound is taken immediately after admission and sent instantly to the laboratory. I examine them on the instant – did 180 in three days – and a bacteriological report was despatched within about half an hour. All the gas gangrene cases were sorted out by this means and the incipient cases were spotted at once and operated according to the severity of the infection as notified by me. By that means we saved lots of limbs, as they were spotted early and opened up in time. So many of the cases where I insisted on immediate operation proved to have early gas formation at the bottom of a deep narrow shell wound that it would certainly be fatal to leave them; they would probably have lost a limb, if not life. So far we have had only 5 deaths and we did 112 bad cases of gas gangrene without stopping. As I did the bacteriological work in batches of 20, my excellent girl orderly did yeoman service in collecting the swabs and preparing of the specimens, I was able to take a hand in the theatre and plied between the lab and the operating table without ceasing day or night.[25]

For the surgeons there could be no system of shifts. The second theatre was now in full operation. Junior surgeons, in addition to their work admitting and classifying the wounded as they came in, doing the dressings of those that had been operated on, watching the patients closely for signs of deterioration which could occur with dramatic suddenness, were also performing the smaller operations, and assisting the chief surgeons.

That first night they were operating continuously till 7 a.m. and, with only an hour or two of rest, they were back. The urgent priority was to check the spread of gas gangrene. This involved in some cases immediate amputation – in others they had to open up the wounds, and remove damaged tissue and tattered clothing which had been driven deep into the wounds and was a potent breeding ground for gas gangrene organisms. Only these most urgent procedures were carried out in the first instance. During the succeeding eight days several of the women had no more than sixteen hours of sleep all told. 'Three hours consecutive sleep was an unbelievable luxury.'[26]

Miss Ivens was under pressure, not only from the constant inflow of patients, but also from the authorities who were making fresh demands upon her. She telegraphed to the Committee on July 3rd: 'Service de Santé nous demande augmenter hôpital très urgent blessés arrivent constamment

Ivens'. The reply came from the Committee: 'Glad agree whatever necessary'.[27]

On July 16th she found a moment to write – a typical letter with an emphasis on practical considerations:

> We are hard at work. We have had in nearly three hundred cases during the last fortnight and they are nearly all *grands blessés* – cases they cannot send any further. As you know we were at once asked to double our beds – I was able to arrange this at once.

The army supplied the actual beds – she put 50 in the cloisters and nearly 100 in the refectory, which was then named the Canada Ward:

> Everyone is working very hard and I am hoping you will soon be able to send us the nurses and orderlies as soon as they can possibly come with or without uniforms. It has been a case of day and night for many, and of course they cannot keep it up. There is every prospect this rush will last for several months. They seem to think that we can be of the greatest value to Creil as we take in heavy cases of gas gangrene to whom a few more hours means a fatal end. The wounds are dreadful. Last year was child's play to it, but so far we have got over the ground well. Refectory makes a lovely ward. M. Pichon has arranged a little stove and taps etc in adjoining store room, and three extra lavatories. We have got in two French helpers for cleaning temporarily. I must not stay for more. Every moment is precious.[28]

Collum elaborated further on the work in the wards and how orderlies throughout the hospital rose to the occasion:

> The wards were an unforgettable sight. Light dressings and gallows splints were the order of the day. Morning dressings were no sooner over than evening dressings had to begin. Stretchers were constantly coming and going from the receiving rooms, the theatre, the operating rooms. It must have been heart-breaking to nurses accustomed to the clockwork round and the neat rows of counterpaned beds in civil hospitals at home. To the girls who were serving as ward orderlies – and during this period of stress had to play the part of staff nurses – it must have been a long drawn-out period of dreadful strain and physical fatigue. The day staffs would work on till nearly midnight to help the night staffs; and the night staffs, instead of going off duty at 9 a.m. would work on in the wards till dinnertime to help the day people. In the same way the kitchen staff, the laboratory orderly, the storekeepers and Vestiaire clerk, would wait up every night till long after midnight, working as a volunteer stretcher squad to carry the stretchers backwards and forwards between the wards and the operating theatre. When they went to bed the cases

were carried by the theatre Sister and her assistants; and if they were too busy swabbing up a too slippery floor, the surgeons would carry them themselves. Several of the poor fellows died, the only wonder was that they had lasted so long, wounded as they had been, after an exhausting struggle, and then sent on that long journey by ambulance and train from the Somme railheads to our clearing station.[29]

Cicely Hamilton records that 121 cases were admitted in the first 24 hours, July 2nd/3rd. During the first week over 200 were admitted, 231 bacteriological and 406 x-ray examinations were made and 160 operations performed. 'The greater number of the cases have been exceedingly grave – some of the men have arrived actually dying. We are serving the Army of the Somme District where fighting is incessant and shows no sign of abatement. Every struggle and advance on the Somme means added work for the hospitals in the rear of the Somme line – of which Royaumont is among the largest.'[30]

It must have been with enormous relief that the Unit welcomed the arrival of two more doctors in July. Dr Hodson, who qualified in Edinburgh in 1900, had been working with the Croix Rouge Français in charge of some of their hospitals in France and was therefore able to transfer rapidly to Royaumont in the emergency. Dr Martland was a young but brilliant graduate from the London School of Medicine for Women. She had been working in a children's hospital and came out to tackle the very different work in a busy war hospital. She was the only doctor at Royaumont to have red hair – a point of some significance in her later history as we shall see.

A third new arrival – but not until September – was Dr MacDougall, a Gold Medallist from Edinburgh, who had been in Serbia with the Scottish Women's Hospital with Dr Elsie Inglis. She had been taken prisoner by the Germans, and after many adventures and much hardship she had eventually been repatriated via Zürich in February. She had had a grim time, but she seemed to be ready for more when she volunteered to come to Royaumont.

On August 9th a much-needed reinforcement of four nurses and three orderlies arrived from the Scottish Women's Hospital in Ajaccio in Corsica to bring some relief to hard-pressed staff.[31]

Although the hospital remained very busy for the next three months, the most acute period was when they increased their occupied beds from 5 (for they had evacuated almost completely in preparation for the expected rush) to nearly 400 in less than three weeks. This was the period of greatest strain for the staff. One more sharp peak of activity occurred on August 30th when they were warned to evacuate as many as possible and to receive 80 *grands blessés* in one day. Miss Ivens was desperate for more pairs of hands and telegraphed the Committee: 'Wounded arriving orderlies urgently required'.[32]

Miss Ivens herself was probably the most resilient of all the staff. On

August 13th she was writing: 'Many thanks, I am quite fit, and ready for another rush'.[33] And to her stepsister, on a postcard: 'We have had a great time with 350 *grands blessés* from the Somme. Day and night for a bit. Everyone was splendid'.[34]

She realised nevertheless her staff did not all have her phenomenal stamina:

> There was a good deal of illness in the staff ... with all those to nurse we
> are very short of orderlies, and while we can just get on with only 200
> beds occupied another rush would be somehow disconcerting.

There was a tendency among the orderlies – some of them anyway – to express themselves in verse. In the absence of diaries or letters from orderlies describing their experiences in cold prose, here is Geraldine Mackenzie's version of events (she was an orderly from April 1916 to May 1917):

IF-

(With apologies to Rudyard Kipling).

Dedicated to the night orderlies at Royaumont and particularly in memory of June, July, August and September, 1916.

> If you can make your walls of dusty sacking,
> And in an unswept barn by daylight sleep;
> If you can laugh when furniture is lacking,
> And keep your things in one ungainly heap;
> If you can smile when gramophones are braying,
> And Etienne shouts at Cardew till he's blue;
> If you can listen to the black boys laughing,
> And make allowance for their laughing too.
>
> If you can hear the staff who stamp and clatter
> When Buckley calls her fire-brigade to arms;
> If you can bear it when the sisters chatter
> To fetch the tea they find so full of charms;
> If you can hear the victims in the theatre,
> And only pity when they groan and scream;
> If you can know the cars have just been sent for,
> And weave it all into a blissful dream;
>
> If you can rise though no one comes to call you,
> And share one candle with five gloomy friends;
> If you can eat cold porridge in the cloisters,
> When in the darkness salt with sugar blends;
> If you can feed your sister to her liking
> On eggs or coffee, jam, or something roast;
> If you can answer wisely when our Binkie
> Offers a sausage on a piece of toast:

If, when the marmite fire sinks lower,
And, spite of all your efforts, goes quite dead,
You then can face St John in gusty moonlight
And calmly meet the ghost without a head;
If, when the men are restless, and the kitchen
Echoes with laughter and resounding fun,
You still can keep your temper mid the turmoil,
And whisper gently – 'Think of Blanche – or Jeanne?'

If you can carry stretchers by the dozen,
Polish the brasses, count three hundred sheets;
If you can work with all your heart, though knowing
The day staff always disbelieves your feats:
If you can crowd the unforgiving minute
With three hours' work and never feel the strain -

Yours is the world and everything that's in it,
But – though I seek you – it is still in vain.[35]

(Etienne was a former patient who stayed on to help with mechanical problems. Mr Cardew was employed as a chauffeur and mechanic. Buckley was the radiographer who was also studying medicine. 'Binkie' was Constance Birks, an orderly 17.2.16 to 22.8.17. Later married: (1) Mrs Goodale, (2) Mrs Dunsmore. The 'black boys' were the Senegalese, renowned for their cheerfulness. St John was presumably one of the Royaumont ghosts. Blanche and Jeanne were wards full of seriously wounded soldiers). Geraldine Mackenzie, later Mme. Potez, died tragically in a road accident in Switzerland in 1923.)

The following poem is 'Anon', but must surely speak for all who were at Royaumont during the Somme Push:

I wish I were a little rock
A-sittin' on a hill,
And doin' nothin' all day long
But just a-sittin' still.

I wouldn't eat, I wouldn't drink,
I wouldn't even wash;
But sit and sit a thousand years
An' rest myself, by Gosh![36]

Miss Ivens was particularly appreciative of the work of the orderlies and urged the Committee:

Some of them have had a considerable amount of experience, and could be trusted to act as seconds in the wards ... they should be promoted to Auxiliary Nurses, be given a salary of £20 and wear Army Sisters' caps with ordinary uniform which would make a distinction. I am sure that some feel that they do not get promotion here, and really they do more work, and with more intelligence, than an inferior type of fully-trained nurse. In this way we should gradually replace some of the sisters (viz those who are sisters in name only) by some of our own training, and I do not think the work would suffer in any way. Miss Duncan [the Matron] quite agrees.[37]

And of the chauffeurs Dr Erskine from the Committee reported: 'Their work appeared to me quite excellent, and during the rush it must have been very hard'.[38] Miss Ivens now wanted them to have an allowance for their uniforms, and, as they were very much 'in the public eye' she did not want uniforms sent out from home 'which were badly cut and of poor material'. They could use a uniform allowance to go to a good military tailor in Paris. They were all volunteers and as Mr Cardew, who got a salary of £60 per annum, was leaving, the three chauffeurs should have a salary of £20. Cardew 'was not as good as the girls who got nothing'.[39] Later, in 1917, this led to quite a major confrontation with the Committee.

The welfare of the hospital and the fair treatment of staff was high on Miss Ivens's list of priorities. She was aware of the major fundraising efforts that were being made at home, and that when the SWH scheme was initiated no-one expected the war to go on so long. She herself had a secure position behind her with her consultant practice in Liverpool, but many of the volunteers, working without pay, were beginning to have financial difficulties. When the Committee offered to increase her honorarium, again she refused it, but asked them to increase Cicely Hamilton's salary to £200 from her present £50.[40] Cicely had two old aunts particularly dependent on her, and was having problems. At the same time she was an absolutely key person in the hospital, and was in practice taking on more and more of the administration from Miss Loudon who, delightful person though she was, was finding the administration difficult. This was done.

Miss Ivens was now worried about the quality of the food. On August 19th she was writing to the Committee:

We shall only be paving the way for more serious trouble if sufficient palatable food is not supplied ... Bread and tea is a very poor preparation for a morning's hard work, and I know myself that I have felt quite faint in the middle of a morning after such a repast.[41]

This was reinforced by Dr Erskine in September:

The margarine was uneatable ... and the bread was unpalatable, dark and sour. ... The staff were very badly fed – after the rush so run down that it was found necessary to have wine at the mid-day meal [though she hastened to add that it was used very sparingly].[42]

She warned the Committee that they must be prepared for increased expenditure on food. Her other concern was the lack of washing facilities for staff: 'The staff feel the lack of a bath very much … They do not mind carrying up the water to fill it if there could be some mechanical means of emptying it'.[43] This must have touched the hearts of the Committee as a consignment of tin baths was despatched almost immediately. (The records do not say how they were in fact emptied, but there is a story that two orderlies narrowly missed the matron when they tipped their bath water out of the window.)

One or two practical problems arose during, or resulting from, the rush, both of which were solved with the help of M. Delacoste, always a good friend to the hospital. The incinerator was proving inadequate to cope with the enormous quantity of used – and dangerously infected – dressings, and the all too numerous amputated limbs which had to be disposed of. M. Delacoste sent along a number of his workmen to build a new, large and efficient *déstructeur*. That problem was solved.[44] The second difficulty arose from the change of use of the refectory to become the Canada Ward. This had been the staff dining room. In the first instance they were able to eat outside in a corner of the cloisters not occupied by patients, and this arrangement continued until winter had pretty well set in, by which time those who had them were donning their fur coats for their meals. They must have been very grateful when M. Delacoste built a wooden hut adjoining the main building and fitted it with a stove.[45]

Mrs Robertson, a member of the Committee, described the experience later in the year:

We are still [November 3rd] having all our meals out in the cloisters except the doctors' breakfast and tea, and on these moonlit nights it is a striking sight to see the trembling lights round the long white tables, and the moonlight striking on the grey arches and plashing fountain. We all wear fur coats for supper. Of course the blessés are never exposed like that, they get all their meals indoors, but now the refectory is Canada Ward so there is nowhere else for the staff to feed.[46]

And as late as November 14th:

The doctors are still having dinner and supper in the cloisters, and though beautiful it is still very cold in the evening and we usually all sit in furs. If you are not very punctual the food is ice-cold. Everything is put on the side table by the door to the kitchen and you help yourself on an enamelled plate. When you've finished your soup you put aside the spoon and take your next course on the same plate. No matter who comes, Prof. Weinberg, Lord Esher or the Embassy chaplain – or the Comtesse de la Rochefoucauld – they all do the same – No one has seemed surprised.[47]

The morale of patients and staff was boosted, as Miss Ivens well knew, by ceremonies and visits, and some of these were particularly valuable. She arranged a formal opening of the new Canada Ward, so called because the money for equipping it was raised in Canada. Mme. D'Haussonville represented the French Red Cross, and Mlle. Montizambert came from the Canadian Red Cross to perform the opening ceremony on July 18th, bringing with her a large Canadian flag to decorate the ward. Weak and ill as they were, some of the men managed to raise a cheer.

On August 25th M. Doumergues, the French Minister for Colonial Affairs, arrived to visit the Colonial troops being treated in the hospital, chiefly Senegalese and Arabs. What this visit meant to these troops, who had very little idea of what the war was all about, why they were involved in it and why they were paying such a very heavy price, must remain obscure; but perhaps they did appreciate in some way that important people were regarding them as important people too. Of more practical significance was that M. Doumergues had some funds to distribute and 10,000 francs were passed over to be spent on their welfare.

Another visitor was Miss Katherine Burke, collecting material for her highly successful fundraising tour of the United States and Canada. She was so good at this task that she became known as 'the pound-a-minute girl'.[48]

Of great significance for the prestige of the hospital was the visit of the President of France, M. Poincaré, with Mme. Poincaré, on September 22nd. There were 330 patients at the time and both the President and his wife spoke to every man. In addition Mme. Poincaré gave each man a little bag of presents (history does not relate what was inside), and a message 'Jusqu'au bout'.[49] This could be, and no doubt was, interpreted in different ways, but it was certainly intended to be encouraging! The Presidential tour took them through Millicent Fawcett Ward, the cloisters, Queen Mary Ward, the new Canada Ward, Marguerite d'Ecosse and Jeanne d'Arc Wards all on the ground floor. Then upstairs to Blanche de Castille (the former monk's library), and on to the top floor for the London and Elsie Inglis Wards with the Arab and Senegalese patients. They certainly did a thorough and conscientious tour. The occasion was heightened by a band playing throughout, and by the crowd of local villagers and local VIPs who lined up to see their President.[50]

Press comments were helpful:

French visitors marvel that this huge Abbaye with all its inconveniences and its eight wards so beautifully kept, is staffed entirely by women, and by so few of them. If the staff have been worked almost to breaking point since the Somme offensive began it may congratulate itself that the hospital can come through an inspection like this with compliments to spare for the British attention to cleanliness and order. It has only been by dint of each individual doing just a little more than her utmost. The wards of

Mrs Robertson, member of the Executive Committee of the Scottish Women's Hospitals Committee.
(By courtesy of Mrs Ailsa Tanner).

Royaumont bear eloquent testimony to the desperate character of the fighting ... Chasseurs-à-pied from the Corps that turned the German offensive on the Marne and withstood the siege of Verdun – and veteran Colonial infantry – Algerians and Tunisians and Senegalese whose special work it was to clear out the first line trenches.

What more could be done to amuse and occupy the minds of the patients? On August 27th Miss Ivens asked if the Committee would send out Mrs Robertson 'to organise raffia and basket work for the *blessés* and little entertainments to keep their minds off themselves'. Another reason, which Mrs Robertson indicated later, was to help settle certain 'diplomatic questions and difficulties'.[51]

Mrs Robertson duly arrived to the obvious relief of the staff and patients and to those over 80 years later who are interested in the daily life of the hospital and the individuals who worked there. She stayed two months and wrote a series of vivid letters home.

She arrived on October 25th in the motor lorry, driven by Mr Cardew, along with Mrs Hacon, an orderly and 'piles of cabbages, eggs, skinned rabbits etc etc'. With the tyres fragmenting, and in constant expectation of a burst, they finally arrived safely:

Splashed and bumped up to the front entrance of the Abbaye in great style ... They were all at lunch in the cloisters, but came very soon to the hall as soon as ever the news spread – at least Dr Ivens and Miss Loudon did and also Miss Hamilton just behind ... Dr Ivens seemed genuinely glad to see me, and Miss Hamilton too; both have given me a great welcome – it's nice to feel that people like that want you with them.[52]

She had long discussions that first day with Miss Ivens, Miss Duncan and Miss Hamilton ('Miss Hamilton is splendid'.)

One of her tasks – and one that she found very pleasant, was compiling 'histories' of the named beds which would be published in the Common Cause (weekly journal of the NUWSS) and relayed back to the donors – and so keep the contributions flowing in. With the great rush of patients this had fallen behind, and it was time to take it up again. She described a session with Miss Hamilton in Canada Ward distributing name-plates to the beds. It was a gay occasion for them all:

All the blessés wanted 'des dames ou des demoiselles' over their beds – but there were not enough to go round and some had to take Colonels, Sirs – Mr and Mrs or even Railway Coys. When I had hung all round the walls and on the pillars there were still many beds in the centre, but these were for the time being unoccupied. I found at the end I had still two cards with ladies' names – So I went up the ward calling 'J'ai encore deux dames à placer, qui désire des dames?' All the men who had colonels or CPR shouted and we had great fun exchanging them in the end ... It interested the men greatly as they had always felt jealous of the other wards having named beds and they not. So now there is great letter writing going on to the American donors.[53]

Mrs Robertson had many assorted duties. Her good knowledge of French was very useful in carrying out necessary business in Paris – helping Dr MacDougall, for instance, who had no French, to get items of x-ray equipment; errands for the patients; purchasing materials for the laboratory; business at the tailor's, and several trips to track down a French cook (they were in difficulties at the moment though the situation was soon to change dramatically for the better with the arrival of the French chef, Michelet, in November).

Apart from the bed histories she took her turn with the 'dévouements'. This was the rather unpopular duty of touring the hospital with the seemingly endless stream of visitors. The doctors shared this duty between them, and if one did an extra turn to help out she would expect to be repaid. Mrs Robertson had

> helped Miss Wilson with some bores of hers the other day, so was very
> much injured because the hockey match prevented her repaying her
> dévouement debt. However Mrs Hacon nobly invited us to the hockey tea
> which was also the opening of the new mess-hut in the yard
> (M. Delacoste's contribution it will be remembered). Scotland won the
> hockey match, so great was the rejoicing and we had a very merry tea.[54]

Hockey was a serious matter in the Unit: one orderly was a hockey international.

On All Saints' Day there was a ceremony and service at Asnières cemetery to which the convalescents and as many of the staff as possible were to go in military procession. An attack of bronchitis prevented Mrs Robertson from attending herself; in any case Miss Ivens wanted her to stay to cope with any visitors who might turn up. On this occasion the visitors were what she described as 'three specimens of the ancienne noblesse'. Two of them had the whole direction and arrangement of the female stretcher-bearers and infirmarians for all the military hospitals in Paris, where women were rapidly replacing men. They wanted to see how Royaumont coped. One positive benefit for Royaumont was that they managed to turn up an under-cook:

> I went to Marguerite among the men, after seeing the procession start off,
> first of all the blessés who cd (sic) with crutches and sticks, then the
> sisters in their veils, and orderlies in uniform, and lastly the doctors, Miss
> H[amilton] and Miss L[oudon]. I believe the little ceremony in the
> cemetery was most impressive. The maire and the curé going to each

grave of those who had died of wounds here and pronouncing a little oration, and Sisters laying wreaths on the graves. There was special mention made of Sister Gray who died here last year.

And then:

> When the party returned from the cemetery General Sieur from Paris arrived to confer the Médaille Militaire and Croix de Guerre on two men in Canada, and we had a very pretty little ceremony there. Miss Ivens loves a ceremony in which she is at one with the French people.[55]

Mrs Robertson found that she had come in for the 'Gay Season'. After the stresses of the Somme rushes this must have been not only welcome but therapeutic. The first party was 'Hallowe'en', a new experience for the men. It was held in the beautiful Blanche de Castille Ward:

> The sisters and orderlies take no end of trouble in decorating their wards and getting up a little programme of entertainment to which the men themselves contribute a large number of items. On Friday night we had Halloween potatoes with all sorts of things stirred in them, rings, buttons, badges, and even British threepenny bits – One poor chap got both a button and a thimble in his little lot and great was the fun and teasing when he was told that he would certainly never get married! 'Tant pis' he said sadly – but was not at all consoled when I suggested that it might be that he was to have two wives – 'Oh, no, one is enough'. Another man was the proud possessor of two threepenny bits. A few of course got nothing, but we made it up to them otherwise. We had games too, hunt the slipper and musical chairs without the chairs, when you flop on the ground when the music stops and the last left standing goes out. It was so funny to see the 'niggers' at the games. [This word jars on the modern ear, but in 1916 it did not carry the same racist implications.] They love the parties better than anything and enter into the games with the greatest enthusiasm. Poor boys, they are so young, and have been fighting for a land which is of course alien to them. Little Sali Fon is 16, and has lost his right arm from the shoulder. He is a fine-looking boy as black as ebony, with dancing eyes and a splendid upright carriage. Another black man has lost his left arm. These two and several others go round to all the parties, they are charming guests, enjoying everything with much gusto. It was a young French sergeant who was the victor at the musical chairs after a tough tustle with an orderly who is an international hockey player. Hunt the slipper gave an opportunity to those of us who are better with their arms than their legs. Then we had a great sing-song, all the men's favourite trench songs 'Le Petit Chapeau', 'Tipperary' etc – and ended with the 'Marseillaise' and 'God Save the King'.[56]

A few days later it was the turn of Canada Ward:

> This was a most gorgeous halloween party. When we arrived they were
> ducking for apples. Imagine the scene – the Canadian Ward is the old
> refectory. It was most beautiful with its lights shaded with red, and
> Chinese lanterns hanging from the grey stone arches. A space had been
> cleared in the centre between the pillars, and all round were the rows of
> beds with their red coverlets; each containing a smiling blessé. In the
> cleared space there was a motley gathering of blessés, convalescents in red
> jackets, sisters in flowing veils, Senegalis (*sic*) with coal-black faces and
> flashing teeth and eyes. Doctoresses in uniform, Zouaves, Arabs and
> orderlies in their pretty pale blue uniforms and frilled caps, and a sprin-
> kling of civilian guests including young M. Gouin in full evening dress
> of the beau monde. Many of the men were ducking for apples with the
> greatest gusto in a big round shallow bath pan and catching them in
> their teeth most cleverly – amid shouts of laughter. Cigarettes, chocolates
> and biscuits were passed round the beds and among the blessés at inter-
> vals. Songs were sung and games were played. About a dozen of the con-
> valescents were dressed up in fancy costumes and some were very clever.
> A witch with high black peaked cap and red gown with cabalistic signs
> struck terror into the hearts of the blackies. There was a stalwart
> Highlander in a kilt made from a travelling plaid and housemaid's brush
> for a sporran. Uncle Sam in a wheel chair, a sailor, a Mees (the patient's
> word for an orderly) and a Sistaire etc etc. What delights the men most is
> to dress up in the sisters' and orderlies' uniforms and play at being
> nurses.
>
> Sir Roger de Coverley was a great sight danced here in this wonderful
> setting and by this motley gathering. Surely quite unique in the world's
> history and typical of the contrasts in this world war. There was Miss
> Loudon tripping down the middle with a huge negro from Martinique,
> demure little orderlies and one-armed French poilus, Mr Ed Gouin and
> fat Mrs Hacon, the kitchen superintendent – Dr Wilson with a Senegali,
> Miss Courtauld with her white hair and gold eyeglasses and Sali-Fon
> Kanara with a red fez stuck jauntily on his black wool, and his pink-
> striped pyjamas tucked into his socks while one sleeve was pinned up
> over the missing arm. I went up in the little musicians' gallery and
> looked down on the wonderful scene. We all joined hands round the
> immense ward, including the bed people when it was possible and sang
> 'Auld Lang Syne' – and surely it never was sung under stranger circum-
> stances. Of course all our parties end with the Marseillaise and God Save
> the King.[57]

And the next day (truly this was the gay season):

When I got back [she had been in Paris trying to find a cook and had
had a nasty fall down a steep flight of dark stairs and was feeling
distinctly shaken] – the preparations for the Sisters' party were in full
swing, and there was also a party going on in Mary [Queen Mary Ward]!
I had to go and give prizes to the men as usual and then one of the sisters
dressed me up as an Arab lady from the Arabian Nights with sheets and a
gorgeous turban and veil and I joined the party in the sisters' room. My
head was very stiff but I thought I'd better turn up in case the Sisters
were disappointed. The costumes were wonderful, but the 'clou' of the
evening was Miss Hamilton as a tank. She had got inside her zinc bath
wh(*sic*) is a long oval and about 18 inches deep. She had big boots on
both hands and feet, and a tremendous noise and rattling going on inside.
She came in lolloping and crawling under it. Another successful do was
Dr Nicholson as the wolf from Red Riding Hood all in grey woollen and
with a big grey wolf's head made out of cardboard. Dr McDougall was
Red Riding Hood. Miss Loudon Rose Red all in crinkled paper. There
were the three bears, Haroun al Raschid, the Babes in the Wood, a Red
Indian Squaw etc etc. We ducked for apples, danced, and I told fortunes
in my lair for a franc a head for the blessés prizes or rather I read hands
wh.(*sic*) I know nothing about, but I made some lucky hits.[58]

And the next:

A wonderful party in Marguerite, for that ward and Jeanne always go
together. This was one of the most successful parties we have had at all,
with one of the cleverest and funniest charades I've ever seen all made up
on the spur of the moment and acted by two or three orderlies and some
patients. They embodied all the little hospital jokes and 'took off' the
Sisters and the ward discipline and the objection of the men to fresh air,
and their amusing ways of getting round the meeses to perfection – also a
scene in the cinema was very funny. The Scots Thistle bed patient
Buhlman yodeled most beautifully – he is Swiss and sang the Ranz (*sic*)
des Vaches and of course we had all the favourite songs and choruses.[59]

A slight pause in the round of gaiety, and on November 14th it was the turn
of Salle Elsie on the top floor which held the Senegalese and the Arabs:

... I made a point of going up ... nothing would have induced me to dis-
appoint Sister W[illiams] and Miss Courtauld their 'first Mammy' who
always pretends she is not fond of them, and makes fun of Sister
Williams' enthusiasm, but who was fussing over them all evening like a
beneficent hen lest they should hurt or over-exert themselves with the
games. One of the Mohammuds (*sic*) was capering about with a tube in
his lung – a man whom she had insisted with wee McDougall two days
previously was too ill to be taken down to the x-ray room! And grandpère

with his just-healed thigh rushing about and dancing! These Arabs are so very live and graceful and so quick on their feet even with their wounds – The Senegalis are heavier and more deliberate, except of course the two young Sali Fons who have each lost an arm! All the Senegalese and Arabs had dressed up as they love to do. My big Kuli Bali as a 'soldat écossaise' copied from the picture postcard I gave him. Sali Fon was a girl of the period with a feathered hat and pink-cheeked mask. His black neck and hands below the mask and fine feathers was very funny. Naephle was a bear, a dancing bear, led by Abdulla who beat a cymbal in time to the gramophone and led the bear on a long chain as it danced about in a big fur coat and a bear's head. They played games, twos and threes and hunt the slipper, and danced 'Sir Roger' which is always very funny here. The proceedings ended by a distribution of prizes as usual. I had got something for each man in the ward, games, cards, briquets, little mirrors etc etc. Then there was three cheers for 'Maman Anglaise' (me), 3 cheers for Maman Camerade [possibly Miss Courtauld] – for Mees, for Sistaire Nuit and Mees Nuit, and finally for the chef who had made the cakes for the party. How this is done is as follows (the cheers not the cakes) the victim is hauled into the middle of an excited gesticulating dusky group and almost torn to pieces in their enthusiasm. We have no piano up in Elsie but the men love the gramophone and keep it going from 6 in the morning. They play cards, draughts and dominoes and love the cinema when it goes to their ward.[60]

Mrs Robertson leaves us a vivid description of a decoration ceremony – another welcome diversion for the patients, and indeed for the staff:

– a decoration with great pomp and ceremony. 'Queen Mary' ward was the scene and it looked just beautiful. All the men who could be moved were there, either in their beds or carried in on stretchers and lying on cane lounges or sitting up on benches. The red coverlets and scarlet flannel jackets of the men made warm patches of colour under the grey vaulted arches, and the frosty November sunlight streamed in through the mullioned windows. The military band from Boran was there and a detachment of soldiers so the whole affair went off with military éclat. Guard of Honour for the General presenting arms and saluting, and a fanfare of trumpets before and after each decoration. Two of our men received both the Médaille Militaire and the Croix de Guerre. Kuli Bali Marmahdon, the Senegali of whom I have already spoken so often, and Molle, the occupant of the Crawfordlane Glen bed, who has had his left arm amputated also. There was another man from Boran also. A greater contrast than the three as they stood up before the general cd (sic) not be imagined – Kuli Bali [Mrs Robertson has a variety of spellings, but as I have no way of knowing which is correct I have used them as she did] –

over 6 feet in height, straight, well-made, coal-black, Molle such a nice looking boy (only 22) bright-faced and clear-eyed, medium height, slim and fair, and the little stranger, a typical little French 'Caporal' in a long blue turned-back coat and a kepi, a regular Bantam in size, lithe, alert and dark. Molle wore his red hospital jacket, Kuli Bali was glorious to behold in a powder blue flannel suit and puttees wh. Sister Williams had unearthed from somewhere and a scarlet fez on his black wool. Sister W. was just like a mother whose son has distinguished himself – her eyes filled with tears of pride and delight.[61]

That was not the end of the day:

Lord and Lady Esher came out from Paris for it [the ceremony] bringing with them a party to give the men a concert. They had a gifted Russian violinist, Mrs Harben, who sings divinely and a conjuror. The latter gave the blessés the greatest possible delight. The niggers were one flash of white teeth especially when he ended by producing from a silk hat quantities of flags of all nations (Allies of course) wh. he afterwards distributed among the blessés. The men had coffee and cakes and cigarettes, and we took the Esher party up to our sitting room for tea. It was a most successful little do. Miss Prance (chauffeur) and a canteen girl from Creil had come up for the party and Miss P played the violin on the balcony of Canada wh. was the musicians' gallery of the old monks' refectory [actually it was for the reading of holy books during meals], and there was another concert for those who had not been able to go to Mary.[62]

There has been no mention of the raffia and basket work which Miss Ivens had been suggesting for the amusement of the blessés. Their amusements seem to have been much more exciting!

She describes taking the 'niggers' for a walk:

Imagine about a dozen coal-black convalescents in pyjamas and blue overcoats most of them minus an arm with scarlet caps on their black wool and a varied assortment of injured Arabs, little Sister Williams and myself, tramping through the woods and over ploughed fields – marched to the orders of Sallifon (sic), Moussa or Couli Bali (sic) who being only privates in the ranks love ordering us to 'form fours' or 'right about face.' The funniest thing was when in the middle of a ploughed field we got the order to 'kneel'! We made each of them 'command' in turn. We had the two dogs with us – Smith and Jack the puppy, and dozens of pheasants rose whirring quite close to us – at wh. the blessés threw their sticks. Smith had a swim when we got to the Oise and shook himself all over us, and we returned bearing sheaves and great branches of Autumn leaves and scarlet berries for my room, wh. the Arabs loved getting and carrying. Our boots were loaded with yellow mud, and our pyjama legs not free from it either, but we were sent round by the kitchen to take a few layers off.

Later she looked out of her window as she heard great shouts of laughter:

> I found Sister Williams and one or two orderlies surrounded by the blacks and Arabs playing a kind of cricket with a big india-rubber ball I brought them the other day from Creil. The runs and the batting were the funniest things I have seen for a long time, and Sister in her flowing veil like a beneficent little dove darting about seeing that everyone of her black charges get a fair chance and fair play. Each day I am more lost in admiration and astonishment at the work she has done.[63]

Back in June 1915 a patient had been admitted who was to play a very important part in the life of the hospital. His wounds were not serious, and before long, as his condition improved, he was found to be disappearing from his ward and drifting towards the kitchen which seemed to have an irresistible attraction for him. From visiting he was soon lending a hand and gradually taking a greater and greater share in the preparation of the meals. This was Michelet – soon to be known as 'Michelet of Royaumont'. He had been called up for service from his occupation as a chef – a renowned and brilliant chef – to a Paris millionaire. Miss Swanston, who was in charge of the kitchen at the time, wrote:

> He is now convalescent and helping in the kitchen, and we are charmed … I feel confident indeed that this man is first class, and unlike most chefs, he will prepare the vegetables or do anything and the cooks are delighted to have his help with the staff cooking.[64]

Unfortunately Michelet was getting better. According to Navarro there were attempts to deceive the authorities that his state of health did not warrant discharge, but they were not so easily fooled. The sad day came in August (1915) when Michelet had to return to his unit. Miss Loudon reported to the Committee: 'Michelet the chef left us on Monday to the great sorrow of the whole hospital. He wept, and we very nearly did'.[65] Miss Ivens, however, recognising the enormous benefit such culinary skills could bring to the morale of the hospital, exercised her charm and not inconsiderable powers of persuasion in getting Michelet seconded to the hospital for the duration. Of course at that time no one expected the war to last so long. He returned in November 1916, and Royaumont soon became known as the best-fed hospital in France. He was well and truly welcomed. Mrs Robertson reported:

> Our military chef, Michelet, a former patient, has now arrived and started work. He has been granted to us 'on military service' so there is unlikely to be any further change in the management. He was most delighted to

return here, and was received with open arms by all the kitchen people. He will undertake all the catering and marketing, and has the experience and knowledge of the markets and prices necessary for this work ... The paid French help in the kitchen will be reduced, in fact to vanishing point. [It will be remembered that Mrs Robertson had had to spend a considerable amount of time chasing down elusive French cooks.] Miss Rolt has done splendid work in the kitchen since Miss MacPherson left. [Rolt was to distinguish herself in the next world war (Part Three: Envoi).] There is a very happy and hopeful spirit prevailing in the kitchen just now with Michelet at the helm. There is no doubt that our cooks and orderlies prefer working by themselves with a capable chef at the head to having these French women of a different class from them.[66]

Miss Ivens took the opportunity to remind the Committee of the crucial importance of food. They had been through a period of difficulties and shortages, no doubt at least partly due to the serious military situation. This was now easing somewhat as the fighting decreased with the advent of winter:

Economies must be made by careful buying, careful distribution and avoidance of any waste or leakage and not by suppressing or curtailing articles necessary to the well-being of either patients or workers. The splendid results obtained at Royaumont are, I feel sure, in great measure due to the good feeding of the patients.[67]

But to return to Michelet himself. He had a way with potatoes – he had a way with meat – and he knew how to rise to an occasion. Dr Henry tells us in her reminiscences:

Once we were warned that 250 walking cases were en route, they had been on the road three days without food, going from one field dressing station to another. They sat on the stone benches all round the cloisters, were given water and towels, then Michelet our chef lived up to his reputation and provided a good meal before they moved on.[68]

Just before Christmas 1916 Mrs Robertson wrote:

There are about 250 men in and Michelet is surpassing himself to give them the best Christmas fare available in war-time. Michelet is really splendid – he showed me with great pride last night his rows of turkeys all stuffed and ready.

And he colluded with all the little private parties the orderlies and sisters organised for themselves from time to time.

Sister Adams, who admitted that she had no great personal affection for him, relented somewhat when he presented her with a plate of apple fritters when she passed through the kitchen. As an old lady she remembered how 'Michelet was a great source of entertainment ... He continually told me how he loved the 'doctoresses, the Meeses and the Sistaires'.[69]

'Little Simpson' (head cook in 1918), visiting the old kitchen in 1961, recalled how Michelet used to

> spin the cocottes like curling stones across the stone floor to the sinks. Woe betide feet and ankles in their path! There I pictured him in the dusk, when all was quiet, as we awaited the night staff, cross-legged on the window sill playing his flute with the crickets for chorus, or again, in the darkness slipping furtively in from the park, with several pheasants tucked inside his coat – pour les docteurs, pour les misses! What wonderful suppers we all enjoyed.[70]

Summerhayes (an orderly who later qualified in medicine) remembered him dancing on the enormous kitchen stove.[71]

It would be pointless to deny that friction did not arise from time to time as the weary war years rolled on. The question as to who was in charge in the kitchen was never completely resolved. Cicely Hamilton, when she became Administrator after Miss Loudon, was always careful to define her powers and responsibilities. 'Who is the authority as regards the kitchen?' Mrs Russell had pointed out that 'unless Miss Ivens went herself to the kitchen there is no one of any authority to administer between Michelet and the other people working there'.

The situation came to a head in June 1918 when Simpson had repeated quarrels with Michelet following the departure of Miss McLeod who had preceded her in the kitchen, and who had also had problems with Michelet. The matter was brought before the Committee who asked Miss Ivens to consider very carefully the question of his employment 'as it seems rather hopeless to send out women cooks to work in the same kitchen with him'.[72] Miss Ivens spoke up for him – 'Michelet has his faults but cooks meat splendidly, and is devoted to the patients'. She resolved the issue – so far as it was resolvable – by using a hut as a second kitchen for the staff cookery and the night cookery, with British staff in charge, and Michelet in control of the men's cooking – at that time, in 1918, a very large commitment with up to 600 beds occupied.[73]

It would have been strange if the solitary man in the kitchen – and one who was a superb chef – had not felt some degree of frustration from time to time. But during the Armistice celebrations the orderlies chaired Michelet shoulder-high round the Abbey. After the war, when minor irritations were a thing of the past, the Association was united in fêting him at its twelfth annual dinner in 1931. He made a 'great oration' and pointed out that he was himself a Royaumontite. He was also the proud possessor of the medal of the Scottish Women's Hospitals. What's more, and a great comfort to the Dinner

Secretary, he approved of the dinner and sent a message of congratulation to the chef.[74]

Christmas came round once more and Royaumont traditions had to be upheld. Their friends in the Army bakery in Boran donated a large Christmas tree which was erected in the great refectory. The patients, those who were able, brought in armloads of evergreens from the forests to decorate it. Michelet's turkeys were consumed and guests, with their children, invited from the nearby villages. Medals were awarded to three of the patients, carols were sung by a small choir of orderlies — some of them professional singers — Père Noel arrived on a sledge bearing gifts for every patient and the day ended with a concert given by a group from Paris.[75]

For the Unit the year 1916 had been one in which periods of intense activity had alternated with quieter times — as is so often the case in war. The records indicate that after the frantically busy time the rate of admissions dropped (the hospital being full to capacity) and normal routines were re-established. The gay round of parties and entertainments suggests that there was still plenty of energy around. And there was certainly a degree of pride as they reflected how, after all, they had coped, and met the challenge.

They had gained valuable experience in the 'rushes' (or 'flaps') in 1915 and this served them well in the greater demands of 1916. The volume of work carried out in a comparatively small hospital was certainly impressive. Miss Ivens gave some of the figures in a paper she published at the end of 1916.[76]

From January 1915 to October 13 1916:

Soldiers admitted	2267
Of these, Wounded	1694
Sick	229
Surgical, unwounded	229

Of the 1694 wounded cases 464 were infected with tetanus and gas gangrene organisms.

At the peak, July 2nd, 127 cases were admitted in 24 hours. Gas gangrene was present almost without exception.

676 patients were examined under x-rays in the month of July, and in the second half of 1916, almost 3000.

As the year drew to a close many must have wondered what was in store for them in the year to come. In the words of Collum:

During the Battle of the Somme the strain on us was terrific — physically, psychologically. We were stretched taut, and not a strand of the rope was frayed. We held![77]

The Kitchen, now one of the most beautiful rooms of the Abbey. The orderlies are hard at work. Note the heavy iron stoves which the cooks found so difficult to manage. No trace of these remains.

(By permission of the Imperial War Museum).

References

1. ML. Tin 12, 'Impressions of Hospital at Abbaye de Royaumont' (source not stated).
2. *CC*, 21.1.16. Reported by Miss Loudon.
3. ML. Tin 42, C. Hamilton to Kemp, 17.2.16.
4. ML. Tin 42, Mrs Laurie and Mrs Robertson. Report, April 1916.
5. ML. Tin 42, F. Ivens to Kemp, 28.2.16.
6. ML. Ibid.
7. ML. Tin 42, FI to Russell, 2.4.16.
8. ML. Tin 42, Loudon to Kemp, 13.3.16.
9. *Leven Advertiser*. Obituary notice, Jan. 1916.
10. ML. Tin 42, *ibid*.
11. ML. Tin 42, 7.4.16.
12. *CC*, C. Hamilton, 18.8.16.
13. ML. Tin 42, FI to Hunter, 21.6.16.
14. ML. Tin 42, FI to Russell, 21.5.16.
15. ML. Tin 42, FI to Russell, 18.6.16.
16. ML. Tin 42, 16.6.16.
17. ML. Tin 42, FI to Kemp, 12.3.16.
18. ML. Tin 12, 4.7.16.
19. 'Skia', *Blackwood's Magazine*, March 1917, pp. 339–40.

20. 'Skia', *Ibid.*, pp. 340–342.

21. 'Skia', op. cit., November 1918, p. 622.

22. 'Skia', op. cit., March 1917, p. 346.

23. *Ibid.*

24. ML. Tin 42, Savill to Russell, 4.7.16.

25. Dr Elsie Dalyell, letter Sydney and *NSW Daily Telegraph*, 22.1.18.

26. Navarro, *The Scottish Women's Hospital*, p. 165.

27. ML. Tin 42, FI to Kemp, 3.7.16.

28. ML. Tin 42, FI to Kemp, 16.7.16.

29. 'Skia', op. cit., March 1917, p. 342—343.

30. *CC*, C. Hamilton 4.8.16. p. 215.

31. ML. Tin 41, 9.8.16.

32. ML. Tin 42, 30.8.16.

33. ML. Tin 42, FI to Kemp, 13.8.16.

34. Dora Pym, 'Patchwork from the Past'. Unpublished memoirs by kind permission of her daughter, Mary Pym.

35. NL 1936, pp. 5–6.

36. NL 1964, p. 9.

37. ML. Tin 42, FI to Kemp, 19.8.16 and Tin 12, FI to Laurie, 12.8.16.

38. ML. Tin 42, Erskine to May, 19.8.16.

39. ML. Tin 42, ibid.

40. ML. Tin 12, FI to Laurie.

41. ML. Tin 42, FI to Kemp, 19.8.16.

42. ML. Tin 42, Erskine to May, 16.9.16.

43. ML. Tin 42, ibid.

44. *Ibid.*

45. ML. Tin 41, Executive Committee Minutes, 20.12.16.

46. Mrs A.M. Robertson. Letters home, 3.11.16. By kind permission of her granddaughter, Mrs Ailsa Tanner.

47. Ibid., 14.11.16.

48. *CC*, 25.8.16; and FL. Box 305, 19.8.16.

49. *CC*, 25.8.16, p. 248.

50. McLaren, *A History of the Scottish Women's Hospitals*, p. 40.

51. ML. Tin 42, FI to Kemp, 27.8.16.

52. Mrs A.M. Robertson, ibid., 25.10.16.

53. Mrs A.M. Robertson, ibid., 14.11.16.

54. Mrs A.M. Robertson, ibid., 12.11.16.

55. Mrs A.M. Robertson, ibid., 1.11.16.

56. Mrs A.M. Robertson, ibid., 29.10.16.

57. Mrs A.M. Robertson, ibid., 29.10.16.

58. Mrs A.M. Robertson, ibid., 31.10.16.

59. Mrs A.M. Robertson, ibid., 2.11.16.

60. Mrs A.M. Robertson, ibid., 19.11.16.

61. Mrs A.M. Robertson, ibid., 19.11.16.

62. Mrs A.M. Robertson, ibid., 19.11.16.

63. Mrs A.M. Robertson, ibid., 4.11.16.

64. 'The Call of our Allies and the Response of the Scottish Women's Hospitals for Foreign Service', June 1915, p. 14.

65. ML. Tin 42, Loudon to Marris, 6.8.15.

66. ML. Tin 42, Mrs Robertson to Marris, 23.11.16.

67. Ibid.

68. Dr L.M. Henry. Reminiscences, by kind permission of her daughter, Mrs Anne Murdoch.

69. NL 1970, p. 6.

70. NL 1961, p. 2.

71. Dr Grace MacRae. Personal communication.

72. ML. Tin 42, Russell to FI, 3.7.18.

73. ML. Tin 42, FI to Russell. No date but probably 15 or 16.7.18.

74. NL 1931, p. 9–10.

75. *CC.*, 19.1.17, p. 536.

76. F. Ivens, *Proc. Roy. Soc. Med. 1916–1917 Part 3. Surgical Section*, pp. 29–110.

77. 'Skia', *Blackwood's Magazine*, November 1918, p. 621.

CHAPTER FIVE

The Patients

It seems appropriate to interrupt the chronological history of the hospital at this point and to switch from the events of the hospital, the administrative problems, the organisation and treatment of the wounded and the experiences of the staff in order to examine more closely the background of the ordinary *poilu* as a private in the French Army. Other nationalities will also be considered.

The name 'poilu' or 'hairy one' was said to have arisen from the fact that at the beginning of the war he looked more like a poacher or a trapper than a soldier. The name stuck even after much of the facial hair was reduced. Many of the *poilus* were simple uneducated peasants for whom life in the Army must have been an extraordinary and bewildering experience.

It has to be said that the *poilu* had a pretty raw deal. Conditions for him were considerably worse than they were for his British or German counterparts, though some improvements did occur when Pétain stepped in and reorganised aspects of his life which had been so seriously neglected in the first two years of the war.

One easily identifiable hardship was his extremely low pay; twenty sous a day (equivalent to two old pence), which compared badly with the British Tommy's far from generous 1/- per day. This meant that he was totally dependent on the services the Army provided for him – he had no means to help himself if the supply of food failed; he had no means of finding a bed if transport arrangements broke down as happened all too frequently; and there was a woeful deficiency of canteens and rest centres. One instance has already been given where a large group of men, on foot, almost collapsed into the Abbey after they had been on the road for several days. This was not an isolated occurrence – it was repeated in 1917 when Michelet fed another large contingent of 180 soldiers marching on foot from one posting to another.

A French account[1] describes the supply of food to the trenches. The 'homme de soupe' carried the food from portable kitchens behind the lines. It arrived cold, if it arrived at all. If a shell exploded nearby the whole meal could be lost, or it could be mixed with generous supplies of soil and mud. The meal normally consisted of rubbery macaroni, solid rice and what they called 'singe' (monkey). This was a stringy tinned beef in coagulated fat, greatly inferior to the British 'bully'. In 1916 during Lent they were served with salt cod which resulted in torments of thirst. The man detailed for fatigue duty was slung around with water bottles containing 'jus' (black coffee, weak, but well sweetened). He also carried the 'pinard', the rough red wine, of which the regulation allowance was 'un quart' per day. The *pinard* was the 'source of comfort, of happiness and endless chat'. Water was always in short supply in the trenches though plentiful enough behind the lines. Discarded food ended up in the 'feuillées' (French latrines), whose upkeep, and even existence, depended on the sector being quiet.

On the march the *poilu* was exceptionally heavily laden. Alastair Horne[2] lists the articles he was supposed to carry – amounting to some 85 lbs. His kit would consist of two blankets rolled in a ground sheet, extra boots, a sheepskin or quilted coat, a shovel or a pair of heavy scissors for cutting barbed wire, a mess tin, a large water bottle containing the 'quart of pinard' (probably one of his more acceptable burdens), 200 cartridges, 6 hand grenades, a gas mask and his personal belongings.

It seems that relations between officers and men were often poor though Navarro reported[3] that officers did visit their men in Royaumont and the men were glad to see them. The tradition in the British Army where the junior officer was expected to have a personal care for his men's wellbeing (instanced by the daily regular foot inspections, and a listening ear for his men's personal problems) seems to have been largely absent in the French Army. The German Army as well as the British had a tradition of personal care for the men by their officers. In the French Army Horne describes how, when they were out of the line, whatever accommodation was available was occupied by officers and NCOs. The men had to fend for themselves. By 1916, he believes:

> The division between officers and men was probably wider than it had ever been. Allied observers were often shocked at the way in which French commanders, after a successful attack, left their troops lying out on the destroyed enemy position for days and nights after they should have been relieved.

Class distinctions were upheld. For instance: 'W.C. pour Mm les officiers, Cabinets pour les sous-officiers, Latrines pour la troupe'.[4]

A French Colonel (le Colonel Champagne) is on record as having said: 'At the Front the soldier may be a hero; in the rear he is merely tiresome'.[5]

Leave periods ('permissions') were few and irregular. Transport arrangements were often so muddled and unreliable that the unfortunate 'permissionaire' might barely reach his home before it was time to return. The lack of canteens, which were generously provided by the YMCA and other voluntary bodies for the British, was a great hardship. This was realised by 1917 when the French authorities called upon the SWH and other British voluntary organisations to help.

However, it was his appalling experiences of trench warfare which formed the horrible background of the *poilu's* life. He might live for days and weeks at a time in the trenches. It was only after Pétain's reforms of 1917 that the men received regular periods of respite behind the lines, though this was routine procedure in both the British and the German armies. Apart from the actual fighting the *poilus* had to suffer extremes of heat, cold and wet. The soil was more often than not waterlogged, their feet could be constantly in the mud, their boots always wet, and often their clothing as well. Deep holes made by shell explosions filled up with water, and turned to mud in which men could actually drown (as Starr's patient told in 1915, this was not at all an isolated incident). Lice, rats, the smell of decomposing bodies (on which rats waxed fat and bold), the lack of sanitation (hygiene in the French trenches was particularly poor and neglected), the irregular supply of unpalatable food, the shortage of water, and often during battles, the agonies of extreme thirst: this was the physical background to their lives.

A first-hand account from a French soldier paints a grim picture of entering a new trench:

> A poisonous smell seizes our throats ... In torrential rain we find the
> walls stuffed with canvas. Next day at dawn we discover our trenches are
> in the middle of a charnel house. The canvas had hidden the corpses.
> Several days of burning sun brought flies. Appetite disappears. When the

*Decoration ceremony in the cloisters. Doctors on right, sisters (or auxiliary nurses) in
centre, chauffeurs in uniform, wearing brassards.
(By courtesy of Mrs Anne Murdoch).*

rations of beans and greasy rice appear we balance them on the parapet.
Only the pinard and 'gnole' (spirits) are welcome. The men's faces are
waxy, their eyes hollow (my translation).

Another describes the rats and flies which abound among the unshaven,
unwashed men; piles of straw with the indescribable acrid smell of urine –
rubbish everywhere; the never-ending search for 'totos' (lice); the constant
torment of the rats when one tries to sleep (the authorities were paying one
sou for every rat tail, so regular chases were organised).[6]

A third French soldier wrote:

> I've spent ghastly nights wrapped in my ground sheet and greatcoat – I
> feel these filthy beasts all over me. Sometimes there are 15 or 20 on each
> of us. After they have eaten our bread, butter and chocolate, they start on
> our clothes. It's impossible to sleep in these terrible conditions.

Others described the rats as 'enormous, fat with human flesh'.[7]

If he were wounded and unable to make his way to the nearest dressing
station the *poilu* depended on the stretcher-bearers. Collection of the wounded
from the battlefield was appallingly difficult – it was generally done under
cover of darkness. The stretcher-bearers were a group of men of often outstanding courage who, together with the men who carried food and water
into the trenches, were said to have the highest casualty rates of all. Once collected by the stretcher bearers and field dressings applied, the wounded man
bumped painfully in a two-man hand cart to the nearest casualty station
where little could be done in the sense of any real treatment and he was sent
– if he survived that far – in a primitive ambulance (solid wooden tyres and
unyielding springs) on a long and painful journey to the rail station. He
would then be piled a into coach, often a cattle truck, fitted with shelves.
Sanitation was almost non-existent, and even water, for which the wounded
men were desperate, was in short supply.[8]

Miss Ivens, writing a medical account of the hospital's experience of dealing with gas gangrene[9] reported that out of 107 cases only 36 were admitted
within 24 hours of being wounded. The remainder experienced much longer
delays, even up to 12 days (though some of these might have had limited
emergency surgery in a field ambulance). Only a few of her cases were in a
'tolerable' condition; some were collapsed and desperately ill; a few were
moribund.

The majority of wounds in the First World War resulted from shellfire.
The shells were larger than any that had been seen in previous wars. On
explosion they shattered into great ragged pieces of metal causing horrific,
usually multiple, injuries. In previous wars (apart from disease) bullets caused
the greatest number of casualties; they resulted in relatively clean wounds,
usually single, and far simpler to treat.

Horne comments:

> It was only astonishing how much mutilation flesh could suffer and sur-
> vive! To cope with these mutilations on so massive a scale, medical ser-
> vices were singularly ill-equipped. In this respect France was notably, and
> notoriously, behind both Britain and Germany. She remained so through-
> out the war. Her medical services had been prepared in 1914 for a short,
> sharp war and were hopelessly caught out ... Of the three Western powers
> France led with easily the highest rate of deaths to wounded: on top of a
> total of 895,000 killed in action, 420,000 had died of wounds or sick-
> ness.[10] [There is considerable uncertainty about casualty figures in the
> French services. Those quoted here may well be underestimates.]

It was no wonder that the men who had the good fortune to be admitted to
Royaumont called it 'The Palace', or, as Private Breuilh wrote: 'Ce charmant
hôpital Ecossais, que les poilus appellent "Paradis" '.[11] Caporal Mathieu
wrote: 'Si par hazard le noir cafard nous guette, les gentilles Miss bien vite
nous l'enleveront car ici tout le monde a le coeur en fête'. [If by chance black
gloom lies in wait for us, the kind Miss (es) soon take it away because here
everyone has a happy heart.][12]

In 1917 one of the staff overheard the exchange: 'Qui est-ce?' 'C'est une
des dames Ecossaises, le bonheur du poilu'.[13] The records are full of such
affectionate tributes but one of the most moving came from a badly injured
patient at the end of the war:

> Après cinq longs mois sur mon lit de doleur, je vous prie d'être mon
> interprète auprès de Mme la Commandante et de toutes les dévouées
> Doctoresses; car, Madame, *il y a des choses qui ne s'oublierent pas* (my italics).
> [After five long months on my bed of pain, I beg you to be my inter-
> preter to Mme la Commandante and all the devoted doctors, because,
> Madame, there are things one does not forget.][14]

On a lighter note one clearly less seriously wounded man declared that he
'wouldn't mind being wounded again if it meant going back to
Royaumont'.[15]

In the early days of 1915 Sergeant Treilles expressed his appreciation in
verse – 'Aux Fées de Royaumont'. The whole poem is not transcribed, but
those whom he picked out for mention should be named here:

> 'Nymphes de Royaumont! qui des doigts divins,
> Avez bati ce nid au milieu des sapins,
> Je ne veux pas quitter ce joli coin de France,
> Ou les anges et les fleurs guérrissent la souffrance,
> Sans dire à tous merci!.
>
> L'acier le mieux trempe des armes meurtrières,

Se transforment vous mains en lames humanitaire,
Et vos doigts délicats douce Miss Nicholson,[1]
Dans les corps palpitants s'enforcent sans frisson,
Tandis que dans un rêve Miss Ivens, Miss Heyworth,[2]
Sur la table lugubre, votre patient s'endort,
Sous le charme confiant que votre science inspire,
Je le vois au reveil rechercher ce sourire,
Baume reconfortant que sur les plaies saignantes,
Vous répandez sans trêve femmes compatissantes.

Je n'oublierai jamais ce dévouement constant,
Tous ces soins maternels et ce zèle touchant,
Que l'intègre Maxwell,[3] la bonne Jeffries[4]
Prodiguent à toute heure aux pauvres corps meurtris.
J'emporte en m'en allant un souvenir précieux,
De la franche gaieté, de vos charmes gracieux,
Suave Miss Harley5, aimable Miss Allen,[6]
L'éclat de votre rire, coquette Miss Chapman,[7]
A l'oreille charmée resonnera encore a côté de celui de la belle Miss Moir.[8]

... And so on ...[16]

A very free translation of the poem runs as follows:

Nymphs of Royaumont! whose divine fingers have built this nest among
the pine trees [N.B. There are few pines at Royaumont], I cannot leave
this beautiful corner of France, where angels and flowers unite in healing
the suffering, without saying thank you.

The well-tempered steel of murderous weapons is transformed in your
hands to healing blades, and your gentle fingers, sweet Miss Nicholson,
enter the trembling body while, Miss Ivens and Miss Heyworth, your
patient sleeps on the table, confident in your science. See how he wakes
seeking the smile which brings soothing balm to his bleeding wounds.
Your compassion is infinite. I will never forget the constant motherly care
and the touching devotion of worthy Maxwell and good Miss [Jeffrey]
poured out continually on poor wounded bodies. As I leave I take with
me a precious memory of your gaiety, your gracious charm, gentle Miss

---

1. Miss Nicholson was the surgeon, second-in-command.
2. Miss Heyworth was the anaesthetist.
3. Miss Jean Maxwell, sister, December 1914 to ?.
4. Miss Mabel Jeffrey, sister, 27.3.15 to 13.3.16.
5. Miss Edith Harley, orderly, January 1915 to ? 1915.
6. Miss Dorothy Allan, orderly, February to May 1915.
7. Miss Marjorie Chapman Auxiliary Nurse, 6.5.15 to 22.3.19.
8. Miss M. Moir, orderly, February to August 1915.

Harley, kind Miss Allen. The brightness of your laughter, dear Miss
Chapman, will ring in my delighted ear, with that of lovely Miss Moir.

There was one patient in particular who impressed himself upon many members of the Unit. We do not know when he was admitted with his jaw wound
but after his discharge he returned frequently to the hospital and did so many
odd jobs for them that he earned the title of 'le Spécialiste'. One of these tasks
they remembered was opening the casks of *pinard*.[17] After the war he corre-
sponded for many years with some members and he was an honoured guest at
one of their reunion dinners where he was said to have made a splendid
speech. After the war his widow, remembering his attachment to 'his family'
at Royaumont, wrote to record his death.[18]

There was an easy friendliness between many of the French patients and
their 'Meeses'. They could share jokes together as when, on April 1st 1917,
Chapman ('coquette Miss Chapman' of the poem) and two other orderlies disguised themselves as blessés. With heavily bandaged faces and wearing
French *horizon bleu* uniform, they got themselves admitted into a ward and
put to bed – and all before the inevitable discovery. The patients loved it –
'Oh, naughty Miss' was their delighted comment.

The patients had their own sense of fun and Chapman relates one such
incident. It was the custom to surround the ward commode ('le cabinet') in a
discreet covering of bright red material. When a French general came on a
visit of inspection, clad in glorious technicolour, as French generals loved to
do, a patient was heard to cry out 'Ah, le cabinet, le grand cabinet!' It was to
be hoped that the general did not catch the allusion.[19]

Another incident in Chapman's time was the fire in Elsie Ward. It was not
a serious affair but the orderlies on fire duty got up in the middle of the night
and donned their dressing gowns to extinguish the fire. Subsequently the
patients remembered la Colonelle's blue silk dressing gown 'C'etait un bon
rêve!'[20]

Naturally a large proportion of the patients were French, but there were
also significant numbers of French colonial troops. These would be largely
Senegalese, and Arabs from North Africa. There were a few from the West
Indies, and soldiers from the Foreign Legion included a number of nationalities, particularly Spanish. There was an occasional Russian or Swiss serving
in the French Army. Later in the war there were British, Canadians, and
Americans, and a few German and Austrian prisoners of war. The monument
in the Asnières cemetery commemorating some of those who died at
Royaumont includes one 'soldat inconnu'.

Relations with the French patients seem on the whole to have been happy.
Professor Weinberg said in a lecture he gave in Glasgow in March 1916 that
'the men were inclined at first to rag the ladies a little', but that seems to have
been a passing phase. The men were quite aware how fortunate they were to

be in a hospital like Royaumont, and that any serious misbehaviour would be punished by transfer elsewhere.

Collum wrote glowingly of the French soldiers' courage. It was her job to make thorough radiographic examinations, and this often involved positioning the patients – painfully – on a hard x-ray table to take the necessary pictures. She described one such patient:

> To endure all that after hours of tense waiting for the attack, more strenuous hours of fighting, the noisy hell of a modern bombardment; then with those two shattering wounds and the long wait, under fire, for succour; and after that the painful journey to the dressing station, and then the long journey by ambulance train and motor! He has the Médaille Militaire now and is doing well.[21]

There was one young French officer who should be mentioned – Lucien Campora. He was from Algeria. He and Mary Peter, described by Sister Rose-Morris as 'my once tireless orderly',[22] provided a Royaumont romance. In later years members remembered seeing Peter pushing Lucien in his wheel chair in the furthest corners of the Abbey grounds.[23] They married in 1920, settled in Algeria where Lucien built up a successful milling business. The last news the Unit had of them was that they were celebrating their golden wedding in 1970 together with their four children, all of whom had done well.[24]

There were naturally a wide variety of types among the French troops: officers and men, educated and simple peasants; élite troops like the Zouaves and Chasseurs-Alpin, and men from the Punitive Battalions (jailbirds and military prisoners who were given an opportunity in the Army to redeem themselves). Collum, whose spectacles were inclined to be rosy, writing near the end of the war, seems to have admired them all: 'They behaved always like the gentlemen they were – and the kind of gentleman a French poilu can be is a very fine gentleman indeed'.[25] At the age of 98, Dr Grace MacRae, formerly orderly Summerhayes, remembered: 'The poilus we liked very much indeed – not really the officers much – but the poilus – yes, they were nice chaps'.[26]

Of the civilian patients who have been recorded there was M. Fox, an Englishman living in Asnières and married to Mme. Fox who was such a tower of strength to the *vêtements* department and elsewhere. He was suffering from cancer, and died in the hospital, having been given every care and nursed in a private single room.

Madeleine was a French girl who was working in a munitions factory in Compiègne when she was very seriously injured in an explosion. Mrs Robertson had a very soft spot for her and enormously admired her courage. She was nursed in one of the two small rooms they reserved for women (and called St Damian's). To quote Mrs Robertson:

The poor girl was brought in in a dreadful condition, her limbs absolutely mangled. Miss Ivens had to amputate her left arm at once as it was only hanging on a thread, and her right leg seemed hopeless too. She is the bravest thing that ever lived, is Madeleine. As she was alone in this hut where it happened (at this work of hers each is alone), when she came to herself she dragged herself out along the ground until she was found! During the journey here and the painful dressings before and after amputation, never a murmur. She has a beautiful mind and keen intelligence, is full of appreciation and gratitude, in fact she personifies to my mind all that is best in the French woman's character. She is improving most marvellously, her legs are left to her and her right arm minus a finger and she is most grateful and says that she knows that there is work for her to do in the world yet. Her French is so beautiful and the way she expresses herself, and she is full of natural refinement.[27]

Mrs Robertson spent as much time as possible at her bedside and a great affection sprang up between them. When Mrs Robertson had an attack of bronchitis which kept her in bed for a few days, Madeleine wrote – with some difficulty as her hand was encumbered with dressings -

J'apprends à l'instant que vous êtes souffrante, j'en suis desolée aussi chère Madame, je voudrais bien pouvoir être près de vous, et vous entoure de mes soins les plus devoués. [I have just learnt that you are ill and I am distressed, dear Madam, I would like to be near you and surround you with devoted care.]

\She went on:

Hier, Doctoresse Wilson a fait le pansement de ma jambe de laquelle elle m'a sorti de petits éclats (qu'on m'a mis dans une petite boîte) et puis un bout de bois que je donne pour chauffer l'hôpital. J'aide ma douce Doctoresse en criant et pleurant bien fort. Je crois qu'on pourra me déserver la Croix de Guerre pour mon courage! [Yesterday Dr Wilson dressed my leg from which she took some little fragments (which I have put into a little box) and then a piece of wood which I am giving to heat the hospital. I helped my kind doctor by shouting and crying very loudly. I think I deserve the Croix de Guerre for my courage.]

Dr Courtauld told Mrs Robertson of a poor boy from Martinique:

He was so badly smashed up when he arrived and gas gangrene had made such awful inroads that it was impossible to do anything; he was surely doomed. Still the impossible almost was done to relieve him, and Miss Courtauld sat with him herself by the bed away beside the window in Elsie. He lived for an hour after coming up from the operating table where his awful wounds had been cleaned. The details Miss C. gave me

Sister Williams with one of her Senegalese patients in the cloisters.
(By courtesy of Mrs Crowther).

were sickening. And shortly before he died he turned to her and said with
an expression of unutterable longing in his eyes: 'Dans mon pays, la
bonne Guadaloupe, il n'y a pas de guerre!' There was sunshine without
and the Oise was stealing in a silver thread through the lush meadows
but France for him was a land of bloody battlefields and unutterable woe,
and his thoughts were with papa, Maman and Babette his little fiancée of
whom be babbled unceasingly.

In the previous chapter there has been plenty of evidence of the way the
Senegalese entered wholeheartedly into all the entertainments in the hospi-
tal, and the extraordinarily good relations they had with Sister Williams. Mrs
Robertson expands on this:

Now I want to tell you something about the dusky patients of Salle Elsie,
who are the spoilt children of the whole hospital. Dr Courtauld is in

charge there and they call her First Mammy. Little Sister Williams simply
adores them and they reciprocate it. If she is 'pas contente' with them
they weep and howl. She is about the size of tuppence, but they obey her
lightest word. She has found out somehow a great deal about their family
history – how many wives they had etc, which is very astonishing as they
speak little French and no English, and she speaks less French still, but
they certainly do understand each other, and the discipline and fine feeling in that ward is very wonderful. When they came here the first time
months ago they were absolute savages and their manners and habits were
deplorable, but now they behave like gentlemen, have learnt self-control
and nice manners and their attachment to the hospital, and everyone who
has to do with them is quite pathetic. Of course they are having the time
of their lives, and dread leaving Royaumont. And no wonder for there
will be a poor welcome in Senegal for limbless heroes.

Also:

Sister Williams wants to take all the niggers off to a farm in Wales and
look after them. The Senegalese are all to be evacuated to-morrow and no
one dare tell them till the last minute – it seems like sending babes out
into the cold.

When she was ill for a couple of days, the Senegalese and the Arabs insisted
on coming to her door with Sister Williams who had helped them to write a
letter: 'To Maman Camerade, Dear Madam, We are sorry you are ill. With
love from All'. And all signed. 'In the open doorway there was a group of
dusky figures and flashing white teeth, each pushing forward to salute, and
the Arabs also. Sister said she just had to bring them, nothing else would
please them'.
    Collum writes that during the Somme rush when they had a large influx
of Colonial troops:

These poor black fellows from Senegal, and the Arabs from Tunis and
Algeria were very severely wounded: men with less iron constitutions
must have died where they fell of such wounds. Yet the agony of their
wounds was as nothing to the terror of their minds when they realised
that a visit to the operating theatre often meant the loss of a mangled or
gangrenous limb. They spoke only a few words of pigeon French, and the
horrible legend spread among them that the first visit to the theatre
meant incisions – mere senseless slashings of the surgeon's knife, to their
unsophisticated intelligences; the second, amputation; and the third the
slitting of their throats. It was days before their terror subsided, and
weeks before their suspicious fear of the white women with sharp knives
and wicked-looking forceps gave place to the dog-like devotion and

gratitude that characterised their attitude to surgeons, nurses and orderlies, eventually. One broad-nosed woolly-headed giant, black as ebony,
awakened from the anaesthetic on the operating table; he looked round in
abject fear, though the instruments were all in the tray and the orderly
had almost finished bandaging him: then his eyes lighted on the Chief
Surgeon (divested of her gloves and gauze mask) who, as it happened, had
dressed him in the ward and evidently gained his confidence. A black
arm shot out towards her as she made towards the door, and clutched her
hand, which he grasped and laid against his cheek, closing his eyes con-
tentedly once more as he murmured, 'Mois connais toi' (I know you).[28]

One little fellow of 21, with a face like a child's golliwog had enough
shrapnel in him to kill three men. His arm – both bones shattered
beyond repair, and so full of metal that it would have been impossible to
put a six-penny bit on any clear part of the x-ray photograph and not
have covered a piece of shell – was amputated; but his thigh, from knee
to buttock, equally full of bits of metal was left, since the buttock itself
had been equally torn away. Yet five months later this black boy was
tearing round the hospital park like a young deer, full of the wildest
spirits, and reconciled apparently to his one-armed condition and his
uneven gait by the fact that his French comrades regarded him as quite a
little hero and that he was to receive the Croix de Guerre.[29]

Dr Courtauld, writing in 1918, comments on the way the Senegalese reacted
to their injuries:

Some very bad patients just now. I have three niggers all badly wounded,
one very bad, but such a nice boy. All the niggers have the generic name
of Sambo by the staff. My three lie side by side and talk in their own
language. One is an immense man with a badly fractured skull. He ought
to be quite still, but sits bolt upright in bed and seems impervious to
pain.[30]

Navarro describes the problem they caused to those looking after them by the
casual attitude they took towards their dressings, splints, drainage tubes and
so on:

Among the Senegalese, the most curious and alarming experiences are the
moments of recovered consciousness when the patient, curious as a child,
tears off bandages, tubes and splints to see the effect of a missing limb or
the result of a minor operation – the combined strength of surgeons and
nurses ridiculously inadequate against the savage determination of the
patient. One giant black who had three times in succession torn off his
splints (six bad wounds in his two legs), murmured each time with satisfaction, 'Bon! très bon!'[31]

Abdulla ben Ati looks down to the cloisters from the terrace.
(By courtesy of Miss Heather Mackay).

Dr Henry remembered that among a convoy of Senegalese troops, there was one they called Snowball, as 'black as ebony'. He was a big powerful man and wore a 'gold band coiled like a snake around his arm'. Somehow

> he had got hold of a kitchen knife which he placed under his pillow. He planned to use it on anyone who came near to dress his wound. He was tamed a few dressings later, ready to respond to every kindness showered on him. On the day of evacuation he announced with tears in his eyes that he would never beat his wives again.[32]

Navarro describes one particular Senegalese, reported to be a king,

> who was discovered one day seated on his bed, head bowed, weeping copiously. Beside him lay the body of a young Senegalese who had just breathed his last. Later, the king appeared suddenly within the screened enclosure (still weeping), explained that the deceased was one of his subjects, and expressed a wish that a ring on the young man's finger should

be given to him as a memento. The nurses suggested showing him the face of the deceased. 'Non!' he answered, with arresting dignity, 'Non. laissez-le! C'est un grand guerrier!'[33]

Less has been written about the Arabs, but Collum writes:

> The Arabs were very different patients: highly strung, nervous, complaining of their sufferings, they nevertheless bore them bravely enough when they became almost more than human nature could support. Their mental pain must have been acute when the strange foreign women, rather than let them die in possession of their shattered limbs, took them off, and thereby closed for ever the gates of Paradise against them should they succumb after all. If they recovered, the loss of a limb troubled them little; but when they came face to face with death, it must have been bitter for the orthodox to face eternal banishment from Paradise as well.[34]

On a lighter note Dr Henry remembers:

> One Arab, enamoured of an orderly, used to follow her around with adoring eyes, and proclaimed that after the war was over if she'd come to Africa, he'd make sure that she would have potatoes every day. [Potatoes were always very popular with the troops.]

One of the auxiliary nurses remembered how the Arabs used to sit up in their beds, clap their hands and sing just like the bagpipes being tuned in.[36] Richmond recalled her embarrassment when she donned a white wig for a play they were putting on. She was to be an old gentleman. When the Arabs uncovered her disguise, they 'used to follow me around the hospital, slapping their thighs and roaring with laughter'.[37]

They were a little confused when they met modern (or fairly modern) sanitary arrangements for the first time. Figgis describes one such incident:

> A newly arrived blessé (I think he was an Arab) was told to go and have a bath, the salle de bains being indicated by a wave of the hand from the 'Seester'. A few moments after, on entering the salle de bains to see how he was getting on, we found him inside the marmite pacing up and down with all his might, the temperature of the water gradually increasing every minute! We hauled and got him out – and he was none the worse for which we were truly thankful.[38]

There are few specific comments about British patients – they were few in number and they did not represent different cultures and values to arouse interest. But one British patient – astonished to find himself in a hospital with a totally female staff – thought there could be only one explanation. 'S.W.H.', he decided, with a sudden enlightenment must mean 'Still Wanting Husbands!'[39]

A particularly fascinating story concerned an American patient and Dr Martland – a story which was only told 38 years later when Dr Martland had retired and was living quietly in Dorset after a distinguished career as a pathologist. She tells the story herself in 1954:

> One day last February two Americans called at the London office of the Medical Women's Federation with an unusual request. They had been asked to trace, on behalf of the National Broadcasting Corporation of America, an Englishwoman who had worked as a young surgeon at a French hospital in the First World War, and they had been given 24 hours in which to do it. They were vague as to the locality of the hospital: nor did they know the name of the surgeon. They were sure, however, that she had red hair. Undaunted by these meagre data the Federation's secretary got down to the problem with vigour and resource, and by the end of the morning was able to identify the hospital with the Scottish Women's Hospital at Royaumont, and to offer my name as a strong probability. The first I heard of this was an incomprehensible telephone call mainly concerned with my once red hair. This was followed by a visit from the two Americans who explained the reason for their mysterious interest in myself. A nation-wide appeal for the American Red Cross was to be launched in a broadcast speech by President Eisenhower. In the half-hour preceding the speech, a television programme called 'This is your Life' would celebrate the life of the Executive Director of the Red cross in New York, Mr J. Harrison Heckman.

In this programme a compère would confront him on TV with people who had played a notable part in his life:

> This was where I came in though I had never to my knowledge heard of Mr Heckman. It appeared, however, that he had been badly wounded as a young lieutenant of Marines in France in the First World War, and that he often spoke of an English girl whom he believed had saved his leg from amputation. 'This is your life' was on the trail of this nameless young woman from Mr Heckman's past, and seemed to have found her in me. I did not remember the incident specifically, but I remembered a convoy of American wounded that turned up at Royaumont, quite by mistake, in the chaos of the last German advance in 1918. The officers had been under my care; and certainly I fought in those days to preserve many a gas-infected limb. The facts fitted and luckily I was the only redhead on the surgical staff. 'If you'd been mousy,' said my visitors, 'we'd never have found you.'

And so she was flown to Los Angeles where the unsuspecting Mr Heckman was busy on Red Cross business. He was lured on to the stage and the game began. After recalling incidents from his past life, the compère suddenly asked:

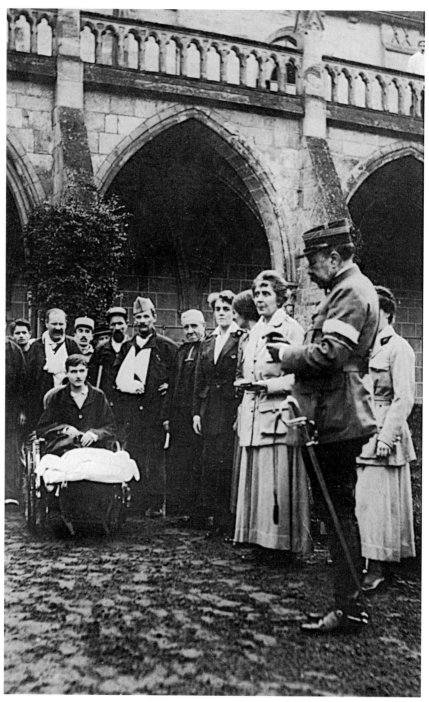

Miss Ivens with some of the doctors and the Curé look on as a poilu receives his decoration.
(By permission of the Imperial War Museum).

'What did you feel like when you found yourself in a hospital run by women?' 'I thought my last chance had gone,' was the reply. 'But you were well looked after?' 'Indeed I was, by a bit of a red-haired girl who wouldn't let anyone take my leg off. I've often wished I could see her again.' I still lurked behind the curtain, finally alone. At last I was brought on by way of the great blood transfusion centre organised by Mr Heckman in New York. 'You could have done with some of that blood yourself, long ago at Royaumont,' I said from behind the curtain. Mr Heckman looked puzzled, as well he might. 'That is the voice,' said the compère, 'that you have not heard for 38 years. And now, after the greatest woman hunt 'This is your Life' has ever staged, here is your doctor of Royaumont, brought from Dorset, England.' The surprise was indeed complete as I stepped through the curtain, and this rich experience has come to me through the gratitude of a young American soldier half a lifetime ago.[40]

The orderlies seem to have had mixed feelings about their American patients. Proctor wrote:

We have some Americans too, some are nice but on the whole they are not half as nice to deal with as the French tommies. They expect a great deal and are inclined to grouse if we are simply through lack of staff and time unable to give them what they want. They are not considerate patients like the French.[41]

Summerhayes (later Dr MacRae), didn't particularly like the Americans – 'they thought they'd won the war and were swanking about' (this of course was in 1918), but it was their weight that she really held against them. Compared to the often underweight *poilus* they were so very heavy to carry – that was her main complaint.[42]

In the confusion of the 1918 battles Dr Henry recalled three little 17-year-old American boys (who must certainly have lied about their age), who were admitted from the French trenches and became lost. It was months before they were located and finally had contact with their families – all eventually made good recoveries.[43]

There were some Germans also in 1918. Dr Courtauld had two very badly wounded in her ward – 'quite decent youths' – but also a 'terror of a German officer'.[44]

Dr Henry found her young German soldiers were 'happy, full of courage and adjusted well', but she had little respect for the Prussian captain in an adjoining room. When she told him about his German companions, he 'asked about their rank and explained that as he was a high-ranking officer he felt pain more'.[45]

Collum considered the German private soldier 'plucky enough' but was highly critical of a German officer who complained of everything and addressed his nurse as 'Schwein'.[46] Summerhayes recalls that only sisters were permitted to nurse the German officers 'because they spat at us' (i.e. the orderlies).[47]

To return to the *poilus* – many were the letters that were written from grateful patients to their sisters and 'Misses': some more grammatical than others – some serious, some emotional, some even flippant. Even as late as 1938 some of the orderlies were still receiving news from old patients who looked back with affection to their stay as patients in the hospital. For them as well as for the staff it had been a significant experience in their lives. As Miller wrote long afterwards:

> We all remember with affection the souvenirs of 'yesteryear' – the hundreds of very touching verses from our kindly and very grateful poilus, verses that always evoke a smile, sometimes a laugh, pen drawings, water colour sketches, excellent of their kind, sheets of paper on which dried lily-of-the-valley (there was plenty of it at Royaumont) and other local wild flowers, were gummed down in artistic form – all very touching, but, alas, fleeting memories.[48]

References

1. Ducasse, Meyer & Perreux, *Vie et Mort des Français, 1914–1918*, p. 78.
2. Horne, *The Price of Glory*, p. 71.
3. Navarro, *The Scottish Women's Hospital,* p. 210.
4. Horne, *op. cit.*, p. 71.
5. Ducasse *et al, op. cit.*, p. 81.
6. Ducasse, *et al, op. cit.*, p. 79.
7. Ducasse *et al, op. cit.*, p. 99.
8. Horne, *op. cit.*, p. 74.
9. F.M. Ivens, 'Clinical Study of Anaerobic Wound Infections. Analysis of 107 cases of gas gangrene', *Proc. Roy. Soc. Med. 1916–1917, part 3. Surgical Section,* pp. 29–110.
10. Horne, *op. cit.*, p. 75.
11. IWM. Georgina Cowan Collection, Pte Breuil to GC January 1918.
12. IWM. G C Collection, Cpl Matthieu to GC January 1918.
13. FL. Box 309, 9.4.18.
14. ML. Box 49, 1.1.19.
15. *CC*, 15.2.18.
16. *CC*, 12.11.15.
17. NL 1964, p. 9.
18. NL 1945, p. 9.
19. Personal communication from Miss Heather Mackay (niece).
20. NL 1965, p. 11.
21. 'Skia' (V.C.C. Collum) *Blackwood's Magazine*, March 1917, p. 346.

22. NL 1964, Sister Rose Morris.

23. NL 1965, p. 10.

24. NL 1970, p. 8.

25. 'Skia', *Blackwood's Magazine*, November 1918, p. 624.

26. Personal communication from Dr Grace MacRae (née Summerhayes).

27. Mrs A.M. Robertson. Letters home, by kind permission of her granddaughter Mrs Ailsa Tanner.

28. 'Skia', *Blackwood's Magazine*, March 1917, p. 34.

29. *Ibid.*

30. Dr Elizabeth Courtauld. Letter to her sister Ruth, 28.8.18, by permission of her nephew, Mr Samuel Courtauld.

31. Navarro, op. cit., p. 189.

32. Dr L.M. Henry. Reminiscences. By kind permission of Miss Helen Lowe.

33. Navarro, *ibid.*

34. 'Skia', *op. cit.*, March 1917, p. 345.

35. Dr L.M. Henry, loc. cit.

36. NL 1936, p. 9.

37. NL 1960, p. 2.

38. NL 1967, p. 11.

39. NL 1973, p. 7.

40. Dr E.M. Martland, 'Half a Century Ago', *Manchester Guardian*, 16.1.57.

41. IWM. Letters of E.H. Proctor transcribed by Dr Leah Leneman and made available to me and used by permission of her nephew, Mr David Proctor.

42. Personal communication, Dr Grace MacRae.

43. Dr L.M. Henry. Recollections recorded on tape and kindly sent by her daughter Mrs Anne Murdoch.

44. Dr E. Courtauld, loc. cit., 27.6.18.

45. Dr L.M. Henry, loc. cit.

46. 'Skia', *Blackwood's Magazine*, November 1918, p. 637.

47. Dr Grace MacRae. Interview recorded by Dr Leah Leneman and kindly made available to me, June 1993.

48. NL 1968, p. 1.

CHAPTER SIX

1917: Strange Interlude

The Military Situation

The 'rushes' experienced by the hospital during the great battles of the Somme were a direct result of the desperate situation of the French army in the fighting round Verdun, and the urgent necessity of relieving some of the pressure on that sector of the Western front.

The terrible conditions in the Verdun sector resulted in a collapse of morale which can be well understood when one considers what the army went through week after bloody week, month after bloody month, from February 21st to 18th December, 1916.

The French troops had experienced intense bombardment, air and gas attacks – including exposure to the new and very fatal diphosgene gas. They had been assaulted by the new flamethrowers which resulted in terrible burns. They had had almost continuous exposure in the trenches with few, if any, periods of relief behind the lines. For all their efforts and for all their suffering they could see little effect, and indeed there was very little.

French official statistics, notoriously unreliable, suggested total casualties of 377,231 of whom 163,208 were killed or missing. This is almost certainly a considerable underestimate. One of the aims of the German thrust towards Verdun had been to bleed France white. In this they were only too successful.

For those who were wounded their care was totally inadequate. Horne writes:

> There were never enough surgeons, never enough ambulances, and often no chloroform with which to perform the endless amputations of smashed limbs. The dressing stations overflowed with badly wounded who had already been waiting for treatment for several days. ... All the equipment was hopelessly inadequate – exacerbated by the poisonous environment virulently contaminated by thousands of putrefying corpses.[1]

By the end of 1916 when winter put a temporary end to all but sporadic fighting, the infantry were beginning to question their role. They were depressed; they had lost faith in their leaders; they even began to resent the artillery who, they felt, were not called upon to suffer anything approaching what they had to endure. Horne sums up: 'The great battles of 1916 were the seeds of mutiny, revolution and despair'.[2] The military deadlock was unbroken.

1917 dawned with no realistic prospect of any change. Neither the Somme offensives nor the operations around Verdun had produced results in any way proportionate to their costs. The troops were weary of being continually called upon for ever more sacrifices – to throw themselves against barbed wire and machine gun fire. They knew better than their commanders how useless it all was. Stalemate, exhaustion and depression signalled the opening of 1917.

On March 16th 1917 the Germans took the sensible decision to eliminate a big forward bulge in their front line and retreat to a shortened, straightened, well-prepared line. They destroyed everything in the vacated area: houses, trees, roads. They contaminated the wells and laid booby traps by the hundred. The ground, on which the Allied forces had been fighting so desperately, was now yielded up, but the Germans were stronger and the Allies weaker as a result. The disputed ground was so destroyed that any subsequent fighting there became almost impossible. It seemed the last straw to the demoralised French troops, but more was to come with the failure of an attack round Reims on April 16th.

In May mutinies broke out in 16 corps of the French army; desertions rose to over 21,000 men. The men were absolutely disgusted with their commanders: 'We will defend the trenches, but we will not attack'. And: 'We are not so stupid as to march against undamaged machine guns'.

It was a lesson for the leaders which they were forced to heed. Pétain was the man to save the situation. This was probably his greatest achievement in the war, for which he deserves great credit. He was appointed Chief of General Staff. He spent a month visiting every division, listening to officers and men and taking note of their grievances. He introduced reforms which paid attention to the welfare of the men which had been so badly neglected in the first two years. He formulated the important principle that fire power should never be used indiscriminately as hitherto, but only with the express object of conserving manpower. Any tactic which required the wholesale slaughter of men could never achieve a military objective – the numbers were not limitless and they needed to be conserved.

Gradually the French army regained some degree of confidence, but for many months to come its delicate state of health dictated that the main burden of the fighting on the Western Front was to be borne by the British. In August the French, now recovering their morale, had this further boosted by regaining some ground that had been lost round Verdun, and in October the successful recovery of the Chemin des Dames (a ridge that had always been of great strategical importance) was another big step on the road to increased confidence.

From May onwards Russia was weakening and it was becoming clear that it would not be long before she was out of the war, and Germany would be strengthened by the transfer of troops from the Eastern to the Western Front.

Russia formally capitulated in October. To offset this America entered the war on April 6th 1917, though it would not be before 1918 that her contribution would have any significant effect on the conduct of the war. Nevertheless it was a great morale booster, and morale in the French army was higher at the end of 1917 than at the end of 1916. This, of course, was not the case with the British army which had borne the brunt of the fighting throughout the year and endured the horrors of Passchendaele.

At Royaumont

These events affected Royaumont to a very appreciable extent. The mutinies were a closely-guarded secret; certainly at Royaumont they knew nothing of them. They could not understand why their hospital was now so quiet – why were they not receiving casualties? After the high excitement of the Somme 'rushes' life was beginning to feel rather flat. They knew that further north the British were having a terrible time. The third battle of Ypres opened on June 7th – at first successfully, but success was short-lived, and it ended miserably in the 'bath of blood and mud' that was Passchendaele. At Royaumont many of them felt that they had outlived their usefulness where they were – and that they should close the hospital and move north to succour their own countrymen. There is a letter, probably sent to the Committee, undated and unsigned, which spells out their concern and dissatisfaction (remember they had no knowledge of the mutinies). They were seeking an explanation for their lack of activity. To quote the letter:

> I don't know if it has become common property or not at home, but there are strong reasons for supposing that all this District is now definitely out of the track of the evacuations of the wounded French.

Hospital trains were no longer coming to Creil, and all they were getting was an occasional trainload of evacuated patients, two or three weeks old, either slightly wounded or 'reported sick': 'There are, of course, wounded, hundreds and thousands of them, somewhere. They don't come our way'. The writer had studied the railway map and speculated that their rail route was possibly being kept free for the transport of supplies which always take precedence over the wounded. Another factor that she (or they?) thought might be responsible for the scarcity of cases was the new method of dealing with battle casualties. In 1916 they got their patients from Creil, usually within 48 hours of being wounded (90% already infected with gas gangrene), and were able to save many lives and limbs. If Royaumont had not been where it was, and if the Royaumont surgeons had not been able to keep up with the flow by operating by day and by night, the casualties would have been faced with still greater delays, and certainly with greater mortality as a result.

The importance of avoiding delay in the initial treatment of casualties was, as a result of their experience, now recognised by both French and British medical services, and in 1917 a new system was devised and put into action. This was to erect very large wooden, barrack-style hospitals as close as possible to the front, where cases could be dealt with rapidly, though not necessarily definitively. For instance, wounds could be cleaned up, dead tissue cut out, drainage of wounds initiated and foreign bodies removed, provided they could be easily located. This undoubtedly decreased the development of full-blown gas gangrene infection, and saved many lives which would certainly have been lost by the delays endemic in the old system where the emphasis had been on transport to base hospitals before any but the most rudimentary treatment was given – in many cases just a field dressing. They had an erroneous impression that a 'rest' would be beneficial to the patient before transfer to hospital.

The writer of the letter reports that in December 1916 Miss Ivens had asked the Service de Santé that, if the distributing centre were to move, the hospital might be permitted to move with it so that it could continue to be useful. There does not seem to have been any response to this approach. The writer continued: 'Well, here we are, killing time, sitting idle almost, while the biggest offensive of the war is on, while England is sending out appeal after appeal for nurses, doctors and VADs'. The writer claimed that it was the general feeling among the staff, that they should switch to 'our own people who are crying out for help'. Yet, she says,

> Miss Ivens persists in sticking to the French. Sometimes she is hopeful that if the head man at Creil were 'energetic' he would insist on wounded being sent round by his town in order to fill our District. Sometimes she thinks it is bad organising ... at other times she thinks it would be a pity to close Royaumont and that the Committee would like it kept open as a sort of convalescent home.[3]

Miss Ivens herself had a hunch that fighting would return to the Aisne region. She was of course quite correct. There was clearly some dissatisfaction. The staff did not want things to be too easy for them, and the idea of a convalescent home had absolutely no appeal.

Royaumont entered 1917 with the gaiety that had characterised the party season in the previous two months. They celebrated New Year with a fancy dress dance and orderly Morgan displayed all her talent in organising the *pièce de résistance*. Dorothy Carey-Morgan was but one of the many gifted women who served at Royaumont. She later became a successful artist in London and South Africa and played a noteworthy part in the Royaumont Association's canteen in France in the Second World War. Her aquatints and etchings of Royaumont, now in the Imperial War Museum, were an early indication of her later celebrity.

This *pièce de résistance* was a performance of Three Blind Mice. Fat and with a round face, Berry (orderly Berry, not Dr (Mrs) Berry) was the farmer's wife armed with a large wooden knife covered with silver paper. The mice were clad in grey knitted helmets, long gray operation stockings, grey sateen costumes, tails of dressing gown cords, pink sateen ears, and – a gift from Michelet in the kitchen – whiskers from the straw casing of a champagne bottle. Holding each other's tails, and with Berry flourishing the knife, gleaming in sinister fashion in the lamplight, they burst into Canada Ward, squeaking with fright, leaping on and off beds, dodging behind tables and chairs, with Berry hacking at their tails. A moment's surprised silence, and then a roar of applause from the delighted patients.[4] We do not know which of them enjoyed it the most.

January set in with very hard frosts, and it remained bitterly cold for the whole of that month. Life wasn't all fun and games. There was more serious business concerning the running of the hospital to be sorted out as the staff settled down to steady, more routine, work, 'Useful, but a little monotonous' as Collum described it. 'We had won a high name for surgery', she said, but now 'we received large convoys of sick and unfit men whose condition required surgical intervention of a more conventional order'.[5] With their spare capacity they were now treating many civilian patients.

Cicely Hamilton became the Administrator in place of Miss Loudon, and was soon demonstrating her efficiency. She was concerned to be absolutely sure of her powers and sought guidance from the Committee. She had run into difficulties with the kitchen staff and the chauffeurs. Mrs Russell (of the Committee) had pointed out that 'unless Miss Ivens herself goes to the kitchen there is no one with any authority to administrate between Michelet and the other people working there'.[6] Miss Winstanley (now the Matron) controlled the supply of orderlies, and also discharged some of the duties of housekeeper. It was agreed that Cicely Hamilton should have financial control, otherwise Miss Winstanley was to be in charge. All housekeeping departments were to report to Cicely, to keep a watch on finances.

Cicely had complained of the conduct of the chauffeurs. She spoke of their 'laziness and insolence' and told the Committee that 'for the general comfort of the place it would be an advantage if the garage were a little more polite and obliging – good manners are not incompatible with good work and the ability to drive a car does not necessarily absolve its possessor from the ordinary rules of courtesy'.[7] There must have been a major row. Cicely Hamilton was known to have 'famous rages', but when the Committee ordered that she should have authority over the chauffeurs on all matters affecting the administration of the hospital, she hoped for improved relations, and 'it would be better to start without an upheaval. The situation is difficult and the other day it seemed nearly hopeless, but I have been firm, and I believe tactful, obdurate but cheerful'.[8] We do not have the chauffeurs' version of these quarrels.

It was becoming difficult for some of the staff who had enrolled as volunteers to continue without any salary. They, like most of the population, had not expected the war to last so long. The chauffeurs in particular were now feeling the pinch. The nature of their work meant that they had many calls upon their purses which were unavoidable. They even had to supplement their uniforms. There was now plenty of paid work available for women chauffeurs. Young and McGregor 'felt they simply could not continue to work voluntarily'.[9] Miss Ivens fought hard to retain them. In March she wrote to the Committee requesting a salary: 'Their work here has made them expert and they are very important members of the Unit as they are very careful drivers and are known and trusted at Creil',[10] and in May she sent a telegram: 'Personally supplementing allowance for Young and McGregor cannot carry on otherwise'.[11] The Committee were not moved. They would pay (at the rate of £12 per annum) for three months but after that new volunteers must be sought. Miss Ivens was not pleased:

> I am extremely disappointed and worried by the refusal of the Committee to grant my personal request for the continued services of our two reliable and skilful chauffeurs. New people are not the same as those who know everybody and who know every bump in the road. Miss H's personal dislike of the chauffeuses (sic) is very unfortunate but it is not likely that she can be very popular with them when they know she never speaks to them but in the most violent manner. It is an obsession. I believe they were inconsiderate but never swore, and their work is excellent. The manners of many members of the Unit leave something to be desired. But the important thing is that I do not want to be left stranded and should prefer the Committee to give me chauffeurs I know and trust rather than these helpless people who keep on coming out one after the other saying they can do things when they only spoil and ruin their cars and are a risk to the patients.[12]

I have already stated the reasons which made me wish to have girls accustomed to the French rule of the road, Paris traffic and the transport of the wounded along bad roads. The length of our runs, and the fact that we have no mechanic also makes it essential that the chauffeuses should be capable of dealing with small adjustments that our old cars now require. I must reluctantly ask the Committee to be allowed to entirely disassociate myself from any censure from the French military authorities in the event of an accident, or responsibility should they in future decline to permit our chauffeuses to conduct the cars. It was with great difficulty that this permission was originally obtained in the Army Zone and I consider it most regrettable that the prestige of the hospital should be jeopardised for the sake of a few pounds a year, which I am quite willing

to supply if there is such a shortage of funds. I am convinced the
Committee does not realise the gravity of the situation![13]

She fought hard but it was to no avail.

Young and McGregor left in July to work with the Canadian Army Corps,
though Young took the first opportunity open to her, in November 1918, to
return to Royaumont and see the hospital through to its final closure. Such
loyalty was further emphasised in 1940 when she was involved with Morgan
(and a few others) in the Royaumont Association's canteen behind the
Maginot Line (see Part Three, Envoi).

Some odd jobs came their way. In early April they were requested to send
a car to Amiens to help with refugees from the Somme fighting areas. Cicely
Hamilton and McGregor took sacks of food and clothing and helped to distribute these in the town centre where the Société de Secours aux Blessés were
attempting to deal with over 2000 refugees who had had their homes totally
destroyed when the Germans shortened their front line and destroyed everything in the abandoned area. The Sisters had organised a collection and this
money was spent on food for those who were to face a further 24-hour train
journey to, for them, unknown destinations.

Their valued friend, Madame Fox, 'directrice-adjointe du bureau de vêtements de l'hôpital 301 de Royaumont', now widowed (her husband had died
in the hospital), was finding life very lonely, and was anxious to come and live
in the hospital. Miss Ivens thought this was a splendid idea. It would save
petrol, which was scarce and the men's clothing could be repaired on the spot;
she would be invaluable in dealing with tradespeople and 'it would encourage the nurses to speak French if they had someone who could not speak
English who would help them'.[14] Madame Fox had said she would 'dearly
like an orderly's blue uniform and a white cap'. This was arranged and she
entered upon a very useful career both at Royaumont and at Villers-Cotterets
(the new advance hospital).

Cicely Hamilton left.

It is very likely that the undated unsigned memo already referred to was
written by Cicely Hamilton, probably after discussion with other members of
the Unit. She now came to her personal decision. In April she was writing to
the Committee asking to be released. She 'was influenced in my decision by
my doubts that Royaumont has outlived its usefulness'. 'The need is not
pressing ... and it seems doubtful to me whether it will be pressing again.'
She wanted more action and a change of work, but:

> I want you to believe that it is with a very full heart that I say my good-
> byes to the Committee of the Scottish Women's Hospitals. I think that
> they have always understood that I was proud to be allowed to work with
> them; and I know that they will believe that I go from Royaumont only
> because it seemed to me to be right to go.[15]

She was to pass the remaining years of the war acting with the Lena Ashwell Players in Abbeville, Amiens and other parts of northern France, and, in 1919, for British troops in Cologne and the Devastated Areas. Some of the talented orderlies from Royaumont were to join her there after the closure of the hospital in 1919.

Her departure led to some new thinking about the post of Administrator. Miss Ivens felt that the creation of such a post had added to the difficulties of organisation and had never been successful 'in spite of the personal qualities of the persons who had held that position'.[16] She felt a good Secretary was all that was needed and strongly recommended that:

> Miss Ramsay-Smith, who is 32, possessed of unusually good judgement, and who has been very well trained in the complicated office-work by Miss Hamilton should be given the post of Secretary at an increased salary (say £100). Her knowledge of French and book-keeping and her acquaintance with the intricate workings of the Croix Rouge Service de Santé and her knowledge of the authorities make her particularly useful here.[16]

Miss Ramsay-Smith was appointed, but the titles of Secretary and Administrator seemed to be used interchangeably in subsequent records. Whatever she was called, the appointment was highly successful.

As far as the rest of the staff were concerned, the departments were 'organised very completely under responsible heads who report to the Office'. The Matron, Miss Winstanley, 'has the hospital staff in excellent working order and we have never been so comfortable as we are now from that point of view'.[17]

Nevertheless there were grumbles from some of the Sisters, not about the hospital, but about the action of the Committee at home. They strongly objected to the wording of an advertisement for nurses which the Committee had published which asked for 'some nursing experience'. To understand their concern it is necessary to realise that it is not until 1919 that there was any registration of nurses. Many of the Sisters at Royaumont had been through a full three years' training at recognised schools of nursing, and were justifiably proud of their expertise. But nursing had not yet reached the status of a profession, and there was considerable disquiet that the hundreds of VADs who were nursing during the war would slip into civilian nursing after the war was over and dilute both standards and job opportunities for those who had come up the hard way.

On June 6th they wrote:

> We fully appreciate the difficulties the Committee may have in obtaining trained nurses for foreign service, and we have no wish to depreciate fever-trained nurses whom the Committee engage as such. We object to

the 'not fully trained nurse with good general experience, and of robust health', who, very likely, has failed to get her three years' certificate, but who is apparently to be put into practice, and have the appointment of a sister. The point is we are anxious to raise and keep up a high standard in the nursing profession – and we hoped and expected the Women's Suffrage Movement to understand and help us to realise it. The advertisement in question is hardly likely to bring the best under the Suffrage banner – rather the contrary.[18]

And further, and impatiently, on July 31st:

The Trained Sisters at Royaumont have waited patiently for an answer to their last letter. As they have had no satisfactory answer to their protest anent the advertisement they now feel justified in sending the correspondence to the Suffrage and Nursing journals, drawing attention to their grievance.[19]

The Committee evolved a scheme to settle ruffled feathers. Nurses, who had not had a full three years' training would be 'Assistant Sisters', and orderlies who were promoted to Auxiliary Nurse would be 'Staff Nurses'. New salary scales were introduced to take these distinctions into account:

Matron	£120 Annual increment £10
Fully-trained nurses	£75 Annual increment £5
Not fully-trained nurses	£70 Annual increment £5

The fuss settled down. They had made their point, and in 1918 they were so busy that there was never any time to return to the subject.

It seems strange that Miss Ivens, who was second to none in advocating the rights of women in the medical profession, was less than sympathetic to the anxieties of the nurses. She referred to this later as 'the agitation created by Sister McKnight', and she clearly found it rather tiresome.

New Challenges

Largely as a result of the mutinies the French authorities were now becoming aware that something must be done to make life more tolerable for the *poilu*. This included the provision of canteens, until now seriously neglected. On returning from leave, the *poilu* was not entitled to any rations until he actually rejoined his regiment, and with ill-co-ordinated troop movements this could mean considerable delay and long periods without food. Even if he had a bit of cash in his pocket, the shops would often be shut and he would have to bed down where he could, tired and hungry. The lack of a canteen was not only unjust, it was inefficient. General Pétain recognised this in the reforms which he was introducing. The problem for the French was – who was to provide them? They turned to the London Committee of the

Rouge Croix to ask the British to supply 40 new canteens. The SWH Committee was approached and they agreed to set up two canteens, one at Crèpy and one at Creil. These did not involve Royaumont. Miss Ivens was approached more directly.

It happened this way. On a visit to Soissons she met the local Commandant. He told her that in his opinion the most immediate and urgent need in Soissons was that of the 'permissionaires' (soldiers on leave). He would take the opportunity there and then to beg the Scottish Women to come to his aid. Collum reported:

> Large numbers of soldiers returning to their sectors from leave passed
> through the town, and many of them had to spend a day and a night
> there. Being isolated from their regiments they were not entitled to draw
> rations. Soissons, he reminded them, was still within the range of the
> German heavy guns, and had only been completely restored to the French
> since April. There is not a house that has not been shelled; comparatively
> few civilians have gone back to their half-ruined homes since the German
> bombardment which followed the evacuation, hence there is absolutely no
> means of getting food. ... So, if the Scottish Women wished to help
> French soldiers here was the opportunity. Outside the Bureau at that very
> moment there were groups of men, haggard-looking after a long journey
> and a sleepless night on an open railway station. Piled on the
> Commandant's papers were some loaves of bread which he himself kept
> handy for the more urgent cases, and more securely hidden there was a
> little heap of tinned sardines. He could do nothing as Commandant; as an
> individual he could, at least, distribute these to the more hungry. To
> make a long story short, Miss Ivens came back to Royaumont that night
> having committed herself and the hospital to come to the rescue, tem-
> porarily at least.[20]

She wired the Committee to regularise her action: 'Urgent appeal for small canteen in front necessity grave will committee undertake starting provision-ally tomorrow is kitchen car available immediately writing'.[21] Her private comment was: 'Isn't it queer that the French women do nothing?'[22] The Committee responded, authorised the canteen and despatched the 'motor kitchen' as a back-up. This arrived in the first week of July.

It was good to feel, back at Royaumont, that there was an urgent task to be done, and the four that Miss Ivens selected to go to Soissons were much envied. Tollitt[1] (store-keeper) was to be in charge, with Rolt,[2] Chapman[3] and Etta Inglis[4] (a niece of Dr Elsie) to assist her. They loaded up the lorry with all the equipment they were likely to need and a small stock of provisions. This was just as well because, although they were authorised to order what-ever they needed from military stores, the inevitable red tape meant a few days' delay before this could be put into effect.

Auxiliary nurse Etta Inglis leaves Royaumont to set up the canteen at Soissons
on June 6 1917.
(By courtesy of Miss Heather Mackay).

They were given an abandoned schoolhouse, full of débris from the shelling but, in contrast to the job of getting the Abbey into order in December 1914, there were soldiers detailed to help them. Furniture was supplied by the mayor, and Tollitt was soon able to report back to Miss Ivens that they were getting 'comfortable'; they had planted salad stuffs in the garden, had been inspected and had served 797 meals (free of charge to the *poilus*), and they were greatly appreciated by the men. With so many shelled and empty houses they were able to raid the gardens for flowers and fruit. They did not confine themselves to the provision of food. A small bath and a piece of soap was placed in the yard by the pump, and papers and magazines and writing materials were supplied inside.

One visiting officer told them they had no right to be there. The local Commandant had exceeded his authority in inviting them to help in the emergency – only the Grand Quartier General[5] had that power! However, now they were there, he went on to point out that they equally had no right to leave Soissons!

Being close to where the action was, they experienced nightly air raids – never hit, but several near misses – and they had to sleep in the cellars. Nothing, perhaps, to compare with the experience of many in the Second World War, but for them it was new and certainly exciting.

After seven weeks of satisfying work when they had served 1681 meals, the need had largely passed as the military were now supplying lorries to take the men directly to their units after coming off the trains.[23]

In December 1918, at a big ceremony to distribute the Croix de Guerre medals to members of the Unit, Inglis, Chapman and Rolt were decorated with the following citation: 'Ont assuré avec zèle et dévouement le service de la cantine militaire de Soissons, malgré les nombreuses bombardements de cette ville'.[24] It seemed very unfair that Tollitt missed her award because, at the time of the ceremony, she had already left the Unit, called home to look after ailing parents.

Changes in the Medical Staff

In June Dr Courtauld left Royaumont to undertake the duties of Chief

---

1. Miss Florence Tollitt, orderly, 1.6.15 to 24.7.18.

2. Miss Agnes Louise Rolt, Auxiliary Nurse, 25.11.15 to 28.2.19.

3. Miss Marjorie Chapman, Auxiliary Nurse 6.5.15 to 22.3.19.

4. Miss Etta Helen Maud Inglis, Auxiliary Nurse, January to March 1915 and 30.11.15 to 22.3.19.

5. The GQG was the powerful body of military advisers who surrounded Joffre at the HQ in Chantilly. It came to be recognised that its influence on the war was not entirely beneficial.

Medical Officer of the Scottish Women's Hospital in Corsica on a temporary basis until a more permanent appointment could be made. The work at this hospital – for Serbian refugees – was very different from that to which she had become accustomed at Royaumont. It was mainly medical, with a large proportion of tuberculosis patients. Her experience was such that she was only too delighted to return to Royaumont, which she loved, to her friends and the work which she found so much more congenial.

Soon after her arrival in Corsica Mrs Robertson (who was visiting on behalf of the Committee) wrote enthusiastically:

> The whole Unit is like a new world and Dr Courtauld's presence here alone for a few weeks, is just the last thing needed to complete the work. [The hospital had been through a difficult period.] She is able to put into force the various internal improvements which no lay person can manage, and I think the Committee ought to write and thank her very gratefully for thus stepping into the breech and helping us.[2]

Later she wrote with a different view:

> I had a long talk with her – about the possibility of her accepting the post of CMO here. She agrees with me about the inadvisability of it – i.e. she is not interested in this kind of work, does not recognise its value, has no sympathy with the Serbs, thinks Europe would be better if they were wiped out and is not a linguist. But quite apart from that she has no desire to leave Royaumont, or rather the Unit, and wishes to continue working there.[26]

Just before Dr Courtauld left Corsica early in August, Dr Erskine (also from the Committee) wired back 'Courtauld unsuitable here'.[27] And so the interlude closed with satisfaction on both sides, and subsequent history vindicated the wisdom of this decision.

One newcomer, and a most welcome one, was Dr Leila Henry who arrived on July 27th. She remained to the end, a period which she later described as the happiest of her life. She had been the first woman to qualify in medicine in Sheffield in 1916, and had subsequently gained valuable experience in Sheffield Royal Infirmary dealing with accidents from the munitions factories – experience more appropriate to the work at Royaumont than could be offered by most women at that time. Hers was a most successful appointment.

Throughout July and August the number of doctors fluctuated between seven and eight. In September and October, with Villers-Cotterets becoming functional, the number increased to eleven. The other newcomers were Dr Florence Inglis in September and Drs Walters and Manoel in October.

Dr Florence Inglis qualified in Edinburgh in 1914. She was a niece of Dr Elsie Inglis, the founder, and joined her two sisters, Etta and Violet, who were

Early days at Villers-Cotterets. No duckboards, no rose bushes, roofs under repair. The
arrival of the post.
(By courtesy of Mr David Proctor).

already working there as auxiliary nurse and orderly respectively. Later they
were all three at Villers-Cotterets.

Dr Enid Walters had qualified in London in 1908. Little is known about
her early experience; possibly she had done some general practice work before
serving with the RAMC in Malta in 1916. After a short period there she
worked temporarily as an Assistant Medical Officer in Hull.

Dr Manoel was a Rumanian and a bacteriologist, who had been working
in the Pasteur Institute in Paris. Her specialised knowledge and expertise
were of great value to the hospital and she well deserved the Croix de Guerre
which she received later. There was some confusion about her status at first.
Miss Ivens requested the Committee to pay her a salary the same as the doctors received, not realising that she was, in fact, medically qualified. She
seems to have fitted in remarkably well with the British staff and kept in
touch with many of them after the war when she went back to Rumania.

With the temporary departure of Dr Savill in November, there were ten
doctors working at the end of 1917, divided between Royaumont and Villers-
Cotterets.

Villers-Cotterets

During the summer Miss Ivens was considering the Unit's response to a request from the French medical authorities. Having won their complete confidence both in their high degree of surgical skill, and equally in the efficient organisation of the hospital, Miss Ivens was invited to organise and staff a new advance casualty clearing station close to the front line. The purpose of such new-style hospitals was to provide early operative treatment and reduce the delays which so greatly increased the mortality from gas gangrene and other complications.

As early as April Miss Ivens was exploring possible sites. One of the chauffeurs – Young – recorded how she drove Miss Ivens, Mrs Berry and Miss Nicholson to search for a suitable base.[28] On terrible roads they drove northward from Royaumont – first to an old chateau dating from the time of *François premier*, and belonging to the family of a patient who had been in the hospital. Not surprisingly it turned out to be quite hopeless. Then they looked at a deserted hospital near Soissons, but it was far from a railway so could not serve the purpose of a casualty clearing station. The Hotel de Ville in Soissons itself was far too ruined from the recent shelling, as also was the Abbaye de Soissons. Another chateau and some 'indescribably filthy' old ironworks were impossible. Almost despairing, they came to Villers-Cotterets and there they found a deserted wooden-hutted evacuation centre right beside a railway station. This seemed to be the answer and negotiations were begun.

Collum reported:

> There our new hospital sprang up, mushroom-like. Nothing could have been more different than this ultra-modern baraque hospital from our own ancient Abbaye. Rows of wooden huts with oil-papered windows and composition roofs, on either side a new road sweeping through the camp to the railway line at the back, each with its smartly cut trench, its duck board and bridge. It made no mark to the eye at even a very little distance, the ploughland coming up to it in waves, the forest screening it.[29]

In July an advance party went up to Villers-Cotterets, about 40 miles away, to direct the necessary alterations and enlargements. They found two rows of huts, one behind the other. The wards in the front row were named after the Allies: Serbia, Belgium, Italy, Portugal, Rumania and Britain. A covered way opened directly into the railway station so the wounded could be lifted directly from the trains and along the covered way into the wards. In the second row of huts – also accessible by the covered way, there were three wards: Russia, France and America, the operating theatre, x-ray installations, other offices and staff accommodation.

On July 2nd Miss Ivens was asking the Committee for more staff. She wanted one doctor, three sisters, five orderlies and two more cooks. Later in the month (July 25th) she was able to report: 'They are working splendidly at Villers-Cotterets, but of course it is hard rough work'.[30] She asked for another four-stretcher ambulance as the authorities wanted them to be independent for transport.

On August 8th, 211 beds were prepared and there was still space for another 60. They had a staff of 33 and were expecting the first patients in the next few days. Another generator was needed urgently as the one they had was too small to cope with the x-rays. The hospital was now named 'Hôpital Bénévole 1 bis 6ième Région (SWH)'.

Madame Fox was proving 'a splendid quarter-master and tries to keep the German prisoners and *infirmiers* [soldiers unfit for military duty] up to the mark. We are allowed 12 infirmiers and a caporal. They will do the rough work, but need a great deal of looking after'.[31]

Miss Winstanley was Matron-in-charge and wrote proudly of the progress they had made (August 12th):

> I have been four weeks getting the hospital ready and I do so wish the Committee could see it and hear a little of the praise we have received from several French generals concerning the transformation of the dirty barracks into a most beautiful hospital. The wards are really beautiful with their clean white-washed walls and red covers. We have had some difficulty with the sanitary arrangements but we are getting that well-attended to. The roofs have all been recovered and the theatre accommodation exceeds Royaumont by a great deal.[32]

Dr Savill had now returned and was supervising the preparation of the hospital as well as the x-ray equipment:

> Everything here promises well. Our great difficulty has been lack of men to do the work – General Descoings* came last week and commanded the various men here to leave all other work in the town in order to finish our hospital. The French authorities would have given us patients long ago had we been ready. That is the difficulty – to get ready when labour is so scarce. We have plenty of unskilled labour but so few skilled, so few who can do carpentering or plumbing. All the stoves and all the piping is being done by two men and all the working men are below par in health or would be in the Army. We have also ten German prisoners who work on the roofs. For the present most roofs are now – (at last) – water-tight with tarred paper covering but until all can be painted over with a layer of tar they cannot be guaranteed to stand much rain. General Descoings spoke most severely to the various men about, that it was a disgrace to

---

* General Descoings was their 'own' general – in charge of their area – and a great friend to the hospital.

the French that they had not finished the hospital long ago. He ordered an important Army man in the town to seek for us where we could have washing, milk, cheap meat and vegetables and every other necessity as rapidly as possible. We are to begin with water carried by the men daily in big tin reservoirs to each ward, and by Autumn a pipe *maybe* laid from the big reservoir at end of camp to each ward – that is the only hope; but everyone is ready to work with the minimum of luxury. I have been a sort of Miss Ivens here. I go about all day between the huts and see how things are progressing, interview local authorities and military visitors – am referred to by plumbers, electricians, carpenters etc. Without Madame Fox, who knows every man's name, it would have been thirty times more difficult. She is a first rate aide. Dr Henry has now joined me to clear up the drainage system – most essential as we were eaten up by flies. The French have left some of the filthiest primitive cabinets we ever saw. No wonder we had flies. Our x-ray hut is huge, magnificent, all provided by the military genie. General Bon (responsible for distributing the blessés to the various hospitals) says we will be the show hospital of the neighbourhood. Though I have not had the rush of work I had expected I know I have been of some use in quite as important a way to Dr Ivens.[33]

Summer 1917 at Villers-Cotterets.
Two rows of wooden huts face each other, each ward named after one of the Allies.
The row on the left also contains theatre, x-ray, laboratory, administration and
kitchens as well as staff accommodation. Order has already been introduced to the
derelict buildings, roses planted and duckboards laid, but report had it that rats were
never eliminated. All was destroyed in 1918. The Forest of Villers-Cotterets reaches
right up to the hospital. It provided cover for troops of both sides in the summer of
1918 as the tide of battle swayed to and fro.
(By courtesy of Mr David Proctor).

She wrote privately to Mrs Russell, delighted with her work:

> I have installed a lovely x-ray room here and with the aid of a very smart
> mechanicien (*sic*) I have made such charming accessories at a few shillings
> cost. [Were these decorations to soften the clinical atmosphere, or
> technical improvements? Whatever they were, they do not seem to have
> impressed her successor in the x-ray department.] We shall get plenty of
> work here. It is going to be a very important centre. They mean to let us
> have grands blessés.[34]

Ramsay-Smith, newly appointed as Secretary, explains some of the feelings of
the Unit as they waited for action to commence:

> At present there is a great lull – whether it is the quiet before the storm,
> or whether the French are not going to take the offensive after all [i.e. the
> expected attack on the Chemin des Dames] is a point none of us can
> quite make out. The only thing to do is to be ready for anything or
> nothing. If nothing comes our way it will be pretty sickening after all the
> preparations and the extra staff we have got out. On the other hand if
> there is a big attack I expect we shall need every ounce of personnel and
> material we can produce.[35]

She was right but their time was not to come until March 1918.
Miss Ivens reported:

> Hundreds! of inspectors have been and all seem to be pleased. We have a
> clearing station for patients arriving by car near the entrance to the hos-
> pital with a doctor (French, male) and 12 brancardiers [stretcher-bearers]
> to sort out the cases.[36]

The expected French attack on the Chemin des Dames did take place in
October and was successful. Because of its success casualties were rather fewer
than had been feared, and Villers-Cotterets, functioning as a reserve hospital,
had only one busy week when 100 blessés were received. Ramsay-Smith commented:

> There have been a few cases sent to us since the attack but not the heavy
> work we expected, but then the French, fortunately for themselves, had
> very few killed or wounded altogether, and their preparation in the way
> of hospitals was on such a large scale that naturally each place only
> received a small number. Royaumont is really very much busier at the
> moment as we have quite a lot of malades and also several very bad civil-
> ian cases which require a great deal of attention.[37]

One senses a little disappointment that they had not had a chance to show
what their lovely new hospital could do.

Miss Ivens was balancing the needs of the two hospitals. For the time being Royaumont was short of actual beds as so many had had to be sent up to Villers-Cotterets but 'we have been rearranging to be of the utmost service'. 'There is no doubt', she went on, 'that the patients are extraordinarily happy and comfortable here' (i.e. at Royaumont). They had had a new Médecin-Inspecteur out from Paris who said it was 'a remarkable argument for feminism'. No wonder Miss Ivens declared him 'charming'.[38]

He also suggested to her that he was considering asking her to move still further forward, which would mean that they would then be functioning as an 'ambulance of the front'. This, in the event, did not materialise, but indicated the confidence the authorities now had in the hospital and what women could do. An astonishing *volte-face* from their initial caution.

There were changes in the x-ray department. Dr Savill, who had seen to the installation at Villers-Cotterets, had to return to her work in London. Collum, who had worked so hard during the 1916 rushes, had returned home on the completion of her three-year contract. Miss Ivens was thankful to procure the services of Miss Brock, who was an assistant of Madame Curie, for three weeks to tide them over. Without her they would, she said, have been in a parlous condition. However, they were joined on November 5th by Miss Edith Stoney who then served continuously until Royaumont closed in March 1919.

Edith Stoney was one of two remarkable sisters. They came from an enlightened family background. Their father and two brothers were all distinguished scientists and all three were Fellows of the Royal Society. Their father had played a major role in giving women the opportunity to register to practise medicine by sitting for the Licentiate of the King and Queen's College of Physicians of Ireland (later known as the Royal College of Physicians of Ireland). This had opened the door to women which had been firmly closed after Elizabeth Garrett Anderson had managed to obtain registration through the licentiate of the Society of Apothecaries. This was not to be tolerated by the opponents of women in medicine and for many years she and Elizabeth Blackwell were the only women on the medical Register, and therefore legally entitled to practise. With such a father it was not surprising that Edith and Florence received the best possible education (privately). Florence qualified in medicine and Edith went to Newnham College, Cambridge and graduated in physics. Both sisters were intensely interested in the new discoveries of x-rays and their potential in medicine. Before the war they acquired their own portable x-ray equipment following a suggestion from Lord Roberts that this might be of use in the event of an outbreak in Ireland!

Edith had been a lecturer in Physics at the London (RFH) School of Medicine for Women until 1915 when she joined the SWH Unit going out to Guevgeli in Serbia, and later to Salonika where she remained until the summer of 1917.

Dr Isabel Hutton (née Emslie) knew her in Salonika. She described her as 'A learned scientist, no longer young, a mere wraith of a woman, but her physical endurance seemed to be infinite; she could carry heavy loads of equipment, repair electric wires sitting astride ridge tents in a howling gale, and work tirelessly on an almost starvation diet'.[39] Another commented: 'She gave the impression of a reed that might snap in two when the wind blew', and: 'She is a funny-looking frowsy old maid with untidy grey hair and large blue eyes – She is a most weird old person'.[40]

Dr Henry left a little thumbnail sketch in a note book:

Grey uniform, grey hair, pale blue eyes, very slight, very intent on her job, – no special friend – no other interests, in and out of the x-ray rooms and developing room – like a moth.[41]

On November 3rd she arrived at Royaumont and went up almost immediately to Villers-Cotterets where she was to be in charge of the x-ray department. She had come with a glowing testimonial from Dr Louise McIlroy, who was Chief Medical Officer in Salonika: 'Her minute and thorough grasp of physics and electricity has made her infinitely more valuable than any graduate of medicine could have been'.[42]

But she also came with a reputation of being a difficult person. However, Dr Erskine (of the Committee) met her soon after her arrival and wrote back:

Miss Stoney is sweeter than honey. Long may it last![43]

When she arrived at Villers-Cotterets Miss Stoney was none too pleased:

Very wet – drifting mist everywhere. I have not yet got the x-rays into working order – damp running down the walls and through the roof of the x-ray baraque – last night flooded the floor and put out the stove. I am very aghast at present at the makeshift way the apparatus has been put up. One is always frightened at a new job.[44]

Nevertheless she worked magnificently at Villers-Cotterets and at Royaumont, as we shall see.

1917 had held its share of sorrow for the Unit when they heard of the death on August 1st of Dr Wilson from acute appendicitis while she was on holiday in the Alpes Maritimes. She was only 36. It was, as Miss Ivens said, a great blow to them all:

Her personal charm and extreme interest and solicitude for her patients gained her their affection in an unusual degree, and after their return to the front they not infrequently walked many miles and spent many hours of their short leave in paying her a visit. In spite of a frail physique, with an admirable spirit, Miss Wilson rose to the occasion during many periods of stress and fatigue – her loss has created an irreparable gap.[45]

After qualifying in Edinburgh in 1906 she had worked as a medical mission-ary in Jaffa and Hebron where she was popular and known as 'El Hakimeh' (the lady doctor). She was a brilliant linguist. She was said to mop up languages as a sponge mops up water – French, German, Arabic, Latin and Greek. Had she lived she would have added Hebrew. She loved best physi-cian's work, but her colleagues rated her surgical skills highly and these were much called into play during her time at Royaumont. When she was decorated with the *Médaille des Epidemies en Vermeil* her patients, proud of their *Doctoresse*, presented her with an address: 'Nous vous addressons nos remerciements les plus vifs pour les soins maternels que vous nous donnez avec une si génereuse abnégation'.[46]

She was said to be rather silent and reserved, with many friends but few intimates, but she had great personal charm. She had wide intellectual interests, including architecture and, while she was at Royaumont, she was studying French history. Music, colour, books, flowers and lace-making were among her hobbies. She also loved horse-riding and played a notable part in the hockey team. One friend wrote of her: 'She was so rare, she was so fine –

Miss Ivens, wearing her decorations, stands outside one of the wards at Villers-Cotterets.
Duckboards were essential for walking between the wards.
(By permission of Miss Helen Lowe).

and she had not the slightest idea of it'.[47] Another wrote that she had a special gift for 'helping men suffering from shock to regain their balance and control'. On hearing of her death, her patients subscribed 100 francs for a wreath from 'les blessés de Royaumont'. One of them brought it – 'Poor fellow, he could hardly speak'. Her name, together with that of Sister Grey, was later inscribed on the monument erected by the Royaumont Association after the war to commemorate those who had died in the hospital.

A happier event took place on October 3rd when, with great excitement, the Unit learned that their Chief had been awarded the *Légion d'Honneur* – one of the very first to be awarded to a foreign woman.

Dr Henry, many years later (1965), thumbing through her old photographs, wrote:

> But now I hold the Ace in my hand – the Médecin-Chef getting out of
> the Boran ferry. The old ferrywoman beside her has a little old shawl
> round her shoulders. The Légion d'Honneur graces our Chief's uniform –
> so that is why she went off to Paris alone that morning?[48]

Miss Ivens maintained to her step-sister that 'she tried in vain to refuse it, but it was a great honour and earned by the whole staff'.[49] (Did she really protest? It seems a little implausible when it was such a mark of distinction for her beloved hospital!) She learned later that it was the *Médecin-Inspecteur Géneral*, who was their Chief in Paris during the Somme rush, who had proposed her for the award.

In July a new orderly arrived at Royaumont. Evelyn Proctor was a prolific letter-writer and her letters to her mother throughout her period of service (until March 1919) provide us with a fascinating view of Royaumont and Villers-Cotterets from an orderly's point of view. It is disappointing, however (as it was to Proctor herself), that a knee injury required sick leave during some of the most hectic times. She was young, keen and wrote freely – her enthusiasm spills over into her letters. Her change of attitude as she settled into the life of the two hospitals may well have been mirrored by many other young volunteers who left a rather sheltered existence at home for the big adventure.

Her first comments to her mother after arrival at Royaumont are probably typical, and they also bring us up to date with some of the domestic arrangements as they had evolved over the previous two and a half years:

> I've completely lost track of days but I believe today is Friday, for which I
> am very glad as our washing comes back – By the way we have a clean
> sheet once a fortnight ditto towel, so we have to be careful! Did I tell you
> that the sole furniture consists of converted packing cases but we do get a
> bed and a mattress – I share a larger cubicle with a girl called Parkinson
> whom I met at the London office of the SWH before I left. She is quite

nice – for which I am glad. I also have a window my side of the cubicle –
my dressing table is quite smart as it consists of an old door that has been
put on top of an old bagatelle table – and I have bought some stuff which
I am going to hang round it. You will send me a bath as soon as possible,
won't you? The country round here is perfectly lovely – I wish I had
brought my bycycle (*sic*) with me, a lot of girls have them, it is the only
method of propulsion to the nearest village, two miles, Viarmes – I wish
we were not quite so cut off. I am in the ward called Blanche de Castille.
It is a lovely ward with all latticed windows with creepers round and a
vaulted roof. This is a *lovely* old place. Breakfast at 7.30 consists of bread
and butter or jam and coffee. Then lunch (*sic*) at 10, the same, sometimes
cheese instead. Lunch at 12.30, meat and generally fresh fruit or milk
pudding. Tea – bread and jam – Dinner at 7.30, meat and fruit. It sounds
more than it is and I am working as I have never worked in my life
before and generally to be put to bed absolutely dead to the world – We
never wear sleeves – which is nice in the summer only our arms and our
hands are absolutely *disgraceful* to look at – We eat off enamel plates or
the table (generally the table) and we drink out of enamel cups.
Everything is served on the side in the dishes they are cooked in and we
grab what we can – food is served in a hut and we sit on forms – the sisters and doctors all feed together but the sisters have a separate table –
we all smoke and it doesn't matter what one does – some of the people
here have extraordinary manners, and are all between the ages of 24 and
30 ... The 'poilus' are the most charming people – so grateful and gentle
– some of them have awful wounds – poor things – I am in the ward
from 7.30 to 9 and get either from 2 to 5 off or from 5 onwards. The
doctoresse (probably Dr Henry) of our ward is awfully nice, she is quite
new – I do not care for some of them very much – there are ward orderlies (the same as VADs), kitchen orderlies and scullery orderlies – we are
not always kept at the same work – Most of the orderlies are Scotch or
Midland – some are quite nice, but the ones who have been here a long
time are awful – But brothers and friends of people who are here – who
come to visit – nearly all say, that we have to rough it here more than the
officers in the trenches, specially in food and no tablecloths etc. [It seems
unlikely that these officers were in fact in the trenches – more likely in
comfortable quarters behind the line.] But it is extraordinary what one
will put up with when really hungry. The Unit has started an advanced
hospital at Villers-Cotterets near Soissons, and quite near the firing line,
about 40 miles from here – I believe we shall take our turn for a time up
there – it is near Crayonne, where the fighting is bad now – So this hospital is only to have 250 beds instead of 600 as before [it was actually
400 at that time] as there would not be enough staff otherwise to go
round. We hear the guns here and especially at night and see the search-

Orderly Evelyn Proctor at Villers-Cotterets in cheerful mood. Note wooden construction of 'barraque' style building. In 1917 when this picture was taken skirts were getting shorter (compare 1914).
(By courtesy of Mr David Proctor).

lights and yet *Paris* is only 40 miles away! Of course, I don't realise we
are in the thick of things at all, but I shall perhaps when I get home
again.[50]

When she had had more time to look around her, she made her assessments
of the medical staff (August 8th):

Miss Ivens, the Chief, is a funny old bird ... they say a marvellous surgeon, but rather an erratic temperament and she changes her mind from
one minute to another. Then there are eight other doctoresses. Some are
quite charming – and some very odd appearances – typical suffragettes![51]

Proctor's letters also give us an orderly's-eye view of Villers-Cotterets in its
early days. She was sent up on August 9th, only a short time after her arrival:

It is considered by the French very near for women to go – we are not far
from Soissons, about 8 kms, which is under fire. I am the most junior
orderly here. There was an awful lot to be done as the place was left in an
awful mess and everyone of us worked like the dickens with never a
moment off to get the place repaired. There is now a beautiful theatre
and x-ray department and the wards are awfully nice. Our first lot of
wounded came in three days ago – we opened three wards for them – and
I am the orderly for one of them. Each ward has one sister and one
orderly and one 'infirmiere' (*sic*) [a soldier who does the dirty work].
Really we are nurses and not orderlys (*sic*) and they call us nurse up here
– So you see I am really doing the [same] work as people who have been
out here for months as the other two orderlies on the ward are old hands
– But I don't know how we are going to exist in Winter as we have to go
out for everything as the huts do not communicate. I must have some
warm clothes sent. I am hoping they will interchange us with people at
Royaumont as camp life is much harder in lots of ways. This Hosp. is
right on a little railway line and the wounded are brought straight from
the clearing station here – Some of the wounds are awful, but they're
wonderful patients. The British fought all over this country in 1914 –
there are the most beautiful forests here that stretch for miles and miles.[52]

After a short spell in the wards she was moved to the scullery temporarily:

The girl at the head of affairs in the kitchen is an awfully nice girl called
Jamieson [Miss Anna Louise Jamieson, cook, 5.10.16 to 5.1.19] and we
work together. But I shall be put back in the wards as soon as more
orderlies from Royaumont come up, so Matron says. They are using us as
a sort of clearance hospital as we are only allowed to keep the men for a
month and get them straight. I don't like the present set of sisters up
here very much but they soon change. The life is very hard but fascinating. The three Inglis sisters [Dr Florence, Etta and Violet] [Miss Violet

A.H. Inglis, orderly, 28.7.16 to 18.10.16 and 22.9.17 to 22.3.19] are charming people, and all nice-looking and very well off.[53]

By October 1st the camp, she said, 'was beginning to look quite smart now as the gardens were growing up'. Mrs Berry (who was a farmer's wife when she was not being a doctor) had organised the planting of flowers and vegetables).[54]

The hard-pressed Committee at home might have been surprised at the impression created on the young recruit that 'they were an enormously wealthy Society and they don't mind how much they spend'.[55] She could now compare life at the two hospitals:

> The staff get really better done for up here as the life is supposed to be harder. I prefer it personally – as we did not get any comforts at Royaumont, but of course the place itself is so perfectly beautiful.[56]

By October 11th she had clearly settled into the life at Villers-Cotterets and was enjoying herself:

> Am very happy here – play hockey when we can and dances and parties – wonderfully free – not a bit strict about uniform. Sisters keep more to themselves, but doctors and orderlies live together which is very nice as one realises these women – extraordinarily brilliant women – are just the same as ourselves and are so simple and nice and kind – we call each other by our surnames – but we are otherwise entirely feminine! which might astonish some people who might imagine the Scottish women to be suffragettes of the most rabid type.[57]

(Compare this with the letter of August 8th.)

There seem to have been a few young men around – this is the only record of social life outside the hospital environment (apart from visits from brothers and other relatives) which has come to light:

> There is a large Canadian camp near here [Villers-Cotterets] and we often get the officers over, Canadian and Scottish, the Adjutant a Captain McNeill is an awfully nice man and sometimes takes us out in his car – a topping Sunbeam. There is also an American contingent at Longpont about 8 kms from here – they are a fine body of men but they are not too popular with the French, who seem to think they should have come into the war before and I am not sure that they are not right.[58]

She wrote of the terrible noise of the big guns and the huts being shaken, and 'all day long yesterday drafts of wounded being brought in straight from the trenches, wounds not even dressed, half dead from fatigue alone'.[59] She found the cases nerve-racking, but she would soon get used to it: 'one does in an extraordinary way – specially when you get a ward full of bad first dressings and the men shrieking and groaning and taking about 6 people to do the dressing – and fearful blood and wounds and smells and rushing about with sterile instruments etc – that's when life ... [here the letter becomes illegible] ... but she concluded: 'I quite see that they have to have young people for these jobs – one does not feel pain in the same way'.[60]

And later, in December, she was working in a ward 'full of gassed men, 33 of them, all spitting and coughing themselves sick on the floor and running at the eyes all day – Some are pretty bad and are such an awful colour. There is very little to be done for them – and the worst part [for her, that is] is emptying their 'crachoires'! poor things – such is life at the back of the front'.[61]

By December 18th she was making plenty of friends: 'Inglis and I have been tobogganing up hill and down dale in the glorious woods with the deer all round and the sun shining furiously'.[62]

Dr MacRae, recalling her life at Villers-Cotterets when she was the orderly Summerhayes, had vivid memories of the rats in the huts which provided their sleeping quarters:

> We slept on the floor as far as I can remember – I suppose we had a palliasse or something – something raised us a little bit from the rats. The things I remember about the huts were the rats. At night time the bombs used to drop [this was in 1918, but the rats were certainly in residence in 1917] – I didn't wake – awful noises they used to make – some not very far away – but if a rat came – just a scratch – I jumped up and threw my shoes all over the place trying to get these rats – I was much more afraid of the rats than the Germans.[63]

Some excitement was caused in December when a film crew appeared at Villers-Cotterets. This had been 'ordered' by the British Ministry of Information as a propaganda exercise to show the French what the British people were doing for them. Times had changed since the War office had done all it could to stop them going at all!

Proctor told her mother:

> We had to fake all sorts of things, including an 'op' (*sic*) – it was too funny – I had to go out in the middle to produce a 'foreign body' which consisted of a piece of coal'.*[64]

When she saw the film later Miss Ivens said it 'made her blood run cold'.[65] The Unit's unanimous opinion when they saw the film after the war at one of their reunions was 'atrocious'.[66]

Proctor had explained to her mother on December 18th that they were in the throes of preparations for Christmas: 'Such fun – our show is going to be

---

* This film survives on video, but it is difficult to identify either Proctor or the piece of coal.

the most original – it is being run by a girl who is an artist in private life – Carey-Morgan by name and she has the most original ideas in everything – besides being a jolly good actress'.[67]

She left a description of their 'top-hole' Christmas at Villers-Cotterets:

All breakfasted together quietly and gaily at 7.30 in the refectory – then we had a service conducted by Mrs Berry, the pro-tem Médecin-Chef. Then the ward-round – and the patients had their Christmas dinner in the wards – Then while we were having tea some beautiful carols were sung by 6 of the staff which were got up by Miss Martland (my doctoresse). The lights were turned out suddenly and out of the darkness from double doors which lead from the refectory to the carpenter's shops lanterns came held by the carollers who were dressed in long military French blue waterproof capes with the hoods over their heads round which was (*sic*) put white cotton wool pieces so that it looked like snow and the storm lanterns were trimmed with holly and mistletoe of which there is an abundance here – They came singing and sang three carols and then walked out singing as they went through the hut with the snow and continued in each ward in turn. The men [Canadians] seemed quite touched. We forget they are so far from home and things like that must bring it very near to them.

This was followed by a concert with pierrots, Père Noel and presents for all. There was more next day:

On Boxing Day there was a staff dinner party with a fancy dress dance afterwards – Mrs Berry made a very nice little speech – and said that she had spent four Christmases with the SWH but this was the happiest. She was dressed as Cardinal Wolsey awfully good get up and Miss Martland as an acolyte ... Everything of that kind involving any kind of entertainment is of a high standard out here and always original – there are so many really clever people altogether – I don't say all but the standard of intelligence is so much higher than in an ordinary crowd of women anywhere that they are bound to be original and well-carried out.[68]

Back at Royaumont Dr Henry recalled many memories of Canada Ward in the old Refectory:

But none more beautiful than in Christmas Eve 1917, as I stood in the music gallery at the North end .... All 100 beds were occupied, the only lights came from two flickering candles on an improvised altar at the base of the pulpit where the old Curé from Asnières-sur-Oise was celebrating Mass. The silence was broken by the choir of orderlies beside me.[69]

And so a relatively quiet year drew to a close. The war, however, was far from over, and once again they must have wondered what 1918 would have in store for them. But with their two hospitals in good working order they were set to meet the challenge.

References

1. Horne, *The Price of Glory*, p. 71.
2. *Ibid*.
3. FL. Box 305, 'Extract of letter from Royaumont', undated.
4. NL 1935, p. 5.
5. 'Skia' (V.C.C. Collum), *Blackwood's Magazine*, November 1918, p. 623.
6. ML. Tin 42, Hamilton to May, 16.1.17.
7. ML. Tin 42, loc. cit, 19.1.17.
8. ML. Tin 42, FI to May, 24.2.17.
9. ML. Tin 31, 6.7.17.
10. ML. Tin 42, FI to Russell, 18.3.17.
11. ML. Tin 42, telegram FI to Committee, 2.5.17.
12. ML. Tin 42, FI to Hunter, 17.5.17.
13. *Ibid*.
14. ML. Tin 42, FI to Russell, 23.4.17.
15. ML. Tin 42, Hamilton to May, 7.5.17.
16. ML. Tin 42, FI to May, 26.6.17.
17. Ibid.
18. ML. Tin 42, 'From the Sisters at Royaumont', 11.6.17.
19. Loc. cit., 31.7.17.
20. *CC*, V.C.C. Collum, 13.7.17.
21. ML. Tin 41, telegram, 6.6.17.
22. ML. Tin 42, FI to May, 10.8.17.
23. McLaren, *A History of the Scottish Women's Hospitals,* p. 60.
24. *CC*, 17.1.19.
25. ML. Tin 42, Robertson to Russell, 8.6.17.
26. Robertson to Russell, loc. cit., ?date.
27. ML. Tin 42, Erskine ?date.
28. NL 1965, p. 6.
29. 'Skia', *Blackwood's Magazine,* November 1918, p. 624.
30. ML. Tin 42, FI to Craigie, 25.7.17.
31. ML. Tin 42, FI to May, 8.8.17.
32. ML. Tin 42, Winstanley to May, 12.8.17.
33. ML. Tin 42, Savill to Willis, 16.8.17.
34. ML. Tin 42, Savill to Russell, 3.9.17.
35. ML. Tin 42, Ramsay-Smith to Russell, 6.10.17.
36. ML. Tin 42, FI to Russell, 15.10.17.
37. ML. Tin 42, Ramsay-Smith to May, 7.11.17.
38. ML. Tin 42, FI to Laurie, 14.11.17.
39. Hutton, *Memoirs of a Doctor in War and Peace*, p. 134.
40. Information kindly supplied by Dr Jean Guy.

41. Liddell Archives, Leeds University, file of Dr L.M. Henry.

42. ML. Tin 12, Dr Louisa McIlroy, 8.8.16.

43. Tin 42, Erskine to Kemp, 22.11.17.

44. ML. Tin 12, Stoney to Laurie, 21.11.17.

45. Frances Ivens, obituary notice in *Brit. Med.* J., 18.8.17, p. 237 and *Lancet*, 18.8.17, p. 259.

46. *The Englishwoman*, November 1917. Quoted in NL November 1934.

47. Ibid.

48. NL 1965, p. 10.

49 Dora Pym, 'Patchwork from the Past'. Unpublished memoirs, by kind permission of her daughter, Miss Mary Pym.

50. IWM. Evelyn Hope Proctor. Letters to her mother, 27.7.17. By kind permission of her nephew, Mr David Proctor.

51. Loc. cit., 8.8.17.

52. Loc. cit., 29.8.17.

53. Loc. cit., 16.9.17.

54. Loc. cit., 1.10.17.

55. Loc. cit., 30.10.17.

56. Loc. cit.

57. Loc. cit., 11.10.17.

58. Loc. cit., 30.10.17.

59. Loc. cit., 25.10.17.

60. Loc. cit., 18.12.17.

61. Loc. cit., 29.12.17.

62. Loc. cit., 18.12.17.

63. Personal communication from Dr Grace McRae, July 1993.

64. IWM. Proctor 10.1.18.

65. ML. Tin 42, FI to Russell, undated, probably 15 or 16.7.17.

66. NL November 1928.

67. IWM. Proctor 18.12.17.

68. Loc. cit., 29.12.17.

69. Dr L.M. Henry. By kind permission of her daughter, Mrs Anne Murdoch.

CHAPTER SEVEN

1918: Their Finest Hour

The Military Situation

As 1918 opened, the balance of power on the Western Front was changing.

The Germans were reaping the advantage of the ending of the war with Russia and the signing of the Treaty of Brest-Litovsk in December 1917. Large numbers of troops were now available for the Western Front. Between November 1917 and March 1918 it was estimated that the strength of the German Army increased by 30%. However, to set against that, the capacity of Germany's industrial base to maintain military supplies was deteriorating, and shortages of all kinds were becoming a serious problem. The entry of the United States into the war would, from now on, provide more troops and more resources of all kinds for the Allied Forces, and in spite of all the tragedies of 1917, a year which had been a very grim one for the British in particular, there was a certain renewal of hope and lifting of morale among the fighting troops. The US troops arriving, raw and untrained though they were, were steadily getting ready for action, and large fresh consignments were arriving every month.

It was clear to the Germans that if ever they were to make a decisive attack and bring the war to a victorious conclusion, they must launch a major offensive in 1918, and as soon as possible. Never again would they have as much manpower or military material. For them the sands were running out. It was a 'now-or-never' situation.

Ludendorff, the Commander-in-Chief, with his clear numerical superiority, planned an offensive in three different areas; the first two in the Lys and the Ypres areas would be primarily against the British; the third in the Champagne would be primarily against the French. It was this offensive which would result in the dramatic events in the hospitals at Villers-Cotterets and Royaumont.

The first of the attacks was launched on March 21st, and by March 27th had succeeded in reaching Montdidier where the railway line to Paris was cut. By March 30th the Germans were on the outskirts of Amiens. The battle came to an end a few days later, a heavy defeat for the British. Further attacks followed on April 9th on the Lys Front and went on until April 29th.

Then followed the breakthrough at the end of May. All seemed quiet on the Aisne between Reims and Soissons, although the US forces had predicted an attack on the Chemin des Dames. The French did not believe it would

happen. Even as late as May 25th they said: 'In our opinion there are no indi-
cations that the enemy has made preparations which would enable him to
attack tomorrow'. On May 26th two prisoners warned that the Germans were
about to attack, but in spite of that surprise was complete when suddenly, at
1.30 on the morning of May 27th, a 'terrific storm of fire burst on the Franco-
British front between Reims and Soissons along the Chemin des Dames [just
as the US had predicted] ... for three and a half hours the bombardment was
said to be unparalleled even in this war of tremendous bombardments. By
mid-day the Germans were pouring over the Aisne bridges which the French
had failed to blow up, an advance of 12 miles in one day. Liddell Hart wrote
of 'the helpless endurance of the Franco-British troops amid the ever-swelling
litter of shattered dead and untended wounded made more trying by crouch-
ing semi-suffocated in gas-masks'.[1]

On May 29th the Germans made a big advance, captured Soissons, and on
the 30th reached the Marne. On May 31st they turned westwards towards
Paris, and right up to the Forest of Villers-Cotterets. This proved to be the
limit of their advance, and was the climax of this Second Battle of the Marne.

On June 1st Pétain ordered up reserves who checked the advance, and the
Americans, now operational, attacked fiercely and successfully at Chateau-
Thierry – 'an indestructible moral tonic to the Allies'. By now the morale of
the German troops was beginning to slip, and what had seemed to be an inexorable advance had been checked.

Villers-Cotterets was destroyed but Royaumont survived.

French forces were collected and more than 20 divisions (including two
American) and 350 tanks were now hidden in the forests round Villers-
Cotterets. On June 15th the French counter-attacked – the 'Battle of Noyon'.
The result was indecisive. On July 15th the Germans attacked again; the
French counter-attacked once more. All these attacks and counter-attacks
resulted in enormous numbers of killed and wounded – French, British,
American, Canadian, Australian. The flow of wounded into Royaumont was
continuous.

August 8th was the 'black day' (Ludendorff's expression) for the Germans
when it became clear that their army was decisively beaten. Although the
battle went on until August 21st, Ludendorff told the Kaiser that the war
must end. In September the Alliance of the Central Powers began to crum-
ble; the final assaults of the Allies at the end of September broke through the
Hindenburg defences; the Germans were in retreat. On 28th October a naval
mutiny broke out in Kiel; socialist governments were installed in Munich
and Berlin. The people were sick of war. On 10th November the Kaiser
retired to Holland and on November 11th the Armistice was signed in the
railway carriage at Compiègne.

In the Hospitals

One may be sure that the New Year did not come in unnoticed by the staff at Royaumont or at Villers-Cotterets, though no record of any celebration has come down to us. What did not go unnoticed was the terrible cold of that winter – said to be the coldest since 1870.

On January 1st orderly Proctor was writing home from Villers-Cotterets:

We have had 22 degrees of frost in our cubicle, [the cubicles were partitioned off within the wooden huts, and were just big enough to contain a bed and a shelf for a jug and basin]. Sponge, toothbrushes, soap, all frozen hard. Water absolutely hard, even hot water bottles – I believe my hair froze the other night! – But weather is lovely, bright sun on the snow – which is quite deep. I believe people at home would call it hard-ships (*sic*) and I suppose they are but no one ever thinks of grumbling – Frozen tea is a funny sight but frozen café au lait is rather nice! Have you ever had a frozen face? ... It's such an odd sensation.[2]

Chauffeur Banks in 1917. The goatskin greatcoat has now replaced the khaki one, for-
tunately in time for the terrible winter of 1917/1918.
(By courtesy of Dr I. Simmonds).

Etta Inglis (Miss Etta Helen Maud Inglis, orderly, then Auxiliary Nurse, Jan. to March 1915 and 30.11.15 to 2.3.19) described how

> Our breath froze to the sheets, our hair to the pillows, our rubber boots to the floor, our sponges would have seriously hurt anyone if by chance we had used them as bombs, and hot water spilled on the floor would in five minutes be frozen solid. The camp was under snow for three months and huge icicles hung from the roofs of the huts.[3]

Although the staff could take it pretty lightly, it was a serious matter for the troops in the trenches as they shivered on opposite sides of No Man's Land. In a strange repetition of the Christmas truce at Mons in 1914 they agreed they would not fire on men bringing up rations provided they were unarmed.

> 'Guten tag, Fritz'.
> 'Bonjour, monsieur'.
> 'Kalt'.
> 'Ya, pas chaud'.
> 'Et tes officiers?'
> 'Quand il fait froid, officiers sont pas la; ils boivent du champagne'.
> 'Böse Krieg'.
> 'Et pas finie!'[4]

Such was the solidarity and mutual understanding existing between those at the bottom of the military hierarchy. From their level of hardship they would have envied the night orderlies at the hospital who carried food around the wards 'in icy gales, with snow whirling round them, the night as black as pitch, – impossible to keep clear of the deep ditch'.[5] At least they could slip into the wards at intervals to warm themselves at the hot stoves. In spite of the cold they were exceptionally healthy at that windswept barrack hospital, more so in fact that at the low-lying hospital at Royaumont.

Proctor, who has given us her impressions of Villers-Cotterets in 1917, had to return home for medical treatment of a knee injury in early January and her witness for the next few months is missing from the record. She was sad to leave the life she had now come to love, but thrilled when Miss Ivens (who seems no longer to be the 'funny old bird') invited her to re-apply when she was fit, 'for which I was very flattered – because Miss Ivens is fearfully particular who she has in the theatre – only the very tip-top will suit her'.[6]

There was a lull in the fighting and the weekly round of ward concerts proceeded happily enough.

Mrs Robertson braved the cold and paid another visit to the hospital on behalf of the Committee:

> I am very much delighted with this hospital [Villers-Cotterets] as a

whole. I should think the standard of efficiency was a high one. The patients seem most comfortable and well-cared for and the cooking is excellent. Jamieson [Miss Anna Louise Jamieson, cook, 5.10.16 to 5.1.19] is splendid. [She was head cook.] Jamieson has pigs and chickens. One of the pigs was killed and we are at present eating Louisa, who is very good – the hens are laying and Jamieson is setting eggs for her chickens. The men put up both bee-hives and pig sties. It's all quite after my own heart and very well-managed. Sister Lindsay makes a capital Matron, and things seem very happy.[7]

The hospital produced as much of their own food as possible. As soon as they had arrived the previous summer they had planted vegetables and flowers, with much rivalry between the wards. Reporting on Royaumont at the same time, Mrs Robertson said:

Royaumont may cost us a lot but there is no doubt that it is the best fed [since Michelet was in the kitchen] and the best-managed hospital in France.[8]

On February 7th Miss Ivens was reporting:

We now have nearly 300 beds at Royaumont but always keep at least 50 empty – and if a big convoy comes in evacuate in a day or two – Our numbers have never been so high as during the last weeks when the French ambulances in the St Quentin section were evacuated for the British.[9]

The Committee were rather alarmed to hear of 300 beds – they had not given permission for so many and felt they could not be responsible. Little did they know of the numbers which would shortly be pouring into Royaumont.
    Miss Ivens went on:

The civilians again grow visibly in numbers although they are only taken in when operations are necessary. Sixteen women today – It is very gratifying to be so appreciated; one does wonder what will happen to the neighbourhood when Royaumont is no more – American women doctors, inspired by the example of the Scottish Women's Hospitals, are coming for the purpose. (i.e. to teach the French to care for their civilian population!).[10]

By February 20th there were 225 patients at Royaumont and 80 at Villers-Cotterets. Miss Ivens was now disposing her forces before the big German offensive which everyone was expecting in the near future. (It will be remembered that Miss Ivens had always held the view that the Aisne would once again be an important battlefield – she had stuck to that when staff were becoming restive in 1917, thinking that they were missing out on the action.)

Foreseeing the heavy demands ahead, she must have been very thankful when Dr Helen Lillie arrived on February 28th, thus increasing the complement of doctors serving the two hospitals to eleven.

Dr Lillie had qualified in 1914 from Aberdeen University and had distinguished herself as an exceptionally able young resident in Sheffield Royal Infirmary. Probably because of wartime conditions in civilian hospitals she gained extensive surgical experience. When she left Sheffield she went to Ostrovo in Serbia and served under Dr Bennet in the Scottish Women's Hospital. There she collected material for a thesis on malaria which she submitted successfully for an MD degree after the war. Dr Bennet described her as 'the right sort', and after watching her operate 'I felt I had never seen a woman do an operation so deftly and so quickly'.[11]

On 5th March Miss Ivens recalled all doctors who were on leave, and asked the Committee to send out another doctor. On 15th March, still conscious of a shortage of doctors, she recalled Dr Martland, in spite of the fact that Miss Aldrich-Blake, the eminent surgeon, had declared she was unfit to return. She also sent for Collum, now an expert radiographer, who had returned to Britain after serving a full three years already at Royaumont. She explained to the committee:

> An Army order now makes it imperative that all cases must be operated on 24 hours after admission. That is why we must have our own x-ray installations fully equipped and a good personnel and enough doctors to operate within 24 hours.[12]

On March 20th bombs began to fall on Paris; some fell close to the Abbey, breaking some windows.

A rush of work resulted from the offensive starting on March 21st in the Montdidier and Noyon regions. On March 27th beds were drastically reduced to make room for the expected run of casualties. They were down to 25 occupied beds at Royaumont and 29 at Villers-Cotterets. Miss Ivens asked for, and obtained, formal permission to move forward if necessary. On 10th April the Service de Santé asked for 100 more beds at Royaumont (which they would supply). Royaumont was now officially recognised as a Casualty Clearing Station (CCS) for French and British patients. (The British were now sharing a section of the front with the French.) Wounded were arriving steadily, bringing the total of beds occupied to 190 at Royaumont and 77 at Villers-Cotterets by April 17th.

Collum arrived back in early April and was distressed to see the enormous numbers of civilian refugees as she made her way back to Royaumont by a circuitous route. On April 11th she wrote:

> The fierce fighting on the Western Front has had a very marked effect on the work at Royaumont. They are now a First Line Evacuating Hospital

and streams of wounded are constantly passing through. The staff is working night and day and fresh workers are being sent out to cope with the rush. The authorities have increased the accommodation by another 100 beds. The cases are coming from a part of the line where French and British are co-operating – French and British alike are coming to Royaumont. It is a deep satisfaction to the staff and to the Committee to know that for the second time the Scottish Women's Hospitals are serving British officers and soldiers.[13]

Apart from the treatment of the casualties there was a heavy workload for the chauffeurs:

The car work had changed from the time when we got in about a dozen patients every day – now they come 40 to 70 at a time, and we often have to send out 30 to 40 convalescents over the whole day. We also have to help Creil to evacuate other hospitals so that it can be done more quickly.[14]

One of the two new chauffeurs [Probably Miss Katherine Fulton, 10.2.18 to 10.11.18. (The other was Miss Margaret Graham 14.2.18 to 11.11.18] who had recently brought over a new ambulance described how, having had no previous experience of active service, she had 'dropped right into such an intimacy with war as I had never dreamed of':

Troops and guns streamed along the roads, newly cut trenches disfigured the fields. Bomb holes gaped with awful reality within a few hundred yards of the Abbaye itself, and wounded poured in continuously. We were at work night and day: it was like a never-ending nightmare to a newcomer, and what sleep we did get disturbed by constant alarms and air raids. For ten days I lived on my ambulance, and worked like one in a dream. Nothing seemed real, there was nothing familiar for my mind to grip, and as at night I tore along without headlights through the soft blackness with a heavily laden ambulance, or helped to load and unload countless stretchers with their groaning burdens, I used to bite my lips till the blood came to convince myself of the reality of it all.[15]

On April 25th Miss Ivens sent details to the Committee of the work actually carried out. In the month March 23rd to April 23rd: 437 patients were admitted, of whom 8 died; 369 operations had been performed; 851 bacteriological examinations, 404 x-ray photographs and 371 x-ray screenings carried out. (It was not surprising that the radiographer Butler [Miss Marian Ada Butler, 18.10.17 to 3.6.18] was suffering from x-ray burns.) The peak period for admissions was 7th and 8th April when 165 were admitted, and 80 operations performed, with a further 34 operations on April 9th. The cases were all 'grands blessés' who could not travel any further.[16] Royaumont was in the Army Zone under the Directeur-General d'Etaple. The beds now numbered 400. It was clear that a much bigger staff was needed, especially doctors and orderlies. Miss Ivens reported:

> The work here is very heavy and at any minute Villers-Cotterets may be deluged. We have got through so far very well as everyone has worked at full pressure and extremely well, but several are showing signs of collapse.[17]

On April 10th she was asking for 10 more doctors. These clearly could not be supplied. Dr Logan was the only one who arrived in April. She had qualified in 1912 and gained her London MD in 1916. She had experience in obstetrics and gynaecology – the usual specialty for women at that period. Unfortunately, as will be told later, her experience at Royaumont was not a particularly happy one.

Things quietened down to some extent in mid-May. Miss Ivens reported to the Committee that 'the patients (the very bad ones) are just beginning to look a little bit more like Royaumont patients'. Staff, she said, were getting a little rested now, but the cars are still very busy. 'It is rather a comfort at HAA 30 that we can do nothing but be in bed as there is nowhere else to go.'[18] It was not to last.

Some of the over-worked doctors at Royaumont went up for a 'rest' to Villers-Cotterets, the advance hospital, which had been relatively peaceful during the rush, and some of the fresher doctors came down to Royaumont to share the burden there.

Dr Elizabeth Courtauld, who had been administering anaesthetics for days and nights during the rush, as well as looking after a ward of seriously wounded men, was rejoicing in a half-holiday in the surrounding woods with a piece of bread and cheese when she wrote to her sister on April 25th:

> I am sending you a blossom of pulsatilla, I picked it this afternoon ... they grow on a warm bank skirting the forest, and are quite abundant ... we are no longer having hectic days, but fairly steady work. In fact my ward is now quite reasonable, so I can begin to enjoy life and the patients again. I like it much better than the rushes, though the younger ones seem to like the excitement of a rush. [Dr Courtauld, at 50, was the oldest of the doctors, and probably the oldest of the whole staff.] We are having dreadfully bad cases just now and have had 8 deaths in the past month's work. We get men sent to us with bits of shell and bullets in most difficult and dangerous parts, but so infected that an attempt must be made to remove them ... In spite of the cool weather they had to put 60 beds in the cloisters, and for three weeks the staff had had their meals outside in the cloisters, sometimes snowed upon and often disagreeably cold ... If it is at all mild I like having meals out. Many of our cases are

so smelly that to breathe fresh air at intervals is refreshing.[19]

Three other doctors arrived in May: Doctors Dobbin and Richardson on May 4th and Dr Adams on May 23rd. This brought the complement of doctors up to 14, certainly fewer than Miss Ivens could have wished but she was delighted with them: 'We like the new doctors very much, especially Miss Richardson and Miss Dobbin who is a charming little thing.'[20] Dr Adams and Dr Dobbin had both qualified in Belfast in 1917 – presumably they decided to embark on this enterprise together as friends. Neither of them would have had very much experience, though experience could be acquired rapidly at Royaumont and at Villers-Cotterets. Dr Richardson was older, having qualified in Edinburgh in 1907, and been a missionary in the Nizam's Dominions in India.

At Villers-Cotterets

Although the work at Villers-Cotterets had been lighter than at Royaumont during March, April and most of May, it had certainly not been uneventful. Severely wounded men were coming in though not in the large numbers that were flowing into Royaumont.

The hospital, formerly known as 'Hôpital Bénévole', was now to be entirely under Army orders and to be known as 'Hôpital Auxiliaire d'Armée No 30 (HAA 30).' In the event of a 'deluge', as Miss Ivens was anticipating (correctly as it turned out), a selected number of staff were warned to hold themselves in readiness to move at two hours' notice with a pack of essential belongings.

There are few records available to supply details. Summerhayes (Grace Summerhayes, later Dr Grace MacRae, orderly 13.12.17 to 16.8.18), working in the theatre, remembers one particular night – probably the night of April 6th/7th. She describes it as 'that bloody night'.[21] Dr Henry left among her papers a little fragment of a diary she kept at Villers-Cotterets – just a page torn out of a notebook:

> 17 May. Air raid. 4 admissions. 1 officer aviator and his pilot both went up with Boche before and behind. Engine stopped, avion came down. Officer fractured spine. v. ill. Pilot fractured ankle.
> 18 May. 2 other admissions, men bombed at the factory. – (illegible) officer operation laminectomy, died later. Valette died. Resection of head of femur.
> 19 May. Miss M's birthday (?Martland) … (words missing) … Air raid. 2 admissions.
> 20 May. Funeral après-midi Madame V (? Valette) heart br … Officer's funeral … picnic … Enjoyed being alone … V C tonight – wish I were back at R. feeling the heat very much. Whit Monday.[22]

The staff had been distressed by the retreat of tired British troops who rested for a time, amazed to find British women stationed so close to the front line:

> They left behind them a memento – a little old fox terrier dog with an unashamedly vulgar tail that curled over his back. The battery passed on; the little dog was missing and could not be found. Hours later he was discovered, draggled, caked with mud, curled up on the bed of the young 'Vague-Mestre' [Orderly in charge of the post – Miss Kitty Salway, later Mrs Mackintosh, 11.10.16 to 21.1.19] who promptly adopted him as the hospital mascot.[23]

He remained in that important position until the end of the war, and, in due course, and after the necessary quarantine, returned to civilian life in Britain with Dr Courtauld.

The Breakthrough

When the big attack took place at 1.30 on the morning of May 27th Miss Ivens, at Royaumont, 'happened to hear quite unofficially of the attack' and made immediate preparations to take up all available staff during the afternoon. 'When we arrived at Villers-Cotterets it was very strange – they had heard nothing although so much nearer' (in fact they were 40 miles nearer the front line).[24]

Why, one might speculate, did Miss Ivens only hear 'unofficially', and, even more, why had no warning been sent to Villers-Cotterets which was, after all, now 'directly under the Army'? If Miss Ivens had not arrived with reinforcements, the staff would have been in great difficulty. The situation seems almost more bizarre and haphazard owing to the fact that the Army had decided some considerable time earlier that the situation of Villers-Cotterets was so advantageous for a Casualty Clearing Station that they were building another large hospital alongside. At the crucial time, however, this was not ready. Villers-Cotterets stood alone.

Miss Ivens' accounts of the work of the hospitals were always straightforward, factual, usually brief, and certainly not given to hyperbole. She wrote to the Committee on June 30th apologetically for being 'very neglectful', but 'I know you will realise that we have been working at the highest pressure and that it has taken us all our time to get through'. It is worth quoting her report in full. She reports on Villers-Cotterets:

> At 5 p.m. May 27th some badly bombed cases arrived, and at 4.30 a.m. on Tuesday morning May 28th, the stream of wounded began to come in by car. Refugees poured in by every kind of vehicle and on foot, and during the night all the medical staff of a hospital nearer which had been forced to evacuate. We worked practically continuously, and yet the

receiving ward was always full. During the few days, more than 3,000 wounded passed through the centre, and we had 127 of the worst, as the big hospital was not yet equipped for work. At mid-day the Médecin-Principal came to me and said he had very bad news, and that we must be preparing to evacuate. We were dreadfully disappointed but as it was perfectly clear that the wounded could not be kept there, I simply said we should do as we were told, but wished to remain until the last possible moment that we could render service. He said it was inevitable and that we must pack up, and be ready to go and form a hospital on the other side of Paris from Royaumont. I gave orders accordingly, but in the evening he came to me and said that as no other hospital was in a position to work, and as no confirmation of his order had been received, would we stay, as a great many cases were expected during the night. Of course I said we should all be delighted, and the theatre unpacked and the x-rays were put together again in about an hour's time, and work was resumed and went on during the night until the middle of the next morning. [Wednesday 29th.] It was an appalling night. We had to work almost in total darkness for from early in the evening, air fights had been going on and we were a target. Tremendous explosions came from a train of ammunition which had been hit by a bomb, and the whole sky was illuminated. The patients were thick both on the beds and the stretchers in the receiving ward 'France' and we kept on tackling the worst cases. No one showed the slightest trace of nervousness in spite of the horror of the night. I lay down for half an hour but was soon called up by the arrival of more and we began again on Thursday morning [May 30th]. I was in the middle of operating when the Médecin-Principal walked into the theatre and said we must be getting ready to go and must not attempt to do any more operations. A train was expected to evacuate the patients, but did not arrive. When it did only half ours could be put on. The telephone was cut the day before. However, during the morning I had sent down to Royaumont for every available car to come up, sending down at the same time a batch of the younger orderlies, and all the important archives. At lunchtime I told the staff to pack up their valuables to take with them, and the rest of their possessions in their trunks, and to dress to be ready to start at any minute. We then devoted ourselves to getting the patients dressed so that they could be sent off as soon as the opportunity occurred. A train came in, and I was allotted 70 places for the 120, which left me with 50 to dispose of. I accordingly sent off all our three cars with wounded to a little town about 15 miles behind, with instructions to return for more as soon as possible. Then three cars from the American section were placed at my disposal, and I filled them up with wounded. At last our cars from Royaumont began to arrive, very late, owing to the condition of the roads, and we were thankful to pack up the rest of the wounded in them. They were to be taken to S [Senlis] – each car took a sister. A little before I had started off a considerable number of the orderlies and doctors to walk as it was quite clear that it would be night before the cars could get back for them, and they would be picked up as opportunity offered. During the afternoon the shells began to whistle overhead, and the American car drivers told me that it was quite time for us to go as the Boche were only 5 kms away and were coming on very fast. At last all the staff and wounded were off. – We kept the little lorry, and Moore [Miss Evelyn Mercy Moore, chauffeur, 5.5.18 to 6.11.18] loaded it with petrol which at that moment was our greatest need, and we started for C. [Crèpy.]. On the way I met several of our returning cars and sent two or three of them on with orders to help with the evacuation of the big hospital, and if not, to bring any valuables they could. I decided to call at C. where we had sent some wounded, to see if they had left in a train, or what arrangements had been made. It was a station more bombed than any other behind the lines, and a great hole in the station yard greeted us – We looked about and found several of them [the staff] still there, including Mrs Berry and, I think, Tollit [Miss Florence Tollit, orderly, 6.6.15 to 24.7.18]. We continued our journey to S. The country was illuminated. It was just like gigantic fireworks, for air raids were going on in every direction. As we got into S. there was a block – all lights were out. However as we had to pull up, an army doctor came out, – We then made for the hotel where I expected to find most of the nurses. Twenty one were there, and I was very cross on finding them in their beds instead of in the cellars, as the raid was on. We decided to make for R. by a quieter road as we could see the bombs dropping over the one we generally took. It was not a happy selection from that point of view for we met a continuous stream of Foch's reinforcements and understood that was what the bombs were trying for. It was a most reassuring and impressive sight – silent dark shapes moving slowly along towards us in the night with quantities of guns and cavalry. Not a sound and hardly a light (I saw, I think, two cigarettes). After a detour we reached R. at one o'clock, and a very short time after Murray [Miss Elizabeth Margaret Murray, later Mrs Galbraith, chauffeur, 9.6.17 to 7.11.18] arrived with four patients from Villers-Cotterets – The following morning May 31st I returned to S. to see for myself the Médecin-Principal. I arrived during a conference of all the medical authorities involved. S. was to function as a clearing station. We were to fetch and receive our patients from there and HAA 30 was to work at Royaumont. It was all fixed in about 5 minutes. We got a load of wounded and took them back with us. Two extra theatres were arranged. Matron Lindsay [Miss Gertrude Lindsay, Sister, then Matron, 22.3.15 to 20.2.19] took charge of one, and our theatre sister (Sister Everingham)

The 'White Elephant'. An ambulance too big for normal use, but a godsend for the evacuation of patients from Villers-Cotterets in May 1918. (By courtesy of Miss Heather Mackay).

[Miss Winifred Everingham, Sister, 18.8.17 to 30.12.18] from Villers-Cotterets, was to do the night work.[25]

Other members of the Unit recorded their experiences. Considered together, they give us a very complete impression of the days leading up to the evacuation and the evacuation itself.

Dr Courtauld had been working at Villers-Cotterets for about three weeks when the German advance took place. Since the patients had started coming in, 'one has lost count of time more or less, for the staff has been working pretty well night and day. Noise, dust, bombing going on night and day almost so if one did get to bed for an hour or two unless one was dog-tired sleep was out of the question, and one never felt it desirable to undress:

> When the first order to evacuate was cancelled and the new order came on to stay we were glad. It seemed horrid to be told to go and leave things working behind us. All night long we were hard at it, and working under difficulties. Terrible cases came in. Between 10.30 and 3.30 or 4 a.m. we had to amputate six thighs and one leg, mostly by the light of bits of candle held by the orderlies, and as for me giving the anaesthetic, I did it more or less in the dark at my end of the patient. For air raids were over us nearly all the night and sometimes we had to blow out the candle for a few minutes and stop when one heard the Boche right overhead and bombs falling and shaking us. However our camp

remained intact. Next morning about 11 a.m. we were told the whole place must be evacuated and all as fast as may be. Patients had come in all through the night, some practically dying, all wanting urgently operating upon. But we had to stop operating, dress the patients' wounds and splint them up as best we could and all day ambulances came up and we got the patients away. A hospital train was also made and a lot went by that. But heaps of really badly wounded had to start to walk. We also got away a good many of our orderlies and younger doctors and nurses. We sent off a party of lusty young ones walking, just carrying what they could in their hands. We had all been provided with what we called a 'retreating ration' the day before, for emergencies, two hard boiled eggs, one orange, a bit of cheese and a bit of bread. [Another account mentions brandy in the ration pack.] By the evening Miss Ivens, myself, the Matron and only a few orderlies and sisters were left, and only 9 extremely bad patients. At supper came the order that the whole place was to get away as fast as it could. Our Royaumont lorries and ambulances had been sent for ... so directly our patients were got on to stretchers and met the ambulances we rushed to our barrack, picked up our handbags and knapsacks and came straight down in the lorry to Royaumont. I got here about 11.30 p.m. It was an exciting journey part of the way. For reasons which seem pretty clear now, but we did not know last night, the road was likely to be bombed, and at a certain place the car got into the midst of it. The moon had not risen. Our camion is a great heavy thing and can't go very fast, and though it seemed dark to the driver (for we had no lights on) yet the road showed as a white line among the dark forest surroundings, and evidently was a good mark for the Boche. Anyway we had a few sharp minutes and I didn't think we should get through unscathed, but we did, but the brutes seemed to follow along from above. And even when we got here bombs and barrage were booming away all round the district. Royaumont has been almost emptied of patients during the last few days, but I think now we are going to get a lot of these poor things who were evacuated by necessity from the hospitals nearer the line – For five days we have lived through a lot and had hardly any sleep. It is simply horrible leaving so much behind. Things packed up and lying just outside one barrack by the side of the railway ready to come but unless we can get them soon they will be looted. I was there only three weeks and took only a few clothes and have not left much behind, my rubber bath being my most important loss.

She had another regret:

I wanted to dig and burn up all the masses of vegetables the staff have grown, but hadn't a moment. Had picked a bed of radishes for supper, but had to retreat before we could eat them.[26]

Dr Henry remembered those four days 'when time did not exist'. The wounded men coming in were the most severe cases. 'Their wounds were terrible, and in most cases they arrived at the hospital minus even a field dressing.' As for the staff, 'For four nights and three days they worked without ceasing except for meals. We began to lose all sense of time, and worked like machines. On the last morning when we stopped for breakfast Theatre Sister went fast asleep sitting bolt upright upon a bench, and she had to be shaken before she could be awakened – That last week at Villers-Cotterets will ever be remembered by the staff as a terrible nightmare ... The saddest sight of that last week – was the seriously wounded men streaming along the roads dead tired, and in many cases, almost unable to drag themselves along.[27]

Dr Henry was one of those younger doctors who set off with a party of the 'lusty young ones' to walk back the forty miles to Royaumont with orders not to spend the night in any of the villages en route:

> We joined the refugees. We were on the run. Presently an empty train car rolled along the railway line, we crossed the field and signalled. Do you remember the French wagon labelled 'Trente hommes ou Huit Chevaux'? That was ours. It was very dirty but we climbed in and sat on a tightly packed row on the floor, our heads nodding in our tiredness. So we arrived at Senlis where our wounded had been dumped on the station platform.[28]

As an old lady, her daughter tells us, Dr Henry still had nightmares about that evacuation journey[29]

An orderly, acting as second sister in the theatre, described the theatre to Collum who reported it:

> A hell and a shambles. Nine thigh amputations running; men literally shot to pieces: the crashing of bombs and the thunder of ever-approaching guns; the explosion of a train of munitions on the line; next, the destruction of a level-crossing keeper's cottage within a stone's throw of their own siding; the operating hut with its plank floor and the tables and the instruments on them literally dancing to the explosions; the flickering candles, the anxiety lest the operated cases might haemorrhage and die in the dark; the knowledge that the next bomb might get them; the still more awful fear that the French had miscalculated – that the door might be thrown open and a German officer walk in on them.[30]

Smieton [Miss Maud Isolde Smieton (later Lady Sanderson), orderly 4.7.16 to 22.3.19] remembered how she and Inglis (Etta) were seconded to the theatre as orderlies, how Inglis held a candle at one side of the operating table and herself at the other 'trying to keep our hand steady while loud explosions went on outside':

The whole place was a shambles with men lying on the floor everywhere. It was so dark – that it was difficult to know if a man was dead or alive. On our last morning, when we were feeling at our last gasp, Miss Ivens said to me: 'Smieton, go and find another blessé. I shall do one more operation'. There were so many wounded still lying on the floor, mostly badly wounded, it was difficult to know whom to choose. However, I saw a man with a tourniquet on his arm so I had him moved into the theatre.[31]

All this while Georgina Cowan [Miss Georgina Cowan, orderly 23.11.17 to 8.6.18] described Miss Ivens 'Just as cool as could be' [32], and Sister Goodwin [Miss Harriet Elizabeth Goodwin, Sister, 29.9.17 to 15.1.19] remembered her as 'a Rock of Gibraltar'.[33]

Florence Anderson [Miss Florence Amy Anderson (Mrs Longrigg), orderly, 15.8.15 to 27.9.16 and 25.4.18 to 25.10.18], radiographer, was summoned up to Villers-Cotterets on May 28th travelling deviously via Paris, and very tired after many nights of bombardment at Royaumont ('it becomes wearisome'), only to arrive in the thick of the packing, unpacking, and the hectic work which followed right through the night. In her account:

Wounded came in all night. The ward next the x-ray department was a nightmare. Black blankets on the beds. On each men were dying, screaming, unconscious and delirious, the Sisters doing their work the best way they could with lanterns – Miss Ivens operating, operating, operating by candle light. Six amputations of the leg, and all the time the horrible bang bang of the bombs and the munition train, and shrapnel falling sometimes on the roof. Then the weariness! – With a train full of wounded, we got, six of us, to Chantilly, from whence we got a trap. But that road from Villers-Cotterets to Crèpy! Soldiers, transports, refugees, crowds of wounded all on foot, poor fellows, all hanging on to any vehicle they could. In the train we were in a horse box with wounded and refugees.[34]

Another (unnamed) member of staff at Villers-Cotterets wrote:

To appreciate what the work meant it must be realised that at the same time as the wounded were pouring into the hospital, men so badly wounded that everyone of them needed immediate skilled attention, the camp was also a thoroughfare past which streams of civilian refugees were pouring, pushing their possessions in front of them on little barrows, or driving in carts of every kind, and was a refuge for the staff of more than one hospital which had to evacuate in the minimum of time. One company of people in this plight had not even time to get all their clothes, but had to leave in a condition of semi-undress. A party of evacuated nurses were given shelter in our hospital, while the staff of another hospital were given rough lodging in tents by the adjacent French HOE [Hôpital d'Evacuation].[35]

These ladies descending on them were remembered by one member of the Unit, looking back from 1968:

> They floated around in high heels, complete with voluminous veils and Red Crosses and heavy make-up and had no intention of soiling their hands with hard work. They fell foul of Ashton [Miss Eva Margaret Ashton, cook, 5.9.17 to 18.3.19] in the kitchen who afterwards used to refer to them briefly as 'the dam' rouges'.[36]

All the time that this bustle was going on in the camp the real hospital work continued steadily. While the nursing staff attended to the patients, the kitchen, in addition to preparing meals suited to our refugee guests, also acted as an emergency canteen for some of the streams of soldiers passing through.[37]

McLeod [Miss Helen McLeod, cook, 4.8.17 to ?], who worked in the kitchen, wrote later (1947):

> Could one ever forget the one candle in a bottle for light to cook by, the rats slipping out from under one's feet, the windows and doors that opened and shut when no one was there? Miss Ivens appearing from the blackout at 4 a.m. and sitting at the orderlies' table discussing the events of Villers with Jerries hovering overhead. Could one ever forget?[38]

On the evening of the 29th when the hospital was ready to begin work again after the order to evacuate had been rescinded, the unidentified member of staff continued her story:

> As far as the difficulty of the work was concerned that was the worst night we had to cope with. The blessés began coming in between 8 and 9 at night, and almost immediately began a violent air raid. The men were among some of the most terribly wounded we had yet received and in the middle of taking them all in the 'All Lights Out' order was given, and we had to carry on by the light of a few heavily shaded lamps, with the whirr of enemy machines overhead, and the heavy b-o-o-o-mp, b-o-o-o-mp of bombs dropping nearby. The raiders were so persistent that it was found to be impossible to delay the operations till they had passed over, and at the same time the raiders were so near that it would probably have meant disaster if a light had been allowed to be shown anywhere. The solution to the problem was that work in the operating theatre was resumed by candlelight.
>
> About 10.30 the order came to prepare the patients for evacuation. In the air raid of the night before the station of Villers-Cotterets had been

bombed, and was still filled with debris so that no trains could pass
through it till the debris had been cleared away. Consequently the 'trains
sanitaires' which should have taken away the wounded were not available,
and the problem of how to get the men removed had to be met. The less
seriously wounded men who had been spending the night at the French
HOE were started out to go on foot till they could find some better
means of transport, but not one of the men in the Scottish Women's
Hospital could possibly go anywhere on foot, So Miss Ivens sent for the
cars to come up from Royaumont and take the blessés from Villers-
Cotterets to the first available hospital further back. The result of this
arrangement was that everyone without exception in the Scottish
Women's Hospital was evacuated safely, and in addition the Royaumont
cars were able to help to transport some of the men for the HOE. The
British staff, who, according to first military orders, were to have been
taken by train with the hospital equipment, were now deprived of that
means of transport. Like the blessés and the civilians there was nothing
for it but to start on foot, and hope to get some better means of transport
further on. So a large party of doctors, nurses and orderlies were sent off
about midday to find their way as best they could to Royaumont, leaving
behind everything except what they could carry.

Those who did not go with the first company remained to help to look
after the blessés till they left, and to attend to the final packing of the
hospital. By six o'clock in the evening there only remained 8 blessés in
the hospital, and nearly all the staff had left. The end of the evacuation
was very sudden. Two American cars drove into the camp with the news
that the German advance was becoming more rapid, and about the same
time we heard the screech of shells for the first time. The result was an
instant order for the blessés to be put into the American cars, and for the
staff to get into the Royaumont lorry which had just then appeared.
When Miss Ivens drove out of the camp about 8 p.m. the evacuation of
the blessés and the staff, both English and French, was completed.[39]

Miss Stoney had won everyone's admiration for her work during the rush, and
it was characteristic of her and her devotion to her beloved x-ray apparatus
that she made superhuman efforts to save as much of it as she possibly could.
She had packed up the apparatus carefully and methodically on the first order
to evacuate, but she had to work fast to get the x-rays operational once more:

The blessés were already pouring in again. Thanks to the ready and
skilled help of my helpers, Raymond, [Miss Patricia Raymond (later Mrs
Lloyd), orderly, 27.7.17 to 18.3.19] Butler [Miss Marian Ada Butler,
orderly, 18.10.17 to 3.6.18] and Anderson – thanks to the help too of S
[Miss Hilda Mary Smeal, chauffeur, 19.7.17 to 19.9.18], the chauffeuse
who had sometimes helped me before, and of the infirmiere (*sic*) Defarge

[French male orderly] we got all the electrical wiring replaced and the Gaiffe apparatus fully functioning by 11 p.m. Villers-Cotterets (ie the town) was blazing – a woman and children were killed at the corner of our hospital. We dared show no light. But Miss Ivens, Miss Martland, Mrs Berry and the other doctors operated all night by the light mostly of a 50 candle-power electric lamp I had stuck in a cocoa tin to shade it – or candles. The engine had to be run for the x-rays – and the electrician had fled to the fields – we had also to see to the engine. I was sent to bed at 4 a.m. and Berry and Butler were working on when I came on duty again three hours later. We worked on till 4 p.m. Thursday seeing x-ray cases. Then the order came to pack up finally. At 1.30 p.m. Miss Ivens sent off the younger doctors and orderlies walking, and hoping for odd lifts – this included my three assistants, Anderson, Butler and Raymond. Then my last helper, the x-ray infirmière (sic) was needed to carry the blessés – and help with the wounded – the doctors and nurses remaining were desperately busy with patients. The whole of the x-ray equipment was however repacked by 6 p.m. and we went to supper. During supper the shelling began, and the splendid American ambulance men came along for the last of our blessés whom we had not yet been able to evacuate in our own cars. And this left our returning cars free for the last of us to luxuriously drive to Royaumont. We were heavily bombed on the way.[40]

'We were on the road all night', wrote Smeal, one of the 'shovers':

It would have been very thrilling if it had not been so unspeakably tragic. The roads were quite a sight to behold, simply black with troops, convoys and big guns going in one direction and in the other, refugees and the poor blessés who were forced to go on foot as all the cars were needed for the stretcher cases. Some of the poor souls had trudged along for miles and miles, and they did look so dusty and weary – a truly pathetic sight.[41]

One further tale must be told of the evacuation of Villers-Cotterets. 'La Colonelle' always made great efforts to suppress surreptitious livestock – efforts which were not all that successful.

Jimmy and his brother canary were hatched actually within the sacred precincts of the theatre in Villers-Cotterets – presumably the warmest spot in that bitterly cold winter. When the final signal to abandon the hospital was given, the Boche being within 6 kms, the canaries had to be left behind:

When all the Villers-Cotterets people had returned to Royaumont, the malade who had been identified to act as theatre brancardier [stretcher-bearer], failed to appear. There were those who in their thoughts accused Dominique of base desertion. But one day, when Inglis was in the hall, she saw a dusty weary figure stumbling up the path – it was Dominique, with a birdcage in his hand, which he flourished triumphantly, calling for 'Sistaire'. He had walked the whole way from Villers-Cotterets, carrying the birdcage with Jimmy and his brother.[42]

In due course the canaries returned to England with Sister Everingham (whose theatre had served as their incubator).

The safe return of all the patients and staff to Royaumont was not the end of the Villers-Cotterets story. Early the next morning (Friday), Miss Stoney, along with the Administrator Ramsay-Smith (Miss Madge Ramsay-Smith, Secretary/Administrator, 25.5.16 to 22.3.19) and Tollitt (Miss Florence Tollitt, orderly, 1.6.15 to 24.7.18) returned to salvage what material they could – every bit would be desperately needed at Royaumont. Shelling began almost as soon as they reached the hospital. They loaded the car with all it could carry while they themselves walked. With the help of occasional lifts they were almost back when they met two Royaumont cars and returned once more to Villers-Cotterets. Miss Stoney did her best to make up a complete x-ray apparatus to take back with her. Renewed bombing on the road on the way forced the second car into the fields till morning, but they got through. She went back yet again and it was only on strict orders that she ceased in her efforts. In spite of that she had her x-rays at Royaumont set up and working within 24 hours.

Her conscience still troubled her over the inevitable losses: 'I trust the Committee will realise the difficulties before blaming me too much for the heavy loss of apparatus entrusted to my care'.[43] She wrote to her sister Florence (a radiologist employed as a consultant in the Military Hospital in Fulham Road under the War Office) what a privilege it was to help in such work, and later she told Mrs Laurie, the Treasurer of the Committee:

> It was nice in that cold bracing forest air! I loved Villers-Cotterets ... one is so eaten up these days with dread of not getting useful enough work that it has been of the deepest pleasure to me to be on the Western Front these days – and where such very excellent help was given when so des-perately needed – as in both the SWHs of Villers-Cotterets March 21–25 and again May 25–31 and Royaumont ever since.[44]

This was in spite of the fact that she felt she had been very overworked all the winter:

> The engine was old and out of work constantly – and there always seemed to be burst pipes to be soldered – kitchen drains to be seen to – broken windows in the men's barraques to be mended etc – and it was cold – colder even in a way than December 1915 in Serbia – always save when that 80 mile an hour blizzard that struck so badly – ! [Miss Stoney had also served in Salonika with Dr Louise McIlroy where she was

Miss Edith Stoney in her x-ray department in the Scottish Women's Hospital in Serbia.
She is wearing a Serbian decoration.
(By courtesy of the Archivist of the Royal Free Hospital School of Medicine).

reckoned to be one of the most oustandingly useful members of staff.] I
was without an orderly, we were so short of staff – and the stove had to be
lit – the floor washed etc – my hands gave out – and it is not easy to
write with one's hands bandaged up.[45]

We will leave Dr Courtauld to speak for many of those who participated in
the Villers-Cotterets adventure:

> None of us would have missed the last week's work for a good deal. What
> we are rather proud of is that when the great need began to come, we
> Scottish Women were apparently the only hospital in full working order
> and I think we really have done some good work there.[46]

At Royaumont

Meanwhile back at Royaumont those who were left behind were very anxious.
They had had no news for two days after Miss Ivens and her reinforcements
had left for Villers-Cotterets. Then they heard – with relief – that the hospital was to be evacuated to Meaux. This, of course, did not occur, but Miss
Ivens sent them an order to empty as many beds as possible:

> Then silence. On the 30th the news in the communiqué was so bad that
> we felt justified in fearing that Villers-Cotterets was already in German
> hands. We had spent the night of the 29th and the early morning of the
> 30th in evacuating the wounded from our hospital; I think we had
> reduced our number to 16! Then came a message from our Médecin-Chef,
> laconic, unembroidered: 'Send up all cars you possibly can immediately to
> evacuate hospital'. So they were still there! And the enemy, for all we
> knew, on the point of entering the town. How our remaining chauffeurs
> worked! For the two who had taken up staff had not come back.
> Afterwards we learnt that they had been commandeered by the authorities
> to help evacuate Soissons. We beat up every car that could crawl. Our
> chauffeur, with mumps, got up and took the lorry. The mechanic took the
> big American car known as the 'elephant' – we have dropped the adjective
> 'white' – which holds 12 stretchers. Orderlies who could drive took out
> other cars. Our Secretary went up in one car to see what could be saved of
> the equipment. An orderly went in an old car that won't go unless some-
> one sits and pumps petrol all the time, so the hall porter went along as a
> pumper. – I do not know how much they all exceeded the speed limit that
> evening on the stretches of road that were clear. There were miles when
> they had to creep in and out of more slowly moving convoys. As they
> neared Villers-Cotterets they met unceasing traffic – the mixed sad traffic
> of a forced retreat. The Germans were already shelling Longpont, 7 kilo-
> metres distant by forest path from the hospital camp.[47]

At about 10 p.m. the first of the refugees got back [i.e. to Royaumont].
They reported that some had reached Senlis and some Chantilly, some
were on the road, and Miss Ivens and her little band were still at Villers-
Cotterets. I thought they might not be able to leave until late, and might
have to walk, so I got a man to take me in a big brake along the road to
Senlis. We hadn't gone a mile when Fritz paid us his almost nightly
bombing visit, but as he was giving it hot to a certain town through
which we had to pass, I confess I felt rather queer. The mare felt queerer,
and tried to bolt. So we had to turn back. Just as I was about to go back
to the Abbaye, I heard a car pelt up to the garage with lights out. It was
the lorry from Villers-Cotterets. Our people on the lorry had run right
through a certain town in the thick of the raid – running into it before
they were aware – being shouted at to douse their lights – and then
going hell for leather, the bombs dropping along after them, but always
running. Fritz was following the white ribands of the roads, which show
plainly through the dark forest, and bombing at low elevation, anything
he could see, in the hope of a convoy of troops.[48]

One of the new chauffeurs wrote of the evacuation as a period when the first
rush which she had encountered 'paled into insignificance':

Everything on wheels was commandeered for that evacuation. Some of the
cars, hastily patched for the occasion, held together as by a miracle, and
our journey from Royaumont to Villers was a hairbreadth escape from
beginning to end. For miles we had to creep in and out of slowly moving
convoys, on the clear stretches of road we defied all speed limits, and as
we neared Villers the road became choked – The town had been bom-
barded by night and by day, but the hospital had escaped miraculously.
The shelling was continuous when we arrived and the town partly in
flames before we left, to be heavily bombed from the air all the way back
on our return journey.[49]

It was not only the staff concerned with the transport, reception and treatment of the wounded who were working at high pressure. On the night of
the 29th:

The office staff [at Royaumont] had sat up till 4 a.m. getting the papers
done of the men in our hospitals whom we had orders to evacuate. We
got away all but 7 immovable cases on the 30th. Then no one much got
to bed that night, what with our staff from Villers-Cotterets arriving and
the awful raid.[50]

Royaumont was having its share of nightly bombings. Collum continues:

When a big bomb fell in the field just behind us, (the crater is still
there), and a big machine just skimmed the ruined tower above our heads

we plunged into the old monkish cellars beneath the Abbaye and waited tensely. … Instead of a bomb we heard the welcome hum of our own lorry's engine, which came creeping in, all lights out, into the garage yard. All our cars were in by 5 a.m., and all had had adventures.[51]

Royaumont after Evacuation

To quote Collum again:

> On the 31st of May began for us at the Abbaye the period of the greatest stress and strain our staff had ever known. During the First Battle of the Somme we had the consciousness of meeting the crisis fresh, with something in hand. There was never any danger of our organisation being strained to snapping point. This time we were tried up to and beyond our strength. And we started tired. The Villers-Cotterets Hospital was officially evacuated on to us, and carried on in amalgamation with us. Somehow or other we managed to provide 480 beds – they even stood in serried rank all round the four sides of the Abbaye cloisters.[52]

Georgina Cowan (Miss Georgina Cowan, orderly, 23.11.17 to 8.6.18) wrote: 'Where everybody is going I don't know – I am in a barn for six'.[53] Others were sharing beds between day and night staff – a Cox and Box arrangement – and many of the extra staff had to sleep on chairs.

There was no rest for Miss Ivens after her amazing feats of endurance at Villers-Cotterets. As she recorded in her report the very next morning (31st), she drove up to Senlis to discuss the changing situation with the medical authorities there. These same authorities could move rapidly on occasion. In five minutes everything was arranged. HAA 30 (the Villers-Cotterets hospital) was to work in tandem with Royaumont; wounded were to be collected directly from Senlis which was now the clearing station instead of the more vulnerable Creil (though at 15 kms a greater distance from Royaumont). She then and there took back what wounded they could carry and arranged two extra theatres to be under Matron Lindsay and the Theatre Sisters (Everingham) from Villers-Cotterets.

For the next two weeks the chauffeurs had to face daily bombing on their trips to Senlis to collect the wounded, and many of them in addition made tip-and-run raids to Villers-Cotterets to salvage what equipment they could until they were forbidden to take such risks. Fortunately by this time they had been issued with tin hats. In spite of their efforts a vast amount of equipment was lost.

It was not only hospital equipment that was lost. The staff had packed their trunks and stored them in an empty hut, but, as Simms reported:

> After we left the French Army got in and looted everything. One of the

wounded arrived here (i.e. at Royaumont) the other day in a lady's chemise so it looks rather fishy. The chauffeurs brought back the remains of our luggage, but there wasn't anything much worth having. I got my trunk, a pair of socks that I was knitting and a vest, and another girl found nothing but her bathing dress!![54]

Summerhayes lost her precious black shiny leather patent shoes which had been hanging above her bed out of reach of the rats. She firmly believed that it was the local townspeople who were the guilty ones.[55]

In response to the requests of two armies in the neighbourhood Miss Ivens agreed to increase their beds to 600. Huts, beds and 'literie' were all to be provided by the Army, and the whole hospital was to be entirely under Army control.

M. Gouin, the owner of the abbey, and the Service de Santé of the French Red Cross were not happy at this expansion of beds, but a good friend at the Ministère de Guerre, M. Piessac, 'represented to them that it was the fortune of war and politely hinted not to be officially disagreeable and unpatriotic'.[56] Miss Ivens also had to look to the future as the military situation was so fluid and likely to remain so. She suggested to the Committee that they should consider providing a mobile hospital, fully equipped, in tents, 'otherwise when the Army moves we shall be left high and dry – in the present we shall just go on working here'.[57]

Collum, the radiographer, continues the story after the return of the Villers-Cotterets hospital:

In three days we were full to overflowing. In 15 days we had brought in, x-rayed and operated on, 1000 wounded men. On several days our six drivers brought in 100 cases from Senlis and evacuated another hundred to our new HOE (evacuation hospital) for the northern front, 8 kilometres in the opposite direction. I do not know how many men were brought in during that first 24 hours of 31st May – but I know that I personally, made 85 x-ray examinations, and that neither my assistant or the developer in the dark room got to bed until dawn. I went on until the assistant from the Villers-Cotterets hospital relieved me at 9 a.m., and did not go on duty again until noon. We worked at this pressure in the x-ray department until the 4th June when the Villers-Cotterets radiographer rigged up the salved outfit and started in to help us. The heaviest week for the Villers-Cotterets équipe was the one that followed, from 9th June until the 15th, in which period they made 164 examinations, – Our own Abbaye équipe, from the 31st May until 13th July (the period of the Aisne fighting) made 1100 x-ray examinations, against 9000 of its entire 3½ year career, the total figures bringing that total up to 1680 examinations for 6 weeks.

The x-ray and theatre staffs, after the first two or three days, when they fared equally badly in the matter of sleep, roughly organised themselves into shifts working eight hours and resting six. Thus we were able to cope with it but at the cost of much physical and mental strain on those who were already tired with two or three years' work at the hospital, that some of them were worked out by August who might otherwise have carried on till the end of the war. However, they coped with it, and that was the main thing.... Two extra emergency theatres were opened. With three theatres working all day and two of them all night it can be imagined how the surgeons were pressed, and how near the anaesthetists came to being anaesthetised themselves. I do not think the Médecin-Chef or the Second in Command Miss Nicholson ever got more than three hours rest in the 24 during that first strenuous fortnight.[58]

On June 4th the Administrator Ramsay-Smith wrote:

The work here is unending and the cases are so bad that it is heart-rending to see them. The staff is working at full pressure night and day in order to treat as many cases as possible and get them sent on to other hospitals. We have received over 400 in three days and we evacuate as quickly as we can and there is hardly ever an empty bed – using sphagnum pads whenever possible – dressings very heavy – many men have several wounds and as they discharge need very large dressings.[59]

The Committee were getting worried about the quantity of dressings required. They urged using more sphagnum which cost nothing.

During the month of May 31st to June 30th there were 1240 admissions, 891 operations and 44 deaths. This does seem to be an amazingly small number considering the severity of the wounds and the pressure under which the staff was working.

Writing on June 30th, Miss Stoney tells us what Collum herself does not:

Collum has been so badly burned with the old Butt Table's want of adequate protection that she could do no x-ray work. I am very thankful – very thankful indeed – that those working the Butt coil have now a better protected table in this new Gaiffe table.[60]

Collum was not the only one to have trouble from exposure to x-rays: Butler was similarly affected. When the pressure of work is very great, some of the diagnostic work has to be done by screening rather than by photographs, which means a greater danger for the operator. It emerged later that Collum had suffered more than x-ray burns. Her blood had also been affected by the heavy x-ray exposure and Professor Salouraud in Paris, whom she consulted in August, forebade her to go back to x-rays for at least ten years.

In 1937 Collum wrote a moving tribute to Frederick Butt who died at the age of 60 after years of acute suffering resulting from over-exposure to x-rays. He 'paid with his life for the too scant attention given in those earlier years to protection for the operator'. She reminded her readers that:

> more than one of the 'Salle Radio' staff suffered from lack of protection in the little Army pattern 'mule-back' Butt installation with which our hospitals started work and carried on, not only through the 1916 Somme push, but in the heavy work of 1918, when a second and French apparatus was in use. Butt, as a designer and builder of apparatus for war conditions, concentrated on portability and reliable foolproof functioning. Thousands of wounded men have cause to be grateful for the reliability of his apparatus, which never let the radiologist down mechanically, and showed none of the 'temperamental' qualities of, for example, our own more beloved Gaiffe installation.

Looking back on the month of June, Miss Stoney felt:

> It has been huge luck to me to be where help was so needed and so ably given by the surgeons, but that we have had over 1200 x-ray examinations in a month is some excuse if the x-ray staff are tired.[62]

She pays tribute to Raymond and the cook Ashton 'who gallantly and most ably helped us in the worst of the rush when we had night work with the lights not able to be shown because of raids overhead. She has gone back to the kitchen. Anderson (the masseuse) [not certainly identified; could be Miss Mary Mack Anderson, 'dispenser', later Mme Petitpierre, or Miss Alison Fairlie Anderson, later Lady Blood, orderly, 10.2.18 to 11.8.18] has mostly taken charge of the Butt apparatus – Grandage [Miss Katherine Grandage, orderly, 27.11.15 to 31.5.17 and 9.3.18 to 1.12.18] has developed photographs from 8 a.m. to 10 p.m. day after day'.[63]

Edith Stoney's distinguished sister, Dr Florence Stoney, who was in charge of all the radiological work in the Fulham Road Military Hospital in London, wrote proudly:

> It is a marvellous performance. When she wrote [i.e. to Florence from Royaumont], she was waiting to examine another case – she had started on duty at 8 a.m. and had been continuously on duty for 30 hours and was soon going off. She feels very old and tired, but she says she seems to stand it as well as some of the younger ones. The wounded keep pouring in all the time, night and day. She says the surgeons must have saved many lives from gas gangrene by their work. Their hospital was the last to be kept working at Villers-Cotterets. And she says what a privilege it is to be able to help in such work. We may indeed be proud of them all but I fear there will be a heavy aftermath to pay for the great overwork they are undergoing. Here, in London, we think we are busy, but it is a

backwater compared with Royaumont.[64]

There was a welcome increase in the medical staff in June which brought the total up to 16, its peak level. Recently qualified (Glasgow 1917) and recently married, Dr Jessie Grant arrived on June 6th in that first hectic week after the evacuation. Dr Miall-Smith joined the Unit on June 26th. Following a B.Sc degree with first-class honours, she had qualified from the London (RFH) School of Medicine for Women in 1916. Dr Guest, with some years of surgical experience behind her, came on June 16th. She had qualified MBBS from the London (RFH) School of Medicine for Women in 1908, and gained her London MD in 1914. From 1912 to 1915 she was on the surgical staff of the Christian Medical College at Ludhiana in the Punjab, founded in 1894 by Dr (later Dame) Edith Brown, one of the pioneer women doctors. From Ludhiana she went to Malta, and then to Egypt, 'attached' to the RAMC. Most women who served in this way felt keenly the low status and discriminatory treatment meted out to them by the Army authorities.[65] After the war – indeed for long after – this was one of the many unfair practices medical women had to fight. After leaving this 'attachment', Dr Guest worked as Chief Medical Officer in the Scottish Women's Hospital in Corsica from October 1917 to June 9th, 1918.

It seems that Dr Guest joined the Unit almost by chance. She had come over to see Miss Ivens at Royaumont on June 16th, but found them so fearfully busy that when Miss Ivens asked her to stay on, she 'had no doubt which path she was to take'. A few days later she wrote to Mrs Russell:

The doctors and staff all looked very tired out and still the wounded poured in night and day and everyone worked with no time to rest. Until two days ago I just helped wherever I was needed – did dressings, gave anaesthetics or helped to operate. Now Miss Ivens has given me charge of the evacuation ward which before no one had time to organise, and it seemed really to fill a gap when I took it on. The 'admission' and 'evacuation' wards are lively spots in a hospital as near as this [i.e. to the front line]. One has to judge whether cases are fit for the journey and is responsible that they do not die en route or haemorrhage or get anything serious – and still must keep them moving in order to have a 'bed and a welcome' for all who are sent down from the ward preparatory to going. We have only got cases that needed operations at once – or were too seriously injured to go any further – since the advance.[66]

With other experience of war service behind her she was able to say with authority:

The Scottish Women have every reason to be proud of their work here. A Military Hospital who, 'on active service' has much waiting to do would be justified in waiting four years for the work of the past four weeks

alone.... I have the greatest respect for Miss Ivens – and in the same
breath for Miss Nicholson, the whole medical staff is good, but *several* are
exceptional.... I have always felt proud, *really* proud to belong to the
SWH. They have such a dignified capable reputation everywhere I have
been, in England or abroad, here or in America.[67]

She went on to warn the Committee to avoid any cheap advertising so that
'we can always hold our heads up with dignity as doctors, amongst those of
our profession'. Although she was only able to stay until August 5th, her help
at a very critical time was crucial.

One doctor, during that hectic month of June, chose to send in her resignation to the Committee as 'she was not satisfied with the kind of work Dr
Ivens had given her'.[68] Dr Logan also criticised the conditions of work which
prevailed among orderlies and nurses. She left on June 27th. Miss Ivens
responded vigorously. Her version was that she had dismissed Dr Logan
because, she said, she had refused to give an anaesthetic when asked to do so.
If this was so, it could be considered a serious offence in the conditions then
prevailing. With two to three theatres at a time in operation, and the usual
anaesthetics being open ether or chloroform, regular anaesthetists were working very long hours, with heavy exposure to the fumes. 'I am very glad to have
her out of the hospital', she wrote. 'At any rate she did not overwork.' She also
referred to 'poisonous remarks like Miss Logan's about "sweating"'.[69] (Of
course they were all 'sweating' then). There was an argument at the end of
1918 when she was claiming salary and maintenance. This was refused by the
Committee – she objected – but the Committee was firm. In spite of all she
was present at the celebratory dinner in London in 1919, joined the
Royaumont Association, and remained a member until 1954. (One wonders
if she regretted her precipitate action?)

Miss Ivens had some other problems during this stressful period that she
could well have done without. One of the most unpleasant incidents that
afflicted the hospital, fortunately unique, occurred at this time. The story is
worth recounting as part of the history of the hospital for two reasons. Firstly,
it throws some light on the sanitary and domestic arrangements, and secondly
it demonstrates the spirit and the ethos of the hospital.

Perhaps the Committee at home had been hard pushed to find staff of the
necessary calibre, and had not been as careful as they might have been in
checking the attitudes of candidates. Doris Stevenson arrived as an orderly on
May 19th. Ten days later she wrote to the Committee, 'horrified at the quite
unnecessary bad conditions which prevail'. She went on:

This hospital, I understood, was near Paris and had been stationary for
three years. I presumed, therefore, that I was coming to a more or less
hygienic and well-organised institution – I likewise understood Royaumont
was administered by gentlewomen and worked almost entirely by them.[70]

She painted a grim picture of the Salle des Bains – 'absolutely disgusting', four W.Cs for the use of three wards of over 100 beds, two baths scarcely curtained off etc; Millicent ward where there was no kitchen but one small table upon which 'dirty instruments and mattery tubes are washed, milk, sugar, eggs and drinking water laid down'; milk and water for the wards kept in stuffy cupboards etc.[71] She complained of lack of method, illogical moving of patients up and down stairs, a lack of consideration for the health of the orderlies and unsuitable baths for the staff (this at least was freely admitted); the supply of drinking water was inadequate, the hospital noisy, and 'appears to be a school for women doctors at the expense of us orderlies of good will and intention'. She admitted the food was excellent but doubted whether – even in France – a sanitary inspector would pass the drainage and unhygienic conditions. On June 8th, with the staff reeling under the continuous inflow of casualties, she wrote to Miss Ivens:

> I *cannot* be associated with an institution representative to the French of British enterprise, so instantly and so lacking in organisation and discipline as the domestic side. *It is also most unfitting that white women should attend to natives in the ways we orderlies have to, as it will tend to lower the prestige of the white woman in the East, as anyone who has lived in India well knows* [my italics].[72]

There was no regret at her departure. Matron reported that she was 'absolutely useless as an orderly'.[73] Miss Stevenson, however, was not finished. After leaving the hospital, she wrote again to the Committee:

> The whole spirit of Royaumont is ludicrous to the few of its members who have seen something of the world, the spirit is positively Prussian in its puffed-upness. The lack of humaneness, civilised spirit or even common politeness is very astonishing to a newcomer, who is supposed to be educated and sometimes well-bred.[74]

Her racist views were expressed more forcibly:

> Anyone who has lived in the East knows well that it is not fitting for white women to wait on natives. In practice they are even less ready than the rest for Christianity, and it will only retard matters by lowering the prestige of the white woman in the East. May I quote an instance, in the ward 'Elsie' an Arab got up and simply made use of the floor, after which an orderly had to clear up. In the East this is the work of the lowest and outcast woman. The French *lady, (and infirmière)* will not wait on her countrymen in the particular ways the Royaumont orderlies do, and with good grace, in spite of the lack of means towards modesty – I ask you is this quite fair to the French lady or ourselves?'[75]

This can be contrasted with the attitude of another orderly, Summerhayes, to a similar incident. She describes how she went into a bathroom at night and found an Arab performing on the floor. 'So what happened then?' 'We got a shovel and shovelled it up and put it into the little loos and whoops it came back and was just on the floor again (hoots of laughter) – it wasn't a very good system!' (Personal communication)

Miss Stevenson criticised the reception of the wounded: 'never have I seen such lack of organisation. The wounded lay in the halls and passages for hours – many of the men were in the hospital twelve hours without food of any kind'. She had not been involved in the Villers-Cotterets evacuation but that did not prevent her from criticising, including the charge that wounded had been left behind in spite of one car leaving empty.

It is not surprising that Miss Ivens reacted angrily 'respecting the malicious charges made by orderly Stevenson':

> With regard to the one that wounded were left at Villers-Cotterets I consider it sufficiently damaging for me to place in the hands of the Medical Defence Union. It is absolutely untrue. – It is quite true that Royaumont has no modern conveniences, but the sanitation, if a little old-fashioned, has given excellent results. Single cases of infectious diseases have repeatedly occurred and have, so far, never given rise to any epidemic – when the hospital is full I myself order the clearance of the cesspools at very short intervals.[76]

Later she gave the Committee further details:

> With regard to the latrines! They are just ordinary water closets, and can be kept in perfect order if the orderlies burn rubbish instead of putting it down them. The infirmiers (unfit soldiers) clean them and the renowned Salle des Bains, which is simply the basement room open to the top to the skylights where a marmite and two baths boarded in are installed. The infirmiers have cleaned the Salle des Bains and water closets since the arrival of the HAA 30 infirmiers at the beginning of the rush and the 6 infirmiers we have borrowed from Creil – were fully occupied (to breaking point) carrying coal and burning rubbish as well as stretchers innumerable. Since then they have done their work under the supervision of the Matron who is after them all the time. I have been in the Salle des Bains at all times and hours and have never found the dreadful conditions described by Stevenson. [Here again Summerhayes can provide some confirmation that the Salle des Bains was not all that salubrious. She can remember cleaning it and the grease getting into her nails (personal communication).] I have placed her case in the hands of the L and C Medical Protection Society. One infirmier is now attached to each ward. – Nearly every statement is inaccurate – The orderlies are supervised and their health is considered in every possible way, but in the pressure of work

there is great difficulty in giving individual attention to the delicate ones, – I cannot see in any way where the doctors benefit at the expense of the sisters and orderlies. I consider such a statement as merely malicious and devoid of fact. The doctors have worked fully as hard if not harder than others both night and day.[77]

When the contents of Stevenson's complaints were heard by the Unit, they were as indignant as Miss Ivens herself. Agnes Anderson (Miss Agnes Anderson, Auxiliary Nurse, 26.4.15 to 11.8.18) wrote on behalf of the orderlies. 'They felt', she said, that Stevenson's letter 'is in no way representative of the feeling of the orderlies as a whole.' Regarding the Salle des Bains, she pointed out that a curtain was provided for the baths, but it is not always used:

Some of the new orderlies find it difficult at first to realise that the French attitude towards these matters is entirely different from the British [Anderson had been an orderly since April 1915 so had plenty of experience of French attitudes on personal modesty], but as the patients are, for the most part, uneducated Frenchmen, *it is easier for us to adapt ourselves to their attitudes than for them to understand, for them, a prudish British one* [my italics].[78]

This seems a commonsense and eminently practical point of view. She responded equally practically to the various other criticisms, and also explained that the health of the orderlies was very well looked after though 'Royaumont is not a place for delicate people or those who tire easily – we do not expect to be mothered here, there is no time'.[79]

The orderlies, however, waxed really indignant when they read of Stevenson's remark on the 'Spirit of Royaumont'. 'In three weeks she can scarcely be expected to gauge that'. Anderson's comments on the treatment of the Arabs are worth quoting:

Once a soldier comes into hospital he is merely a patient and is treated as such regardless of nationality and colour. It has always been the pride of Royaumont that the orderlies have been able to do for the Frenchmen and others what their own countrywomen would not or could not do for them. The French themselves realise this and are respectfully grateful – The Director of the Service de Santé had asked other Médecins-Chefs at a recent meeting to 'model their hospitals on Royaumont'. The care given to the Arabs can in no way endanger the prestige of white women, French or English.[80]

Sister Thom [Mrs Jean Thom (later Mrs Pierce), Sister 21.2.17 to 5.12.18] had more understanding of the Arab who had so offended Stevenson for 'using the floor':

He was a head case, operated on the previous night and not responsible. We have a number of Arabs in the ward, all of whom behave very well indeed and give sisters and orderlies no trouble in any way. The Arab Miss Stevenson speaks of is now one of the most helpful and obedient in the ward. In my experience here I find the Arabs in every way as modest as the French.[81]

Miss Lindsay, who had been Matron at Villers-Cotterets, was indignant at the charge that patients had been left behind:

By the evening every patient had been evacuated. As Miss Stevenson was never on the Villers-Cotterets staff I fail to see how she dared to make any statement about our hospital there.[82]

The Committee did, however, respond to the complaints about the baths which had been endorsed by the staff. They ordered 12 canvas baths which would be much easier for them to fill and empty, bearing in mind that all water had to be carried. They suggested enquiring about the feasibility of erecting a bath house, thus picking up an idea from the difficult Miss Stevenson. There is no record that this ever materialised.

The shortage of doctors, and indeed of all staff, was becoming acute after the amalgamation of the two hospitals. Miss Ivens sent repeated telegrams for more staff: on June 6th 'work colossal'; on June 13th 'enormous pressure staff inadequate thousand patients in a fortnight 630 operations -'; and on June 25th 'staff collapsing send reinforcements'.[83]

She could be forgiven for feeling a little aggrieved when she sent a further telegram: 'Staff overworked London offering new hospital in France can they not supply staff for Royaumont instead'.[84]

The explanation is a curious one. 'London' refers to the sub-Committee of the Scottish Women's Hospitals Committee which was based in Edinburgh. They had a good deal of autonomy, were very good at fund-raising and were responsible for the 'London' units which operated in Rumania and Russia, and later the 'Elsie Inglis Unit' in Macedonia. It will be remembered that in the early days of Royaumont, London had raised money for the magnificent x-ray car of which they were so proud, and which had done so much for the prestige of the new hospital in the eyes of the French.

The offer of a new hospital in France had apparently been made by this sub-committee to M. de Piessac in the French War Ministry, and it was on the basis of this offer that M. de Piessac invited Miss Ivens to take over the hospital in Troyes. He assumed, naturally, that Miss Ivens, whom he knew well, and for whom he had the greatest respect, knew all about it and would be prepared to take over another hospital. When Miss Ivens explained to him her serious staffing problems at Royaumont, he was 'very puzzled', as she was herself. She was also resentful that in London they had so little appreciation of what was going on at Royaumont where the staff were working themselves almost into the ground. The 'Unit' proposed by London must have been a myth, she finally decided, and she wrote along those lines to Mrs Russell.[85]

There was now a pressing need for more ambulances to deal with the unrelenting flow of patients into and out of the hospital, and to meet the demands of the Army authorities to help out in other areas. The x-ray car was no longer required as a mobile unit as it had been in earlier years. Now all the hospitals in the neighbourhood were equipped with their own machines. So this car was adapted as an ambulance to carry four stretchers. Nor was the kitchen car, which had been so useful in the Soissons canteen, needed for that purpose. This was transformed into a lorry. The 'elephant' which, before the evacuation, had been regarded as of the 'white' variety, was now coming into its own. It could carry 20 patients. Always ready to use all the talent that was available, Miss Ivens applied for the permanent attachment of a patient who had great mechanical skills (the 'méchanicien'). He was very skilled at keeping their somewhat aged fleet of cars on the road. With so many very bad fracture cases in the hospital, a portable x-ray apparatus for use in the wards was becoming necessary. Miss Ivens and Dr Courtauld went ahead with the purchase, making use of money donated directly to the hospital. Miss Ivens felt she could not ask the Committee, 'having lost so much'.[86]

With so many mouths to feed, it was not surprising that stresses and strains arose in the kitchen. These came to a head when Simpson, one of the chief cooks (Miss Peternia M.B. Simpson (later Mrs Gray), cook, 12.10.17 to 22.6.18), asked, and was permitted, to leave before completion of her contract. There had been repeated quarrels with Michelet. Miss Ivens, recognising that he was not easy to deal with, had asked Simpson to make allowances for his 'temperament and nationality' – not easy when one is tired and overworked. Simpson accused him of frequent drunkenness though she later changed this to 'excitable'. Miss Ivens maintained that he had never been incapable. Unpleasant he certainly had been if Simpson's story was to be believed. During the rush the Matron had asked the locally employed kitchen women to wash their own floor, thus relieving the orderlies who were required for the unending tasks in the wards. When Simpson made these arrangements, Michelet responded by spraying the floor with grease (so Simpson claimed), declaring that he would tell Miss Ivens if she enquired that Matron had refused to have the floor washed, and 'he did not care if it should lie so for two months'.[87] (Perhaps he was 'excitable' at the time!) Miss Ivens thought Michelet's health and temper would benefit from a long convalescence, and sent him off, but was annoyed that Simpson then refused to take charge even with Michelet out of the way. Moreover she would not allow Simpson to work in other parts of the hospital as she wished to do until her contract was completed. Instead she dismissed her. Simpson told the Committee that 'she loved her work and felt that her dismissal was unjust and quite uncalled for'.[88] She may have had a point.

When the Committee asked Miss Ivens if Michelet was really worth all this trouble (he had quarrelled with other cooks), Miss Ivens stood up for him and wrote:

> If you had been here from the beginning you would know that the cooks had always quarrelled [some of these she detailed]. The usual cooks sent out are not capable of running efficiently alone such a big establishment, and chefs are at a premium. Michelet has his faults but *'cooks meat splendidly'* (my italics), and is devoted to the patients.[89]

She did not give in to the Committee but nevertheless made alternative arrangements which she hoped would solve the problem. She discussed it all with Jamieson ('a remarkably fine character' who had been cook at Villers-Cotterets and was also a close friend of Simpson). With Ashton and Madame Jeanne (a French cook trained by Michelet) they decided to use the kitchen hut for the staff and the night cooking, and, when Michelet returned from leave, he could have sole charge of the men's catering in the main kitchen.

On 30th June the steady, almost overwhelming, inflow of patients suddenly ceased. Miss Ivens went up to Senlis to find out why. She learned from the consulting surgeon of the Army that they wanted beds reserved – possibly 300 – for fresh cases from the front line. This was the period of attack and counter-attack. It was agreed that they would do so – the beds officially numbered 600 – with the proviso that the whole hospital would now be completely under Army control. Reporting all this to the Committee, Miss Ivens added: 'For the present we shall just go on working here ... but we should be ready to partially close down here and move when necessity arises'.[90]

During that first month – and longer – they had to work under conditions imposed by the nightly air raids. As Collum remarked: 'They interfered considerably with our work':

> It was impossible adequately to darken vast, ecclesiastical windows, hence we had to put out all lights in the corridors, halls and stairways. Imagine an inky dark corridor full of stretchers of newly-wounded – more stretchers being carried up pitch-dark stairways from unloading ambulances: more stretchers being carried out of theatres with unconscious men on them – the groping in the dark, with the noise of the guns all round, and then the shattering crash and dull quaking of a bomb! And in one of the huge wards [Canada, the monks' refectory] – a vast building in which one could place a parish church, with as many lofty windows – and in the half-open cloisters, nurses groping about in the dark, and men beginning to haemorrhage.[91]

As an orderly Summerhayes remembers how they were desperately short of linen to cope with the unending stream of casualties coming in and being

transferred. 'You put someone into bed with bloody sheets from the last man
– without time or sheets to change – that kind of thing'. She concluded – and
would have agreed with the difficult Miss Stevenson – that hygiene left much
to be desired, but unlike Miss Stevenson she took it in her stride: 'Well, what
did she expect?'[92]

Writing to her sister on June 27th, Dr Courtauld gives us some insight
from a doctor's point of view. She had been called from her bed at 5.45 that
morning to see one of her patients and was using the short space of time available before the daily rounds began again:

> Many of my patients are so bad that calls from one's bed to urgent cases
> are not infrequent – We had a tremendous noisy raid in these parts last
> night … the noise was tremendous with guns far and near and now and
> again the rattle of the mitrailleuse, and in the lull – we hear the horrible
> little 'hum-hum' of the Gothas hovering round. And my room got full of
> powder, reminding me of the taking of wasps' nests.[93]

They were still getting wounded, a score or so a day, but the wounds were
rather less serious and they arrived with only a few hours' delay. (A major
French counter-attack was launched on June 15th – in part from the forests
of Villers-Cotterets which many of them knew well). They were also getting
some German prisoners; she had two very badly wounded in her ward ('quite
decent youths') and a German officer (' perfect terror'). She was much moved
by the death of a young American aviator who died in her ward with his
young wife of only two months beside him.[94]

By July 16th when she wrote again the hospital was emptying – they had
evacuated almost half, in response to the request to hold beds ready for the
next attacks. 'We are ready for anything next', she said, but in the meanwhile
she was 'enjoying the lull immensely'. Her remaining patients were really bad
fractures with 'awful wounds'. This work was very time-consuming.[95]

Miss Ivens, recognising the need to relieve the stress, was trying to arrange
for the staff to get short periods of leave while this respite lasted – this would
also relieve some of the overcrowding for the staff. The younger doctors and
the new arrivals were sharing rooms and a house in Asnières was rented for the
night staff to protect them from the daytime bustle and noise of the hospital.

On July 14th, Bastille Day, the first ward concert took place in the cloisters. A welcome return, though briefly, to the Royaumont tradition.

The coverage in the x-ray department was giving Miss Ivens cause for anxiety, with two radiographers *hors de combat* on account of their x-ray burns. She
sent for Dr Savill to return to help out – she came though she had been ill
and was looking 'absolutely cadaverous'. However, just after her arrival in
July she (Dr Savill) was able to write:

> I am glad to say that I have arrived at a quieter time when all are tired.

Poor Miss Stoney went off duty with a bad varicose leg. She had worked like a Trojan, and what an amount of abstruse knowledge she possesses. We are a very harmonious and congenial x-ray department now. [There was perhaps a sting in the tail as Miss Stoney was known to be difficult to get on with.] My Mrs Large [Mrs Ruby Large (Mrs Wilson), x-ray orderly, 11.7.18 to 9.11.18, her radiographic assistant in her London practice] is a great success – liked by everyone and good at her work too. As no blessés are well enough to help now we have Smieton and Salway to run all the messages, fetching cases and cleaning generally. Anderson is first rate and delightful too. We had the two rooms going today. The tales I hear from all of Miss Ivens' courage, steadiness and superhuman physique in carrying on day and night without rest are really of a super-human creature, and she looks well, handsome and obviously cheerful and happy.[96]

However, on July 30th, orderly Simms was writing: 'Poor Miss Ivens, she has more than she can do now, she is looking dreadfully worn and haggard'.[97]

The long months of strain on top of four years of hard work had finally broken Mrs Berry who had to be sent home on July 7th with a complete nervous collapse. Dr Martland was the next to break down and she went home on August 9th. It will be remembered that Dr Martland had responded to Miss Ivens' appeal in the spring, and returned to duty in spite of Miss Aldrich-Blake's doubts that she was well enough. Whatever the strain she had been under, she had earned the lifelong gratitude of one American patient (Lieut Hickman, whose story is told in Chapter 5). Apart from the physical strain, the emotional demands on all those in direct contact with the wounded must have been great. The doctors, sometimes regarded as 'hard', were not exempt. Simms reported after a particularly sad death of a young American, 'a dear, very badly wounded but so brave and grateful, he died the other night, and *even the doctors wept over it*'.[98]

In mid-August Miss Ivens, with four doctors ill, was becoming desperate and asked the Committee to try again to recruit more doctors even if the appointments could only be temporary.[99] The Committee wired to three doctors but the only response was from Dr Potter. This, however, was very welcome as Dr Potter had considerable experience of battle casualties in very bad conditions with the London Units of the Scottish Women's Hospitals in Romania (Braila) and Galatz with Dr Elsie Inglis – who had described the work there as a nightmare. Latterly she had been at Reni. She arrived on August 16th.

On August 29th Miss Ivens wired for five more doctors to come immediately – those already there were on the point of breakdown, and Dr Grant had given notice. Dr Walters was feeling the strain and she too had to go home on September 2nd. A replacement came for her on September 3rd in the person of the American Dr Grace Hendrick, who had been working in the Medical College for Women at Vellore, South India and who had been one of an interested group of American women who had visited the hospital the previous May. The medical staff total was now down to 14 in August and 13 in September. Miss Ivens felt that the minimum number should be 17. They never reached that total.

A welcome return from the chronicler's point of view was that of the orderly Proctor who had recovered from her knee injury and now resumed her work at Royaumont – and her letters to her mother. She told her mother about the evacuation from Villers-Cotterets and how Miss Ivens was 'operating to the very last absolutely at her own personal risk – they say it was the most marvellous thing'. She had changed her mind from her original impression of the 'funny old bird' and had fallen under her spell, flattered that Miss Ivens wanted her back. She compared Royaumont as it was now with her happy memories of Villers-Cotterets – 'although I like this place it is not half as nice as up at Villers-Cotterets – we were just one big happy family up there – here it is different – military huts in the grounds to accommodate 250 blessés'. 'Several of the nicest doctors have absolutely broken down and have had to go home.' (She was particularly attached to Dr Martland and Mrs Berry.)[100] She went on:

> We have been fearfully busy here – having had convoys of blessés in every day for the last week – the poor theatre staff have been working day and night without ceasing – two poor things died before they could be relieved or undressed – one of our 'babies' died yesterday, poor fellow, it was very sad as he was the only child and such a splendid person – he had shrapnel in his legs, and they at last took him down to the theatre to operate as a last recourse, but he died under the anaesthetic. We are very busy and now we only keep them till they are well enough to be moved – the men come in direct from the line and have their ops done here and are then sent out.[101]

She was now working in the cloisters, 50 beds with a staff of 5; one sister, a senior orderly and herself with two other orderlies, quite new, and who had never even been in a hospital before. They had one male orderly, but he had only one arm:

> We have nothing but heavy surgical cases and the shrieks and groans that go on sometimes are too awful – it's awful to see a strong man yelling with pain at the top of his voice like a demented thing. – Miss Ivens is looking very well, much better than when I came home (in January). She is a most indomitable worker and has done and is doing marvels – so are all the staff.[102]

There were, however, some compensations which must have made her mother green with envy in war-starved Britain: 'Being "militaire" we get all the food we want – little white grapes, peaches, nuts, melons and pears. Butter and sugar are rationed in the hospital but we can buy in the villages'.[103]

Dr Courtauld takes up the tale on August 28th:

I haven't written much lately. One is busy all day, and sometimes most of the night, and hitherto when one does get a moment one is far too witless to write a letter. The French are not making any special attack on our part, so for that reason, and also because we have hardly an empty bed, we have had no new patients for the last two or three days. [After the 'Black Day' for the Germans on August 8th the front line was moving quite rapidly away from them.] But the wards are full and heavy, and one keeps on from morning to late evening, before one can get a moment to oneself as a rule. We are planning a big evacuation soon, 150 patients or so. Then Miss Ivens can ask for a train, one which has a doctor on board, so we can evacuate quite bad cases. So in a few days' time my own patients may diminish from 60 to 30 or 40.

I have some very bad patients just now. I have three niggers, all badly wounded, one very bad, but such a nice boy. All the niggers have a generic name of Sambo by the staff. My three lie side by side and talk in their own language. One is an immense man with a badly fractured skull. He ought to be quite still, but sits bolt upright in bed, and seems impervious to pain. I like the niggers much better as a rule than the Arabs of whom we always have a good many. An American boy in my ward who was terribly wounded died the other morning, and I had two days later to conduct the funeral, the second American I have had to bury. It is so difficult to get a Protestant clergyman here [why should this have been when they were only 30 or so miles from Paris, and visits from Protestant clergymen are recorded in the Visitors' Book?], so one of us has to read the service or part of it at the graveside, and just see the coffin lowered. Generally when I have done it one or two of our French soldiers are being buried. We try to fix the time that my car with the Protestant coffin should come to the cemetery just as our other car with the French soldiers' coffins has emptied itself from the church, and their service finished. But we meet sometimes, and yesterday I joined up with the French party, and after that was over, conducted my Protestant funeral, and in this case had quite an audience, as all the villagers, who had turned out as they always do in a kindly way for our French soldiers, stayed for our American soldier. Of course I read in English so I don't suppose much was understood. A new addition to the village cemetery has had to be made these last two years, and is for soldiers only now; French, a few English and American, a few Arabs and niggers are there and two Germans. The Arabs lie by themselves with their graves dug in the proper way, the head, I think, facing Mecca, and they have Arabic words and a crescent on their stones. The niggers have nothing, only a mound. All the French have stones [The names of 93 soldiers who died at Royaumont are now commemorated on a memorial in the cemetery at Asnières. This represents about half of those who died.].[104]

In October, with Drs Berry, Martland and Walters all having broken down and returned home, the remaining 12 doctors were soldiering on, but the strain was telling.

Dr Savill – already very unwell when she had returned to help out in July – struggled on till the end of September. Miss Stoney was back from sick leave but found her staff was almost completely new and in need of much training. She had to check personally all localisations (of shrapnel etc in the wounds) for the surgeons, and for over five weeks could not get even half an hour out. It was too much. She became ill (it may have been influenza); she had had an argument with Miss Ivens (unspecified, but, she maintained, justified); and she could not get on with the senior sister in the x-ray department. Miss Stoney was always very sensitive about her lack of a medical degree and this seems to have been at the root of the problem:

> The sister did not like to work under me as I was not qualified medically – it is a funny world – that I have four university degrees would count nothing to her even if she knew it.[105]

She decided to leave Royaumont as, with her asthma, she could not face the thought of the 'wet of Royaumont in winter', and went to Cannes for a well-earned holiday. Loving the work at Royaumont as she did, and in spite of the personality problems that beset her, she could not refuse Miss Ivens' invitation to her to return. She saw the hospital through to the end.

Miss Stoney was not alone in suffering from 'la grippe' – influenza. A form of influenza had hit the armed forces in July, but this had been relatively mild. However, in October the desperately serious 'Spanish influenza' swept through France, Germany, Britain, the United States and most of the world – a true pandemic. It continued unabated, well into 1919. The death rate was enormous. There was no effective treatment – and it spread like wildfire. It was reported that 70,000 American troops were hospitalised with the disease of whom one third died. Royaumont, although it did not escape, was comparatively little affected. Many of the staff went down with it as Dr Courtauld reported:

> I am convalescing from an attack of 'grippe', which I had the bad luck to succumb to about a week ago, after two days' work here only. [She had been on leave.] I took over ten sick staff among whom there were a dozen or more (sic) grippe cases, but of course it is everywhere about here as elsewhere. I have had a slight attack and came back out of isolation to a

room with a fire yesterday to my own quarters. It is nice to get independent again – the staff is shorthanded as you can guess with so many ill
and some really bad so there was a lot of staff isolated and nursing the
sick staff. Doctors are rather short – and the hospital crammed just now.
200 patients poured in all the night before last, none, or very few of them
really bad, … but taking notes, examining wounds, dressings, x-rays,
operations (if needed) even on light cases take up hours and hours when
patients flood in like that. – Our idea here is that directly a flu person is
well enough she rises from her bed and crawls along in the sun in the
garden and retires back to bed if need be, for there is no sitting
accommodation provided when one is isolated.[106]

They seem to have been lucky. At least it did not hit them when the worst of
the rush was on, their policy of isolation seems to have been relatively effective, and perhaps they had an advantage over most of the population, at least
in Western Europe, of being well-fed.

The number of patients was declining, but all through October and into
November remained round the 400 mark.

In October 1918 the Germans torpedoed the *Leinster*, sailing between
Ireland and England. 450 lives were lost, among them 130 women and children. This atrocity provoked an enormous outcry and hardened attitudes
against the Germans who had been making some tentative moves towards
bringing the war to a conclusion. Among those who lost their lives was Nurse
Fannin, who was on her way to Royaumont. Although she never actually
served at Royaumont, one feels her name should have been added to those of
Mary Gray and Dr Wilson engraved on the Monument close to the Abbey
which commemorated those who had died in the hospital. Her name is, however, recorded on the Scottish Women's Hospital window in York Minster.

It was typical of Miss Ivens that as the war was drawing to a close she
expressed a wish to 'honour at the Festival of All Saints the memory of the
soldiers of the Allied Armies who had died in the hospital at Royaumont' in
order that 'the tribute of our admiration and the expression of our sorrow
should be brought to those who had fallen in this the most noble cause'. The
ceremony took place in the local cemetery and was also an 'opportunity for
the families concerned – and of the entire country – to express their gratitude
to the Ladies of Royaumont – whose self-abnegation and boundless devotion
call forth our admiration'.[107]

Finally the day they had all been waiting for for so long was approaching,
the day of Armistice. Dr Courtauld:

Well, what can we say more about these gorgeous times than has already
been said? I have never lived through such a fortnight. The suspense of
last week as the climax was gradually reached. The three days of thrilling
suspense during which the fate of the Armistice was in the balance. The

gorgeous news which we got here, thanks to our General [Descoings] who came over himself about 8 a.m. on Monday morning to tell us. 'La guerre est finie', he said. The Germans had agreed to sign an Armistice and at any moment a message might come through that it had been signed. Doctors, sisters, orderlies went from ward to ward to spread the news. In less than an hour the telephone rang. We heard the Armistice had been signed at 5 a.m.

Then the hospital let itself go! From ward to ward went processions of orderlies waving flags, singing, cheering, and beating anything that made a noise. And cheering men greeted them everywhere. 'Vive la France!' 'Vive l'Angleterre!' 'Vive les Alliés!' Impromptu concerts began in odd corners and never ceased till all were in bed by midnight. The rope of the bell on the roof comes down by a patient's bed, and I don't think that bell ceased for five minutes except when food was going. How the cook managed it I don't know, but by 5 p.m. we had an extra spread in our great Canada ward, when nearly every patient in hospital, nearly 300, came in on beds or sat at table, scores of staff and odd maids also, so we must have had 5–600 there. Such a sight of flags and colour and merriment. General Descoings appeared also. Two of his daughters had been placed with us as orderlies. The fun went on fast and furiously. Miss Ivens and two others who have been here from the beginning (Miss Nicholson and 'Disorderly' Gray) were chaired round the place, then M.le Curé, then the cook (Michelet), then the General, all this done with our enthusiastic orderlies. The men had champagne to drink to victory and the General sprang on a chair and made an excellent little patriotic speech. Then the Marseillaise and 'God Save'. I have heard them often here shouted out by hundreds, but last Monday night it was grand. The General stood at the salute at the time we were singing 'God Save'.[108]

Then follows a description which may seem a bit tasteless to our more sophisticated times:

Then the staff and all the patients who could streamed out into the rose garden. There in a large open space had been erected a huge pile of faggots and straw and on top a huge effigy of the Kaiser. Miss Ivens set a match to it and soon the pile was blazing. It was a sight; the straw and wood flamed up high into the air. Then the Kaiser caught. His helmet flamed. A huge ring of a hundred or more went round and round the pile. It was a lurid scene. At last the Kaiser fell backwards and a perfect howl of hate rose from the patients. Some jumped as soon as the fire was at all low on to the burning remains of the Kaiser and tramped him out with curses and execrations. I fancy the French are a more revengeful race than the English. In fact we have often been laughed at for feeling so little personal spite, but then the English have not had the cause the French have.[109]

The evening finished with a concert in Canada Ward.

Dr Courtauld was not the only one to spare a thought for the prisoner patients in the hospital. She and Miss Ivens went in quietly to give the news to one of them, an Austrian. They felt sorry for the man, with his eyes full of tears and looking very depressed. He, however, rallied well enough, and in a few days was almost smiling and asserting that the Kronprinz must be killed and the sooner the better. Another prisoner put on fancy dress and enjoyed himself mightily with the French patients.

> Amidst all the rejoicing she was conscious of the fact that she had come through these years well-fed, and not a scratch, and having had congenial work to do; no sacrifice at all on my part – all on theirs. Two little mutilated boys in my ward who must die and till then a paralysed life as they have dragged out since last June are examples of the end of the war between them and me. One wept, when we were all rejoicing, poor little chap!

> I tell Sister MacGregor, [Miss Jessie Leslie McGregor, Sister, 28.7.16 to 18.11.17 and 2.3.18 to 30.12.18] the one in my ward, Queen Mary, that when the last patient has gone, I and the staff of my ward shall salute the 50 empty beds, salute the flags which have hung there the last four years and then walk out solemnly.[110]

References

1. Liddell Hart, *History of the First World War.*
2. IWM. E.H. Proctor, letters to her mother, 1.1.18. By kind permission of her nephew, Mr David Proctor.
3. McLaren, *A History of the Scottish Women's Hospitals,* p. 44.
4. Decassé et al., *Vie et Mort des Français, 1914–1918,* p. 310.
5. McLaren, *op. cit.,* p. 44.
6. IWM. E.H. Proctor, loc. cit., 27.4.18.
7. ML. Tin 42, Robertson to Laurie, 16.1.18.
8. Loc. cit., 8.1.18.
9. ML. Tin 42, Frances Ivens to Kemp, 7.2.18.
10. Ibid.
11. ML. Personnel Committee File, Dr Bennet to Russell, 7.6.17.
12. ML. Tin 42, FI to Kemp, 15.3.18.
13. ML. Tin 42, Collum to Committee, 11.4.18.
14. ML. Tin 42, FI to Kemp, 15.3.18.
15. 'K.S.B.', 'Through the War with a Motor Car', *The Englishwoman,* Oct. 19, p. 35.
16. ML. Tin 42, FI to Kemp, 25.4.18.

17. Ibid.

18. ML. Tin 49, FI to Hon. Sec., 20.5.18.

19. Dr E. Courtauld, letter to her sister Ruth, 25.4.18, by kind permission of her great nephew, Mr Samuel Courtauld.

20. ML. Tin 49, FI to Hon. Sec., 20.5.18.

21. Dr Grace Macrae (née Summerhayes). Personal communication.

22. Liddle Archive, Leeds University, Dr L.M. Henry papers.

23. 'Skia' (V.C.C. Collum), *Blackwood's Magazine*, November 1918, p. 62.

24. ML. Tin 42, FI to Kemp, 30.6.18.

25. Ibid.

26. Dr E. Courtauld, letter to her father, 31.5.18, by kind permission of Mr S. Courtauld.

27. Dr L.M. Henry. Reminiscences. By kind permission of her daughter Mrs Anne Murdoch.

28. Ibid.

29. Personal communication from Mrs Anne Murdoch.

30. 'Skia', *op. cit.*, p. 629.

31. NL 1968, p. 5.

32. ML. Tin 42, Georgina Cowan to Committee, 30.5.18.

33. NL 1938, p. 14.

34. ML. Tin 42, Florence Anderson to Committee, 1.6.18.

35. ML. Tin 49, unnamed and undated.

36. NL 1968, p. 6.

37. ML. Tin 49, loc. cit.

38. NL 1947, p. 9.

39. ML. Tin 49, loc. cit.

40. ML. Tin 42, Edith Stoney to Mrs Walker, 30.6.18.

41. NL 1968, p. 6.

42. NL 1928, p. 9.

43. ML. Tin 42, E. Stoney to Mrs Walker, 30.6.18.

44. ML. Tin 12, ES to Laurie, 17.7.18.

45. Ibid.

46. Dr E. Courtauld, letter to her father, 31.5.18, by kind permission of Mr Samuel Courtauld.

47. 'Skia', *op. cit.*, p. 628.

48. *Ibid.*

49. 'K.S.B.', *The Englishwoman*, Oct. 1919, pp. 35—36.

50. FL. SWH Collection, Collum to Committee, 5.6.18.

51. 'Skia', *op. cit.*, p. 630.

52. 'Skia', *op. cit.*, p. 631.

53. ML. Tin 42, Georgina Cowan to Committee, 30.5.18.

54. F.B. Simms, letter to her governess, Miss Grignells, 10.6.18, by kind permission of her niece, Miss M.P. Simms.

55. Dr Grace MacRae. Personal communication.

56. ML. Tin 42, FI to Russell, undated, probably 15 or 16.7.18.

57. Ibid.

58. 'Skia', *op. cit.*, p. 632.
59. ML. Tin 42, Ramsay-Smith to Laurie, 4.6.18.
60. ML. Tin 42, ES to Walker, 30.6.18.
61. NL 1938, p. 13.
62. ML. Tin 42, ES to Walker, 30.6.18.
63. Ibid.
64. ML. Tin 42, Dr Florence Stoney to Laurie, 17.6.18.
65. Dr Leah Leneman, *Brit. Med. J.*, 1993, Vol. 307, 18—25, 'Medical Women in the First World War – Ranking Nowhere'.
66. ML. Tin 42, Dr Guest to Russell, undated.
67. ML. Tin 42, Dr Guest to Russell, 21.6.18.
68. ML. Personnel Committee Minutes, 25.6.18.
69. ML. Tin 42, FI to Russell, undated, probably 15 or 16.7.18.
70. ML. Tin 42, D.H.K. Stevenson to Russell, 29.5.18.
71. Ibid.
72. ML. Tin 42, Stevenson to Ivens, 8.6.18.
73. ML. Tin 42, Ramsay-Smith to Russell, 13.6.18.
74. ML. Tin 42, Stevenson to Russell, 12.6.18.
75. Ibid.
76. ML. Tin 42, FI to Russell, 26.6.18.
77. ML. Tin 42, FI to Russell, undated.
78. ML. Tin 42, Agnes Anderson to Russell, 25.6.18.
79. Ibid.
80. Ibid.
81. ML. Tin 42, statement by Sister Thom, enclosed in letter FI to Russell, 26.6.18.
82. Statement by Miss Lindsay, loc. cit
83. ML. Tin 42, FI to Committee, 6.6.18, 13.6.18 and 25.6.18.
84. ML. Tin 42, undated telegram.
85. ML. Tin 42, FI to Russell, undated.
86. Ibid.
87. ML. Tin 42, Miss Simpson to Committee, 5.12.18.
88. Ibid.
89. ML. Tin 42, FI to Russell, undated.
90. ML. Tin 42, FI to Kemp, 30.6.18.
91. 'Skia', *op. cit.*, p. 637.
92. Dr Grace MacRae. Personal communication.
93. Dr E. Courtauld, loc. cit., 27.6.18, by kind permission of Mr Samuel Courtauld.
94. Ibid.
95. Dr E. Courtauld, loc. cit., 16.7.18.
96. ML. Tin 42, Dr A. Savill to Russell, 15.7.18.
97. Miss F.B. Simms, letter to governess, 30.7.18, by kind permission of Miss M.P. Simms.
98. Ibid.
99. ML. Tin 42, FI to Committee, telegram 7.8.18.

100. IWM. E.H. Proctor letters to her mother, undated, by kind permission of Mr David Proctor.

101. Ibid.

102. Ibid.

103. Ibid.

104. Dr E. Courtauld, loc. cit., 28.8.18, by kind permission of Mr Samuel Courtauld.

105. ML. Tin 42, E. Stoney to Laurie, 7.10.18.

106. Dr E. Courtauld, loc. cit., 8.10.18.

107. Account of ceremony kindly supplied by Mr Samuel Courtauld.

108. Dr E. Courtauld, loc. cit., 14.11.18, by kind permission of Mr Samuel Courtauld.

109. Ibid.

110. Ibid.

CHAPTER EIGHT

From Armistice to Closure

The Armistice was signed. It was time to start looking to the future although there were still many patients to be cared for. It was also the time for recognition of the valuable work that they had done. The French were generous with decorations, and as early as November 20th le Maréchal Commandant en Chef Pétain signed the order (11.726D) for the award of the Croix de Guerre to 23 members of the staff at HAA 30.

The ceremony took place on December 12th:

Today Royaumont was en fête ... it was a singularly picturesque ceremony, the beauty of the ancient Abbaye lending a touch of enchantment to the scene, indeed, for where in the annals of history before these last

Croix de Guerre ceremony, December 12, 1918 in Canada Ward. Doctors in dark uniforms at rear left, with other recipients gathered behind. Band of the Chasseurs Alpins on right. Village children in right foreground. Note precarious suspension of chimneys and electric lights.
(By courtesy of Mrs Anne Murdoch).

four revolutionary years is to be found any instance of a Women's Unit receiving military decorations at the hands of a foreign government for direct participation in war?

At two o'clock in the afternoon all the staff were gathered in the great hall now known as Salle Canada. The beds had been cleared away from the centre of the ward, but there still remained a row of them down either side. The staff stood at the far end, with those who were to receive the Croix de Guerre in a line in front. On the right hand side was the band of the 12e Bataillon de Chasseurs Alpins. On the left the infirmiers attached to the hospital were drawn up. General Nourisson, Général Commandant Direction des Etapes de l'Ouest du Groupe d'Armée Maistre, was to give the decorations.[1]

Perhaps they were a little disappointed that it was not *their* own General Descoings, but he had been posted to Alsace, newly returned to France. Dr Courtauld painted the scene:

All the staff who could possibly leave ... stood en bloc in order at one part, the blue and white of the gowns looking lovely ... the Chasseurs' band has a most taking way of giving a swing round and round high in the air to the trumpets which have gay tassels, before beginning ... Full uniform being the order of the day we were as alike as two peas.

General Nourisson and his staff arrived at 2.30, heralded by a fanfare by the Chasseurs with the double flourish of their trumpets above their heads. Then followed the Marseillaise with all the military party standing at the salute. Next, another fanfare and the citation for Miss Ivens was read out. The General stepped up to Miss Ivens, pinned the Croix de Guerre avec palme on her coat, and kissed her on each cheek.[2]

Citations

For Miss Ivens:

Forçant l'admiration de tous, a assuré de jour et de nuit le traitement des blessés français et alliés au cours des bombardements répétés de Villers-Cotterets en mai 1918. A l'approche d'ennemi, a replie sa formation au dernier moment sur l'Abbaye de Royaumont ou elle a continué sa mission humanitaire avec le plus absolu dévouement.

Then came the turn of the doctors, they also received the kisses on each cheek and the Croix de Guerre avec étoile pinned on. The recipients were Miss Nicholson, Mrs Berry, Dr Courtauld, Dr Henry and Dr Martland. It was sad that Mrs Berry was then seriously ill, and Dr Martland had had to go home

Doctors awarded the Croix de Guerre, December 1918. From left to right: Miss Ruth Nicholson, Surgeon, second-in-command, Dr Marie Manoel, Bacteriologist, Rumanian, Dr Elizabeth Courtauld, Physician and Anaesthetist, Dr Leila Henry, Assistant Surgeon and, sitting, Miss Frances Ivens, Médecin-Chef (Drs Berry and Martland were unable to be present at the ceremony)
(By courtesy of Mrs Anne Murdoch)

before the end of the war and so neither could receive their decorations in person. Dr Manoel, who was head of the laboratory services, and Miss Stoney head of radiological services, were also honoured. With Matrons Lindsay and O'Rorke and Sisters Goodwin and Anderson they all shared the same citation:

> On prodigué à l'hôpital des Dames Ecossaises tant à Villers-Cotterets qu'à Royaumont leur science et la dévotion au blessés français et alliés, sous des bombardements répétés.

Smieton, Salway, Armstrong (orderlies) and Daunt (Miss Dorothea O'Neill Daunt, orderly, 18.8.17 to 25.2.19) were cited as follows:

> Malgré un tres grand surmenage, ont continué le transport (sic: traitement?) intensif des blessés sous des bombardements répétés, faisant preuve dans dévouement digne des plus grands éloges.

The work at the Soissons canteen was not forgotten. Inglis (Etta), Chapman (Miss Marjorie Chapman, Auxiliary Nurse 6.5.15 to 22.3.19) and Rolt (Miss Agnes Louisa Rolt, Auxiliary Nurse 25.11.15 to 28.2.19):

> Ont assuré avec zèle et dévouement le service de la cantine de Soissons, malgré les nombreuses bombardements de cette ville.

Tollitt should have been included here, but she had been recalled home to look after ailing parents.

Collum, the assistant radiologist:

> Aide radiologue, zèlée et dévouée, blessée alors elle rejoignait son poste en 1916 à bord du 'Sussex' coulé par sous-marin ennemi.

Ramsay-Smith received her decoration for her work as 'gestionnaire' (Officier d'Administration), 'Doubtless the only woman holding that office in France':

> C'est acquittée de ces fonctions d'administrateur de l'HAA 30 avec compétence, zèle et dévouement dans une période critique et dans circonstances perilleuses.

Finally the chauffeurs, Murray (Miss Elizabeth Margaret Murray, chauffeur, 9.6.17 to 7.11.18), Fulton (Miss Katherine Fulton, chauffeur, 10.2.18 to 10.11.18) and Smeal:

> Ont continuées le transport des blessés avec courage et sangfroid au cours des bombardements de Villers-Cotterets et de Creil en mai et juin 1918.[3]

Decorations, citations, kisses and handshakes; the Marseillaise again, the General's speech, God Save the King and a salute. The staff and guests (there were plenty of them) filed up to the empty Blanche de Castille ward, to a really good Scotch (*sic*) tea, provided by Jamieson – scones and shortbread and wonderful plum cake. 'The French always love our Scotch teas', said Dr Courtauld, 'and try to pronounce "scone".'[4] The band played on down in Canada, photographs were taken, and conversation made (tiring for Dr Courtauld whose French was never all that good).

A great day for them all. *Dévouement* seemed to have been the order of the day – not to mention *zèle*, but they deserved it all. It was unfortunate that Miss Ivens was upset by the account that appeared later in the *Common Cause* (the weekly paper of the National Union of Women's Suffrage Societies). She felt that it did not do the Unit justice. It had been written by Collum, who had never intended it for publication – she had hastily written it out for a friend and was much distressed when she learned that the friend had sent it to the paper without her knowledge. Collum was also upset that her own citation mentioned the fact of her being torpedoed rather than the work she had done at Royaumont.[5]

After the Armistice there were still 141 wounded patients to be cared for and also, with their surplus capacity, they were once more admitting civilians from the neighbourhood. These were now 'flocking in', as Dr Courtauld wrote, 'to take advantage of treatment before we close'.[6]

The remaining doctors carried on their routine medical duties but also had to tackle stacks of paperwork to satisfy the military authorities. These were the dreaded 'Feuilles d'Observation' which had to be drawn up for each patient who had passed through the hospital. They had to follow a rigorously defined format. There were 'thousands' to do, Dr Courtauld reckoned.[7] 10,861 patients had passed through the hospital by the time it closed, and although clinical notes and army records had always been kept carefully, it is likely that a large number of these still required their 'feuilles'.

Two of the chauffeurs (Yeats was one [Miss Monica K.B. Yeats, chauffeur, 5.8.18 to 2.1.19]) responded to an appeal from a French corporal attached to the hospital to rescue his wife and a friend who had been imprisoned by the Germans. They were now free but isolated in the little village of Fourmies, eight miles from the Belgian frontier.

On December 9th they set off with a car and some provisions. Their route took them through Villers-Cotterets, Soissons, the Chemin des Dames (the scene of so much bitter fighting, and from where they had received so many wounded men), and Laon:

> Villers-Cotterets was much damaged and Soissons was in ruins. We passed through the Chemin des Dames and had lunch by the roadside and inspected some of the trenches and dugouts. This part of the front was by far the worst which we saw during the whole run – shellholes quite 30 feet deep and the whole countryside torn up and stripped of its trees, which are only blackened remains. Between Soissons and Laon the desolation was appalling, and all the villages which we passed being just heaps of stone and debris.
>
> Refugees with hand baggage were tramping along, worn out, begging for a lift in the cars which passed. One cannot imagine what these poor people would do when they reached their destination for not a single house was habitable. Also, if they do discover the remains of their village, they will most likely find it a heap of stones and rubble with no place to give them shelter and no possibility of buying food. From Laon to Fourmies, the country and villages are intact but these places were entirely cut off from railway communication and transport, this part being the invaded country.[8]

Arriving at Fourmies that night, the corporal and his wife were reunited after their four-year separation. The chauffeurs found they were the first British to enter Fourmies after the Armistice; they shared their food with the villagers who, in turn, found them a few blankets for the night. Next day, returning by another route, they found the road so bad they had to stop off in a village for the night where they had the choice of a cave, a ruined house or a stable. There was no water – they had to use the water in the car radiator to make their tea – 'and it was good tea too'. Another long drive took them through St Quentin, 'completely destroyed, the railways all blown up and the road for miles around had been ruined every 300 yards and blown up'. German prisoners were mending the roads, filling in mine holes with stones and planks of wood, but they had to make many detours:

> The desolation of all the places we passed through is past description;
> churches, cathedrals, raised to the ground, and all damaged beyond
> repair. At intervals along the roadsides, we came across lonely little
> graves of soldiers who had been buried where they had fallen.

They were distressed that there seemed to be no organisation to help people 'returning to what had once been their homes, without transport or supplies of any kind or means of building or remaking'.[9]

Their report probably had an influence on some of the Unit, as a number elected, after their work at Royaumont ended, to work in the devastated areas. The Committee were also moved and voted £100 for Miss Ivens to use for individual refugee relief. They were all curious to see the scenes of so much fighting, and now some of them were able to satisfy this curiosity – and who can blame them now that the country was at last cleared of the invader?

Dr Courtauld, with Dr Henry and Ramsay-Smith, the administrator, took a short 'congé'. With rucksacks on their backs, bread tickets and 'permission' papers they set off by train from Creil to Compiègne, and then on to Villers-Cotterets which they had known so well. There was no trace of the former C.C.S., only a few shell holes – 'not a patch of our garden to be seen – just waste land',[10] though Proctor reported there was one mud hut with poppies growing on top, where they used to keep butter and vegetables:

> The beautiful forest of Villers-Cotterets as we knew it in 1917 was
> ruined, leaving an occasional shell-torn tree, and scattered graves of
> Scottish Highlanders and English Guardsmen.[11]

(The forest had sheltered large contingents of Allied troops in the Summer of 1918 when the Germans had retreated from the immediate area, and before the June counter-attacks were launched.)

They moved on to Longpont, but it was not the Longpont they had known in early May 1918. Then it had been a

> lovely little village with a beautiful ruined Abbaye, a chateau adjoining, a
> lovely rural scene of buttercups and water meadows, wooded hillsides and
> funny little cottages – Now it is dreadful. I think there are three families
> returned, each to a room in a ruined cottage, the rest all shelled and a
> tumbled mass of ruins.

An unexploded shell still stuck in the wall of the old Abbaye and there were stray graves of German and French soldiers. Above the village the real battlefield was

> strewn with every sort of munition exploded and unexploded, and graves, German, French, and possibly English scattered about, lots with crosses and names, lots without, and often a post with a helmet stuck on top.

They explored the ruined farms:

> Dumps of bayonets, helmets, rucksacks, guns, shells, bullets, clothing, German grey, French blue, English khaki, all mixed together. In one mouldy unwholesome, shell-worn dug-out we found a copy of 'John Bull' of last June and tins of Rowntree's cocoa and Crosse and Blackwells' potted meat, and could easily trace English there.

They reached Soissons and recalled how the first intimation they had had the previous May that the Germans were really in Soissons was from a patient who had a huge iron bolt sticking out of his smashed hand – the bolt had come from the Pont des Anglaises in Soissons, where he had been engaged in hand-to-hand fighting with the 'Boche'. Further on, a big village, now a

> great desolate heap, not even a cat. I don't think I have ever seen such desolation of walls standing in dead silence, and just tree stumps and broken wood on every side. – A steep bank full of dugouts of the weirdest aspect looking across a steep valley to a ruined village – and graves by the roadside and graves even in the dugouts. Germans mostly just here. It is funny somehow to see side by side 'mort pour la patrie' or 'Gefallen vor (*sic*) den Faterland' written up roughly on bits of poles, or shell cases made into crosses. One often sees 'les soldats inconnus'.

By this time they were actually on the edge of the Chemin des Dames. There were miles of desolate country all round – no trees, no tree stems – 'just going on and on'. Trenches, graves, barbed wire, every sort of debris of war. Great dumps of German, French and English munitions. These were the front-line trenches. Then – no more trenches, no more barbed wire or anything at all but shell holes, some big craters, some smaller, and every sort of debris crushed in the mud, or sticking out, or broken down wire. This was 'No Man's Land'.

They came to Laffaux – the cross roads – where so many of their patients had fought:

> An awful scene of desolation – all one great upheaval of earth, – shells and shells and shells – bullets, gas masks and water bottles and boots and cloth-ing and wire and bits of gun carriages and armoured cars trodden into the mud ... and here and there a bit of a cross or a hole showing a grave.[12]

Deeply moved, these were the memories they brought back with them, and never forgot.

They were perhaps lucky that they did manage to return with their memories. Dr Henry, the young one of the trio, had collected sundry pieces of military hardware in her haversack. On enquiring from an officer in the inn as they relaxed beside a good fire, she was astonished when he made a rapid exit and threw them into the nearest pond. They were live hand grenades.[13]

Even after the Armistice Miss Ivens was still asking for more orderlies – she had enough doctors and nurses for the reduced demands of the hospital but orderlies were, in many respects, the backbone of the hospital. They could put their hands to a multitude of various tasks – and with impending closure there were still many tasks to be done.

The Committee and Miss Ivens were planning the closure which was to take place, officially, on December 31st. Mrs Laurie wrote to Miss Ivens on November 30th:

> Is there no possibility of M. Gouin in any way disposing of it [i.e. Royaumont] to Government or French Red Cross for convalescent purposes, such as a home for limbless French soldiers or TB cases or anything of that sort? It is so beautiful and permanently fitted up with its operating theatres, sterilisers, kitchens, with the system of electric light we have put in, along with the sanitary improvements and all the stoves in the different wards, not to speak of the operating tables and instruments, drugs, x-ray rooms and labs. To scrap all these seems such a waste ... to hand them over intact as a gift to be retained in the Abbaye de Royaumont would be a tangible and surely desired gift to the French Nation in acknowledgement of their kindness and graciousness to us during these four years of war.[14]

But on December 13th Miss Ivens wrote back:

> I have had an interview with M. Gouin and he has no intention of establishing any kind of home in the Abbey after we leave. He wishes us to remove everything we have put in (electric installations, stoves, laboratories, fittings etc.[15]

They therefore had to consider the disposal of all their equipment. Mrs Laurie again:

> It should be donated in a handsome way as a lasting memorial of what the Scottish Women have done in the Great War, – it would perpetuate a memorial of Royaumont in a fitting manner.[16]

After enquiries had been made, and with the advice of the French Red Cross Service de Santé, it was decided it should go to Lille which had been occupied throughout the war by the Germans who had taken almost everything with them when they evacuated the town. Not only had they removed all the brass, copper and glass utensils, along with the bedding and other equipment, but they had also broken up the bedsteads and smashed the floors of the wards. Equipment could have been of use to their deprived hospitals back in Germany, but the smashing of bedsteads and floors looked like sheer vandalism. In February 1919 the 'Commission Administrative de Lille' wrote to Miss Ivens thanking her for the gift of 20 railway wagons of equipment for the Hôpital Sauveur.[17] The gift included 400 beds and quantities of medical, surgical, x-ray and bacteriological equipment and other stores. One microscope and a special air pump went to the Pasteur Institute in Lille and another microscope to the Pasteur Institute in Paris. All the non-medical equipment – bedsteads, tables, cupboards etc – was sent to Villeneuves, one of the devastated villages, after the final closure of the hospital in March.

Miss Ivens wanted to do more. She had been asked by the French (and she regarded it as a great compliment) to take on the provision of a canteen at Mayence alongside the big naval base of Toulon – 'the most important and sought-after position for such a venture'. After her four years of working with the French Army, and the excellent relations she had built up, she felt this would be a 'tremendous opportunity to continue the promotion of the entente with France in the most favourable surroundings and also to keep the British end up when the tendency is now for the United States to swamp everything'. When the Committee refused permission she was 'sadly disappointed. We had everything here to fit it out, several girls with very decided musical talent, a cinema in first class order, a little stage – and several workers who speak French fluently – It is distinctly depressing for us to feel that the work we have done for the French is to be allowed to drop completely'.[18]

The Committee's negative response may have been due to their disappointment when the French authorities had been completely unco-operative at Favresse where Miss Jack had been running a SWH canteen. She had reported to them on December 2nd that she had hoped 'to have done something for the good of the poilus, but evidently it is not wanted'. It would seem that now that the war was over the authorities had reverted to their disregard for the welfare of the poilus which had been such a feature before the institution of the Pétain reforms in 1917. The captain in charge of the camp where they were working 'has shown plainly', Miss Jack went on 'that he does not take any interest in our work. It is very disappointing, but we are not appreciated and we are not given the proper position and all my workers feel this'.[19]

The Committee remained firm in their decision. 'The idea of canteens at Toulon was absolutely turned down.'[20] No doubt with the ending of the war many were getting tired – Red Cross activities were closing and a number of people on the Committee felt everything should now stop barring what they had undertaken to do for Serbia. Mrs Laurie, the Treasurer, would have liked to go on with Miss Ivens' plan – 'You cannot get them to understand that by having these canteens, we would get in touch with the Serbian students at Toulon, homeless, friendless laddies, waiting for the boats to take them home, and that this would be one of the best bits of work for Serbia, if it is really Serbia we want to give our assistance to. But there, you know how it is'.[21]

Royaumont being Royaumont, it was not to be thought of that Christmas 1918 should not be an exceptionally magnificent affair.

It began on Christmas Eve when all lights were extinguished and every patient lay in bed. Three big knocks heralded the carol-singers carrying lanterns, accompanied by Father Christmas on a sledge with a present for every man. At midnight some of the orderlies sang Mass in one of the empty wards. On Christmas Day itself there was virtually open house to the neighbourhood for the great Christmas pantomime – one that was to eclipse all previous pantomimes. Preparations had been intensive. The pantomime, 'Cinderella', was written by one of the orderlies, and the whole thing was spoken and sung in French.

There was a host of talent available. Two of the orderlies had been trained by the opera singer Marchesi, and another (Minchin) (Miss Irma Eleanor Minchin, later Mme Steinmann, orderly, 17.10.18 to 30.12.18) was a principal in the Margaret Morris School of Dancing. 'There is nothing', Proctor told her mother, 'she does not know about stage management and make-up and scenic effects, and her own dancing simply brought down the house and the men simply screamed for more.'[22] There had been a sudden panic when the horse's head could not be found. Etta Inglis and Chapman had *always* played the horse. Paris was searched frantically – with ultimate success. Tradition could now be maintained.

As in all good pantomimes, there was plenty of variety. A succession of songs and ballets: Widow Twankey (Howard-Smith), riding astride the Inglis-Chapman horse – 'honestly a second Dan Leno' – and when the horse collapsed in a helpless heap with Widow Twankey underneath – 'simply killing'. There was a splendid pirate scene in which the prince dashes in, killing the pirates and the wicked baron; a court scene with an orderly dressed as a wandering minstrel who played the violin 'absolutely divinely'; there were minuets and Scottish reels, and, as a grand finale, a tableau 'victory': 'A very good-looking sister, all draped in white, with green palms in her hair and holding a shining sword which scintillated and looked dramatic'. Emotion was never far from the surface beneath all the jollification and 'Many people wept'.[22]

Nearly 1000 people watched their pantomime, including two from the formidable Edinburgh Committee who joined in the fun. It was a grand ending to their long years of effort before the official closure on the last day of the year when 200 men were moved on. Only one ward remained open with seven men too ill to be moved. It was a 'lutte contre mort' in Proctor's picturesque phrase, for six weeks, with injections, strychnine and rectal salines:

> It is rather wonderful that these last dreadfully ill patients are being
> entirely nursed and looked after by us orderlies – all the trained sisters
> with the exception of the Matron who was at Villers-Cotterets were sent
> home, even the theatre sister, and we have had five operations – three of
> them amputations since. Of course there are none but the very ablest
> orderlies left who are auxiliary nurses and most of them have been out for
> three years and are covered with Croix de Guerres and other decorations –
> but still it is rather wonderful – isn't it! I am the most junior orderly
> again! There are only twenty of us left! [She was writing some time in
> January] – And up to a little time ago I was among the seniors![23]

Miss Stoney was having problems in the final clearing of the x-ray department – but characteristically made things more difficult for herself than perhaps they might have been. She had handed in her resignation and left
Royaumont on October 24th feeling very unwell after flu and bronchitis. She
'dreaded the wet of Royaumont in winter'. But she had another reason:

> I could not have worked with the Senior Sister – she used language I
> could not have passed over when I tried to show her the Gaiffe apparatus
> and other French things we have – new to her – which she therefore nat-
> urally could not work without getting it out of order. As I was likely to
> have to go in any case on account of my own health I thought it easier to
> go than complain and so force her to go. I don't want you to think that I
> left everything at sixes and sevens – I went over everything very fully
> with the x-ray orderly, Low (sic) [Miss Catherine Lowe, x-ray orderly,
> 22.8.18 to 31.12.18] who will be the person to keep the apparatus in
> order. She is excellent'.[24]

However, after a holiday in the South of France she felt able to respond to
Miss Ivens's invitation to return if she felt well enough. She came back, but
it was a period of great frustration for her as she told Mrs Laurie after she left:

> It was a great rush at the end in the x-ray department – hampered by
> frozen water etc and my assistants had to go on to other work long before
> we had got through the x-ray prints of all the four years – no regular
> record had been made before and one was necessary in case of questions re
> pensions etc. The War Museum of the College of Surgeons is wanting
> copies of all the stereo plates I was able to save – but it was a great disas-
> ter at the close – Miss Ivens put the x-ray plates out of my charge and
> into those of Sister McAlister [Miss Marion Jamieson McAlister, sister,
> 29.7.18 to 16.12.18] – she had not the necessary education to see their
> great value or to keep the card indices etc and Miss Courtauld has a story
> of seeing boxes full of plates thrown out and broken. This was while there

was still a great deal of x-ray work going on and I had all I could do –
but after the Armistice then seeing how things were going on of course I
took over the plates again, but nearly all the stereos had been spoilt –
The sister seems to have thought they were duplicates and destroyed one
of each pair. You must have thought me very slow and careless in closing
up – but I got bronchitis after influenza and that made what depended
on me slower – I had no trained assistant then – Knowing Royaumont
you will understand the delays caused by the cold in January – The water
wheel froze – the sluice gate was allowed to freeze on a very cold night.
This meant no water or electricity for the printing as for the other things.
An emergency operation had to be done on one of the five patients who
could not be moved when the hospital officially closed on December 31st.
The want of water made it unsafe to heat the theatre by its own fires
under an empty boiler – so the chief x-ray room with a good fire had to
be cleared and cleaned out in a desperate hurry – It is, of course, all in
the day's work in a front hospital. But I am only trying to show you why
I was so slow.[25]

It must have been a shattering blow to a conscientious scientist, as Miss
Stoney certainly was, to lose all this valuable material which would also have
been clear evidence of the quality of the work that was achieved by the Unit
during the war. The observer might, however, speculate, if Miss Stoney, with
her difficulty in getting on with people and her own sensitivity, could have
avoided some of this if she had explained what stereo x-rays were all about.

She had had her frustrations also during her service in Serbia with the
SWH. The x-ray car which had been sent out was unworkable (and if Miss
Stoney said it was unworkable it certainly was so) and although she had
shown that she could do x-ray work in Casualty Clearing Stations up-country
from Salonika, the lack of an operational car was sickening. However:

It was luck of lucks to get in for the work at Villers-Cotterets and
Royaumont – If the x-rays could not have been brought down and
installed at once at Royaumont – the huge mass of surgical work coming
in could not have been done anything like as well. Your surgeons are
wonderful – and I think the way Ramsay-Smith and the matrons and
cooks managed with that great increase of work and staff was grand.[26]

After she left in February her sister, Dr Florence Stoney, who was devoted to
her and fought many battles on her behalf, wrote to Mrs Laurie:

She is not at all well – it is the price she has to pay for the help she has
given during the war. Few people realise what the constant strain of x-ray
work in the dark and stuffy atmosphere and with the x-rays about – mean
to the worker – If she had been in the Army she would have had a pension, but *that is one of the things where it is hard to be a woman*. [My italics][27]

Edith Stoney was certainly a complex character, and had many problems with her colleagues – often of her own making. Dr Henry records that she and Dr Berry never got on together:

> I remember Mrs Berry taking me aside one day and begging me to take Stoney for a walk in the forest. 'If you do, I shall get you an egg for breakfast, and if you take her for a walk and lose her, I'll give you two.' And that was when eggs were scarce.[28]

Nevertheless she served Royaumont devotedly, and Royaumont certainly owes her a debt of gratitude. Mrs Berry, a generous and kind woman, kept in touch with her after the war and, as minor irritations faded with the passage of time, described her as 'a saint'.[29]

At long last, in February, Miss Ivens was able to take a proper holiday, her first real break since her arrival in 1914. She went to the South of France with Miss Nicholson and two other doctors – a sufficient indication of the strength of the friendships which had built up in spite of being cooped up together for so long and sharing so many stressful events.

Dr Courtauld was formulating her plans. Her first decision was to take charge of Spot, the mongrel fox-terrier with the comic tail who had been left behind at Villers-Cotterets by a British battery whose mascot he had been. Salway, the devoted orderly who had looked after him, could not take him home with her. Dr Courtauld negotiated his quarantine, and they settled down together for many years at her home in Essex. Her other decision was to 'work for a month or two amongst the devastated villages':

> I have had a fine three years' work with the Unit, and from one point of view it is a grievous business finishing it up and severing connections with one's fellow workers. But the experience will always be something worth remembering. My new work is to be under the American Fund for French Wounded which now really means work among the refugees. I am to be taken to Cambrai next week with a bed and a few household utensils and a dispensary outfit, and, I think, a nurse and an 'aide' are to accompany me. We are to set ourselves up in a ruined village called Caudry, somewhere near Cambrai, and make that our HQ and work other villages from there – giving material as well as medical aid. There are already some workers in Cambrai, so I hope to find out from them how to proceed. It will be rather an 'adventure' and I hope I shall be able to carry on alright. At present the people are coming back to their district, and there is practically nothing for them to set up house with, even if they have sufficient shelter. But in some districts already things are looking up a bit I am told – French doctors coming back and transport getting better, so help from the Allies will not be needed much longer.[30]

After all the adventure, excitement and freedom of their lives at Royaumont some of the orderlies were reluctant to return to a more mundane life at home. Some, like Dr Courtauld, worked for a time in the devastated areas. Others went to join the Cologne Leave Club, where Lena Ashwell's Players were entertaining the occupying troops. Cicely Hamilton was there, and her reputation was still high in Royaumont.

Three orderlies, Cranage (Miss Lucy M. Cranage, later Mrs Costa, orderly, 22.9.17 to 22.6.18), Stein (Miss Netta Hunter Stein, orderly, 2.9.17 to 17.7.18) and Summerhayes, entered the London (RFH) School of Medicine for Women and subsequently qualified. Some wished to continue working for the SWH. Grandage (Miss Katherine Grandage, orderly, 29.11.15 to 31.5.17 and 9.3.18 to 5.12.18) and Tollitt went to work in the London Office; Sister McGregor (Miss Jessie Leslie McGregor, sister, 28.7.16 to 18.11.17 and 2.3.18 to 30.12.18), Dispenser Figgis (Miss Ella Margaret Figgis, dispenser, 5.5.17 to 2.1.19) and Auxiliary Nurse Miller (Miss Marjorie Miller, Auxiliary Nurse, 30.8.15 to 28.2.16 and 9.9.16 to 30.12.18) transferred to the SWH hospital for tuberculosis patients at Sallanches, in France. Mme Manoel (Mme Marie Manoel, doctor, 25.10.17 to 21.1.19) also went there for a few months as bacteriologist before returning to her native Rumania.

Four of the sisters went on to work in SWH hospitals still functioning in Serbia. Two of them devoted many years of their lives to further work in Serbia: Sister Lawson (Miss Jean Henry Lawson, sister, 5.7.18 to 30.12.18) undertook the training of nurses in the American Training School (Serbia had been virtually devoid of nurses), and Sister O'Rorke (Miss Catherine O'Rorke, 25.2.15 to 24.4.16 and 15.9.16 to 5.1.19) worked in the Children's Hospital in Belgrade until her health broke down in 1930.

There were a number of orderlies who got jobs in Paris, postponing their return to a possibly less exciting life at home. As Proctor said, 'The Scottish women are very much sought after as we have a very good name and a good tone'. For her closure was

> desperately sad to think of and we all feel it most frightfully. Life here has been a wonderful experience and one never to be forgotten and funnily enough *Royaumont has closed at the height of its fame, which is a good thing in its way.* [My italics]

She, for one, was now absolutely convinced of the quality of women doctors:

> I could not bear the idea of them at first but that was only from ignorance and prejudice – I expect the idea of women doctors seems awfully odd to you [her mother], specially such young ones, but they are a splendid lot of women out here and work frightfully hard all the time.

Like many of the orderlies, she had matured – 'Women must do more now'.[31]

Mlle Descoings (Mlle Marie Descoings, orderly, 2.8.18 to 26.1.19), the daughter of their own General, who had been permitted to work as an orderly (foreigners were not normally employed), wrote with Gallic fervour of the 'deep regret' she felt at having to leave Royaumont:

> You cannot believe how grateful I am to all and what deep remembrance I keep in my heart. I have passed the happiest years of my life at Royaumont. The union was perfect, all the English were like sisters to me. France will never forget ...[32]

It was the Treasurer, Mrs Laurie, who summed up the contribution of Royaumont to the war effort when she wrote:

> It seems curious that Royaumont is of the past. Despite the hard work and many discomforts it has had a wonderful and glorious record of war work, along with Villers-Cotterets. I do not think even the Committee or public realise what extraordinary heroism and valour were displayed and hardships endured by the staff during the terrible retreat and ensuing weeks of work.[33]

And one patient, desperately ill, must surely have spoken for many when he said:

> Il y a des choses qui ne s'oublient pas.[34]

References

1. Dr E. Courtauld, letter to her sister, 13.12.18, by kind permission of Mr Samuel Courtauld.
2. Ibid.
3. *CC*, January 7 1919.
4. E. Courtauld, loc. cit.
5. ML. Tin 42, Collum to Cooke, 14.1.19.
6. E. Courtauld, loc. cit.
7. Ibid.
8. ML. Tin 42, Report to Committee from Yeats, December 1918.
9. Ibid.
10. Dr E. Courtauld, letter to her sister, 12.1.19, by kind permission of Mr Samuel Courtauld.
11. Dr L. Henry. Reminiscences, by kind permission of her daughter, Mrs Anne Murdoch.
12. E. Courtauld, loc. cit.
13. Dr L. Henry, loc. cit.
14. ML. Tin 42, Laurie to FI, 30.11.18.
15. ML. Tin 42, FI to Laurie, 13.12.18.
16. ML. Tin 12, Laurie to FI, 30.11.18.
17. ML. Tin 41, Hospital Committee Minutes, 1.2.19.
18. ML. Tin 42, FI to Hunter, 30.12.18.

19. ML. Tin 42, Jack to Russell, 2.12.18.
20. ML. Tin 4, Laurie to Robertson, 9.1.19.
21. Ibid.
22. IWM. Proctor letters to her mother, undated, by kind permission of Mr David Proctor.
23. Ibid.
24. ML. Tin 12, ES to Laurie, 7.10.18.
25. ML. Tin 12, ES to Laurie, 2.5.19.
26. Ibid.
27. ML. Tin, 12, Dr F. Stoney to Laurie, 23.4.19.
28. NL 1965, p. 10.
29. NL 1937, p. 10.
30. ML. Tin 42, E. Courtauld to Russell, 24.2.19.
31. IWM. Proctor letters, undated by kind permission of Mr David Proctor.
32. ML. Tin 49, Descoings to Laurie, January 1919.
33. ML. Tin 12, Laurie, undated.
34. ML. Tin 49, 1.1.19.

CHAPTER NINE

Friends and Visitors

During its long service to the French nation Royaumont gained respect and also friendship from many of its neighbours. Some were involved professionally, such as M. Pichon, the architect, and M. Daviaud, that 'Prince among Plumbers'.[1] Apart from his skill in updating the antiquated – or non-existing – sanitary arrangements, Cicely Hamilton described him as

> slight, sensitive, intelligent-looking, discharged from the army because 'poitrinaire'; well-read and well-spoken with a Frenchman's sense of the word. I had many conversations with him besides those relating to his professional duties.[2]

She, and some of the orderlies, kept in touch with him until the second world war.

After the war a few of those who contributed to the Royaumont community were awarded the medal of the Scottish Women's Hospitals. These included Michelet, M. Delacoste, Madam Fox and the Curé.

Some indication of the character of Michelet has already been given in Chapter 7 – his qualities, his efficiency and also his failings – but always, as Miss Ivens declared, he was 'a good friend of the patients'.

M. Delacoste was the owner of a big factory in the neighbourhood and an important man in the district. He seems to have taken the hospital under his wing very soon after its arrival. He was continually coming to the rescue when difficulties arose. When the vêtements department was almost overwhelmed in the early days he sent two of his women workers to help out. When the incinerators proved inadequate to cope with the ever-increasing rubbish, soiled and infected dressings and amputated limbs, it was M. Delacoste who provided them with a new and efficient 'destructeur'. When the staff found themselves with no place to eat after the refectory was turned into Canada ward, and winter was approaching, it was M. Delacoste who built them a comfortable wooden hut – and equipped it with a stove. It was M. Delacoste who built a beautiful tomb for Sister Grey in the churchyard and it was he who, after the war, placed a wreath every year on the monument to commemorate their dead. He was always a very welcome guest at their Christmas entertainments, and received a warm welcome when he attended one of their reunions in London. One of the attractive aspects of M. Delacoste's attitude to the hospital was the way he mingled respect with a degree of amused detachment. He could speak of 'l'héroïque phalange de

The Curé. M. l'Abbé Rousselle, Aumônier (Chaplain) to the hospital.
(By courtesy of Mrs Crowther).

Royaumont et de Villers-Cotterets' but could also refer to the 'Dames de Royaumont' as 'l'Opéra Comique'.[3]

Mme Fox was French, married to an Englishman who lived in Asnières. Her association and work for the hospital extended right through the war years. It began in the vêtements department when she earned the title from Cicely Hamilton of 'Adjointe-Directrice de Département de Vêtements', and later at Villers-Cotterets she was a most efficient manager of the cure workmen. After the death of her husband she became a member of the unit and was proud to wear the uniform.

Professor Weinberg was the leading scientist on gas gangrene infections. He was a frequent visitor for professional reasons but was as popular with the orderlies as he was with the doctors. Indeed they included him in their parties and even devised an entertainment specially for him. He was Russian by birth (from Odessa) but took French nationality in 1901 and from 1900 till his death in 1940 he worked in the Pasteur Institute in Paris where he rose to be Chef de Service. He had a reputation for blunt speaking among his colleagues but they recognised an acute sensibility and great kindness beneath his rough manner.[4] It was this kindness and sensibility that endeared him to those with whom he worked at Royaumont, and on his side he recognised the unique contribution the Royaumont women were making 'to further the work of the women's movement'.[5]

M. le Curé

In any discussion of the friends of the hospital one name stands out above all others. That is M. l'Abbé Rousselle, Curé of Asnières-sur-Oise, Aumônier (Chaplain) to the hospital. He was greatly loved in his parish, greatly loved by the *blessés* and loved and valued by the staff.

Possibly his supreme hour came before the arrival of the hospital during the Battle of the Marne. Collum reminded her readers of the terrible fate that had befallen the town of Senlis in the autumn of 1914. When the Germans entered the town, the mayor counselled submission and, in good faith, assured the Germans that the French troops had left the town. When some concealed French forces fired on them the Germans believed the civilians had deceived them. They took a terrible revenge. Using civilians as a screen, they advanced to clear out the French troops. Two of the civilians were killed. They then took the mayor and six other civilians chosen at random, marched them outside the town, and shot them.[6]

All the neighbouring communes were in panic. At Asnières the mayor and most of the male inhabitants fled the village. The Curé quietly assumed the office of mayor and each day, as the Germans advanced and the sound of gunfire came nearer, he stood at the crossroads on the boundary of his village, intending to plead with the Germans if the need arose.

Collum told the story as she heard it from the old postmistress:

Dawn came, and M. le Curé and Mlle Baignières walked out to the
crossroads, as all thought, for the last time. Would they save the village,
or would the Germans treat them as M. Odent, the Mayor of Senlis was
treated? It was dreadful to see them go, an old white-haired man, and a
tall white-haired lady, walking with a cane – and yet – Oh it was fine!
What a day that was – what suspense! No more refugees came through,
no more troops, – only a straggler now and then. And in the evening the
Mayor of Viarmes, M. Denain, came to tell M. le Curé that the
Commandant had had marching orders which neither of them compre-
hended – for the troops were not to retire to Paris after all, but to swing
across to Meaux. So the troops went, and we were left alone, and the
sound of the guns crept further and further away. Gradually it dawned on
us that a miracle had happened. For the Germans, after a week's
occupation and a week's burning and pillaging, had evacuated Senlis,
evacuated Creil, and their patrols had been withdrawn from the woods
and from Chantilly. The menace to our own little village was removed –
and we all felt very tired.[7]

The Miracle of the Marne had saved Asnières and the Abbey.

It was here at these same crossroads that the Royaumont Association
erected their monument to commemorate those who had died in their hospital, and their own two losses – Sister Grey and Dr Wilson. The inscription
reads:

Le 4 septembre 1914, l'ennemi est venu jusqu'ici. La victoire de la Marne
l'a empêché d'aller plus loin.

A la mémoire glorieuse des soldats français et alliés morts pour la patrie
aux hôpitaux des dames écossaises de Royaumont et Villers-Cotterets
1915–1919.

Les dames écossaises reconnaissant.

It was on the occasion of the unveiling of the monument in 1922 that the
Curé was decorated by the mayor with the Médaille de la Reconnaisance
Française. The citation read:

Aumônier de l'hôpital auxiliaire 301 de Royaumont, Seine-et-Oise, n'a
cessé, pendant quatre ans, de se consacrer aux blessés de cette formation
avec le plus entier dévouement, se rendant presque quotidiennement, de
jour et de nuit, à cette ambulance de 3 kilomètres de sa résidence. A eu
une très belle attitude au cours de l'occupation par les Allemands, en
1914, de cette commune, ou il a fait les fonctions de maire.[8]

M. le Curé was admired for his broadmindedness, for his charity and for his
courage. He was 66 years of age when the war began. He never spared him-

self and showed unceasing devotion to the wounded throughout the war. After the war his health gradually declined and he died on September 11th 1928. Miss Ivens used to visit him during her holidays in France. Quite by chance she came to Asnières on the very day of his funeral. She wrote 'how he had spent himself to the uttermost in bringing peace and comfort to the wounded soldiers of France. I left feeling that I and all of us, had lost a most faithful and sympathetic friend'.[9]

Collum wrote:

> This simple and unselfish old man at once established his influence over the blessés by his practical Christianity. He never considered himself, and he made no difference in his attitude to wounded men who were theoretically anti-clericals, with the results that he disarmed them completely and they soon came to love the kindly old compatriot whom they all respected from the first. His attitude towards ourselves was equally catholic. He never thought of us as outside the church to which he belonged. He loved us because we were doing our best to heal and comfort.[10]

Others remembered him in after years. Dr Henry spoke of 'that dear old man who walked miles every day to Royaumont with his pockets full of cigarettes and candy, and his heart full of love and sympathy'.[11] And Merrilees (Miss Anna Louisa Merrilees, Auxiliary Nurse, 4.9.15 to 6.9.17) remembered how he 'went without a fire for two winters in order to have money to buy cigars (*sic*) for the blessés'.[12] He shared in the rejoicings over the Armistice, and the orderlies showed their affection by chairing him enthusiastically all round the hospital.

In 1915, when blood transfusion was still virtually unknown, he wrote to Miss Ivens:

> Bonne et Chère Madame,
> J'ai vu, hier, le petit cher Salles, que vous disputer avec tant de dévoue-ment à la mort. J'ai pensé qu'il serait peut-être très utile de transferer dans ses veines un peu de sang régénerateur qui pourrait lui donner, avec la force de guérir, le moyen de reprendre toute son energie et toute son activité intellectuelle.
>
> Je me mets, en toute simplicité et toute franchise, à votre entière disposi-tion. Je vous offre tout le sang qui coule dans mes veines. Usez-en, je vous en supplie sans compter. Je suis tout à vos ordres. Vous me rendrez heureux, bien heureux, en acceptant mon offre. Soyez assez bonne, chère et bonne Madame, je vous prie, d'agréer, avec mes hommages très respectueux, l'assurance de tout mon dévouement en N.S.[13]

[Good and Dear Lady, I have today seen little Salles, for whom you are

fighting death with such unsparing devotion. I have been thinking that it
might be well to transfuse into his veins some regenerative blood which
might give him the strength necessary for convalescence and ultimate
recovery. I place myself, in all humbleness and sincerity, at your disposal.
I offer you all the blood that runs through my body. Use it, I entreat you,
to its fullest limit. You will make me happy, supremely happy, by
accepting my offer. I beg of you, dear and good Lady, to accept, with my
respectful homage, the assurance of my fidelity in the Lord. *Navarro's
translation.*]

They were always aware how much they owed to their *Aumônier*. In August
1918, when the hospital had been under great stress, Ramsay-Smith
reminded the Committee:

M. le Curé is a splendid old man who is devoted to the hospital and never
spares himself on our behalf. He comes over most days to see the patients
and writes letters for them ... as well as doing anything else he can for
them. He never asks for a penny for his Church or for himself – and he is
always so nice about the funerals – very different from the Maire. Instead
of paying him any fixed sum we have to ask him to accept a donation
every few months to defray any expenses he may have incurred for the
funerals ... Did the Committee only know M. le Curé as we do they
would realise how much they owe him and what a good friend he is to
the hospital.[14]

At the end of the war he was awarded the medal of the Scottish Women's
Hospital.

Enough has been written about the hospital to indicate how very fortunate
they were in having so many devoted and capable women on the staff. But it
was also fortunate that the hospital found itself in the parish of such a man as
the Abbé Rousselle.

The Visitors' Book

It was the task of the Hall Porter to keep the visitors' book and to record as
far as possible the many and various visitors to the hospital. After the war the
book disappeared. The Association News Letters carried many enquiries as to
its whereabouts. It was all to no avail. It seemed to have vanished completely.

By an astonishing coincidence it was discovered in 1974. M. Henri Gouin,
the son of M. Edouard Gouin, the owner of the Abbaye during the first world
war, discovered it in an antiquarian bookseller's. In 1914 Henri had been a
boy of 14, and had been a frequent visitor to the hospital. With his younger
brothers and sisters he had offered to help when the hospital was being prepared. He participated in their parties and organised some of the entertain-

ments. His close association ceased when he was called up in 1918, but it must have been an exciting find for him, at 74 years of age, to come across this record of part of the history of the Abbaye. It was unfortunate that the discovery came too late for the Royaumontites who would have so much enjoyed poring over it and reminiscing about the visitors. Nevertheless it does throw a little further light on the history of those eventful years.

One thousand, five hundred and fifty one visitors were recorded in a little over four years, though we know from other records that this is an underestimate. It is no wonder that the doctors, whose task it was to show visitors round sometimes, became a little weary of their continual 'dévouements' as they called their guided tours. Villers-Cotterets received its share – 139 during its ten months of operation – and the canteen at Soissons received 38 during its two months.

The Curé opened the book:

> Ai visité avec bonheur l'Abbaye converti si admirablement en ambulance
> militaire et offres à toutes ces dames de la Croix Rouge mes félicitations
> bien sincères et mes respectueuses hommages 19 decembre 1914.

There were many important officials from the Army and civil authorities. Lt-Col Rampont called no fewer than 12 times 'on behalf of General Joffre', the Commander-in-Chief, whose headquarters were at nearby Chantilly. On one occasion he brought a gift of cigarettes for the wounded sent by the Queen of Belgium. The 'Controlleur' of the Marne brought his wife, and in April 1915 the Chief Architect of the Paris police came as a delegate of the Servis de Santé of the Military Government of Paris. He declared himself 'happy and satisfied' and remarked on the 'happy faces of the wounded cared for so conscientiously'. This was when the hospital was, as all admitted, in a pretty disorganised state, with patients arriving faster than the equipment needed to look after them. One visiting General (name illegible) seems to have been very impressed: 'Il y a tout ce qu'il faut ... même les balais pour tuer les mouches!' (brushes to kill the flies)

The 'Directeurs des Etapes' (Area Commanders) of the 10th and 6th Armies came. General Descoings, of the 6th Army, they soon came to regard as their own special general. He and his family were real friends of the hospital, and, as we saw, his daughter in due course became an orderly by special dispensation of the Committee who waived the rule that all members should be of British parentage. With General Descoings the association was no mere formal one. An example of this was that he made a special point of bringing them the news of the impending armistice on November 11th, and stayed to share the celebrations with them. There were officers too at a lower level. One group in charge of automobiles in the Region came to study the organisation of the hospital fleet.

The Préfet of Pontoise, the Consul-General of Paris, mayors and priests of surrounding villages and owners of various chateaux in the neighbourhood all came to call.

The most important visitor of all was the President of France who brought his wife. They signed but left no message. Their visit was in 1916 after the great rushes of the Somme battles when the hospital had won such a high reputation. The visit has been described in Chapter 4.

Some visitors slipped through the net without signing the book. These included M. Doumergues, the French Government Minister for the Colonies, who was particularly interested to visit the Arab and Senegalese troops. He steered a considerable sum of money (10,000 francs) towards the hospital to spend on their welfare.

Naturally enough the hospital was of great interest to women.

The French and British Red Cross came to look, including the Présidente of the Comité des Dames Secours aux Blessés Militaires. Miss Ivens later reported to the Committee that this lady had expressed herself as 'very surprised at the idea of women performing operations'.[15] The Présidente-Générale of the 'Union des Femmes de France' came in August 1916. She was 'enchantée de ma visite et d'avoir vu avec quel dévouement mes (sic!) blessés étaient soignés ici par un personnel de Dames aussi instruit que zèle pour le bien'. The Secretary-General of the journal 'La Française' came with a photographer. Publicity was always useful. The visit of Queen Nathalie of Serbia in 1915 has already been described. She left a message which might have given them some amusement: 'Le coeur de la femme est un trésor d'où Dieu tire ce que l'humanité a de meilleur'.

There were nursing sisters from the French Flag Nursing Corps and from nearby hospitals, including the Hospital at Clichy which was under the patronage of the Gouin family. British women included Dr Mabel Gurney from the Hôpital Gare Maritime at Cherbourg who later worked as a civil surgeon attached to the RAMC. The distinguished surgeons, Louisa Aldrich Blake and Louisa Martindale, both operated on their visits. Dr Octavia Lewin (sister of Dr (Mrs) Berry), and Dr Florence Stoney (sister of Edith) came, as also did Dr Else Inglis accompanied by the Hon. Evelina Haverfield who went with her to Serbia, and later to Rumania and Russia. There were visits from the Womens' Emergency Canteen Corps at the Gare du Nord in Paris and from two groups of American women, in March and May of 1918. These included four women doctors one of whom, Dr Grace Hendrick, later joined the Unit and stayed until closure in 1919. There were visitors from Britain well-known in the suffrage movement, such as Ray Strachey, the Duchess of Atholl and Mrs Millicent Fawcett, the President of the National Union of Women's Suffrage Societies. Mrs Fawcett, unfortunately, was only able to come in January 1919 when almost all patients had left, but she would, no doubt, be shown the old chapter house, the ward named in her honour.

There must have been much eager comparing of notes when seven members of the SWH Unit from Salonika called in on their way home in April 1916. Violet Inglis was one of these and joined the Royaumont staff later that year.

Doctors were rather too numerous to mention, both military and civilian. Most were, naturally, French, but there were also visits from British, Canadian, Serbian and Australian doctors. Increasingly, as the years went by, and the fame of the hospital grew, doctors came from the American Ambulance and Red Cross Units. Some of the French military visitors may have come in response to the advice of Dr Bossières (Médecin-Chef of the Grand Quartier General) to 'model their units on Royaumont'. During the very stressful period in 1918 when the hospital was full of very complicated cases there were a number of specialists who could advise them on specific problems.

As far as clergy were concerned there were Bishops, Army Chaplains and the Minister of the Scots Church in Paris. It seems strange, therefore, that they could not find a Protestant clergyman to read the burial services when they were much needed in 1918. It will be remembered that Dr Courtauld took on this duty (Chapter 8).

Antonio de Navarro came several times to collect material for his book on the hospital which he published in 1917. Another very important visitor for the reputation of the hospital was the poet, Lawrence Binyon, who was writing an account of the British voluntary hospitals in France for his book, *For Dauntless France*. Lawrence Binyon is particularly known for his poem 'For the Fallen', so frequently quoted in Armistice Day services:

> They shall not grow old as we that are left grow old:
> Age shall not weary them, nor the years condemn.
> At the going down of the sun and in the morning
> We will remember them.

Lawrence Binyon was also a volunteer ambulance driver and his poem 'Fetching the Wounded' describes what must have been the experience of many of the Royaumont chauffeurs. He was clearly impressed by his visit and reflected that:

> If there had been difficulties at first, it was amply made up for by the
> warmth of recognition when it was seen how admirably these women of
> Scotland could administrate, organise, operate and nurse.

It has to be remembered that he visited in May 1917, when Royaumont was experiencing its strangely quiet interlude. He was struck by its beauty:

> There is a sense of old and large abundance in the surroundings, the her-
> itage of peaceful centuries ... On this May morning, when the cherry was
> in clouds of white bloom, the impression was one of singular peace and

beauty ... One receives an impression of airy cleanness and order.

The wounded were lying out in the cloisters; convalescents were strolling in the grounds and a merry party was setting off in a boat on the lake. Others were fishing:

> At Royaumont I was struck by the order and discipline that prevailed. The very fact that there are no men in authority over them appeals to the chivalry of the French nature ... One had a sense of happy co-operation between patients and staff.

He was impressed by their ingenuity, such as the pulley for the hauling up of the heavy sacks of clothing to the fifth-floor attics, and the use made of an old sewing machine and a dwarf harmonium to exercise stiffened limbs in the massage department:

> The women of Scotland have cause to be proud of their representatives, who surely will leave a fragrant memory behind them in Royaumont ... If any male doubt the capacity of women to organise, administrate and create a cheerful order, let him go to Royaumont.[16]

The first group to entertain the patients was the band of the 15th Hussars in 1915. Later they received entertainments from a group from the Paris Conservatoire. There were actresses from the Opéra Comique and the Comédie Française with the great Sarah Bernhardt herself. The Gouin family entertained them both at Royaumont and at Villers-Cotterets with a performance of 'English as she is Spoke'. The artist-sister of Mme Gouin wrote of the 'delicieux hôpital de Miss Ivens' (this was Villers-Cotterets).

The final message in the book came from the Curé who had penned the first welcome message in 1914:

> From P/Rousselle, prêtre, curé d'Asnières-sur-Oise et Aumônier de l'hôpital de Royaumont,
> Merci de tout coeur à Miss Ivens, notre médecin-chef, à Miss Nicholson, à Miss Ramsay-Smith et à toutes ces dames au nom de la France pour leurs soins devoués mieux tant maternels donnés tant aux blessés qu'au civils. Asnières-sur-Oise 21 mars 1919.

References

1. NL 1937, p. 2.
2. Hamilton, *Life Errant*, p. 104.
3. NL 1928, November.
4. *Annales de L'Institut Pasteur*, t. 64 No. 6, 1940, p. 461.
5. McLaren, *A History of the Scottish Women's Hospitals*, p. 38.
6. NL November, 1928, p. 5.

7. *Ibid.*
8. *Ibid.*
9. *Ibid.*, p. 4.
10. *Ibid.*
11. NL 1965, p. 10.
12. NL 1964, p. 9.
13. Navarro, *The Scottish Women's Hospital*, p. 209.
14. ML. Tin 42, Ramsay-Smith to Committee, August 1918.
15. ML. Tin 42, Ivens to Committee, January 1916.
16. Binyon, *For Dauntless France*, pp. 243–6.

CHAPTER TEN

The Hospital: An Assessment

The hospital at Royaumont was unique in many respects.

1. It was entirely staffed by women.

    To be accurate, there were two chauffeur-mechanics in the early years. This arose because of initial doubts about whether or not women would be permitted by the French to drive their cars.

    Then there was Michelet, the superb chef, who was seconded by the Army in 1916 following a period in 1915 when he had, as a patient, unofficially seconded himself. There was, from time to time, a recovered patient with a special skill who was seconded. Such a one was Etienne, the 'mécanicien'. Then at Villers-Cotterets some unfit soldiers carried out stretcher-bearing and other duties. Dominique, who rescued the canary Jimmie after the evacuation, was one of these. At Royaumont, in 1918, after the evacuation of Villers-Cotterets 12 infirmiers were attached. Later when the beds increased to 600, they were allowed 20 to 30 men, all unfit for heavy work, but who nevertheless had to carry stretchers, deal with the rubbish, carry the fuel, clean the 'cabinets' and do other unsavoury jobs, though orderlies still had to take their share of the unpleasant tasks.

2. It was under the French Red Cross and latterly under the French Army. It had no connection with the British medical services. It followed that there is no mention of the hospital in the British Official Medical History, and no British decorations were awarded to the staff.

3. During slacker times they treated civilian patients. This was not the custom in other voluntary hospitals.

4. At its peak it was the largest of the British voluntary hospitals in France with its 600 beds. Only the St John's Hospital at Etaples approached it in size with 520 beds.

5. Royaumont was in continuous action throughout the war from January 1915 to March 1919. (Compare this with the other voluntary hospitals listed in Appendix One.)

6. Apart from the St John's Hospital at Etaples, it seems to have been the closest to the front line.

Royaumont and its advanced hospital at Villers-Cotterets were in due course classified as Casualty Clearing Stations.

According to the *Official History* of the Medical Services in the First World War,[1] these were 'the pivot on which the whole system of collecting and evacuating sick and wounded turned'. In the early years this was their primary function. Later, as the importance of early operative treatment came to be recognised, their function changed to accommodate the new thinking. They could now hold casualties for up to a month before transferring them further back to the base. This policy was judged to have saved many lives.

It is interesting to compare the work of British Casualty Clearing Stations, as it had developed by September 1917, with the work done at Royaumont in the critical periods of 1918.

By 1918 the British CCS's were getting larger. – up to 1200 beds (compare Royaumont at its peak – 600). During a battle operations went on continuously day and night (as they did at Royaumont). The major difference was that the medical staff in the RAMC could be supplemented if need be from Base Hospitals (this was not possible at Royaumont). Similarly Base Hospitals could send forward more orderlies for stretcherbearing and other duties. At Royaumont orderlies and chauffeurs had to carry on regardless. In the British CCS's they worked a shift system which seems generous – not to say 'easy' – compared to Royaumont. For the first 24 hours of a battle they worked in the theatre continuously for 16 hours. This was followed by eight hours off. Subsequently they worked 12 hours on, 12 hours off. This was a far cry from the hours worked by the Royaumont women. For instance in the Somme rush (Chapter 4) several had no more than 16 hours' sleep in eight days, and three hours' consecutive sleep was an almost unbelievable luxury.

In the RAMC the record number of operations carried out in 24 hours was held by No. 3 CCS in August 1917. This was 103. The maximum was seldom over 80 in the 24 hours. This was carried out by a team of 12 to 16 surgeons. Compare this with the number of operations and staff available to carry them out at Royaumont in 1918. For example:

April 7th to 8th (24 hours). 80 operations performed.
Between March 23 and April 23. 437 patients admitted; 369 operations performed.
Between May 31 and June 30. 1240 admitted; 891 operations performed.
In April there were 12 doctors in all, shared between the two hospitals.
In May there were 14 and in June, when the two hospitals were combined in the abbey, there were 16. Of these, 11 were surgeons.

In the British Army a scheme was evolved whereby any one CCS was required to admit a total of 150 cases when a battle commenced. When that total was reached, all further casualties were switched to another CCS in the area, so the staff of the first could concentrate on follow-up treatment and disposal of the wounded. A further improvement was then made, whereby two adjoining CCS's shared the first 200 cases, so that both were fully occupied from the beginning of the battle, and not sitting idle while the other filled up. There was no relief of this sort for Royaumont. The flow of casualties remained continuously high for at least a month after the Villers-Cotterets evacuation. As they evacuated, they filled up again immediately. The casualties received at Royaumont and at Villers-Cotterets were as serious as any that reached a CCS.

It does not seem to have been recorded how many of the medical staff in the British forces broke down under the strain. Given the intensity of work at Royaumont in 1918, it would have been surprising if there had been no breakdowns. There were no relief arrangements available to them as there were in the RAMC. That there were only three who broke down is a tribute to the remarkable stamina demonstrated by the majority. Some of them probably did not realise themselves how much stamina they had. Certainly they made it difficult for sceptics to maintain that women were too weak for the heaviest demands in wartime conditions. Miss Ivens herself was a perfect example of stamina in the face of great challenges, but there were also others, particularly Miss Nicholson on whom fell, with Miss Ivens, the greatest burden of the major surgery.

The Work of the Hospital

The total number of patients treated in the hospital (including Villers-Cotterets) was 10,861. Of these, 8752 were soldiers, among whom there were 159 deaths. This gives a death rate of 1.82%. 572 civilians were admitted and a further 1537 were treated as out-patients. Of those admitted, 25 (4.5%) died. They were probably older, less fit and less well-fed than the soldiers (the husband of Mme. Fox was one of these).

Although the great majority of soldier patients were battle casualties, there was also a range of conditions requiring surgical treatment. At intervals there were some admitted sick. Among the civilian patients women and children predominated, and some small rooms were set aside for them if admission was required. There was also the occasional civilian casualty from the munitions factories (Madeleine in 1916 was one of these).

Treatment

The treatment of battle casualties in World War One took place when medical science had comparatively little to offer compared to what is available today. The type of injury had changed from previous wars: more wounds from shrapnel and machine gun fire, and fewer from single bullets or hard steel. New techniques had to be learned. Moreover the conditions in which wounds were received had not been met in previous wars, or indeed in any of the other theatres of war in 1914–1919. The well-manured and heavily contaminated soil of Northern France – all too often a sea of mud – harboured the organisms of gas gangrene, tetanus and the streptococcus, to mention only the most deadly. How to deal with these and other infections was one of the most urgent tasks facing the medical services in that pre-antibiotic era.

The use of antiseptics was soon abandoned as positively harmful. Various fluids were used for continuous irrigation of wounds, and tubes used to enable the fluids to reach the opened-up wounds. At Royaumont they experimented with a number of different fluids, all of which being used in the British Army, and after extensive trials settled on their own preference of 5% saline with 2½% carbolic acid. The principles of surgical treatment were learned including excision of damaged tissue and free drainage of wounds, all to be carried out as early as possible.

Anaesthetics were usually open ether, or sometimes chloroform, though later on nitrous oxide and oxygen were used. The relief of pain was generally inadequate: aspirin, morphia or a general anaesthetic were all they had to offer. They followed a routine of frequent dressings which must have been very painful – nowadays these might be considered excessive and possibly unnecessary. Their surgical techniques would appear to have been of a high standard. They earned the respect of medical visitors and inspectors, including Dr Erskine who visited them from the Committee in September 1916.

They followed new developments – Miss Ivens recalled later how they all studied Sir Robert Jones's classical paper on the treatment of fractures, and how it was referred to again and again. They all became adept in the use of the Thomas's splint which did so much not only to promote healing of lower limb fractures, but also to reduce pain, and mortality. Miss Ivens recalled their distress when a consignment of badly needed Thomas's splints finally arrived – only to find they were all children's sizes.[2] In training the staff Miss Ivens was careful to emphasise the importance of avoiding pressure in avoiding the worst consequences of gas gangrene. The doctors were encouraged to follow their patients to the x-ray department whenever possible to learn, among other things, the detection of gas in the tissues. Through her friendship with Sir Robert Jones she was able to obtain the services of his most highly trained sister who stayed for a month and gave many demonstrations of his methods in the treatment of fractures. When a new technique of 'primary suture' of wounds was introduced by the French Professor Tuffier in 1918, Miss Ivens adopted it in very carefully selected cases. This technique depended not only on very meticulous bacteriology but also on close observation and very sound judgement.

'Masseuses' (the old term for physiotherapists) were employed from the autumn of 1915 until January 1919. Their techniques would be less sophisticated than they would be today. They used certain forms of electro-therapy for the stimulation of damaged muscles and nerves. Dr Savill was responsible for this as well as the x-ray department. Movement, both active and passive, was encouraged. Mrs Berry was recognised to be particularly skilful and patient in the manipulation of damaged fingers and restoring movement. In the massage department, as we learned from the poet Lawrence Binyon, they showed their ingenuity in utilising an old treadle sewing machine and a dwarf harmonium for active exercise of the leg muscles. Where apparatus could not be provided, they improvised.

It is difficult to judge the quality overall of the nursing care. In the beginning there were a number who could not adapt themselves to the very different work and working conditions of a hospital in the unforeseen conditions of wartime. The quality of nurses showed a steady improvement as time went on. However, recruitment of new nurses became increasingly difficult in the last year of the war when nurses were in very short supply everywhere. Miss Ivens met some of these difficulties by appointing the best and most intelligent of her orderlies to be Auxiliary Nurses, and this was highly successful. Throughout there were always some senior nurses who were of very high quality and Royaumont was fortunate in earning their devotion. They worked particularly well in the rushes of 1916 and the prolonged stress of 1918. Many of these went on after the war to rise high in the nursing profession. We know that the medical documentation of the wounded was carried out meticulously as Dr Henry included many nursing charts in her MD thesis on gas gangrene which she wrote after the war,[3] and Miss Ivens was careful to ensure that vital medical records were sent back to Royaumont when it became clear that evacuation from Villers-Cotterets was imminent.

One aspect of nursing care must have been a real problem for the nurses in 1918. Dr MacRae, looking back in her 99th year to her time as an orderly in 1918, felt that though the surgery at Royaumont was excellent the hygiene was not. This is not very surprising when one remembers the rapid flow of desperately wounded patients in May, June and July. The shortage of linen became acute, and she remembers having to put new arrivals in the bloodstained sheets of the previous occupant.[4] However, in quieter periods Royaumont was famous for its cleanliness and order.

Training of the staff was taken seriously. It was particularly successful in the x-ray department. Collum, a freelance journalist on her arrival, only had experience as an amateur photographer to offer, but became a highly skilled technician, especially in the localisation of foreign bodies. Buckley was an undergraduate at Cambridge and had partially completed her medical training when she came to Royaumont and worked in the x-ray department. After the war and completion of her training she became a distinguished radiologist and served in the RAMC in the Second World War as a consultant. Her experience at Royaumont probably determined her future career. Other x-ray orderlies were singled out for praise by Dr Savill and Miss Stoney as 'excellent', and in the laboratory Dr Dalyell had a high opinion of Smieton, her orderly assistant.

In 1915 Royaumont attracted the attention of Professor Weinberg of the

On the left General Descoings – 'their own general' – and on the right Professor
Weinberg of the Pasteur Institute, distinguished scientist and expert on gas gangrene.
(By courtesy of Mrs Crowther).

Pasteur Institute in Paris who was working on the development of anti-gas gangrene sera. He was so impressed with the efficiency of the hospital, and in particular the laboratory work, that he selected it as one of the hospitals in which his new sera were to be tried out as they were developed. 'He had', he said, 'seen hundreds and hundreds [an exaggeration, surely!] of military hospitals, but none, the organisation and direction of which won his admiration so completely'. The gas gangrene trials continued throughout the war, and Royaumont was able, with its high degree of surgical skill, to achieve excellent results. (Details of this work are given in Appendix Two). They had a great advantage here over the British medical services who only obtained sera towards the end of the war, sera which were of far lower efficiency than the French sera.

If the hospital at Royaumont had an advantage over British hospitals in the treatment of gas gangrene, it was at a disadvantage regarding blood transfusion. By 1917 this was slowly becoming organised in the RAMC (the major developments were due to the Americans, many of whom were involved in voluntary units before the United States was officially in the war), but it does not seem to have been available to the French, and it was on the French that the hospital had to rely. They were forced to use less effective forms of fluid replacement though they did seem to have realised its importance.

Apart from the purely medical and surgical treatment, some of the good results that were obtained could have been due, in part, to the generally happy atmosphere, the beauty and peace of that lovely building and the woods surrounding it. Navarro wrote, 'and when evening has come, a night of silence and of stars – the soothing babble of the fountain lulling the nerve-racked sufferers to sleep'.[5] (Navarro, of course, was writing in 1917, before the nightly visits of the Gothas rendered the abbey less peaceful in 1918.)

Open-air treatment was a feature of Royaumont. Another factor which probably contributed to the recovery of the patients was the excellence of the food. There were shortages, of course, from time to time, but overall they were probably far better fed than in almost any other hospital. Some, possibly a very large part, was due to Michelet, not only an excellent chef, but also a bit of a genius at finding supplies.

Unquestionably, on the outbreak of war French services for the collection, transport and treatment of the wounded were very defective. They had envisaged a short war and were totally unprepared for the scale of the casualties. Compared with the British and German armies, over the whole period of the war the French experienced the highest ratio of deaths among the wounded. In addition to 895,000 men killed in action, almost half as many again died from wounds or sickness.

In France public concern rose steadily over the appallingly bad facilities for treating the wounded. This reached a climax in August 1915 when a debate took place in the Chamber of Deputies which almost precipitated a political crisis. The arrangements for dealing with the casualties from the Battle of the Marne (1914) were described as 'most casual'. An example was given where 1200 wounded men were sent to a place where there was not a single bed to receive them. There were no hospital trains, only cattle trucks, and journeys could take days. Hospital equipment was hopelessly inadequate. Linen, clothing, instruments and appliances were all in short – very short – supply. Hospital orderlies had no training, and no effort was made to heat the hospitals. Medical officers were desperate. They were totally dependent on the Medical Department of the War Office. One senior officer received a reply from a lay official in the department – 'Your demands are justified in principle, but they are too numerous, and will end by trying the patience of the Minister'. The debate continued the following week when the Minister claimed that improvements had been made. The Deputies seem to have been unconvinced and endorsed the principle that 'the less non-medical ministers meddled with professional details, the better'. The debate was clearly becoming uncomfortable for the Government. It was continued the following week, but this time was held in camera.[6]

After this disastrous beginning many improvements did occur in the French medical services as the war progressed. The story of Royaumont shows how greatly it was valued by the doctors administering the services in the field, not only for the work it did but also for the example it set.

It was fortunate for Royaumont that it had a determined, effective and conscientious Committee behind it to keep the supplies flowing, often with great difficulty. Naturally there were some shortages from time to time but the records do not suggest that these were ever as desperate as those suffered by the French military hospitals.

The Committee at home learned to appreciate the valuable work being carried out on their behalf at Royaumont. In September 1916 Dr Erskine, a medical member of the Committee, wrote:

To begin with, we would emphasise to the Committee the magnificent quality of the work that is being done at the Hospital. On all sides we found that this was cordially recognised by the French authorities. Over and over again, the Officers of the Service de Santé have expressed their pleased surprise at the number of limbs that have been saved from amputation – and at the numbers of men who recover. They show their appreciation by sending into the hospital the very serious cases that it would be dangerous to send further. During the recent advance of the French all the severe cases of gas gangrene were sent in to Royaumont somewhat to the astonishment of some of the Paris hospitals. Many of these cases were saved by the prompt and skilful treatment they received, the percentage of recovery being wonderfully high considering the severity of the condition.[7]

One of the objects of Dr Erskine's visit was to investigate if there was need-less extravagance. She reported that in this supposition, which she had shared, she was mistaken:

> ... I think the Committee can discount the prevalent rumours of extrava-gance as being without foundation. That the hospital is expensive to run is, unfortunately, true, but the conditions render this inevitable. The initial error lay in fixing on such a building which, though beautiful in the extreme, has certain disadvantages when considered as a hospital. The following are instances:

1. The fact that no hot water is laid on throughout the house – that ward utensils etc have to be carried sometimes considerable distances to be emp-tied and cleansed, thus entailing much labour and a much larger staff than would otherwise be required.
2. That there are no lifts of any sort, so that all food has to be carried from the kitchens by hand, and all patients carried on stretchers up and down stairs when required for operation or for x-ray examination.
3. That to keep the place tolerably warm a large expenditure of fuel is necessary.
4. That the distance from a railway station and the fact that the hospital is situated in a military zone, further enhances the price of supplies which are even dearer than in the country.

The memorial in Asnières Cemetery to those soldiers who died in the hospital and were buried locally. (This is half of those who died. 'Soldat inconnu' is recorded bottom right).

On the other hand the advantages of the place must not be forgotten. The extreme beauty of the surroundings – the spacious airiness of the wards – the facilities for open-air treatment, are points of great value and are in strong contrast to the conditions prevailing in other hospitals in the vicinity. No doubt all of these contribute to the success that has attended the work of the staff.

She saw no way to reduce expenditure – in fact she expected it to rise:

I had to revolutionise my ideas as to the amount of dressings required. I have to admit that I was quite mistaken in my estimate. I went round the wards of the various doctors and saw the majority of the cases being dressed and certainly could discover no waste … But the amount of

The Royaumont Monument, erected after the war, commemorates all those who died in the hospital. It stands one mile from the Abbey at the crossroads where the curé stood to plead for the safety of his village of Asnières in September 1914 as the German advance was halted – 'The Miracle of the Marne'. An inscription on the back records the names of two members of staff who died, Sister Gray and Dr Wilson.

dressings required by these extremely septic cases was certainly a revelation to me. The conditions I found were not at all comparable to anything in this country. ... The Committee have to bear in mind that the work done is probably *on a much larger scale and of greater value than that done in any of the other SWH Units* [my italics]. This arises from the circumstances and must in no way be taken as implying any disparagement of the other units.[8]

When Royaumont finally closed in 1919, Mrs Laurie (the Treasurer) reminded the Committee:

Despite the hard work and many discomforts it has had a wonderful and glorious record of war work, along with Villers-Cotterets. *I do not think even the Committee or public thoroughly realise what extraordinary heroism and valour were displayed and hardships endured by the staff during the terrible retreat and ensuing weeks of work.* [My italics][9]

Reflecting on the hospital in 1928, one member of the Unit wrote:

Women's work will be judged, not by the bravery of the women and their readiness to face danger and death, but by its economic results – by the number of men their hospitals were able to restore to the effective forces, whether in the army or in the militarised industry, for a given number of days of hospitalisation and for a given expenditure of money and personnel. We do not boast when we claim that Royaumont, from this point of view, is in a unique position of having functioned uninterruptedly from 1914 to 1919, and hence of providing the only data that will be of any value to posterity as an example of consistent evolution and well-tested efficiency during an entire campaign.[10]

References

1. *Official History of the War. Medical Services, Vol 2*, pp. 49–50.
2. Frances Ivens-Knowles, *Brit. Med. J.*, Nov. 25 1939, p. 1058.
3. L.M. Henry, 'The Treatment of War Wounds by Serum Therapy'. MD thesis, University of Sheffield.
4. Dr Grace MacRae. Personal communication.
5. Navarro, *The Scottish Women's Hospital.*
6. *Brit. Med. J.*, Aug. 21 1915, p. 301 and Aug. 28 1915, p. 334.
7. ML. Tin 42, Erskine and Low, Report to Committee, 16.9.16.
8. *Ibid.*
9. ML. Tin 12, Laurie, undated (1919).
10. NL 1928, November, p. 3.

PART TWO

The Women

Miss Ivens wearing her Légion d'Honneur.
(By courtesy of the Archivist, Royal Free Hospital School of Medicine).

CHAPTER ELEVEN

Miss Frances Ivens, CBE, MS (Lond), ChM (Liverp), FRCOG (1870–1944)

'Quels yeux, quel esprit, quelle femme.'

It is clear from the history of the hospital that there was a very remarkable woman at its head. This chapter covers her early life and subsequent career, and records an impression of her personality and the opinions of her friends.

Mary Hannah Frances Ivens was born in 1870, the fifth and youngest surviving child of William Ivens and his wife Elizabeth (née Ashmole). Her father was a successful timber merchant – 6' 6" tall and reputedly 'the handsomest man in Warwickshire'. He was described as 'a man of rare ability with a most attractive personality'.[1] Frances probably inherited much of her drive and organising ability from him. When he was only ten and at boarding school, the story goes that he was sent home because he had fainted in class. 'The boy's outgrown his strength, Mrs Ivens', his headmaster wrote. 'Give him port wine and pound cake. Let him go out and help with the hay.' That seems to have been the end of his formal education, and he was apprenticed to a timber merchant. At the age of 17 he was ready to go out on his own with the purchase of a large number of elm trees which had blown down in the grounds of Rugby School. These he sold to the Admiralty, a deal which led to a contract which continued after his own death many years later. He prospered and his family had what could be described as a comfortable background in a handsome house in the small village of Harborough Parva in Warwickshire.

Frances was proud of her mother's descent from Elias Ashmole, founder of the Ashmolean Museum in Oxford in 1683. Perhaps some of her appreciation of beautiful things came from that side of her family. Elizabeth was 21 when she married, ten years younger than her husband. She was 'beautiful, lively and gay, and full of go', but sadly died of consumption when Frances was only seven, and the eldest sister, Edith, barely 15. They all went to boarding schools, and Edith acted as 'mother' to the younger ones until her own marriage in 1883. A close and lifelong friend wrote of Frances when she was 13 as 'heavily built, large and unattractive in appearance'.[2] As a young woman she was reckoned to be less good-looking than her sisters, but 'very attractive, interested, keen and intelligent'.[3] Her photographs during World War One show her to be a very handsome woman – her sisters must have been really exceptional.

She attended a number of undistinguished schools and showed no special distinction herself except for French where she passed second in all England in the Oxford Senior Certificate.

At the age of 20 she was living at home with her father to whom she was closely attached. He suddenly 'announced to the family at the mid-day meal his intention to marry again. They were eating bread and butter pudding (he evidently let them enjoy their first course happily), a pudding Frances could not bear to touch again. The shock was terribly severe.'[4]

He settled his first family in a house nearby while he, his new wife and, in due course, their two little girls continued in the original home.

Frances was a witness of her sister's unhappy marriage, and her close friend, Lillie Robinson, believed that this influenced her 'to put aside all idea of marriage for herself'. There was said to be 'a young man, a lawyer and brainy … who evidently fell for her' whom she met at some relative's, but 'it came to nothing'.[5]

The family were said to be very happy at Pailton, the new house, just 'pottering about'. There were tennis, horses and other country amusements, and Frances was said to have excelled herself at a women's cricket match. Her friend Margaret Joyce wrote of her at that time as 'a healthy girl with lovely brown eyes and beautiful teeth – I do not think she ever spent an idle moment. She was a keen gardener, played the organ at church, ran the village tennis club and other local enterprises, and entered eagerly into all the pursuits of the countryside – she drove a high-stepping Arab horse in a tall dog cart'.[6]

Frances did not seem to have had any idea of working until this chance meeting with Margaret Joyce who was a student of the London School of Medicine for Women. This seemed to have fired her with the idea of making a career for herself in medicine. 'When she told her family they all laughed aloud at the idea of her doing *anything* but she did'.[7]

She took her London matric and entered the London School of Medicine for Women in 1894 at the age of 24. She lived in College Hall during term-time where she made some lifelong friends including Elizabeth Courtauld and the Lewin sisters, Octavia and Jessie Augusta. Jessie Augusta Lewin later became Mrs Berry. Both Berry and Courtauld served for long periods at Royaumont, Mrs Berry from 1914 to 1918 and Courtauld from 1916 to 1919. In vacations Frances lived with her father's second family with whom she was on good terms. Her stepsisters Dora (20 years her junior) and Clare remember 'when she came home at Christmas or Easter or, indeed any time, she seemed to bring a strong breeze from outside. Frances always did energetic things, swept us out for long walks or "turned out" the attic. On one occasion they saw her rushing about saying "Where are my eyes?" Clare and I could not understand this but heard the butcher being blamed. Later we peeped through the dairy window and saw Frances standing at the sink, examining something in a bowl. She told us to run away. She was wearing a white surgical overall'. Dora sums up: 'she was very bright, lively, vivacious, ready to laugh and talk with anyone. So she was generally very popular'.[8]

At medical school she was 'a very happy student. Her brilliant examination results, and the important posts she was given show how hard she worked but then – as throughout her life – she entered with zest into the various activities and diversions of College life. She was elected "student representative", which office she filled with dignity on all formal occasions, and was a successful advocate when controversies arose between the authorities and the students'.[9]

Her fellow-student, Courtauld, remembered Frances as 'a fine student, never content till she had got to the bottom of any job she was doing. I remember watching her in the dissecting room one day and being so impressed by her patience and perseverance as she searched for a small nerve and not satisfied until she had traced it out from its origin to its end. She was a fine worker and determined to get on'.[10]

She qualified in 1900 with the London University Gold Medal in obstetrics, and Honours in medicine and forensic medicine, and graduated MBBS with honours in 1902. In 1903 she became Master of Surgery – the third woman to achieve this degree. (The second was Dame Louisa Aldrich-Blake whose connection with Royaumont has already been noted.) She furthered her experience in obstetrics and gynaecology in Vienna and Dublin. After early training posts in London she was appointed as consultant in gynaecology to the Liverpool Stanley Hospital, the first woman to hold an honorary post in Liverpool. Later she held another honorary post in the Liverpool Samaritan Hospital, and, after the war, at the Liverpool Maternity Hospital. She took a house where she held clinics for the babies of the poor – this was before infant welfare clinics were general.

After her arrival in Liverpool she became, as Dr Catherine Chisholm remembered, a 'protagonist in all our feminist struggles. She was the leader of our younger medical women whom she never ceased to spur on to further achievements. Much fighting for hospital posts was necessary then and Miss Ivens proved a magnificent leader. Manchester and Liverpool met and formed the North of England Medical Women's Society. Miss Ivens was always ready to go almost anywhere in the North ... to read papers for us or to help politically with advice – her social experience was a valuable asset for she took part in everything going on in Liverpool'.[11]

This was her life until the outbreak of war. She was then a woman of 44, highly respected in her profession, and playing a notable role in Liverpool and the women's movement.

On the outbreak of war she volunteered at once for service in Belgium, but had to return without landing because of the rapid German advance. Still determined to serve overseas, she volunteered for Dr Elsie Inglis' Scottish Women's Hospital then preparing for France. A medical woman wrote at the time, 'Elsie Inglis makes a habit of biting off more than any human being can chew – and then of finding other people to go and do the chewing for her'. Collum wrote later:

> That, I think, sums up the history of the Royaumont Unit. No one but the founder could have bitten off such a big piece of military prejudice against the work of women in war. That is just her unique title to fame. The second magnificent thing she did was to find and send Miss Ivens to France to 'chew' this particular war project for her. 'More than any human being can chew.' It was. But – the Chief did it! Had there been no Elsie Inglis there would have been no Scottish Women's Hospitals. Had there been no Miss Ivens there would never have been a Royaumont.
> Royaumont – we are proud of it – was a success from start to finish and all through the four and a half years of its existence it was the Chief who made Royaumont. We only held up her hands.[12]

Preparations went on apace, but it was a measure of the quality of the woman that amid all the uncertainties of her immediate future she did not shirk her commitment to deliver the Inaugural Address to the LSMW students on October 1st 1914 on 'Some of the Essential Attributes of an Ideal Practitioner'. 'I am hoping', she said, 'and I think it is not a forlorn hope, that it will not be long before there is a very decided public opinion formed, that it is not right for an able-bodied young woman, in whatever station of life, to eat the bread of idleness or to allow her brains to atrophy for lack of use'.[13]

She placed high on her list the gift of imagination – 'it will enable the fortunate possessor to place herself in the position of those with whom she is brought in contact, and so to realise the facts of life as they affect another'. There were other attributes she commended to the students but her final advice was 'to concentrate on work when you are working – unwearying sustained effort will be necessary. But above all do not neglect outside interests or limit your horizon, for one of your most difficult tasks is to learn how to deal with people'. And for the weaker students she had a word of encouragement: 'if unsuccessful be patient and persevering. There is a niche for you somewhere'.

How did Miss Ivens prepare herself for the great task ahead? Probably first and foremost in her mind would be the very different surgery she would be called upon to undertake if, as these pioneers all fervently hoped, they would be called on to treat battle casualties. There was much reading to be done – and we know from the books she later donated to the Liverpool Medical Institution that she read widely on different types of injury. She would know, however, that experience would bring more knowledge and the learning process would have to continue. She kept up with the new developments in the treatment of battle casualties as the war progressed and contributed to this herself. She particularly acknowledged Sir Robert Jones' articles in the

British Medical Journal in 1916 on fractures under war conditions. 'They were read and re-read until the pages were ragged.'[14] She was also studying amputation techniques – that surely would be necessary. She became a recognised authority on the treatment of gas gangrene, and kept up with all the advances.

She was already an experienced administrator and probably had little difficulty in that aspect of her work. She seems to have had considerable skills in problem-solving as the history shows.

Miss Nicholson, her second in command, recalled her first meeting with Miss Ivens:

> I met Miss Ivens for the first time in London in December 1914, at the gathering of the Royaumont Unit of the Scottish Women's Hospital preparatory to being sent across the Channel. My first impressions were of a retiring feeble woman, but I was quite wrong and I found that she was suffering from sinus trouble and a temperature. This was not improved by the crossing, the worst known for years, but insisted on by Dr Elsie Inglis, the organiser of the SWH and a very strong-minded woman. Very quickly I found I had misjudged Miss Ivens' character when I saw how she tackled the rather depressing situation which awaited us in Paris. Starting as an unwanted unit under the French Red Cross with a beautiful old abbey as hospital, but without heat, light or sanitation, and equipment still on the seas, she set to work to move all the possible influential powers, French and English. Before long the hospital was ready for inspection by high officials of the Red Cross. Never shall I forget our disappointment when our two top wards were condemned (incidentally they were used to capacity later) and we all, including our Médecin-Chef, had to move huge pieces of furniture belonging to the owners from two large rooms downstairs. Even then, before any soldiers arrived, Miss Ivens had to tour the Casualty Clearing Stations in the neighbourhood, and by persuasion of her powers of fascination she induced the commanding officers to send us cases. The one hundred beds were soon filled and the hospital never again lacked work.[15]

The chauffeur Prance recalled Miss Ivens in the early days of the hospital when those who were there:

> admired perhaps most of all her quiet courage and persistence in overcoming the somewhat understandable hesitation of the high French authorities, who would not at first send high-skilled work to Royaumont. These women surgeons, women doctors, were an innovation, they had still to prove their technical and practical ability in a sphere which they entered as total strangers. With infinite patience Miss Ivens gave herself up to this wearying work. She went round French war hospitals, speaking

with her fellow professors, gradually permeating their minds with growing recognition of her high ability. Without her patient victory and winning of this trust, the Scottish Women's Hospital at Royaumont would
never have made its way, and in this, very specially, she was the creator of
what was to become a bye-word all over France and far beyond, as one of
the finest war hospitals on all the fronts.[16]

After her wartime experiences which have been chronicled in Part One of this
book, she spoke once more to the students of the London (RFH) School of
Medicine for Women and outlined her hopes for the future. 'A great opportunity was coming', she said, 'for medical women. After the years of destruction a period of construction was coming. Things which had been permitted
in the past, neglect of women and children and insufficient hospital
accommodation would no longer be allowed.'[17]

After the closure of the hospital in March 1919 and a well-earned holiday
she was soon taking a prominent part on the Liverpool medical scene. She
returned to her appointments in the Stanley and Samaritan Hospitals and
became a university lecturer in obstetrics and gynaecology. She was said to be
a good teacher with an emphasis on the practical and the ability to draw the
best out from her students. One of her students – Dr Hilda Cantrell –
remembers her as 'a very charming person. She was very good-looking and
carried herself well and wore beautiful clothes. She tried to remember everybody's name and particulars and if she didn't she worked round it until she
found her way'.[18]

She was involved in the planning of the new Maternity Hospital and
helped to found the Crofton Recovery Hospital for Women (no longer existing) and the Liverpool Women's Radium League. She was already a member
of the Liverpool Medical Institution, one of the oldest medical societies in the
country. The Liverpool Medical Institution was ahead of its time in its
attitude to women. As early as 1888 the society admitted Dr Lucy Craddock,
one of the first generation of medical women. This did not suit all members
and in 1889 a resolution was put that 'Miss Craddock's presence at the
meetings of the Medical Institution having been found inconvenient or objec-
tionable by a large number of members she should only use the library and
cease attending meetings'. The President, however, upheld the honour of the
Institution and declared the resolution illegal. Gradually more women were
admitted and by 1916 there were seven (of whom Miss Ivens was one), and
the first woman was admitted to the Council. Miss Ivens was an active
member and became Vice-President in 1926, the first woman to hold that
position.[19]

She also played a leading role in the Medical Women's Federation, serving
on the Executive Committee from 1921, and as President from 1924 to 1926.
During this period the MWF was engaged in the battle for the status of

women doctors and ensuring better medical services for women, particularly maternity services.

In 1929 the University awarded her an honorary degree of Master of Surgery (ChM)

> to recognise the valuable professional services which Mary Hannah
> Frances Ivens rendered to the Allies during the war, as Surgeon-in-charge
> of the Scottish Women's Hospital, her self-sacrificing devotion to public
> and charitable work, and her endeavours to promote the advancement of
> her profession amongst medical women.[20]

In the same year she was made a Commander of the British Empire. (A number of women who were employed by the War Office during the war in military hospitals, or who served overseas as 'attached' RAMC were awarded CBE or OBE, but these were not given for those serving with the French Red Cross or French Armed Forces.) Nevertheless Miss Ivens' late award may probably have been, like her ChM, a recognition of the totality of her achievements.

After this double recognition she astonished all her friends by announcing her decision to marry. She was almost 60 years of age, but was ready to begin a new life. She had been happy in her work and now a new happiness awaited her. The man who was to be her husband she had known for many years, in fact since student days. Charles Matthew Knowles was a barrister in the Home Office and a widower. His first wife had been another pioneering woman, unusually successful for a woman of her period. Lilian Tomn was a close friend of Frances – it is likely they met when living in the same student residence. She was then attending the London School of Economics after a brilliant career at Girton College, Cambridge. She later became a Professor of Economic History in London University. The three remained close friends and Frances was godmother to their only son.[21]

The Unit was thrilled. There must have been many of that generation who were unable to marry following the enormous loss of young men during the war years, and they revelled in the romance of their beloved Chief.

The wedding was celebrated with considerable style in the Lady Chapel of Liverpool Cathedral, and it was perhaps typical of Miss Ivens that she gave a party for 250 of her poorer patients. Fifteen members of the Unit flocked to Liverpool to form a guard of honour and shout 'Vive la Colonelle' as she came out. The day before they had presented her with a beautiful diamond and sapphire jewel, 'to demonstrate the esteem and affection in which our Chief was held by all who had served under her'. They had a glorious reunion in Miss Nicholson's house:

> Every now and then we stole a glance at one another to make sure it was
> not all a dream. We are such creatures of habit. La Colonelle seemed to
> belong so exclusively to Royaumont, to sit so much apart, to be so

entirely the supreme and unique head. And now, after two decades of professional work, at a time when she was beginning to toy with the idea of retiring from her honorary posts and her strenuous life in Liverpool, we had heard her, that very day, making solemn vows to obey …! And we had watched her go out on a new adventure, to start a new life, with as much zest as she had gone off to Royaumont in 1914. We wish her many days of happiness in which to enjoy to the full the new and complete comradeship which is now hers.[22]

She lived in London for a few years, working, but probably less intensively than in Liverpool, until her husband's retirement when they moved to Killagordon, near Truro, which had been the family home of his first wife and was now theirs. Here Frances became a great gardener, devoting as much thoroughness to her garden as to all her other activities. Margaret Joyce remembered seeing her,

> accompanied by her head gardener and his underlings, set out upon her daily round. She was dressed in an overall, arms well away from her body, (this can be seen in the film shot at Villers-Cotterets), hands encased in rubber gloves, wrists flexed and fingers spread out so as not to contact anything – exactly in the attitude of a surgeon about to begin an operation. Each plant was visited in turn – a top dressing would be prescribed for one, a leaf mould or a mulch for another. I was never sure whether I was awake in my deck chair or dreaming when I heard her say to the head gardener – 'And now, Godrich, about the Maurandia. Nothing seems to make it thrive; we will have it up to the theatre and get to the root of the matter'. One of the men once said to me, 'There are none of us as good at a ditch as the mistress'.[23]

Just as Royaumont had been described as the 'crack hospital' of the war in France, so did the Killagordon garden become famous in its turn.

Apart from the garden Mrs Ivens-Knowles, as she was now known, took part in many public activities in her adopted county. She was a County Medical Officer for the Red Cross, head of the Women's Section of the Truro British Legion, and a governor of the High School. When war came in 1939 she became Chairman of the Cornwall Committee of the Friends of the Fighting French, and played a leading role in activating the Second World War activities of the Royaumont and Villers-Cotterets Association both in Britain and in Canada with her old ally Dr Henry.

She was active to the end and died after a short illness in 1944 at the age of 73. Because of wartime conditions few old Royaumontites were able to attend the funeral, but a wreath was sent and Dr Hancock, now Mrs Barfett, one of the first doctors at Royaumont, represented the Association and the Medical Women's Federation. The 'Royaumont jewel' (the wedding present from the unit) was sold in aid of the Emergency Loan Fund still functioning for the benefit of old Royaumontites who had need of financial help. She would have been pleased.

It may be asked what part religious faith played in her powerful motivation for service. There is no record of any mystical experience such as has been recounted of Dr Elsie Inglis sitting beneath the statue of Joan of Arc in Notre Dame Cathedral in Paris in the early months of the war. We can only guess what religion meant to her. She was brought up as a regular church attender in rural Warwickshire – a conventional upbringing. When her young step-sister Dora visited her in Liverpool while a student at Cambridge, Frances felt she was becoming too involved in the Student Christian Movement. 'She told me to read Robert Browning whose expression of Christianity could not, she thought, be bettered.'[24] At Royaumont daily prayers were held, but they seem to have been most often led by Dr Courtauld, and it was Dr Courtauld who read the burial service over the British and American soldiers in the absence of any Protestant clergyman in the neighbourhood. Her wedding in Liverpool Cathedral suggests that she was probably a regular attender, as she certainly was at Truro Cathedral in her retirement.

Such was the life of this remarkable woman. But what was she really like? There are many stories that could be told, but perhaps an overall impression can be gained from Collum's speech at their first reunion dinner on November 28th 1919, when almost 100 members of the Unit met to honour 'The Chief'. In her speech she asked:

> However did she achieve this superhuman success? Not by courting popularity. She never cared a tinker's curse whether we liked her or not. She did it always by putting the hospital first. She was ready to sacrifice us all to it. She was ready to work us to death for it. And when the call came we quite contentedly fell in with her views – and just let her! Why was it? Because we all knew our Chief never asked any of her staff to do anything or face anything that she would not do, endure or face herself. She beat us all into a cocked hat in endurance, in fortitude, in singleness of aim. The certainty, the ruthlessness, with which she went straight to her objective was the certainty, the ruthlessness of a tank. But now that the war is all over, we know that the objective was worth it – all France knows it, and pays her homage. I think no woman and few men in the Allied Medical Services worked so hard and so unremittingly as our Chief – or got so much work out of her staff! Few lived so simply. Very few preserved through those long four and a half years that extraordinarily sensitive human sympathy with the wounded men themselves. They all had implicit confidence not merely in her skill, but in her human understanding of their personal pains and fears. And yet, some of you who did not know the Chief very well, used to think her hard. She was – hard as

Aberdeen granite on the outside, and it was a pretty thick outside. It had
to be. How could she have gone on getting us to do impossibilities by
simply ordering us to do them and then expecting them to happen, if she
had not wrapped herself in a coat of steel? What I would like to make
clear tonight is that some of those who knew her better – most of us who
had known her in the beginning before the hospital got so big and
unwieldy – had discovered that there was a very *human* human being
inside. Afterwards – well, her isolation was the isolation of a captain of a
great battleship. The Chief, I grant you, could be a hard-hitting enemy.
But – I can tell you that she can also be a very staunch friend ...[25]

Collum has indicated several themes to follow in seeking to identify different
facets of her character.

First, her very human understanding towards her patients. Many of the

*Miss Ivens in her office. Note the economy – the fire is laid, but unlit – and her feet are
in a muff.*
(By courtesy of Dr Christopher Silver).

Royaumont women – whether doctors, sisters or orderlies – showed sensitivity and understanding. We can think of little Sister Williams with her Senegalese and Arabs; Marjorie Starr and her 'man with the mouth', Collum with her terribly wounded men on her x-ray table, Mrs Robertson from the Committee with her deep feeling for Madeleine, Dr Wilson, whose patients spent part of their precious leave coming back to visit her, and who had a special gift for bringing comfort and peace to those who were mentally shattered by their experiences. An unnamed orderly provided a picture of Miss Ivens as she appeared to the patients:

> They were not so astonished at their own particular 'doctoresse' being
> interested in them, but that 'La Colonelle' should know and name them
> ... always amazed them. It was small wonder they loved her. During one
> of the worst rushes of 1918, a boy was brought in with a dreadful leg,
> and as gas gangrene had set in, amputation was necessary. The poor lad,
> however, was too far gone, and there was no hope. He knew he was
> dying, and kept asking for 'la Colonelle'. Sister eventually went down to
> see if Miss Ivens could spare time to come and see the boy. Miss Ivens had
> been operating night and day for days past and, as it happened, was just
> going to rest for half an hour. But she came to the ward and sat with the
> boy, doing everything for him herself till he died.[26]

Dr Henry recalls how she would get up in the middle of the night to bestow a medal on a dying *blessé*. She also told a story of her deep humanity. After the war she and Miss Ivens had been invited to attend a conference in Brittany on gas gangrene. They were the only two women in the group of medical men. The party was returning by train from watching a 'Pardon' (a religious festival unique to Brittany), when a young boy fell off the roof of a crowded train. Out of the whole group of doctors, Henry and Ivens were the only ones who made any attempt to save the boy's life. They were, unfortunately, not successful – but they could not pass by.[27]

We saw some evidence of her 'hardness' in her annoyance and impatience with those sisters in 1917 who were protesting to the Committee about advertising for nurses who were not fully trained. She perhaps saw their dissatisfaction as a threat to the smooth working of her beloved hospital; but, however it was, her attitude did seem unsympathetic to a body of women who had not yet achieved even the limited measure of security in their profession that medical women were – just – beginning to win for themselves.

A second instance of her 'hardness' which affected, not the hospital, but the status of medical women was shown in the deliberations of the Medical Women's Federation after the war when she was President. On May 8/9 1925 the Council considered the motion 'That any woman who accepts a black-listed post [i.e. blacklisted by the Medical Women's Federation and the British Medical Association because it offered lower rates of pay for women] be ineligible for membership of the Federation, and if already a member be automatically suspended'. The motion was lost as many members felt it went too far. Many women at that time were facing very heavy competition from men and were not in such a favourable financial position as Miss Ivens with her successful practice and secure honorary consultant work in Liverpool. She was no doubt right in principle, but others could not accept the hardship that would be imposed on many. The battle for equal status continued but this somewhat ruthless measure was abandoned.[28]

Miss Ivens was always eager to supply amusements for the men – for this she had the enthusiastic support of her Unit which always seemed to include a number of extremely gifted people. She made a point of attending all the parties she possibly could that were such a feature of life at Royaumont. Probably her early life in the Warwickshire countryside was a useful experience for the rather socially isolated life at Royaumont where amusements had to be made on the spot and from their own resources.

With her care for the amusements of the men she was also watchful for her orderlies for whom she felt some responsibility. She asked Miller, whose French was up to the task, to examine the words of the *poilus'* songs and exclude those which were 'pas convenables'.[29]

She appears to have handled efficiently the problems which sometimes arose between the different nationalities under her care. Navarro relates how she was summoned to the top of a cold staircase where a proud Algerian had stubbornly installed himself because a Frenchman in the next bed had called him a pig. She never scolded, but sorted out the problem quietly, with tact, and to everyone's satisfaction.[30]

Her care for the morale of her staff was high. One recalls how she encouraged her deeply discouraged staff when the hospital which they had worked so hard to prepare failed the first inspection by the Service de Santé in December 1914. With Cicely Hamilton and the willing assistance of the two cooks she organised splendid Christmas festivities.

She had a 'forceful personality, refused to have any fools around her and had a unique power of stimulation', said her (non-Royaumont) friend Dr Chisholm.[31] Her second-in-command Ruth Nicholson wrote of her 'social charm and tact, as well as her indomitable character and boundless energy which carried her through all obstructions'.[32]

Some thought she lacked a sense of humour – others strongly denied this. Dr Estcourt-Oswald, who had known her since student days in 1897, was one who did not agree. 'She was one of the most brilliant and delightful women I have met ... a most unselfconscious being, with a great sense of humour.'[33] Mackay, who was a clerk from January 1915 to July 1917, said, 'what endeared her so much to us all, and especially to the orderlies, was her sense of humour, for she would laugh wholeheartedly at all our vagaries'.[34]

The admiration of her staff has been described in many different ways. 'She made it her business to know everyone in the hospital from the oldest hand to the latest inarticulate newcomer.'[35] She knew which of them was working well, but she could also detect the slacker. A few she sent home as unsuitable, but she fought hard to retain the chauffeurs in whom she had great confidence, and did not hesitate to voice strongly her differences with the Committee. To the orderlies she was 'Auntie' or sometimes 'Fanny', but we may be sure this was behind her back.

The French admired her greatly. She was a new experience for them. The French 'Directeur' stationed in the Abbey described her as 'une femme tout-à-fait supérière'. The quotation at the head of this chapter ('Quels yeux, quel esprit, quelle femme') was heard by the porter Daunt spoken by a departing French general.[36]

Her generosity was great, much of it known only to the Committee at home. She repeatedly refused the increases of salary offered her and was prepared to dip into her own pocket to retain the services of the two chauffeurs who could no longer afford to work as volunteers. She was generous in providing champagne and splendid food (when possible) for special occasions. After the war, in 1922, a few of them went over to Royaumont for the ceremony to unveil the monument to commemorate those who had died in the hospital. When she discovered that the young Belgian sculptor had given his services free, she asked the Committee to send him the amount they had budgeted for her personal expenses.[37]

She had a gift for friendship and many were the holidays, chiefly in France, that she spent energetically with old Royaumont colleagues, and she maintained links with her French friends.

Collum was speaking for the whole Unit when she spoke of her at the first reunion dinner as 'so entirely the supreme and unique head'. She had 'a genius for scrounging talent and holding on to it'. 'Our Chief led gallantly and greatly' and 'Her lexicon knew no such word as fail'.[38]

References

1. Dora Pym, Unpublished memoirs, 'Patchwork from the Past', by kind permission of Miss Mary Pym.
2. Mrs Lillie Robinson to Mrs Dora Pym, August 7 ?year. By permission of Miss Mary Pym.
3. Writer unknown – footnote to above letter.
4. Dora Pym, loc. cit.
5. Robinson loc. cit.
6. NL 1945, p. 3.
7. Dr Hilda Cantrell, taped recording kindly sent by Dr James Carmichael.
8. Dora Pym loc. cit.
9. NL 1945, p. 3.
10. NL 1945, p. 4.

11. Dr Catherine Chisholm, *Journal Medical Women's Federation*, 1945, p. 41.

12. V.C.C. Collum, speech at First Royaumont dinner, 28.11.1919, transcribed and kindly made available to me by Miss Mary Pym.

13. Royal Free Hospital School of Medicine Press Cuttings Book 4.

14. Frances Ivens, *Brit. Med. J.*, letter December 1939.

15. *J. Med. Women's Fed.*, 1945, p. 42.

16. NL 1936, p. 12.

17. RFHSM Press Cuttings Book, p. 139.

18. Dr Hilda Cantrell, loc. cit.

19. Information kindly supplied by Mr D.M. Crook, Librarian, Liverpool Medical Institution.

20. Information kindly supplied by Mr A. Allan, Assistant Archivist, University of Liverpool.

21. Mrs Lillie Robinson, loc. cit.

22. NL 1930, p. 6.

23. NL 1945, p. 3.

24. Dora Pym, loc. cit.

25. V.C.C. Collum, loc. cit.

26. McLaren, *A History of the Scottish Women's Hospitals*, p. 53.

27. L.M. Henry, tape recording kindly supplied by her daughter, Mrs Anne Murdoch.

28. MWF Minutes, 1925.

29. NL 1970, p. 5.

30. Navarro, *The Scottish Women's Hospital*, p. 198.

31. NL 1945, p. 3.

32. NL 1945, p. 2.

33. NL 1945, p. 4.

34. NL 1945, p. 1.

35. Ibid.

36. *J. Medical Women's Federation*, 1945, p. 198.

37. ML. Tin 49, 1922.

38. V.C.C. Collum, loc. cit.

CHAPTER TWELVE

The Doctors

Dr Elizabeth Courtauld, LSA (1901), MD Brux. (1903) (1867–1947)

Dr Elizabeth Courtauld was an important personality in the history of Royaumont. Her wonderfully vivid letters to her sister Ruth which have been quoted extensively in the story of the hospital have given us an insight into what it felt like to be part of all the stress and turmoil which was the life of the hospital in 1918. Secondly, as the oldest member of the staff, she represented one of those pioneer women at the close of the nineteenth century whose slowly developing interest in the possibility of a career in medicine is an important part of medical history.

Elizabeth Courtauld came from a well-known Huguenot family who had been long established in Essex where they founded the large and successful silk industry. Her family had a strong tradition of social responsibility. In 1858 one member of the family (a woman) founded a day nursery, a hostel and a night school for women working in the local silk factory.[1] Elizabeth's father, George Courtauld, founded the Halstead General Hospital in 1884. Elizabeth herself was a generous benefactor of the hospital and to many good causes locally and nationally.

Elizabeth, the third child in a family of nine, was born on December 2nd, 1867. When she began her diary at the age of 16 her mother was dead. She had completed her formal education at a school in Wimbledon and was then living at home, where she had some private tuition from a series of tutors. She refers to lessons in botany, music, drawing, geography, French, German, geology, 'sums' and Euclid. Apart from her occasional lessons she led a life that must have been very common for girls living in well-off families in rural communities, and one that was not dissimilar to that led by Miss Ivens before she considered a career in medicine. Social events, gardening, 'doing the flowers', tennis, reading and card games in the evenings filled her time, but a certain rather endearing enthusiasm lightened the earnestness of many of her diary entries. She was 16 when she wrote: 'I ran nine times round the garden without stopping', and 'went on the common and jumped'.[2]

Three years later, when she was 19, she took up her diary again. She still had music and drawing lessons, but now she was also housekeeping and teaching the younger children. Sometimes, however, she just 'muddled about'. Visits to London for concerts and theatres were highlights in her life.

The pattern was broken when she was 21. Her father suddenly announced his intention to marry again. She said little, but for the next few weeks the diary entries were brief or absent altogether. 'Did not go out' or 'in bed all day'. Soon after the wedding, which she did not attend, she went off to friends in Germany for a month.

On her return home she began classes in nursing and physiology and 'ambulance' (but 'forgot to go'). She bought a clinical thermometer, learned bandaging and heard lectures on digestion and psychology. Her ideas were slowly taking shape. She went up to St Thomas's Hospital to 'discuss nursing plans'. Nothing seems to have come of this. Instead she went back to Germany on a prolonged visit. There she had a gay time skating, snow-balling, sledging ('many tumbles but very exciting'). There was also plenty of dancing – 'Had plenty of partners – not in bed till four'. Then after Christmas she began serious nursing studies at the Deaconess's Hospital at Kaiserswerth where Florence Nightingale had gone many years earlier on a similar search for practical nursing experience. She took this seriously, worked hard, improved her German and enjoyed life.

After a year on the Continent she returned home. A diary entry records 'Talk about my being a doctor. Ways and means'.[3] Dr Courtauld later told Dr Henry that her father had strongly disapproved.[4] She seems to have renounced the idea (this was in 1890) and instead began to attend the local hospital regularly, saw as much as she could, helped where she could, visited the sick, and, finally, made her decision to follow a career in nursing. In January 1891 she began work in Cheltenham Hospital where she remained for the next four and a half years.

Before she left home she records that she and her sister had 'called on Miss Cooper, a lady doctor. She was not at home but Miss Bedford was'.[5] A few days later Miss Cooper returned the call. Little did either of them know that years later they would both be serving with the Scottish Women's Hospitals: Elizabeth Courtauld in France and Dr Cooper in Serbia.[6]

The next we hear of Elizabeth Courtauld is on her entering the London School of Medicine for Women in the autumn of 1895, after passing an 'arts' examination in English, Latin, German, arithmetic, algebra and Euclid. She was now 28 years old – but she had finally reached her goal of committing herself to a medical career.

At the LSMW Frances Ivens and Augusta Lewin (known at Royaumont as Mrs Berry) were her fellow students. Elizabeth and Frances had adjoining rooms in the student hostel and shared their cocoa in the evenings after the day's work.[7] They had much in common – similar backgrounds, a search for a more fulfilling life which had led them towards a career in medicine, and a shared experience of a dearly-loved father's second marriage.

Elizabeth Courtauld qualified in 1901 by sitting for the Licentiate of the Society of Apothecaries which entitled her to be entered on the Medical Register. She followed this with a Brussels MD in 1903. (She did not have the necessary qualifications to sit for the London University degree.) After qualification she worked as a junior doctor in the New Hospital for Women (later known as the Elizabeth Garrett Anderson Hospital), and as an assistant

Dr Leila Henry, the youngest, and Dr Elizabeth Courtauld, the oldest, doctor on the terrace above the cloisters.
(By courtesy of Mrs Anne Murdoch).

anaesthetist at the Royal Free Hospital. Her experience in anaesthetics later proved invaluable at Royaumont. Her next move was to South India to the Church of England Zenana Mission Hospital in Bangalore. Apart from her war service she spent the remainder of her professional life there. She described herself as 'an independent worker, not a missionary'.

She loved her work in India which provided medical women with greater scope to use their training and talents than was often possible at home. In 1909 she sent an account of her work and her patients to the Royal Free Hospital School of Medicine for Women (RFHSMW), written with her characteristic mix of humour, impatience and affection. After a night struggling with a difficult maternity case she wrote: 'A successful maternity case, followed by an Indian sunrise, makes life very well worth living'.[8] In 1924 she was still urging young women to go out and wrote of the work waiting for women in India. 'Until the coming of the English lady doctor millions of women living under the purdah system 'just suffered'.[9]

She was a devout Anglican and at Royaumont conducted the daily morning service for staff in the St Louis Chapel until this had to be abandoned in the rush of work in 1918.[10] It was she who conducted the funeral services in the local cemetery when a Protestant clergyman could not be found.

She was on leave from India when Miss Ivens invited her to join the Unit. She accepted and worked there from January 1916 to March 1919.

She became one of the members of the Unit best loved by the staff and by the patients. She was remembered later as 'Miss Courtauld with her white hair and gold eyeglasses'.[11] She was affectionately teased by the younger members. She was to take part in an Armistice party in Blanche ward, and Minchin had the task of doing the make-up:

> When Miss Courtauld was told that make-up was necessary for the plays she refused point-blank. I told the others to 'talk her round'. Finally she consented, and I went to her room to do the deed *in private*. I explained that under powerful lights, if she had none on, she would look very ill indeed. So, with a mirror firmly grasped in her hand, I started. When I got to the rouge and the lipstick my impatient protegee kept backing her head away and shuddering at the very idea – but – *I got it on*.[12]

Her Senegalese patients called her their 'First Mammy', and although she liked to pretend that she did not like them, she was in fact devoted and during one of the ward parties 'was fussing all over them all evening like a beneficent hen'.[13]

Ruth Nicholson remembered her first appearance at Royaumont in January 1916:

> A quiet little grey woman with spectacles half way down her nose. Soon she made her way into all our hearts by her kindness, her understanding,

her unselfishness, her sense of humour, and, above all, her simplicity, and had bestowed on her the well-loved name of 'Mammie'. Whenever there was any work, unspectacular, rather dull but necessary, of the nature of filling the breach, she volunteered to do it and did it well. And yet she was shrewd and practical and full of common sense and so respected she was never imposed upon. We used to find her invaluable as an adviser in cases of 'pyrexia of unknown origin' where the soldier came from the East, and in midwifery, of which she had great experience in India. [It will be remembered that in slacker times the hospital admitted civilian patients from the local community.] I remember her thoughtfulness when I first settled in practice in Birkenhead and was trying to make ends meet and she insisted on coming as a (very profitable) paying guest for some weeks. It is not everyone who knows how to use riches in the unostentatious way which she had mastered.[14]

Dr Potter, one of the surgeons, knew her work at first hand. She wrote:

although frail physically she was always at work and took practically no time off – she did not object to other medical officers taking time off but was merely mildly surprised that they should want to do so.[15]

Dr Henry remembered her as 'that sweet woman'. 'E.C. was amazing – looking so frail yet a tower of strength. In times of stress when a convoy of badly wounded arrived we had to work in the operating theatre without let-up until all was done. E.C. was our chief anaesthetist and she could outstrip many of the younger colleagues when they were visibly tiring after long hours.'[16]

After leaving Royaumont and working, as has already been told, in the devastated areas of Northern France, she returned to her beloved hospital in Bangalore until her retirement in 1927.

Then followed a period in her native village in Essex where she immersed herself in the affairs of her church (she was a churchwarden), and the local hospital. She built a playground for children and interested herself in local housing. She was a generous benefactor to the hospital and to the Marie Curie Hospital for Medical Research. On the outbreak of the Second World War, while preparing her barn for the storage of medical supplies, she fell and broke her hip. That proved to be the end of her active life. She became increasingly disabled, suffered much pain and died on December 26th, 1947, shortly after her eightieth birthday.[17]

Her hospital work was only a part of the immense service she rendered to those who had worked at Royaumont and Villers-Cotterets. In 1920 Collum discussed with her the possibility of forming an 'Association to maintain and strengthen our wartime comradeship'. She welcomed the idea enthusiastically, provided the finance for all the initial expenses and the first of a long series of Newsletters which continued almost without interruption till 1973. Apart from keeping old Royaumontites in touch with one another, the Newsletters provided a rich source of personal experiences and comments for a future historian. Miss Ivens was the first Chairman, followed by Ruth Nicholson, and finally Lady Sanderson (Smieton the dispenser). Dr Courtauld was Vice-Chairman until her death in 1947.

Many old Royaumontites found some difficulty in establishing themselves back in civilian life. Collum had reason to be grateful to Dr Courtauld for a temporary loan which enabled her to embark on a literary and archaeological career. When she was able to repay it she suggested to Dr Courtauld that it might be used to set up an Emergency Loan Fund which could give temporary help to other old members in difficulty. This was done and a Trust was established in 1926.

In 1954 Collum reported that 14 old Royaumontites had been helped since it had been inaugurated. Among these fourteen grants, outright gifts had been made to three sick and dying members to enable them to pass their last days in comfort.[18]

Thus Dr Courtauld's generosity and foresight continued after she herself had died. As Collum wrote: 'There were many who had cause to be grateful to "Mammie" who made it all possible'.[18]

References

1. Moberley Bell, *Storming the Citadel* p. 18.
2. Elizabeth Courtauld, unpublished diaries, 1883 by permission of Mr Samuel Courtauld.
3. E. Courtauld, diaries 1886, 1888, 1889 and 1890.
4. Dr L. Henry to Mr Samuel Courtauld, 15.3.79, by permission of Mr Courtauld.
5. E. Courtauld, diary 1890, December 10th.
6. Williams, *No Easy Path* and Leneman, *In the Service of Life.*
7. NL 1945, p. 4.
8. E. Courtauld, Session Papers, RFHSMW 1908–1909, p. 25, 'Sketches from a South Indian Hospital'.
9. Courtauld, Edinburgh *Evening News,* 25.7.24
10. Dr L. Henry to Mr Samuel Courtauld, 15.3.79, *loc. cit.*
11. Mrs A.M. Robertson, letter 29.10.16, by kind permission of Mrs Ailsa Tanner.
12. NL 1964, p. 7.
13. Mrs A.M. Robertson, letter 19.11.16.
14. NL 1948, p. 2.
15. 'L.M.P.', *Brit. Med. J.* 1948, Jan 17th, p. 129.
16. Dr L. Henry to Mr Samuel Courtauld, 15.3.79.
17. *Halstead Gazette* and *Times*, Jan 2, 1948.
18. NL 1954, p. 5.

Dr (Mrs) Agnes Savill, MA, MD (Glasgow), FRCPI (1875–1964)

Dr Agnes Savill was one of the original group of women doctors who went out to Royaumont at the beginning of December 1914 and who was an eye-witness to and participant in its many vicissitudes throughout its history. She was a woman of great intellectual brilliance, charm and vitality. She contributed to the hospital her professional expertise, often at great personal sacrifice, and her colourful personality enriched the community at Royaumont.

She was born Agnes Forbes Blackadder in 1875, the daughter of an architect. She soon showed her intellectual calibre by graduating MA at St Andrews University in 1895 at the early age of 20. She then went to Glasgow and enrolled in Queen Margaret College for Women, graduating MB ChB in 1898. She gained her MD in 1901 and became a Member of the Royal College of Physicians of Ireland in 1904. She was only the sixth woman to achieve this distinction. Her clinical experience followed what was a common pattern for women doctors at that time – resident house appointments in a maternity hospital, a children's hospital and Medical Officer in a workhouse infirmary – all posts for which there was not much competition from the men. After her marriage in 1901 to Dr Thomas Savill she moved to London where she began to develop her interest in skin diseases, electrotherapy and radiology. At some stage she went abroad to gain further training in her specialties. By now she was among the most highly qualified women in the country, and in 1907 she had the rare (possibly unique) distinction at that time of being appointed to a consultancy at a hospital which was not exclusively for women. This was at St John's Hospital for Skin Diseases. In addition she was a consultant to the South London Hospital for Women. Her husband died in 1910. With great courage she continued not only her own work but also undertook the editing of her husband's standard textbook, *Savill's System of Clinical Medicine*, and continued editing this right up to 1942.

Her strength of character is shown by her actions which led to her dismissal from the staff of St John's Hospital which was then going through a difficult and unhappy time. This was an act of considerable courage for a woman. A member of staff had complained about the actions of the Senior Physician. Many members of the staff agreed and endorsed the complaints. Dr Savill was one of these. They were all called upon to resign, and when they refused 'were given imperative notice of dismissal'.[1] This unhappy episode did not, however, appear to have damaged Dr Savill's subsequent career.

She was very much in sympathy with the suffrage movement, and in 1912 published papers in the medical journals on the forcible feeding of suffrage prisoners on hunger strike.[2] The Home Secretary had maintained that the procedure was carried out with safety and without pain to the prisoners. An investigation was carried out by Dr Savill in association with two of the leading surgeons of the day – Mr Mansell Moullin and Sir Victor Horsley. Dr Savill was the principal author of the report. The report considered 102 prisoners, 90 of whom had been subjected to forcible feeding. A large number of prisoners were also examined personally after they had been released under the 'Cat and Mouse Act'. This Act declared that when a woman's health was so far damaged she was released until she had recovered sufficiently to allow her return to prison to continue her sentence. If she still refused food, the whole horrible process would be repeated.

The information they acquired themselves and which they had obtained from physicians who had attended the women after their release 'give the direct negative to the Home Secretary's assertion that forcible feeding as practised in Her Majesty's prisons is neither dangerous nor painful. We are confident that were the details of the statements we have read, and cases we have examined, fully known to the profession, this practice, which consists in fact of a severe physical and mental torture, could no longer be carried out in prisons of the twentieth century'.[3] The accounts of the procedures used, given in horrifying detail, and the physical and mental injuries suffered, add up to a formidable indictment of those carrying out the feeding, the medical profession who took part and the Home Office which was ultimately responsible.

On the day war was declared on August 4th 1914, Dr Savill records how she held in her hands a ticket for a holiday in Germany. 'With hourly news of doom the first terrible weeks crept past – long months of black depression followed.'[4] Her response to this depression was to volunteer for the Scottish Women's Hospital Unit which was preparing to go to Royaumont. She was to be responsible for the installation and operation of the radiological equipment and for the training of the radiographers, which she did to a high standard of efficiency.

She records her impressions of Royaumont:

> So impressive was its architecture that during all the long sad years it
> never failed to arouse a wondering joy in the hearts of those who dwelt
> within its walls. Custom never dulled one's appreciation of its beauty, nor
> did long familiarity with the passage of the years ever blur the sense of
> satisfied delight aroused by the peaceful proportions of its cloisters, its
> arches, its great grey pillars and groined roofs.[5]

Dr Savill did not remain continuously at Royaumont. During the winter months when there was a lull in the actual fighting, the corresponding slackening of hospital work enabled her to return to her practice in London; but as spring approached, she recalls her sense of eager anticipation:

> Every return to Royaumont from 'home leave' was accompanied also by
> profound gratitude that once more one was safe within these lovely
> stones, once more privileged to live among beauty so rich that the early

waking thought would acclaim it as a dream too fine for reality.
Royaumont was beautiful at all times of the day and night; that one
never ceased to be aware of and grateful for this beauty was one of the
strange facts of the situation.[6]

Her eyes were not closed, however, to more unglamorous aspects of the old
abbey. She commented in August 1915: 'Royaumont drainage smells worse
than ever'.[7]

Professionally her work was of a high order. Her pioneering studies of the
x-ray appearances of gas gangrene are described in Appendix Two.

Her dedication to her work was demonstrated by her rapid response to the
request to return from home leave to oversee the introduction of the new x-
ray car in 1915. She installed the x-ray equipment at Villers-Cotterets
Hospital in 1917 with her usual efficiency and enthusiasm. Again in July
1918, in response to the then desperate need for a radiologist, she came back.
She had been ill, and on her return Dr Courtauld commented: 'She does look
ill, absolutely cadaverous'.[8]

She was active in the cultural life at Royaumont. She it was who introduced Antonio de Navarro in 1915, and gave him much assistance in his
writing of the early history of Royaumont.[9] She contributed in another way
to the richness of the Royaumont experience. This was the result of her great
and absorbing love of music, a passion with a most curious and unusual history which she records in her book, *Music, Health and Character*. She tells of
her conversion from a period of active antagonism to music combined with
sheer boredom, to a full commitment. As recently as March 1913

> came the unforgettable day when I learnt that piano music was capable of
> communicating not merely a passive state of pleasure but an active
> experience of vivid and creative joy. There came about a change in my
> whole attitude of mind that it can only fitly be described by the word
> 'conversion'.[10]

This 'conversion' resulted from hearing Busoni playing Chopin preludes in
the Queen's Hall.

She followed this up with a period of intense self-education and detailed
study, all fitted into a very full professional life. The means to do this she
found with the pianola. So overwhelming was this interest that she borrowed
a pianola for Royaumont from a Paris firm, and set it up in the great refectory. Starting with the Appassionata sonata of Beethoven and some Chopin
works, several members of staff and some patients spent hours practising,
practising, practising, gradually perfecting their technique and finding relief
from the difficult conditions of their daily life. When the refectory was
turned into Canada ward in 1916, the pianola had to be moved into a
corridor, and in 1917 it had to be returned to the firm which owned it. The

ward concerts, always a feature of life at Royaumont in the quieter intervals between rushes of intense activity, gained enormously by the introduction of classical music and were greatly appreciated by the *poilus*. This was not a normal feature of life in a military hospital.

Dr Savill's own involvement with music continued and developed after the war – to the extent that before long she was helping young musicians to get established, often through musical soirées held in her own house. She was a pioneer in the use of music as therapy. Her book, *Music, Health and Character*, published in 1923, caused a stir in the musical world, a lively correspondence in *The Times*, and later led to the foundation of the Council for Music in Hospitals.

In 1944 she was elected a Fellow of the Royal College of Physicians of Ireland – the sixth woman to receive this honour. She continued with a distinguished professional career certainly well into her 70s and possibly even into her 80s.

Returning to her early interest in the classical world, she published, in her late 70s, *Alexander the Great and his Times*.[11] This was an immediate success, went into three editions and led to a request from the publishers of the *Encyclopaedia Britannica* for an article on Alexander. She had begun writing during a period of convalescence. She recounts that it was with her as it had been for King Alphonso of Naples who asked his physician for something to distract his mind from his illness. He was given a book about Alexander and became so absorbed by it that he was able to exclaim 'Fi des médecins!' It must have been effective therapy for Dr Savill also, as she went on to live to be 88.

The work was for the benefit of the general reader. It is highly readable throughout but was nevertheless based on an exhaustive study of many writers from ancient to modern times. The most recent work she consulted had been written only eight years previously. She described how she was intrigued by Alexander's exclamation that he was 'seized with a longing' – by which he meant that he felt impelled to attain some apparently impossible goal and must translate his emotions into practical achievement. In her beautifully lucid account of the contribution of Ancient Greece to European culture she includes a passage from Plato's *Republic* which must have had a particular meaning for her:

> Musical training is a more potent instrument than any other because rhythm and harmony find their way into the inward places of the soul, on which they mightily fasten.

Perhaps some of her own philosophy is summed up in her final paragraph:

> When the urge from the unconscious is accepted by the intellect, it has a clear path; in that personality there is in truth a vocation, a call to follow, a mission.

With all her many accomplishments throughout her long and fruitful life, one must conclude that her 'urge' had indeed been accepted by her intellect.

She published the third and last edition of her book when she was 83. Some of the longer-lived of her fellow-workers from Royaumont kept in touch with her. Dr Henry records that at the age of 83 she was still seeing patients, but recouping her strength by spending weekends in a nursing home.[12] She died in 1964. Truly an indomitable woman.

References

1. St John's Hospital for Diseases of the Skin, 1863 to 1963, pp 31, 32. By courtesy of Dr I.R. White, Hon Archivist.
2. A.F. Savill, C.W. Mansell Moullin and Sir Victor Horsley, *Lancet* July 13 1912, p. 119; and *Lancet* August 24 1912, p. 549, 'Preliminary Report on the Forcible Feeding of Suffrage Prisoners'.
3. *Ibid.*
4. Savill, *Music, Health and Character* p. 48 *et seq.*
5. *Ibid.*
6. *Ibid.*
7. ML. Tin 12, AS to Committee, 6.8.15.
8. Dr E. Courtauld, letter to Ruth, 16.7.18, by kind permission of Mr Samuel Courtauld.
9. Navarro, *The Scottish Women's Hospital.*
10. Savill, *Music, Health and Character.*
11. Agnes Savill, *Alexander the Great and his Time.* Rockcliffe Publishing Corporation, 1955.
12. Dr L. Henry, memoir on Dr Savill written in April 1964, by kind permission of Mrs Anne Murdoch.

Dr (Mrs) Berry, MB (Lond) 1904 (died 1956)*

'A deal of Ariel, a streak of Puck
And something of the Shorter-Catechist.'**

Apart from Miss Ivens and Miss Nicholson, Mrs Berry served at Royaumont longer than any other doctor. She arrived on 30 November 1914 and remained until August 1918 when her health broke down under the strain of that stressful year. Because her long association ended on a note of sadness, it seems right to record something of her special contribution to the Unit.

Known as 'Mother', there were many new – and often homesick – orderlies who had reason to be grateful for her sympathy and kindness. Although

---

*Some confusion has arisen from her name. Our Mrs Berry had no connection with the 'Berry Unit' in Serbia where Sir James Berry's wife also served as a doctor.
**On R.L. Stevenson by W.E. Henley, quoted by her friend, Dr Martland.

some of the medical women might give a first impression of 'hardness', this was never the case with Mrs Berry. An unidentified orderly, writing home in January 1915, remembered:

> Last night I waited on the doctors and staff, all indifferent to anything save food, except for one doctor, Mrs Berry, who beckoned me to sit down, pointing to a chair by the door. She has such a sweet face and is so different from the others.[1]

Collum remembered her as 'always a kind friend of the orderlies, ready to overlook their occasional unprofessional conduct and to sympathise with their troubles'. She was equally sensitive to the unspoken needs of the patients. One example is told by Mrs Hacon, technically the housekeeper, but who liked to describe herself as the 'Head Char'. 'Mother Hacon,' Dr Berry said, 'make something to amuse that poor boy in Jeanne.' The result was a rag doll, 'Tommy', a complete success for the lonely wounded boy. With a handkerchief tucked under his chin, 'Tommy' shared all his foster-father's meals.'[2]

Mrs Berry was born Jessie Augusta Lewin. She entered the London School of Medicine for Women in 1894. With her older sister Octavia she was a fellow-student of Miss Ivens and Dr Courtauld though she herself did not qualify until 1904. Little is known of her career after graduation, though Miss Ivens referred to a career in public health. In 1911 she married Mr Grosvenor Berry, a Norfolk farmer. It was probably at the personal request of Miss Ivens that she joined the Unit in November 1914. Miss Ivens later described her (together with Nicholson, Ross and Savill) as 'a prop of the hospital from the beginning'.[3] Ruth Nicholson remembered her as 'one of our most loved members. She was a woman who put her hand to everything from ward dressings and toe-nail cutting to cleaning out drains and cutting wood. She also had a fine brain and a very tender heart'.[4] Collum remembered her as an enthusiastic and hard-working doctor as they laboured together getting the *vêtements* department into some sort of order.[5] She also concerned herself with the hospital hygiene – an uphill task considering the primitive nature of the sanitary installations. 'I can see her now,' wrote Dr Martland, 'in her white coat and gum boots, up to her ankles in water, endeavouring to 'débouche' the choked drains.'[6] Although she did no surgical work, she had a gift for restoring function to wasted limbs and fingers after surgery.[7]

Mrs Robertson, visiting on behalf of the Committee in the autumn of 1916, wrote that she was 'the funniest thing on earth', but:

> she is very sweet and unselfish and would do anything on earth for the patients, and a very skilful and devoted doctor, but utterly unpractical. One man in her ward told me he owed his life to her spending whole nights attending to him when he had frightful haemorrhages, and the men in 'Mary' simple adore her.[8]

She also looked after the health of the staff, a task she carried out with great devotion. Mrs Robertson saw her in action when a number of staff were suffering from 'chills':

> The funniest thing was Mrs Berry, or Mother as we call her, being 'dévouée' to the invalids. In our sitting room was a scene of wild confusion. The fire raked till it was half out, an enormous saucepan with a huge iron spoon in the embers, the spoon having on the end of it one speck of Oxo, another sticky cube on the mantelpiece among Dr Ivens' notes on gas gangrene. Each chair had a piece of burnt toast, and a plate, cup and spoon. Some burnt milk was in another saucepan, and Mother was found coming upstairs with a loaf of bread under one arm, and a third saucepan with an excessively greasy soup in it – and a raw egg in the other. Miss Martland locked her door [her 'chill' was apparently of the gastric variety], and firmly refused the sight of anything Mrs B. could produce. She had been warned off attending to Mrs Robertson in the food line and so she limits herself perforce to odd cups of tea, very cold and slopping which she puts down on the mantelpiece and forgets. Whenever anything in the house is missing – medical papers, things from the wards or x-ray room, a book that one is reading, a pet hot water can, the one bottle of red ink in the establishment which belongs to the lab etc, etc, it is found in Mrs Berry's room, after she has denied all knowledge of it.[9]

She cared little for her appearance – 'a frail, unprofessional-looking figure, uniform worn anyhow and hat askew'.[10]

As befitted the wife of a farmer, she was a prime mover in the cultivation of flowers and vegetables at Villers-Cotterets. She was Médecin-Chef *pro tem* at Villers-Cotterets over the bitterly cold winter of 1917–1918 during the lull in the fighting. Orderly Proctor remembers the Christmas festivities when she conducted the Christmas Day service, and on Boxing Day, dressed as Cardinal Wolsey, and with Miss Martland as her acolyte, made a speech at the dinner. She recalled her four Christmases in the Unit and declared this was the happiest yet.[11]

She was noted for her wit, gaiety and fun. Dr Martland recalled her first sight of Mrs Berry when she arrived, 'young and bewildered', in June 1916. She came into the cloisters while they were at supper:

> having been in Paris on business for the Médecin-Chef. Suddenly the whole sombre atmosphere changed, and in a moment the doctor's table was rocking with laughter with her fantastic tales of the day's adventures told with rare and delicate wit. But someone said 'Mrs Berry will have a headache tomorrow,' and sure enough she paid for her brilliance with a formidable migraine next day. That was a characteristic episode. Hers was a spirit too intense and sensitive for the tragedy of war. But she threw

herself into the life of Royaumont with passionate energy, sparing herself nothing.[12]

Besides her gaiety she also had a 'driving sense of duty that could on occasion be puritanical. She could not rest while anything remained to be done – so she never rested'.[13]

Perhaps it was this driving sense of duty, her highly strung and sensitive nature and the terrific pressures of the spring and summer of 1918 which became an increasing and ultimately intolerable strain upon her, leading to her collapse. She had to return home in August. Her illness seems to have been a serious one. In April 1919 her husband asked the Committee to write to her as warmly as possible about her work. The chief cause of her depression, he said, was the feeling that she had been of no use to Royaumont.[14]

Eighteen years later Collum met her by chance and found her 'as amusing as ever'. Her chief interest now was in restoring old cottages. Collum reminded her fellow Royaumontites that:

> for years we have all refrained from breaking through the tacitly accepted
> barrier erected when Mrs Berry left us, broken down by overwork in
> 1918, and like so many of us, feeling miserable and angry with herself for
> having thus failed to 'stay the course'. We heard that she had not wanted
> to be reminded of the war. I am sure now that she would love to meet
> any of us who knew her well, specially in the more leisured days of 1915.
> Shall we ever forget how charming she looked in the part of Marguerite
> d'Ecosse at a famous Royaumont fancy dress party?[15]

Perhaps the wounds healed eventually – one can but wish that this very lovable woman found some happiness in later life, and realised that her work at Royaumont was, if not spectacular, of real value to the total wellbeing of the Unit.

She died in 1955:

> For some of us she lives on in memory shedding a radiance upon the years
> at Royaumont.[16]

References

1. NL 1956, p. 5.
2. NL 1961, p. 5.
3. McLaren, *A History of the Scottish Women's Hospitals*, p. 39.
4. NL 1956, p. 2.
5. NL 1931, p. 2.
6. NL 1956, p. 5.
7. *Ibid.*, p. 2.
8. Mrs A.M. Robertson, letter 14.11.16, by kind permission of Mrs Ailsa Tanner.
9. *Ibid.*

10. NL 1956, p. 5.

11. IWM. E.H. Proctor, letter to mother, 29.12.16, by kind permission of Mr David Proctor.

12. NL 1956, p. 5.

13. *Ibid.*

14. ML. Tin 30, Mr Grosvenor Berry to Mrs Laurie, April 1919.

15. NL 1937, p. 10.

16 NL 1956, p. 5.

Besides Miss Ivens, Dr Courtauld, Dr Savill and Mrs Berry, there were other doctors who served at Royaumont for shorter or longer periods whose experiences after the end of World War One throw an interesting light on the career possibilities open to women at that time.

Miss Ruth Nicholson, MB BS (Durham) 1909, M S (Liverp), FRCOG (1884–1963)

Ruth Nicholson was an important member of the Unit from its arrival in December 1914 to closure in March 1919. She was second-in-command and the principal surgeon after Miss Ivens herself.

She was the eldest of a large clerical family in the North of England. Unlike Miss Ivens and Dr Courtauld, she made her decision to study medicine at a very early age when her father took her to an exhibition of medical missionary work in Newcastle. Her mind was made up and she pursued her aim with singleminded determination. At medical college in Newcastle she was the only woman in her year (though there were a few in other years). She graduated in 1909, and after work in a dispensary in Newcastle she went to Edinburgh where she became an assistant to Dr Elsie Inglis in the Bruntsfield Hospital. Like many women of her generation, she saw the mission field as an opportunity to gain wider experience than was easily available at home. Until the outbreak of war she worked in Gaza in Palestine. Wishing to participate in the war effort, she returned home and joined a voluntary unit. Standing on Victoria Station about to depart, she had the bitter experience of being turned down by the doctor in charge who refused to have a woman on his staff. 'Imagine the feelings of a strong feminist', her sister commented.[1] This rebuff, however, was a fortunate one for the Scottish Women's Hospitals, for Royaumont, and for Miss Ivens herself who gained an assistant on whom she could, and did, utterly rely.

Work at Royaumont certainly gave her a wonderful opportunity to develop her surgical skills. After the war, and with the strong encouragement of Miss Ivens, she determined on a career in obstetrics and gynaecology. 'She gave me all my chances', she wrote later in a tribute to Miss Ivens.[2] After a period in general practice in Birkenhead while she prepared herself, she gained her own consultancy appointments in the same Liverpool hospitals as Miss Ivens and successfully developed her own practice. She inspired confidence in her patients and was well-known for her sympathy and dedication.* Perhaps more unusually, she was 'a great favourite with the nurses. Her visits to the ward always gave pleasure, and the mornings in the theatre left no nervous wrecks behind'.[3] She succeeded Miss Ivens in her University appointments when Miss Ivens left to get married in 1930 and in 1933 she became one of the earliest Fellows of the new Royal College of Obstetrics and Gynaecology. She became the first woman President of the North of England Society of Obstetrics and Gynaecology and earned the respect of her male colleagues. One of them commented, 'I think we have picked a winner'.[4] As might be expected, she played a prominent part in the Medical Women's Federation.

She was a popular member of the Royaumont Unit and was known for her liveliness and sense of fun. They were impressed by her 'scarf dances', and her role as a 'dancing dervish' was remembered with pleasure. After she settled in Liverpool, she made her home with two friends with whom she shared many intellectual interests and undertook strenuous walking tours. Her energy was famous. On retirement to Devon – still with her two friends – she devoted herself to gardening and to her hens, and was famous for her baking.[5] A hip operation was unsuccessful and she became increasingly disabled and suffered much pain. She was cared for by Miller,* a friend from Royaumont days, until increasing disability and pain put an end to her active life. She died in 1963 at the age of 79.

References

1. NL 1964, p. 4.
2. NL 1945, p. 2.
3. NL 1964, p. 4.
4. *Ibid.*
5. NL 1950, p. 2.

Dr Elsie Jean Dalyell, OBE, MB (Sydney), ChM (1881–1948)

Elsie Dalyell was one of the most distinguished of the Royaumont 'doctoresses'.

She was born in Sydney, Australia, in 1881. She first intended a career in teaching, but the 'shattering blow' of a hysterectomy, with the interruption

---

*The writer has heard from no fewer than three ladies who have had personal experience of her obstetric skill, one of them being an extremely complicated case.

of an incipient romance, led to her decision to study medicine.[1] As a student she was said to be 'an extremely attractive girl with corn-yellow hair, a fair (some said 'apricot') complexion and blue eyes. The combination of her personal attractiveness, her general charm and her brilliant intellect quickly caused the young male graduates to dub her 'the Yellow Peril'. Her fame as a fast rider on a motor bike may also have contributed to the sobriquet.[2] She graduated with first-class honours in 1909, and in the following year graduated ChM.

She became the first woman resident in the Royal Prince Alfred Hospital and later the first woman to be appointed to a full-time post in the medical school. She was described as a 'superb teacher with tremendous enthusiasm'.[3] In 1912 she became the first woman in Australia to be appointed to a Beit Research Fellowship at the Lister Institute in London.[4] She was then well-set on a promising career.

On the outbreak of war she offered her services to the War Office. Not unexpectedly she was refused because she was a woman. Instead she joined the Serbian Relief Fund Unit which was leaving for Skopje in Serbia where an epidemic of typhus was raging. Her appointment was as bacteriologist, but with only two doctors available she had to turn her hand to much other work.[5] After the typhus epidemic had subsided there was a continuous inflow of all types of infectious diseases. The hospital was finally overrun by the

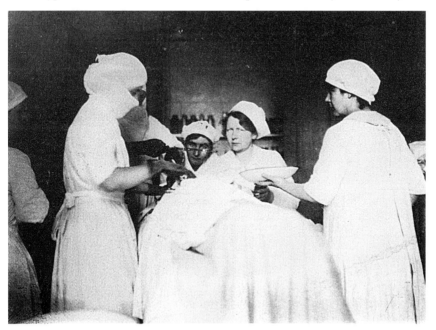

Dr Elsie Jean Dalyell, the bacteriologist, lends a hand in the theatre by giving an anaesthetic.
(By courtesy of Mr William Dalyell).

Bulgarian Army in October 1915.

In May 1916 she went to Royaumont to take charge of the bacteriological laboratory where she remained until October. The focus of her work was on the complicated bacteriology of gas gangrene and other infections of war wounds. Her own brief account of her work at Royaumont is given in Chapter 4. After the rush resulting from the Somme battles was over she volunteered for the RAMC. Being a woman, she was only 'attached' to the RAMC with no real status in the male-dominated British Army. She served as a bacteriologist in Malta and Salonika, and after the end of the war went to Constantinople (as it was then called) to deal with an outbreak of cholera. Her work with the RAMC was recognised with two 'mentions in despatches' and the award of the OBE in 1919.[6]

She returned to the Lister Institute in London and then embarked on her most important contribution to medical science. With Dr (later Dame) Harriet Chick, Dr Helen Mackay and an experienced hospital nurse, Miss Henderson-Smith, and with the support of the Lister Institute and the Medical Research Council, she went to Vienna. Vienna at that time was experiencing most extreme conditions of poverty and deprivation. The knowledge of the role of vitamins in human nutrition was then in its infancy and many questions remained unresolved. It was not even known at that time whether rickets was due to a deficiency or to a low-grade infection in debilitated children. Vienna provided the ideal test conditions for exploring the various theories.

With great tact, and thanks to Dr Dalyell's proficiency in French and German, the group was able to 'establish emotional relationships', in Harriet Chick's phrase. The result was the offer of 60 cots by the medical authorities where they could try out their ideas. Over a period of two years they were able to demonstrate conclusively not only that the addition of cod liver oil to the diet could prevent the development of rickets and promote healing when rickets had already occurred, but also that sunlight and ultra-violet light could also have a beneficial effect. This cleared up much of the confusion that had existed previously, and led to an important leap forward in public health policy.[7,8] Her deep compassion for the suffering children of Vienna was illustrated by her action on returning from home leave. She discarded all her equipment in her surgical suitcase and took it back filled with butter.[9]

On completion of this important research project Dr Dalyell returned to Australia.

One might speculate how her career might have developed had she been a man. Probably she would have reached great heights in academic medicine. As Richardson comments, 'she was still too far ahead of her time and suffered a regrettable lack of scope for her talents. On 2nd January 1924 she was appointed to the Department of Public Health where she remained until her retirement in 1946: as senior assistant microbiologist she became the highest paid woman in the public service in New South Wales, but it was inadequate use of a splendid mind and a forceful and most engaging personality'.[10] Her nephew reported that she herself felt frustrated and that the work did not give her the satisfaction she could have wished.[11] This is in no way to denigrate her work, but emphasises that career possibilities for women were different from those available to men. She developed a clinic and laboratory service for the treatment of venereal disease in the Rachel Foster Women's Hospital, work which could only effectively be done by a woman. She did this with her customary skill and dedication so that her clinic, and the methods she employed, were copied all over Australia. When World War Two broke out, in addition to her routine work, she organised the Red Cross Blood Transfusion Service.[12] She died in 1948 at the age of 67.

Her friends remembered her 'frame-shaking chuckle'. Her brother remarked that 'it seemed an eclipse of the sun had occurred'.[13] Her old friend, Dame Harriet Chick, wrote that she was an inspiration to those privileged to call her friend, and all so privileged realised how greatly her friendship had enriched their lives.[14]

She was typically modest about her achievements. During a short visit to London in 1920 she was entertained by 60 of her colleagues. In reply to a toast she 'disclaimed all credit in connection with the bacteriological successes attributed to her, and insisted that, with the anti-dysentery serum, for instance, the entire honour was due to an old woman who was found to have an absolute genius for nursing the sick rabbits on whom the experiments were made'.[15]

She was a very popular member of the Royaumont Unit and was remembered with great affection. She kept in touch with a number of old Royaumontites who had settled in Australia, and one of them, Mrs Hayward (Miss Jean Lindsay, orderly, March to September 1916 and 9.3.18 to 16.9.18) visited her only five days before her death. 'I liked her so much', she wrote.[16]

Dr Martland wrote of her:

Whatever time she may have spent in that remote attic up the spiral
stair, she certainly became a ubiquitous and beneficent presence throughout Royaumont. If a medical officer was wanted to give an anaesthetic or
evacuate a batch of blessés, there was Dalyell, a calm, fair, massive figure,
always available, utterly efficient, never in a 'flap'. She had a genius for
appearing in any place where trouble was; that soft Australian voice mur-
muring, 'Can do, honeyeee?' (sic) in a tight spot, is one of my most
blessed memories of Royaumont. Another good memory is of her divert-
ing a bunch of depressed 'doctoresses' by quick-change impersonations of
Scottish Women in the incredible variety of tartan-trimmed garments
which Edinburgh considered suitable as uniform. Her gaiety was one of
her best gifts to Royaumont. I never saw her gloomy, though sometimes

saddened by the waste and muddle of war. Just to speak of Dr Dalyell brings a sense of healing to the spirit – that is the kind of woman she was.[17]

References

1. *Australian Dictionary of Biography. Vol 8. 1891–1939.* Melbourne University Press, pp. 201–202.
2. G.D. Richardson, 'The Dalyells and their Kin'. 1988. By kind permission of the author.
3. *Ibid.*
4. *Australian Dictionary of Biography, op. cit.*
5. E.J. Dalyell, Letter to Professor Welsh, University of Sydney. May 31st 1915.
6. *Australian Dictionary of Biography, op. cit.*
7. Post-graduate Bulletin, University of Sydney, May 1958, p. 48.
8. Harriet Chick, Margaret Hume and Marjorie McFarlane, *War and Disease: A History of the Lister Institute.* Andre Deutch, 1971, Ch. 15.
9. Mr William Dalyell. Personal communication.
10. G.D. Richardson, *op. cit.*
11. Mr William Dalyell. Personal communication.
12. University of Sydney. Centenary Book, Faculty of Medicine, 1984, p. 234.
13. Mr William Dalyell. Personal communication.
14. M. Hutton Neve, *This Mad Folly.* Library of Australian History, Sydney, 1980, p. 144.
15. D. Richardson, *op. cit.*
16. NL 1950, p. 9.
17. NL 1950, p. 5.

Dr Lydia Manley Henry, MB ChB, MD (Sheffield), DSc (Hon) (Sheffield) (1891–1985)

> 'I have never lost the spell it had on me'
> 'The happiest years of my life'
>
> (L.M.H. on Royaumont)

Dr Henry arrived at Royaumont on July 25 1917 just one year after graduating when she was 26. She was then the youngest doctor to be taken on the staff – a fact which may have owed something to her winning personality and the impression she conveyed to a somewhat reluctant Committee of her unusual ability. Her future career demonstrated that their judgement had been sound.

Dr Lydia Manley Henry (or Leila as she liked to call herself) was the fourth and youngest child of William Patterson Henry and his wife Lysbeth. She was born on 30 June 1891 in Macduff, Banffshire, Scotland. Her father had been a tea planter in Ceylon, but had returned to Scotland with tuberculosis and died when Leila was only two and a half years old. The older children went to public schools and 'Little Leila' stayed on in Macduff with her aunt who was the local postmistress and a widow with children of her own. Leila attended the local school until she was 14 years old when she went down to Sheffield to join her mother. Here she attended the Sheffield High School for Girls.

Leila's mother must have been a remarkable woman. She was one of the early women graduates of St Andrews University. Her granddaughter has in her possession a letter to Macgill University written when she was 17 in 1873 requesting entrance to study medicine. Not altogether surprisingly nothing came of this. After her husband's death she had to earn a living and took up a post as the only full-time lecturer in the Day Training College for teachers in Sheffield. She was so successful in this that when the College closed owing to financial problems in 1905 she was appointed Vice-Principal of the new City Training College which took its place. She served for many years with distinction in that capacity.

The medical school in Sheffield was founded in 1829, and as Leila was leaving school was just opening its doors to women.

Apart from the first two years' slog in physics and chemistry she thoroughly enjoyed her training, though she was amused that she had to have separate instruction from the men in pathology, obstetrics, gynaecology and urology. Her period at medical school did not pass entirely smoothly. One of the bodies provided for dissection had not been properly prepared. A fellow student developed an acute dermatitis, and she an acute streptococcal infection – a very dangerous condition at that time without antibiotics or anti-streptococcal sera. Her brother, who was a bacteriologist, treated her with an autogenous vaccine. She recovered but had to miss a year of her studies. During this time she lived in a cottage, high up on the moors above the city in the care of an old woman ('who looked like a witch'). She spent her days out on the moors and her evenings studying.

On returning to college she found that many of her fellow students and a large number of junior staff had gone to serve in France – inexperienced as they were for life in the trenches and without any knowledge of military surgery. This was to the benefit of a keen student as she was. She could gain experience that was available to few, and would have turned green with envy the women pioneers who had such difficulty in getting any practical experience at all. The hospitals in which she worked, the Sheffield Royal Infirmary and the Sheffield General Hospital, were close to a munitions works and there were many serious casualties which must have been splendid training for her later work at Royaumont. Only one aspect of her training was less than satisfactory, and this, curiously enough, was in obstetrics. Out of the 20 midwifery cases assigned to her no fewer than 16 required Caesarian Section on account of severe rickets. She became aware then of the dreadful conditions of life in the slums.

She graduated on her birthday, 30th June, 1916, the first woman in Sheffield to do so, and next day became the first woman intern. Her intern year was an exceptionally heavy one owing to wartime conditions and shortages of staff. Zeppelin raids and accidents in the munitions works resulted in a strenuous workload, made even more so by the fact that she was a woman. As such she was required to live out, apart from her night shifts on casualty, and had to walk several miles after her day's work – 'not very pleasant' – was her comment. This was an example where it was hard to be a woman – but it proved her stamina.

During 1916 it became clear that VD was rampant. The Royal Infirmary responded by setting up free clinics for men and women. Leila Henry became the first woman assistant in the female clinic. Looking back on this experience in the 1960s she wrote 'I doubt if we ever see now such horrible lesions as we had to treat'. She learnt the current methods of drug treatment, knowledge which served her well after the war in her work in Blackburn.

The day after she completed her one-year internship she responded to the appeal of the Scottish Women's Hospitals Committee for women doctors to serve in France. She was refused on account of her age. Nothing daunted she travelled up to Edinburgh to plead her cause in person and was accepted.

She returned to London, collected her grey cotton uniform and crossed to France. Her views on that uniform and Miss Ivens' response have already been recorded (p. 29).

At Royaumont she was an assistant surgeon and, with Sister Rose-Morris, had charge of the Blanche de Castille ward. She immediately found her place in the Unit. Of Courtauld and Savill she said 'although twice my age they gathered me into their group'.[1] Before the hospital closed in 1919 she, Ivens, Nicholson and Manoel spent a strenuous holiday together in the South of France. When she was working in Blackburn in 1921 to 1923, there was a room in Miss Ivens' house in Liverpool known as 'Henry's room'. She kept up her friendship with all of these and with others. She deeply regretted her inability to visit Dr Savill in her extreme old age owing to her own ill-health – 'one of my big sins of omission for which I have never forgiven myself'.

She played a full part in the work of the hospital, in Villers-Cotterets and in Royaumont during the rushes of 1918. In later life she recalled one incident from her days at Villers-Cotterets which shows the affection which patients had for the hospital:

A few nights before we retreated I was called to one of the wooden huts: a patient was haemorrhaging. It was moonlight and as I was walking along the duckboards between the huts, a tall figure appeared: as I got closer I recognised him as a French sergeant we had as our patient in Royaumont. I asked him how he had got to our CCS and he told me the trenches all round us were filled with French soldiers. 'I came to see if my

Royaumont doctoresses were all safe.' He left as suddenly as he came and I walked into the hut – but I had not realised until then that we were right in their midst.

Her friendships were not only with doctors. She and Sister Rose-Morris watched the burgeoning romance between the orderly Peter and the French officer. Years later Henry became godmother to the first of their four children, and Sister Rose-Morris on her part 'cared for them all as deeply as if they were her own'.

After the war she obtained several offers of employment. Dr Louisa Martindale employed her as a locum in her practice in Brighton and wanted her to settle there. She had another offer to pursue a surgical career. Both these she turned down in favour of more academic studies. She applied for a Beit Fellowship. There was only one dissentient voice. This was that of Sir Edward Mellanby as 'she would only get married'! She did undertake academic studies in University College, London and prepared her MD thesis on gas gangrene. This she submitted to Sheffield University in 1920, becoming one of the first two to receive a Sheffield MD and the first woman to do so.

She switched her interest to the fast-growing area of public health and obtained the post of Assistant Medical Officer of Health in Blackburn, Lancashire, an industrial town with many problems. This was a new and important post – 'I had a free hand in virgin soil'. In addition to organising clinics in preventive medicine she did a great deal of public lecturing to women and girls. She was the only woman doctor in the area. She saw the ravages of a high rate of criminal abortions and she had to use most of her allotted number of hospital beds to restore the damage. Many midwives were untrained, some almost illiterate, though fortunately trained midwives were beginning to make their appearance. As far as public health was concerned she was amused – and dismayed – to see the dustcarts going up and down the old cobbled High Street while the milk was being delivered into the open jugs and basins waiting to receive it on the window-sills. She was able to organise a (limited) supply of pasteurised milk before she left.

She made such a success of this post that she was invited to head the Social Services Department at the King's College for Women in the University of London in 1923. She was a lecturer and a member of Senate. In 1924 she was invited to participate as a lecturer on maternity and child welfare for the British Association for the Advancement of Science in Toronto. The following year she resigned her post, went out to Canada, married and spent the remainder of her life there. Until then she had always maintained that being a woman had never stopped her from doing what she wanted. But this changed when she went to Canada.

It seems that her medical career was at an end and her daughter describes this as a period of some frustration for her. Nevertheless she had a happy life

– 48 years of marriage, two children and nine grandchildren in whom she took great pleasure and had many other interests. In 1978 Sheffield University Medical School celebrated its 150th anniversary. To mark the occasion the University, with great imagination, awarded Lydia Manley Henry an honorary D.Sc. degree, their first woman graduate and first woman MD, as one of whom they could be rightly proud:

> We are privileged to discover in this anniversary that our first woman graduate was pre-eminent in courage, in academic potential and in the art of living.

In World War Two she busied herself in providing warm clothing and other comforts for the British minesweeping crews and Free French sailors in North-East Scotland. She lectured extensively on the war effort at the request of the Canadian Government, and she raised Canadian support for the Scottish Women's Hospitals canteens in France in 1940. She maintained her wartime friendships and made many contributions to the Newsletters. Her health declined gently, though her last year was somewhat disturbed by her memories of the Villers-Cotterets evacuation which seemed to haunt her. She died in 1985 at the age of 93.

References

Information from Dr Henry's own papers and tape recordings very kindly supplied to me by her daughter Mrs Anne Murdoch, who has also added some further information about her mother. I am indebted also to Dr Harold Swan, Honorary Lecturer in the History of Medicine in Sheffield University, for the citation for her honorary degree and information about her mother's career in Sheffield.
1. L. Henry to Mr Samuel Courtauld, 15.3.79, by kind permission of Mr Samuel Courtauld.

Dr Edna Mary Guest, OBE, MB BS (London 1908), MD Toronto (1910), MD London (1914) (1883–1958)

Dr Guest's career spanned three continents.

She was born in 1883 in London, Ontario. When, in her late teens, she determined on a medical career, the University of Toronto had not yet opened its doors to women. Accordingly she enrolled in the London (Royal Free Hospital) School of Medicine for Women in 1901 and gained her MBBS degree in 1908. It is possible that she met Frances Ivens who had qualified in 1900. Her student years suggest a remarkably wide range of interests and enterprise. She contributed articles to the college magazine, for example 'Some British Antiquities in Orkney'. Though still in her early years as a

Dr Leila Henry wearing her Croix de Guerre medal.
(By courtesy of Mrs Anne Murdoch).

medical student, she did not hesitate to proffer some useful advice to her fellow students: 'A great opportunity for medical antiquarians, for there are several medical appointments in the Islands'. But she warns of harsh conditions – 'if she cannot face these things she had better leave these problems in the hands of the Society of Antiquaries'. Other articles followed: 'Stone Crosses of Britain', 'The Mechanism of a Great Library', and, intriguingly, 'Mrs Chapone: her letters on the improvement of the Mind addressed to a Young Lady, 1773'. More seriously she reported on a visit to Professor Osler, the great Canadian physician.

After qualifying in London, she crossed the Atlantic and took her Canadian qualifying degree in Toronto in 1910. She worked as an intern in the Women and Children's Hospital in Boston, Massachusetts and in private practice in Toronto. In 1912 she went to the Christian Medical College in Ludhiana, Punjab, in India as 'Adjunct Lecturer in Anatomy and Surgery' where the pioneer Dr Edith Brown was her chief. She stayed until 1915, greatly enjoying the work and the splendid opportunities she got for major surgery, not all of it gynaecological, and above all for her freedom of action – 'it makes life so much pleasanter than in many of our institutions at home'.

In 1915 she returned to England and joined the RAMC (in an 'attached' capacity) in Malta, Egypt and a military hospital in Northamptonshire. She then joined the Scottish Women's Hospital in Corsica where she was Chief Medical Officer, and followed this with a short period at Royaumont (already described in Chapter 7). After Royaumont, service in a military hospital in France with the RAMC gave her experience in venereal disease. On her return to Toronto in April 1919 she headed the VD section of the Women's College Hospital, where, after further study in Britain on the diseases of women, she became Head of Surgical Services. She introduced a Cancer Detection Clinic and a separate Department of Obstetrics and Gynaecology. In 1928 she gained her Toronto MD and in 1932 a Diploma in Surgery from the University of Vienna. Also in 1932 she was awarded the OBE.

She was said to have held 'radical views' and played a prominent part in medical politics. In 1933 she was the first woman to be elected to the Academy of Medicine of Toronto. She became president of the Federation of Medical Women of Canada in 1940, and first Vice-President of the World Federation of Medical Women. She was actively involved in preventive medicine, particularly in all aspects relating to women's health. She was a popular and much sought-after speaker and was involved with many women's organisations. She supported the concept of 'wellness' 50 years before it became fashionable and she was a strong supporter of women standing for parliament.

On her death in 1958 it was said of her and two of her contemporaries: 'without them it is doubtful whether so many women would be in general practice now all over Canada, in various branches of medicine and in research work. These are positive gains for our society and Dr Guest will be remembered for what she did to make it possible'.

In many ways her career in Canada ran along similar lines to that of Miss Ivens in Britain.

Sources

Royal Free Hospital School of Medicine, Session papers, 1903–1908; Material from the archives of the Women's College Hospital, Toronto, by courtesy of Ms Margaret Robins, Archivist; *Canadian Who's Who, 1936/37*, p. 454; *Journal of Canadian Medical Association*, vol. 79, 1 July 1958, p. 74.

Dr Edith Marjorie Martland, MB BS (London) (1888–1962)

Dr Martland was another of the Royaumont doctors who achieved consultant status after the war.

She was born in 1888 in Oldham, Lancashire, where she was the eldest child of a medical family. In 1906 she went to Newnham College, Cambridge where she obtained her Natural Science Tripos in 1909. From Cambridge she went to the London (Royal Free Hospital) School of Medicine for Women, qualified LRCP, MRCS in 1914, and took her London MBBS with Honours in Surgery in 1915. After a year as an intern she went to Royaumont as an Assistant Surgeon in July 1916. The hospital was then extremely busy as a result of the enormous influx of patients from the Somme battlefields. She proved to be a very competent surgeon, and enjoyed the work so much that she toyed with the idea of making her career in surgery. It became clear to her, however, when she broke down in the late summer of 1918, that her physique was too frail for the rigours of such a life. Instead she switched her interests to biochemistry and pathology, joined the Elizabeth Garrett Anderson Hospital for Women and in addition worked at the Lister Institute. She soon rose to be consultant pathologist. On the outbreak of World War Two, when the hospital was evacuated to Barnet under the Emergency Medical Service, she organised a highly efficient and widely admired pathology service under very difficult conditions. After the war she moved to Salisbury, again as consultant pathologist, until her retirement in 1954. She moved back to Cambridge where she had been so happy during her student days. She died in 1962 at the age of 73.

At Royaumont orderly Proctor regarded her as 'a brilliantly clever little thing and one of the nicest people you could meet anywhere, and a clever surgeon'. The American officer, Lieut Hickman, never forgot his 'doctor with the red hair who wouldn't let anyone take his leg off'.

Their enthusiastic judgements were endorsed by her more knowledgable peers:

an excellent brain, clear and accurate and her intellectual honesty and capacity for going to the root of the matter made her a most stimulating professional colleague and friend … she had a shining integrity which made her loved and respected by all who knew her … She loved music, painting, and literature, especially poetry … Her gaiety and love of life made her the best of friends. She moved through life a little aloof, yet warm and loving, poised and clear-cut, yet warm and compassionate.[2]

References

1. IWM. E.H. Proctor, letters to her mother, 1.1.18.
2. *Lancet*, April 7 1962; *Brit. Med. J.*, March 24 1962, pp. 885–886.

Dr Helen Lillie, MA (1910), MB ChB (1914), MD (1920) (1890–1977)

Dr Lillie's career took an unusual turn in later life.

Helen Lillie was born in Caithness in 1890, a daughter of the manse. We do not know what influenced her towards a medical career but when she qualified in 1914 from Aberdeen University she had carried off a large number of the prizes and won the coveted Gold Medal in Clinical Medicine. She was 'very well-known as the most distinguished student of the university', as one of her chiefs recorded. Her early experience was gained in the Aberdeen Children's Hospital and later in Sheffield where she was valued for her exceptional operating abilities, her common sense, tact, bright disposition and keen sense of humour.

In May 1917 she joined the Scottish Women's Hospitals and went out to Macedonia, working in the America Unit under Dr Bennet. There she gained such an extensive knowledge of malaria that she was able to make malaria the basis of the thesis she submitted in 1920 for her MD to Aberdeen University. In February 1918 she arrived at Royaumont in time for the great pressure of work from March of that year onwards. An extra pair of surgical hands was desperately needed and warmly welcomed.

After the war she prepared herself for work in India. She worked in the Jessop Hospital for Women in Sheffield and studied for the Diploma in Tropical Medicine and Hygiene which she passed with distinction. In 1920 she went to the Dufferin Hospital in Calcutta in the Women's Medical Service and in 1925 to the Church of Scotland Mission Hospital in Sialkot in the Punjab. Here she married the Rev John Garrett who was Principal of the College.

After the Second World War she and her husband returned to Scotland where his sudden death in 1948 left her with the need to find some means of earning a living. Having been abroad for so long, she seems to have failed to find medical employment – the job market was difficult at that time with large numbers coming out of the forces. Instead, with an extensive knowledge of languages, and some librarian experience in her husband's college in India, she obtained a temporary post in Glasgow University Library. She remained in this 'temporary' post for the next 12 years, acquiring a librarian's qualification on the way and adding yet more languages to her repertoire. She must have been an extremely valuable member of staff in the periodicals department.

Her active life ended in 1963 with a very serious car accident in Poland where she had gone to a conference as a representative of the History of Medicine Society. She survived, but with failing eyesight and failing health. She died in 1977 at the age of 76.

Information kindly supplied by her son, Mr William Garrett.

Some General Reflections

In spite of forming only a small section of the women doctors of their time, the experience of those who served at Royaumont could be seen as illustrative of the experiences of women doctors in general.

Women in Medicine in World War One

By the time the war began women had won the battle for registration and were slowly becoming accepted in the profession and by the public. In 1911 there were 477 women on the medical register; in 1915 there were about 1000; and in 1921 there were 1253. Before the war 1500 women were commencing medical studies each year. By the end this number had doubled to around 3000.

Service at Royaumont

In all 36 doctors served at Royaumont. Of these, two, Ivens and Nicholson, served for the whole period. Savill's attachment was intermittent, but spanned the whole period until Armistice. Berry's attachment which dated from the beginning was only terminated by her breakdown in 1918. Wilson was at Royaumont for 21 months until her death. Courtauld and Henry who arrived in 1916 and 1917 respectively stayed to the final closure in March 1919. The normal contract period was for six months. Apart from those mentioned above, 17 stayed over six months, and four stayed over a year. Two resigned before completion of their contract and one was dismissed. Others who were at the hospital for less than six months left because the war was ending.

They had qualified in no fewer than nine British Universities. These included 10 from London, seven each from Edinburgh and Glasgow, three from Belfast, two from Aberdeen and one each from Durham, Liverpool, St Andrews and Sheffield. Three obtained their qualifications abroad in Sydney, Philadelphia and Rumania.

Dates of Registration

Five had qualified in 1900 or earlier; 14 between 1901 and 1910; seven between 1911 and 1914, and eight between 1915 and 1917. The date of qualification for the remaining two doctors is unknown.

Marriage

Six of the doctors were married before they came to Royaumont (Dr Savill was a widow). A further 12 married during or after the war. This includes Miss Ivens and Dr Estcourt-Oswald who both married in later life. The fact of marriage does not appear to have had a major impact on their careers. Twelve continued to work after marriage; three did not, and for three it is not known.

Missionary Work and Work Overseas

With opportunities for work still limited at home, work overseas held a special attraction.

Before the war five had worked in the mission field. Nicholson and Wilson were in Palestine; Guest spent three years in the Christian Medical College in Ludhiana in India; Courtauld was in Bangalore, and Hendrick in the Christian Medical College in Vellore, India.

After the war Courtauld returned to her hospital in Bangalore. MacDougall went to a mission in Peru for a short period before her health broke down. Heyworth went to a mission in Swatow in China where she later married the Bishop of Foochow. Richardson went to the Nizam's Dominions in India (Hyderabad) and Meiklejohn to a hospital in Northern Rhodesia. Lillie went first to the Women's Medical Service in Calcutta and later to a mission in Sialkot, Punjab. The orderly Cranage who qualified after the war went to a mission hospital in Kenya.

Some worked overseas though not in missions. MacDougall practised in Ghana after her marriage. Cranage (Mrs Costa) practised in Italy after hers. The orderly Summerhayes who also qualified after the war entered the Government Colonial Service in the Gold Coast. She, as Dr MacRae, recounted the story of her appointment to Dr Leah Leneman, to whom I am greatly indebted for permission to quote here:

> I went to the interview by all these ancient men sitting around at the
> Colonial Office – they outlined all there was to do if I got the job – (i.e.
> to be in charge of the new Government Maternity Hospital in Accra), –

And they said 'Do you think you can do this?' I said 'I think I'm just *per-fect* for it'.

Work with the Armed Forces

Six of the Royaumont doctors had experience of serving with the Armed Forces. Dalyell, Rutherford, Newton-Davis, Walters and Guest were 'attached' to the RAMC and served abroad while Estcourt-Oswald, also 'attached', served in the Military Hospital in Colchester.

As a result of her experiences Estcourt-Oswald proposed to the Medical Women's Federation in 1919 that the Federation should seek private discussions with the War Office on the status of women vis-à-vis the Armed Forces. She listed 11 points of serious inequality and unfair treatment from her personal experience (see also Leah Leneman, *Brit. Med. J.*, 1993. 307. 1592–1594 and *Medical History* 1994 38. 160–177). She proposed that women, if employed as doctors with the Armed Forces, should receive 'Temporary Honorary Commissions' as had been available for men. Nothing came of this proposal; the war was over, everyone had lost interest and the women themselves had other more pressing concerns. It was not until the Second World War that some action was taken, and full equality with the granting of the King's Commission took even longer.

Careers after World War One

A few of the doctors held higher degrees before the war but afterwards several went on to gain further qualifications. Two who intended to work abroad took the DTM and H (Diploma of Tropical Medicine and Hygiene); six gained the DPH (Diploma of Public Health) and three the MD. Two of the theses submitted for the MD were based on experience acquired from service with the Scottish Women's Hospitals: Dr Henry's on gas gangrene at Royaumont and Dr Lillie's on malaria in Macedonia.

The careers followed by those who remained at home reflect the openings available to women at that time. Public health work of various kinds was the most common. This included maternity and child welfare, school health, health education for women and girls and venereal disease. A few, but probably only a few, did general practice. Some followed various specialities such as anaesthetics, ophthalmology, occupational therapy, pathology, bacteriology and radiology. (Buckley, who qualified after the war, became a distinguished radiologist, having had her early experience as an x-ray orderly at Royaumont.) Three – Ivens, Nicholson and Guest – became consultant surgeons in obstetrics and gynaecology.

Ten of them published papers in medical journals or books on medical topics, and 13 at least belonged to medical societies such as the British

Medical Association, the Medical Women's Federation and the Society of Medical Officers of Health.

Some involved themselves in a number of other activities. For instance Dobbin was adviser to the Women's League of Health and Beauty; Hawthorne, among her other work for women and children, was adviser on child psychology to the LCC; Logan became President of the Travelling Medical Board of the QMAAC (Queen Mary's Auxiliary Army Corps); and Potter became Director of the Section of Child Welfare of the League of Red Cross Societies in Geneva. Proctor was head of the King's College Department of Household Social Studies, and examined in Bristol and London Universities.

Medical Women's Federation

At least six were members of the MWF. Miss Ivens herself was President from 1924 to 1926. Apart from Estcourt-Oswald's proposal, Miall-Smith raised an important issue in 1921. She had been requested to resign from her post as Assistant MO to the St Pancras Borough Council on the grounds that she was a married woman. This was but one instance where things were becoming very difficult for married women. In 1921 Glasgow Corporation decided that they would dismiss all married women whose husbands were in regular work, and in 1924 the LCC declared they would employ no more married women doctors. The employment of married women was to prove a contentious issue in many professions and for many years to come. We can only note here that doctors were not exempt and that it was a Royaumont woman who brought the issue forward.

The Effect of the War on Women Doctors

What did their wartime experiences do for women doctors themselves?

In the early days the women pioneers had to overcome a certain feeling of delicacy in looking after men. Working in Poor Law Hospitals (which was sometimes the only work available) helped them to get over that, and their work with desperately wounded men in difficult circumstances would certainly further that process. There were enough high achievers in the first and second generations of women doctors to give them confidence in their own intellectual and practical abilities. Their administrative abilities, gained from their involvement in setting up new hospitals and clinics for women and responding to women's special needs, were also of a high order. They may have been unsure of their physical strength, but the war demonstrated to themselves, as well as to others, that they could cope in stressful conditions which were at least as demanding as those faced by men. Moreover, in France at least, they had to cope without the back-up support available to men.

As a result of their war work it became difficult for others to say that they were not competent. They had shown that they were able to undertake military surgery without previous experience, and, in other theatres of war, to manage epidemics of disease. They were able to run large institutions effectively and economically. Sir James Berry, the eminent surgeon who led a medical team to Serbia, said of them: 'Their jaws were stronger and their bite was better when they were not spoon-fed'. Indeed they had little experience of spoon-feeding at Villers-Cotterets or at Royaumont.

After the war there was certainly a tendency for women to return to their more traditional areas of work and there was a tendency for some doors that had been opened during the wartime shortage of medical manpower to close. Many of the London hospitals that had admitted women students during the war reversed this policy (page 334). Nevertheless things were never quite the same again.

Looking back in her old age, Dr Henry reflected with understandable satisfaction: 'The breakthrough for women in every branch of medicine was made 62 years ago and showed the British Government what women could do'.

And who dare say she was wrong?

CHAPTER THIRTEEN

Other Royaumont Personalities

V.C.C. Collum, Chronicler

It could be said that it was due to V.C.C. Collum more than to any other single member of the Royaumont and Villers-Cotterets Units that, apart from the official archives, so much information about the women who worked in them has come down to us. It is therefore only fitting to add some notes about Collum herself.

Her articles in *Blackwood's Magazine* under the pseudonym 'Skia' and her contributions to the *Common Cause*, the magazine of the National Union of Women's Suffrage Societies, record some of the story as or shortly after it occurred. She was also one of the moving spirits who set up the Royaumont and Villers-Cotterets Association after the war 'to maintain and strengthen our war-time comradeship'. This resulted in regular Newsletters keeping members in touch, arranging reunions, stimulating memories and sharing news of current activities. The Newsletters continued almost uninterruptedly, until 1973, almost 60 years after the opening of the hospital.

Collum was an only child. Her childhood was not a happy one. The remarriage of her widowed mother was a shock and she never managed to get over her dislike of her stepfather.[1] Throughout her life she threw herself into one enthusiasm after another: for Japan, where she seems to have become interested in Eastern religions, the suffrage movement, and then Royaumont. This last enthusiasm, fortunately for us, lasted her whole life. After the war other enthusiasms followed but never displaced her love for Royaumont.

On the outbreak of war she was earning her living as a freelance journalist and was also working in the Press Department of the London office of the National Union of Women's Suffrage Societies (NUWSS). There she fell under the spell of Dr Elsie Inglis, and arranged the newspaper and other publicity to help her get the Scottish Women's Hospital project off the ground. She persuaded her friend Cicely Hamilton (a friendship rooted firmly in the women's suffrage movement) to volunteer for the first Unit departing for Royaumont in November 1914. She looked on rather enviously as other recruits left for Royaumont but on February 28th 1915 she was able to follow them and realise her ambition. She was then 30 years of age.

Her first assignment was to the *vêtements* department and then, when her interest in photography became known, Miss Ivens moved her into the x-ray department where she received her initial training under Dr Hawthorne, and advanced training under Dr Savill. She was enthusiastic, devoted to her work and to her patients and became a highly skilled technician. She performed magnificently during the Somme rush (Chapter 4) in 1916 and again in 1918 (Chapter 7) until injuries from exposure to x-rays forced her to leave in July. She developed a very strong empathy with the French, *poilus* and officers alike. She felt deeply the suffering she sometimes had to cause them as she positioned them on the table so that she could take her pictures to reveal and localise the shell fragments and other foreign bodies in their wounds. Her strong sense of duty brought her back to Royaumont as soon as possible after suffering serious injuries in March 1916. These arose from being torpedoed in the *Sussex* as she was crossing the Channel coming back from leave.

She wrote of her experience:

> In a moment the whole earth and heaven seemed to explode in one head-splitting roar. In the thousandth part of a second my mind told me 'Torpedo-forward – on my right' – and then the sensation of falling, with my limbs spreadeagled, through blind space. When I came to myself again I was groping among a tangle of broken wires, with an agonising pain in my back and the fiercest headache I had ever known. My hair was down and plastered to my chin with blood that seemed to be coming from my mouth. There was more blood on my coat-sleeve. I was conscious that I was bleeding freely internally with every movement. My first definite thought was 'If only it is all a ghastly nightmare!' But I remembered. My next thought was a passionately strong desire not to die by drowning. I crawled free of the wires that were coiled about me and stood up. In one unsteady glance I took in a number of things. Near me a horrible piece of something, and a dead woman. I never heard a sound – I had been deafened. So I had been blown up to the top deck, to the other end of the ship. I swayed to and fro and looked for a stairway, but could find none, and began to be aware that I had only a few moments of consciousness left me. – I found I could not speak.[2]

A boat was lowered and men were climbing down into it. She took hold of a loose davit rope and, making a mighty effort, managed to slide down until she was just above the water. She waited till the roll of the ship brought her near enough to the boat to catch hold of another rope and so lower herself into the boat:

> Men were pouring into her. I saw a man's knee hooked over the side of the boat where I sat. I could not see his body, but it was in the water between us and the side of the Sussex. As in a dream I held on to his knee with all the grip I had left. I could do nothing to help him in, but so long as I remained conscious, his knee-hold should not be allowed to slip. No one took any notice of either of us.

The man whose knee she was holding was eventually pulled into the boat which was now dangerously overcrowded. Three oars were produced – they had to get away from the steamer. Their boat was taking in water; it was now up to her knees. Between cries of 'Ramez!' (row) and 'Mais non! Videz l'eau! Videz l'eau!' she tried to guide the oars of a young Frenchman who had no idea what to do and was gazing vacantly before him. The balers could keep the water from rising further, but they could not lower it. And then:

> I saw our steamer riding quite happily on the water with her bows clean gone. Afterwards I learnt that the torpedo had cut off her fore part, to within an inch or two to where I had been standing, and that it had sunk.

In her boat hysteria broke out. Some wanted to row and get away; others, including Collum and a Belgian who seemed to have been the only effective one in the boat, thought they should return to the *Sussex* before they were swamped. The sight of another boat returning to the *Sussex* decided the cooler heads to go back to the steamer and get the captain's advice. The boat had to be turned. No one knew how. 'Ramez au sens contraire', Collum cried, this being the nearest she could get to 'backwater'. Her Frenchman was too dazed to understand:

> So I simply set my teeth and pulled against him. With my injured back and inside I could only just compass what I did. A mutinous mood came on the boat. Every few minutes they wavered and prepared to flee again. It was like a political meeting. The boat followed the wishes of those who shoutest loudest. When the oars ceased dipping I called out as encourag- ingly as I could 'Courage, mes amis! Ramez! Ramez! Courage mes enfants!'

Later she realised, with some amusement, she had been following French newspaper accounts of how sergeants encouraged their men in battle. But it worked: 'No one thought it odd. The dazed ears heard, the nerveless arms worked again'. They drew alongside the *Sussex*. The Frenchwomen in the boat appealed for Collum to be taken off first as she was the only one who was injured. In spite of that she was left behind alone apart from the one Belgian. The boat was floating away. She could not stand. The water came over the gunwale, poured over her legs to her waist, soaked through her thick great-coat and chilled her to the bone. Help came from the same Belgian who had done more than anyone to control the boat, and, with the help of sailors from the *Sussex*, he hauled her up by the arms 'like a sack' and propped her against a wall.

The Belgian gave her what help he could. A man with a wounded head sat patiently in a corner; a girl, in great pain, struggled down the stairs, lay on a couch, and never moved or spoke again: 'She died bravely and silently, quite alone'. There followed long hours of waiting:

It is nerve-racking work lying helpless in a damaged vessel wondering whether the rescue ship or another enemy submarine will appear first on the scene.

A French fishing vessel drew alongside. Her Belgian friend, with the help of a young Chinese, carried her up to the rail but they were too late. The boat had already sailed. Half an hour later a destroyer was on the scene and this time she was lucky. The crew got her on her back as far as the ship's rail: 'British sailors grasped my arms and pulled me over. For one sickening second my legs dangled between the two ships, but the sailors hauled me in before the impact came'.

She was now safe in the hands of the British Navy. Early next morning she was transferred to a hospital ship: 'I was in very great pain and suffering physically more than I have ever suffered in my life, but my memory of those hours between dark and daylight is one, not of personal misery, but of the beautiful tenderness of those Nursing Sisters'.[3]

She spent a few days in a local hospital after landing in England and then went by ambulance train to 'one of the great London Hospitals'. She had a smashed foot, a fractured lumbar process on her spine, strained muscles in back and thigh and some internal injuries.

She considered herself almost a professional radiographer and took a great interest in the beautiful x-ray apparatus in the hospital. But at the same time she felt a thrill of pride that 'our radiographs, though our installation is small and comparatively cheap, are as good as any I saw in the show frames that day'.

Three months later she was back at Royaumont – 'going back to a life I loved, to a Chief I delighted to work with, to comrades proven in long months of alternating stress and monotony and to a little group of friends'. She was back in time to play a heroic part in the tremendous rush of work which commenced on July 2nd in the first Battle of the Somme (Chapter 4).*

After Royaumont

After the war Collum pursued two major interests. One of these was an intensive study of ancient religions. This probably originated in her early travels in Japan and other parts of the Far East before the war.

---

* 386 passengers were on board the *Sussex*, 270 of them women and children. The Captain and the 50 crew members were French: 53 died in the attack. The Captain stated later that if people had only stayed on board the steamer when the bows were shot away, the loss of life would have been confined to those killed in the actual explosion. Thirteen passengers, of whom Collum was one, were seriously injured.[3]

Her first publication was an essay in 1926[4] which she called 'The Dance of Çiva' (*sic*), one of a series, 'Today and Tomorrow', to which many well-known writers of the time contributed, for example J.B.S. Haldane, Bertrand Russell and Robert Graves, to mention a few. In this essay she contrasted the thought of East and West, maintaining that the West should learn from the East and acknowledge their underlying unity. She was groping towards a philosophy that would satisfy her need to make sense of the world and the individual's role within it.

In 1933 she published *The Music of Growth*,[5] a further attempt to harmonise the philosophies of East and West. The range of knowledge revealed in the book was remarkable, including the latest theories in physiology, physics, crystallography, endocrinology, anthropology, archaeology, prehistoric art and the interplay of religious and artistic influences in different parts of the world. Part of her journalistic work in 1925 had included interviews with many of the leading thinkers of the day which had probably helped her to achieve this wide perspective. However, when she came to form her conclusions the modern reader might feel a certain lack of sympathy: 'It is biologically sound to allow the fit to fight for and defend the community if need arise' (she was arguing against pacifism), 'but it is suicide for the fit to allow the unfit in the community to feed upon their vitality. The parasite itself can survive only while the host lives'. And yet this was the woman who never spared herself to help others. There are many instances of her sympathy with the suffering which had little in common with this bleak statement.

She was still searching for the truth in 1940 when she published *Manifold Unity*[6] which she described as 'The Ancient World's Perception of the Divine Pattern'. It was altogether softer in tone than the previous work, and she referred to 'those of us who still believe in the ideals of Religion and Humanity'. It seems that although she did not subscribe to any one form of religion, there was much in Buddhism that appealed to her. Among a collection of her own poetry there are lines written on a Khmer head of a Bodhisattva which to her was a complete revelation of the love and peace of the saint.

Her other great enthusiasm, apparently beginning in the 1920s, was for archaeology. She took part in a number of excavations and became a Fellow of the Royal Archaeological Institute. She came to the notice of Sir Robert Mond who was a very gifted scientist in various branches of chemistry, a Fellow of the Royal Society, a philanthropist, a collector of antiquities and an archaeologist who conducted his own excavations. He was also a very wealthy man. For many years in the 1930s Collum had charge of his excavations in Brittany and published reports in 1934 and 1935 illustrated by her own beautiful photographs. She concluded that the megalithic monument with which she was concerned did not date from several centuries BC, as was currently believed, but from the period of Roman occupation and represented the 'Cult of the Great Mother', then practised by the Armorican Gauls. It must have been a great disappointment to her that her conclusions were not accepted (there is still no support for her theory). In her will she left all her research material to an executor in the United States in the hope that it would find some acceptance there. She had been lucky in working for two chiefs whom she could wholeheartedly admire – Miss Ivens and Sir Robert Mond. Through the generosity of Sir Robert she was able to pursue the work she loved without financial constraints. However, her archaeological work ceased after the death of Sir Robert in 1938.

The outbreak of World War Two found her active in fostering the contributions Royaumont members could make to the war effort through canteens in France and the welfare of the Free French in Britain. She was earnest in defending the French nation which had been betrayed by the Vichy regime:

> France cannot do without Britain and Britain cannot do without
> France ... The whole point about Royaumont standing for France now is
> that thousands of people all over the country do already trust les dames
> de Royaumont because of what we were to them last time: not just an
> efficient auxiliary hospital but proven friends and loyal comrades.[7]

She was no pacifist. She had strongly criticised Vera Brittain's *Testament of Youth* in 1934 for its emphasis on the 'exquisitely painful experiences she and her circle had suffered, but she had forgotten 'the unfortunate peasant soldier who stolidly fought as though obedient to destiny and died of wounds'. 'Royaumont', she maintained, 'saw war through the less sentimental, not at all hysterical, and more realistic eyes of French youth.' 'We who saw that comradeship and knew it among ourselves during the war, let us at all events keep it untarnished – the "Testament of Maturity"'.[7]

During the war her great energies were diverted to soil fertility research – she was indeed a woman of many achievements. Sadly her health deteriorated seriously after the war and she died after much pain in 1957 at the age of 72. She left her body, a typical gesture, to the Royal College of Surgeons of England.

Her friend of over 40 years, 'Big Andy' (Miss Agnes Lang Anderson), who was an auxiliary nurse at Royaumont from April 1915 to August 1918 (corresponding almost exactly to Collum's service), wrote: 'It is difficult to know where to begin, or for that matter stop. Her interests were so wide-ranging, her enterprise so great, her nature so complex'.[8]

References

1. NL 1958, p. 2.
2. 'Ski' (*sic*), 'Torpedoed!', *Blackwood's Magazine*, May 1916, pp. 690–698.
3. *Times*, 25.3.16 to 30.3.16.

4. V.C.C. Collum, *The Dance of Çiva: Life's Unity and Rhythm*, Kegan Paul 1926.

5. V.C.C. Collum, *The Music of Growth*, Scholartis Press 1933..

6. V.C.C. Collum, *Manifold Unity: The Ancient World's Perception of the Divine Pattern of Harmony and Compassion*, John Murray 1940.

7. NL 1934, February, p. 3.

8. NL 1958, p. 2.

Ciceley Hamilton, Playwright, Actress, Writer, Suffragist, Administrator (1872–1952)

Cicely Hamilton, who worked at Royaumont for two and a half years from December 1914 to May 1917, is one of the outstanding personalities among the many striking and interesting women who brought their talents and dedication to Royaumont during the four and a half years of its existence.

Cicely's life is well documented both in her own writings, those of her friends and colleagues, in her autobiography, *Life Errant*[1] and a biography, *The Life and Rebellious Times of Cicely Hamilton*, by Lis Whitelaw.[2]

On the outbreak of war Cicely was 42 and had already achieved fame as an actress, a playwright and a leading character in the suffrage movement. Her early years had not been happy ones. Her father was a distinguished soldier in the Gordon Highlanders (no doubt she was happy to wear the Gordon flash on her uniform when she joined the Scottish Women's Hospitals). Cicely's mother had faded from family life shortly after the birth of her fourth and youngest child though no record is available to explain what happened. Cicely was ten years old at the time and there followed what was probably the most miserable period of her life when she and the other children were fostered by an unkind and unsympathetic family. Financial losses had reduced the family income to her father's army pay, wretchedly low even for a high-ranking and much-decorated serving officer. The children knew they had to make their own way in the world, and Cicely, being the eldest, knew it was for her to set the pace. With some family help and the loving support of two aunts she obtained an education in England and Germany. She tried teaching as a career, one of the few openings for middle-class women in the 1890s. She soon found this to be intolerable. Enthralled with the theatre, she then embarked on the hard, chancy, exhausting and financially unrewarding career of acting, supplemented by occasional articles and stories for magazines. Later she extended her literary work to writing plays, and achieved particular success with *Diana of Dobson's* which brought her fame and some acting engagements on the London stage.

Her experiences of the problems of an unsupported woman finding an opening for her talents led to her involvement in the growing movement for women's suffrage. At this time, in the early years of the century, there were two main wings of the movement. One was consolidated in the National Union of Women's Suffrage Societies under the leadership of Mrs Millicent Fawcett, a younger sister of the pioneer woman doctor, Dr Elizabeth Garret Anderson. They believed in pursuing their aims through constitutional means. The other wing, under the leadership of Mrs Emmeline Pankhurst and her daughters, was the Women's Social and Political Union (WSPU). They felt the constitutional approach was getting them nowhere and advocated aggressive, disruptive and militant tactics – a policy which earned them the title of the 'militant suffragettes'. Cicely Hamilton wrote later:

> I had more sympathy with the constitutional suffragists than with the 'militants' who so heartily despised them; the more I thought of it, the more it seemed to me there was a lack of logic in the militant belief in violence. The acceptance of violence as the best means of obtaining political ends implied a secondary importance for the vote itself.[3]

And again:

> I never attempted to disguise the fact that I wasn't wildly interested in votes for anyone ... if I worked hard for women's enfranchisement, and I did work hard, it was because the agitation for women's enfranchisement must inevitably shake and weaken the tradition of the 'normal woman'. (i.e. marriage, motherhood and housekeeping). My personal revolt was feminist rather than suffragist.[4]

This was the theme she explored in her book, *Marriage as a Trade*, published in 1909, which attracted a degree of notoriety.[5]

In 1908 she was a co-founder of the Women Writers' Suffrage League (WWSL), and later in the same year of the Actress's Franchise League (AFL). Both of these organisations involved a large and effective group of women prepared to use their particular talents in the cause. She never believed that obtaining votes for women was anything more than a step on the way towards a fundamental review of society's attitudes. Her personal concern, she said, was 'social justice, not the vote'. Indeed when women over 30 were granted the vote in 1918 Cicely's response was very low-key. She knew only too well that there was still a long way to go before social justice was achieved. She died 40 years later at the age of 80, and one can speculate, if she were alive today, whether she would have been satisfied that the marginalisation of women was really a thing of the past.

One further initiative, the Women's Tax Resistance League, was set in motion by Cicely in 1909 in association with Dr Louisa Garrett Anderson (a daughter of Dr Elizabeth) who herself had a distinguished career. With Dr Flora Murray, she was in charge of a Military Hospital in Endell Street, London, for most of the war, a hospital staffed almost entirely by women. 'No taxation without representation' seemed to them a reasonable point of view though the tax authorities did not agree. An amusing battle went on for some time till the outbreak of war when Cicely decided that enough was enough. This must have been a relief to the tax-men.[6] In these pre-war years she employed her very considerable skills of speaking and writing, using humour, satire and drama.

This was her situation at the outbreak of war in August 1914 when she found herself involved, as was the entire country, in an upsurge of patriotic feeling. Her previous strenuous life of campaigning, acting and writing lost its savour. She felt the need to participate and to direct her talents in a new direction – to assist the war effort and show in a practical way what women could do.

Her friend, V.C.C. Collum, who was then working in the Press Office of the NUWSS, suggested to her that she might consider volunteering for one of the SWH Units which Dr Inglis was then planning. This suited Cicely's ideas and she offered her skills – an adequate knowledge of French and, curiously enough, book-keeping. The offer was accepted and she was engaged as a clerk at the princely salary of ten shillings a week. She herself recorded some of her early experiences at the abbey in *Common Cause*.[7]

How did this strongly individualistic woman fit into the life of a community such as Royaumont? Cicely had, for years, been accustomed to associating with women who were talented, intellectual and professional. At Royaumont she clearly enjoyed the companionship of the medical women all of whom had come up the hard way and had had to struggle to a greater or lesser extent for their qualifications and experience in a man's world. They, in turn, appreciated her as an efficient member of the team, first as clerk, later as administrator, and as a lively and entertaining colleague. The rather rigid hierarchy which required the orderlies, the sisters and the doctors each to have their separate sitting rooms and dining tables was waived for Cicely who shared with the doctors. Miss Ivens in particular relied enormously on Cicely for her meticulous keeping of accounts (Dr Inglis considered this was not Miss Ivens's strong point), and for her knowledge of French, specially before Miss Ivens became fluent herself.

Miss Ivens expressed her appreciation in August 1916 when she requested the Committee to raise her salary to the same level as that of the doctors – £200 per annum. She wrote:

> Her work has been so invaluable I think it would be disastrous for the
> hospital if her services could not be retained for pecuniary reasons. We all
> use her brain so much that even a temporary absence on leave makes us
> feel extremely helpless. I should like the Committee to realise how much
> the hospital is indebted to her, not only for the accurate and scrupulous
> accounts, but for the tactful and clever letters she writes for me to many
> of the French officials with whom I have to conduct negotiations.[8]

She was also the perfect morale booster, as was clearly demonstrated in what might have been a very gloomy Christmas in 1914 when their Herculean efforts had been rebuffed by the French authorities. She laid on a pageant of the history of the abbey enlivened by her own humorous comments. She was the prime mover and inspiration of many other shows during the slacker periods of the hospital. Mrs Robertson, a member of the SWH Committee in Edinburgh, visiting the hospital in 1916, after describing Miss Hamilton's entrance disguised as a tank at one of their parties, wrote: 'Miss Hamilton was brilliant that evening and afterwards. She sometimes keeps us all in fits. She is so clever and witty'.[9]

Cicely, however, had her moments when the restrictions of communal life must have been very irksome. Mrs Owen, the first administrator, who had difficulties with Miss Ivens and with her job, recorded an 'extraordinary exhibition of temper from Miss Hamilton'.[10] Mrs Owens's successor, Mrs Harley, however, wrote to the Committee in March that she was 'a delightful person to work with and so helpful to us all'.[11] Dorothy Littlejohn, one of the somewhat disgruntled cooks in the kitchen in 1914, wrote home of

> A Miss Cicely Hamilton, a thorough Bohemian … a most understanding
> person and fortunately sees the funny parts. Certainly if you could see
> Miss Swanston and me simply weak with laughter you would be able to
> comfort yourself that I am not taking life too seriously, but if we did not
> laugh we would probably do the other thing.[12]

But it was not all fun. One of Cicely's saddest duties was attendance at funerals in the local cemetery when doctors and nurses were too busy to spare the time. 'It was a duty I never got hardened to.'[13] She felt deeply the suffering of ordinary people caught up in the horrible wastage of war. She describes in her autobiography a scene she witnessed when medals were being bestowed by the French military authorities:

> Among the soldiers there was an elderly man in a clean and tidied work-
> man's suit. That meant a dead son whose cross he was that day receiving.
> – When the ribbon was pinned on the workman's coat, a woman beside
> me stirred and drew a breath – a young woman dressed all in black; then,
> the ceremony over, she slipped under the rail, and went forward to meet
> the old man. I remember a thin fine rain was falling and they said not a
> word as they met; but the woman took out a square of white handker-
> chief, unfolded it, spread it on her hands, and stood waiting. The father
> unfastened the cross from his coat and laid it on the linen, and they stood
> in the rain and looked down on it – all they had received for the life of a
> man! Then slowly, she folded the handkerchief and covered it, and they
> walked away together, still without a word; she carrying the medal as a
> priest might carry the Host.[14]

Other experiences brought her face to face with the tragic realities of war – twentieth-century war – rather different from the experiences of her father when, as she saw it, war had been played by certain rules. She visited the town of Senlis which had been overrun by the Germans in September 1914 (whose story has been told in the account of the Curé of Asnières in Chapter 9). She was so moved by what she saw that she wrote an account in her book *Senlis*.[15]

Cicely recorded how

> The regimental herd life has never appealed to me, and in the SWH I often felt as if I were at school again, longing for the holidays ahead; which does not mean that I did not like and respect many of those with whom I was called upon to work. The fact that I did like and respect so many of them was one of the compensations of life at Royaumont – apart from the hope that one was being of some little use to the hospital.[16]

She could take an objective view of life at Royaumont when her period of service came to an end in the spring of 1917:

> The characteristic of a war hospital is the irregularity of its work. There would be 'rushes' when the ambulances went again and again to the station at Creil, where the trains from the front discharge their wounded, when every ward was full and doctors and nurses were never out of the operating theatre, and you wondered how they kept going. And there would be other times – long stretches – when beds were vacant and operations few, and the staff in general had plenty of leisure to remark on each other's shortcomings; as invariably happens in any institution when there is not enough work to go round![17]

She disliked wearing uniform, and whenever she could wore a working man's 'blouse', which puzzled Miss Tod, the first Matron (Chapter 3). She rode her bicycle in the woods which was not allowed by the French authorities. (Later this regulation was quietly ignored.) She enjoyed long conversations with the local plumber, M. Daviaud, who did many much-needed jobs in the hospital, and whom she described as 'slight, sensitive, intelligent-looking, well-read and well-spoken with a Frenchman's sense of the word'.[18] Another close friend she made among the local village people was Mlle. Baignières – she who had stood beside the Curé at the crossroads in September 1914 when the Germans were approaching (Chapter 9).

Her bicycle rides led to an extraordinary experience which she recorded in her autobiography. Riding home one evening she saw

> a woman, some yards ahead, walking in the same direction as myself – walking swiftly at the side of the road. She wore no hat, her dress was dark and, in the dusky light, looked black. I took her for some young woman of the village to whom, as I overtook her, I should call the cus-

tomary greeting. I was just drawing level with her, when – she cut across the bend diagonally by darting out into the road and right in the path of my bicycle; I saw we must collide, shouted something, took my foot off the pedal and put my brake hard on. And then – nothing happened. The blackness of her dress was against my front wheel – but the wheel went on without impact! My impression – my belief – was that I and my bicycle had passed through the figure.... I believe wholeheartedly that I saw a ghost and rode through that ghost but I don't expect those who read of my adventure to share my personal belief![19]

She had other experiences in the autumn of 1916, this time in the Abbey itself. Night after night the handle of her door was rattled – and there was no one there. She tried leaving the door open, but taps and knocks around the room took the place of the handle-turning. She never spoke of these events, but one day, as she was going through the housekeeping accounts with a member of the staff, 'there came the familiar twist of the handle; I tried to ignore it but my companion, when it was repeated, rose to open the door'. As usual there was no one there. Finally there was 'a final and violent wind-up of the manifestations'. She went to bed early and an orderly (this was Margaret Davidson, 23.5.15 to 29.8.17) who was accustomed to putting a hot water bottle in her bed, came in and started chatting:

Suddenly the door of my room was rattled as I had never heard it rattle before – with an energy suggestive of anger or desperate haste. D. jumped up promptly and made for the door; from the inner side it opened easily enough, and she had it wide in an instant. This time I had not recognised my visitor – his furious way of making himself known was new – but I wasn't so surprised as D. when the open door revealed nothing but an open door. She looked up and down the corridor and turned and looked at me; and I think I said something rather lamely about wondering who it was, and why they had run off like that – knowing all the time it was quite impossible for anyone to vanish so quickly. Whether she accepted my attempt at an explanation I don't know, but she shut the door, came back to my bed, and sat down again; but hardly had she done so than my visitor came back, and more thunderously. This time he left the handle alone; his assault was on the door itself. Judging by the sound a man, and a heavy man, was hurling himself against the door which (this I will swear to) actually cracked on its hinges. For a second or two I think we were both of us staggered; then D. naturally was the quicker of the two. Before I was out of bed she was back at the door, and once again flinging it open – with the same result as before – I don't know what we said about it but I know it wasn't much – D. respecting my obvious desire to avoid discussion and after a few minutes taking herself off to her own quarters. When she had gone I got up – the new developments had made me uneasy (she had had bad news that morning about the health of her old aunt), and stood outside my door. A nurse came out into the corridor and as she walked away I called after her 'Sister, did you hear someone banging on my door a few minutes ago?' 'No, I didn't hear anyone', and departed down the corridor. Was it really possible that thundering noise had been audible only in my room? It was a piece of good luck that I had a companion when the battering on my door took place; if D. had not been with me I might have had doubts about my own sanity when I discovered that the noise had been heard only by myself. For outside my room it had passed entirely unnoticed; I made sure of this after the sister had left me, by calling on the occupant of a room on the other side of the corridor, and exactly opposite my own. The said occupant was a visitor to the hospital. She also had gone to bed early and, as I expected, I found her awake and reading. She also had heard nothing unusual ...[20]

It so happened that the visitor was none other than Mrs Robertson who has left her own account of the incident when Cicely Hamilton arrived in her room utterly distraught:

That night after I had gone to bed a very odd thing happened. It was a wild stormy night with the wind howling among the trees in the park. I was lying in bed trying to read myself to sleep, and listening to the wind. I would have heard any sound in the house as I had heard every step which passed along the passage previously. About 12 o'clock a tap came on my door, and Miss Hamilton came in looking very pale and disturbed. She said 'I saw your light and thought I'd ask if I might sit by your fire a little as you were not asleep'. After a little she asked me if I'd heard anything peculiar and told me that twice a great blow had fallen on her door like a mailed fist, and that though the door had been opened instantly, – the second time was just before she came to me – and though her door is just opposite mine, I had heard nothing at all! She was completely upset, so much so that we dragged her mattress and bed-clothes into my room and she slept here by the fire beside me. It's funny, but though we did not mind the window wide open to the universe we carefully bolted up the latch of the door! Miss Hamilton is wonderful. We had a splendid talk till about 2.30 a.m. and then slept till after 6 a.m. when we dragged all the bed things so the orderlies should not talk. They have great tales of a monk who 'walks' in the upper corridors, and there is a presence in the bacteriological lab which can be felt quite distinctly, if not seen. I, however, am ghost-proof, and see and hear nothing.[21]

Although it does not strictly concern Cicely Hamilton, it might be appropriate here to comment further on Royaumont ghosts.

Ambulance in 1915. From left to right, unknown figure, Miss Loudon, Administrator, unidentified doctor, Miss Ivens in white coat and rubber gloves, Cicely Hamilton (sitting) and Chauffeur Williams in her khaki greatcoat.
(By permission of the Imperial War Museum).

In 1938 an orderly, Ramsay-Smith (later a most successful administrator), recorded an experience she had in July 1916 while she was on night duty in Canada ward. About midnight

> the door into the passage was suddenly shaken violently as if someone were endeavouring to get in, and could not get the handle to turn. But there was no one there and the shaking ceased. I gaped at it vaguely and then I decided it must have been one of the Royaumont ghosts. 'So', I thought, 'if it happens again I will open the door for it and ask it to come in.' Sure enough, in a few moments, the same rattling came once more. In what I hoped was the grand manner, I flung open the door and cried 'Entrez-donc!' to the empty air. There was no movement – nothing – and for the rest of my time on night duty the ghost did not return. 'At least', thought I, 'I have brought peace to one restless spirit.'[22]

She goes on to recount two other incidents she experienced later, one on the North-West Frontier of India, and one in her own home in the South of Scotland. In all these three experiences the doors rattled in an identical manner, and in the second two they were definitely due to recorded earthquakes. 'I am now convinced that my ghost at Royaumont was only a double earthquake shock, not a ghostly vision.'[23] Could this explain Cicely's ghostly visitor?

The orderly Daunt (Miss Dorothea O'Neill Daunt, 18.8.17 to 28.2.19) worked as a hall porter – a lively Irish girl with plenty of the Irish blarney and much loved for her sense of fun. She took delight in making the flesh of new arrivals creep with her ghost stories told with all the horrifying details she could think of – but she only arrived after the experiences reported by Cicely and Ramsay-Smith.

Dr Leila Henry had a theory that the Royaumont ghosts could be explained by the thundering of horse's hoofs on the Chantilly Race course transmitted through the ground by some quirk of geology. But there could not have been much in the way of horse-racing at Chantilly in July 1916 during the Somme offensives, or in November in the middle of the night, so we may rule that out. Another explanation might be the peculiarities in the plumbing system installed in the old buildings combined with Cicely Hamilton's psychic tendencies. We shall never know, and there is no one left to tell us.

In the spring of 1917 Cicely Hamilton was feeling the need of a change. She had served two and a half years, and the hospital was going through a quiet period. She wrote to the Committee:

> I should like to say this, those of you whose work lies at home can hardly realise [Royaumont's] indirect effect for good upon the men and women with whom we have come in contact. I do not judge by official compliments – which are always flowery – or the polite remarks of visitors; I judge by all the little things I have seen and heard, the interested and often puzzled questions of my French friends and acquaintances. So far as my observation goes, the work of our countrywomen in France stands high in public estimation; we are still accounted curious, we are, occasionally, a jest, but it is always a kindly jest; if we are not always understood we can say with truth we are trusted. It is something to have served for two years and a half with those who have proved themselves worthy of trust; and for that alone I shall always remember Royaumont.[24]

She joined Lena Ashwell's Players, returning to her old love of acting. They performed in Abbeville and Amiens till the end of the war and then, in 1919, in Cologne and the Devastated Areas.

In 1920 she went to Austria on behalf of the Save the Children Fund and in Vienna observed 'the children stunted for lack of nourishment, the shabbiness and beggary and the queues at the soup kitchens'.[25] Did she, one wonders, know that Dr Elsie Dalyell (the bacteriologist) was also in Vienna carrying out her important work with Dr Harriet Chick on the nutrition of children? There is no record that they discovered each other but it is interesting that two old Royaumontites were engaged in the same humanitarian work for children, using their different talents to the same end.

She found the post-war period depressing. She wrote:

> There are certain epochs of my life that I think of unwillingly and as sel-
> dom as possible – specially of those from an ugly epoch, the first years
> that followed the war – years of disillusion and hope falsified ... The war
> seemed to have become a habit with us; instead of hating by nation we
> hated by party and by class.[26]

Her experiences in the war led her to fear the evil men (and women) could do when they were part of an organisation and acting for that organisation – evil they could never do as individuals. She was acutely aware of the dangers of demagogy. Unlike many of her contemporaries she had a very sceptical attitude towards the League of Nations.

Nevertheless she campaigned tirelessly on women's issues right through the '20s and '30s. She was active in the 6-Point Group urging equality between men and women and she was a founder-member of the Open Door Council. She wrote extensively in newspapers and magazines. She was a regular contributor to *Time and Tide* and was a highly respected figure among the leading feminists of the day. She wrote several novels, for one of which she won the Femina-Vie-Heureuse Prize, a number of plays and a series of travel books on Modern Europe, including the USSR. In Leningrad she met Daunt (she who told the ghost tales), who was then the sole administrator of Lady Paget's Fund for Distressed British Subjects. These were mostly old governesses stranded in the USSR, having lost all their property in the revolution. She (Daunt) wrote to Miss Ivens in 1931, very tired, describing the difficult conditions in which she had to work, and added, 'I must be the last of your flock still wandering around Russia in a uniform'.[27]

Cicely remained a faithful member of the Royaumont Association until her death. As she grew older she ran into financial problems. When she was 65 she was awarded a civil list pension of £80 per annum, later increased to £100. She died at the age of 80 on 6 December 1952, having been helped in her final months by a grant from the Royaumont Emergency Loan Fund which provided her with a few extra comforts. So Royaumont paid back a little of its debt to her who had done so much for its success and reputation.

On her death Ruth Nicholson spoke of her as 'the person who kept us sane'. 'So lovable, so interesting and entertaining, so erudite, always friendly and so brave. She was the one who really understood the French and guided us on the right path.'[28]

In her autobiography, published when she was 63, Cicely summed up her life: 'The bye-paths of interest have sometimes been such happy little bye-paths; and if the aim of life is its living, then I haven't done so badly for myself. I have had pleasures and thoughts and experiences that would have been denied me on a straight arterial road'.[29]

References

1. Hamilton, *Life Errant*.
2. Whitelaw, *The Life and Rebellious Times of Cicely Hamilton*.
3. Hamilton, *Life Errant*, p. 66.
4. *Op. cit.*, p. 65.
5. Cicely Hamilton, *Marriage as a Trade*, Chapman & Hall, London 1909, reprinted The Women's Press, London 1981.
6. Whitelaw, *op. cit.*, p. 104.
7. Quoted in Part One, Chapters 2 and 3.
8. ML. Tin 12, FI to Laurie, 12.8.16.
9. Mrs A.M. Robertson, letters home, 31.10.16, by kind permission of her granddaughter, Mrs Ailsa Tanner.
10. ML. Tin 12, Mrs Owen 2.2.15.
11. ML. Tin 12, Mrs Harley to Committee, March 1915.
12. IWM. D.H. Littlejohn, letter to fiancé, 11.12.14, by permission of her daughter, Miss Rachel Hedderwick.
13. Hamilton, *Life Errant*, p. 106.
14. *Op. cit.*, pp. 110–111.
15. Cicely Hamilton, *Senlis*, Collins, London 1917.
16. Hamilton, *Life Errant*, p. 109.
17. *Op. cit.*, p. 108.
18. *Op. cit.*, pp. 104–5.
19. *Op. cit.*, p. 230.
20. *Op. cit.*, pp. 233–236.
21. Mrs A.M. Robertson, letters home, 29.10.16, by permission of Mrs Ailsa Tanner.
22. NL 1938, p. 5.
23. *Ibid.*
24. MacLaren, *A History of the Scottish Women's Hospitals*, pp. 41–2.
25. Hamilton, *Life Errant*, p. 201.
26. *Op. cit.*, pp. 186–7.
27. NL 1932, p. 11.
28. NL 1953, p. 2.
29. Hamilton, *Life Errant*, p. 205.

CHAPTER FOURTEEN

Orderlies and Sisters

The Orderlies

Miss Ivens regarded her orderlies as the mainstay of the hospital. She formed this opinion when she witnessed the enormously heavy work they carried out in the initial period of preparation and, in spite of the occasional misfit, had no reason to change this opinion throughout the subsequent history of the hospital.

Collum wrote of them:

> The orderlies were untrained, raw material, most of them lacking even the personal discipline that comes from going down into the world's arena and competing there for a living. Even in the matter of physical strength they came up to a male standard. Throughout the rush of work that came to the hospital during the Somme battle, when the convalescents who usually give a hand had been evacuated, and the wounded poured in all day and all night long in a steady stream, every stretcher had to be carried upstairs to the wards, the x-ray rooms and the operating theatre, by women.[1]

These opinions were in stark contrast to those of John Masefield (later Poet Laureate) when he worked as a volunteer orderly in the spring of 1915 in a hospital in Arc-en-Barrois, Haute Marne:

> We have a lot of catty young minxes here and they have catty ways of wheedling when it is a question of carrying stinking blood in a bucket ... There were a lot of lady probationers who have lived idly and luxuriously and who are now, in the main, useless nuisances.[2]

The Royaumont orderlies, for the most part, came from similar backgrounds. What made them so different?

Perhaps it was in part due to the fact that the hospital was so very experimental, employing only women. They were on their mettle. They were as keen as the doctors to prove what women could do. There were no men to fall back upon to do the unpleasant tasks. They had to get on with them and they did. They also knew that those in charge were observing the work and determining where their particular talents lay. It was possible for an orderly to train as a radiographer or a laboratory technician, or to take overall charge of different departments – *vêtements*, stores, linen, housekeeping, pharmacy and so on. Those who proved themselves particularly valuable in the wards could be upgraded to the rank of Auxiliary Nurse with a salary and a defined status and to wear the White Cap. ('We used to respect the White Caps', Dr Macrae remembered when she was the Blue Cap orderly, Summerhayes.)

These Auxiliary Nurses did not have the knowledge that a fully-trained nurse might have had, but they knew, very thoroughly, what was appropriate for the military nursing at Royaumont.

Orderlies had to be sufficiently well-off to give their services voluntarily. Only uniforms, travel expenses and board and lodging were supplied. They came from a variety of backgrounds. For instance, Trail was the daughter of an Aberdeen professor; Banks and Littlejohn came from medical families; Summerhayes and Nicholson ('Nicky') had clerical backgrounds; Stewart and Daunt were 'landed gentry' and did not 'work'; Allan came from the shipping family and Denny from the Denny shipbuilding firm. Some already had their own profession. Davidson was teaching modern languages in Dornoch Academy; Norah Neilson-Gray was well-embarked on her successful artistic career (she was one of the famous 'Glasgow Girls'); Buckley and Almond were medical students; and Woodall and Freeman interrupted their studies at Girton College, Cambridge; Don was training to be an opera singer; and Minchin was in the Margaret Morris School of Dancing; Collum was a free-lance journalist; and Mrs Hacon had been at the centre of a cultured circle of writers and artists. There were a few widows, some of them the result of the war. Proctor had lost her fiancé in the Royal Flying Corps, and there may well have been others in a similar situation. Some had had previous VAD experience in military or voluntary hospitals in Britain; some no experience at all. A few, in the later stages of the war, came from other SWH hospitals in Serbia or Corsica. Moffat's sister, speaking of Royaumont, where her sister was an orderly, and later physiotherapist, said it was a very popular place.[3]

In spite of the then current French view that the women at Royaumont must have been among the most ardent of feminists, the facts do not bear this out. Cicely Hamilton, Collum, Mrs Hacon and Miss Loudon among others were involved in the suffrage movement. Norah Neilson-Gray certainly held strong feminist views. After the war she was commissioned by the Imperial War Museum to paint a picture of life at Royaumont. She was adamant that her painting should not be included in the Women's Work Section of the proposed exhibition.* Some, like Littlejohn, were heartily opposed to women's

---

* She described her picture as 'a view of soldier patients ... (seen by a woman if you like) – It was painted from within and absolutely true to fact. The scene would be unfamiliar to anyone who has not worked in a first-line hospital in France. It was unlike the pictures of rows of tidy beds which usually are the subject of hospital pictures'. She believed the Imperial War Museum should have a record of 'what was done by the British for the French Army in the way of hospitals'. This picture, 'Hôpital Auxiliaire d'Armée 30, Abbaye de Royaumont', is now in the Dumbarton District Library. Her other big picture, 'The Scottish Women's Hospital', was commissioned by the Imperial War Museum and painted after the war. It can still be seen there. See dust jacket.

suffrage. Starr's fears that some of the more outspoken and unconventional orderlies might be 'militant suffragettes' seem to have been without foundation. Summerhayes was actually ashamed to have an aunt who chained herself to railings (though on reflexion she thought she ought to have been proud!). As the war years passed, agitation for the vote faded and when it was actually granted in 1918 to women over 30 the event seems to have passed without comment so far as surviving records show. On the whole it was not women's rights that drew women to work at Royaumont. It was rather the opportunity to spread their wings, to escape from the restrictions of life at home, to answer the call of freedom and adventure with the added attraction of serving overseas. The Gamwell twins, who arrived in 1914, were 'very anxious to get to business and have a go at the Germans'.[4] Summerhayes tells us how the war relieved her of a rather uncongenial job at home:

> I was teaching in a little school up in the north. I hadn't settled what I was going to do, but my father, having seven children, in the days when the state didn't pay for you, ... I pushed out on my own and taught in this little school, and that was when war broke out, when I was up there. And I was so glad the war came because it released me. I taught English, I taught history, I taught hockey – I don't know what I didn't teach – I taught Latin, I taught everything. And praise be, the war came, and I got called up and I was able to leave without dishonour. I didn't let the school down.[5]

For Smeal, a Scot living in California, it was the sinking of the *Lusitania* which persuaded her to volunteer.[6]

Discipline was slack, but disciplinary problems were few. Having worked in a British military hospital before coming to Royaumont, Summerhayes found the lack of discipline strange, and considered it could not have worked with a 'less-committed set of orderlies'. Mrs Manson (Orderly Starr) agreed:

> An enthusiastic band – some very knowledgeable, others, like myself, willing but inexperienced. There was a fine feeling of camaraderie but always a helping hand in a difficulty. We were not surrounded by red tape. There was mutual trust and respect, and there was never any thought of abusing this.[7]

They had little idea when they arrived at Royaumont what might lie ahead of them. On landing in France for the first time, Proctor 'felt alone and homesick, far from England and home and safety. I was on a great adventure – the greatest of my life'.[8] She was not the only one to feel homesick. Berry, an early arrival in January 1915, was 'awfully homesick and shocked by the unconventionality and extreme discomfort at that time and said she wouldn't stay'.[9] Nevertheless stay she did, going on to be an expert radiographer, affectionately known as 'Granny B' (why, one wonders?).

They could smile later at their naïveté. Another of the first arrivals in December 1914 wrote:

> Do you recall our youthful enthusiasm in those early days, our keenness starting out for France with vague ideas of rescuing soldiers in the trenches (otherwise why take wellington boots?) and finding ourselves not on a battle field but in a lovely old Abbey with other strange women and a few chronic cases of bronchitis. You had, perhaps, pictured yourself wearing your wellington boots and tartan-trimmed coat, bringing comfort and relief to some poor poilu, instead, at first, it seemed rather problematical whether you would ever see a poilu, let alone look after one. Certainly you wore your wellington boots, but in the scullery where, ankle deep in water, you washed dishes and wondered why the cooks were so disagreeable. They too, no doubt, had dreamed of other sorts of kitchens in or near the front line, run by trained men orderlies.[10]

Looking back, it was the fun they remembered most clearly. (Possibly the painful memories were suppressed.) The picnics, often shared with sisters, doctors and patients, are a recurring feature of their photographic collections. Their memories included outings to Paris, long cycle rides to Chantilly, Soissons, or even as far as Chartres, sledging in the snow, skating on the lake, long walks in the woods, meals in the Cheval Blanc at Viarmes, and private supper parties. They were indefatigable at devising amusements for themselves and for their patients – and with the variety of talents among them these could be of a very high order. Armstrong produced some 'stirring dramas' – a skill she later developed in Australia. Warren was a brilliant pianist ('Mees Piano' to the blessés), and several of them had very good voices. Don was an opera singer. Perhaps it was a little disappointing for Watt ('le miss qui rit') to be told by a French officer that although her voice was beautiful her French accent was dreadful and she should stick to singing in English.[11] Minchin, a pupil of Margaret Morris, was well-versed in all the details of stage management and was, in addition, a beautiful dancer. Richmond had already embarked on her acting career under Sir Henry Beerbohm Tree when she came to Royaumont, and later pursued this successfully in London, Australia and in the BBC. She became co-director of a drama school and wrote a successful Textbook of Stagecraft. She was remembered by her Royaumont friends as the 'personification of gaiety and happiness', and for her rendering of Irish folk songs.[12] Moore got some of her experience at Royaumont which could have prepared her for her eleven years in The Mousetrap! Cicely Hamilton's dramatic productions have already been described.

Their easy relations with their patients are typified by the exploits of Chapman and her friends on April 1st 1917 when they disguised themselves as blessés and got themselves admitted to the ward (see Chapter 5).

They sometimes got themselves into scrapes. Summerhayes remembers a spot of trouble shared with her friend Simms over the huge 'marmite' in the bathroom in which water was heated. On night duty:

> We used to have to clear it out, it was really rather an awful task, and the only thing to do was to laugh because if not you'd have cried, really, digging out all these ashes. And then we used to put them in a bucket, and then we left them, and one day the bucket set on fire and we found the fire brigade rushing madly round the abbey saying 'Where is the fire coming from?'. I said, 'Quickly, Simms, quickly, put it outside in the cloisters, we can't be had up for this! So just in time we were able to get rid of our incriminating ashes which were burning through the bottom of the bucket. It was a good thing to have a good pal there. We had great times.

They coped in varying ways with the suffering they saw. For many there was no gentle introduction. Watt found her first night in the ward 'terrifying' as a soldier lay dying. Summerhayes' first task was to carry the body of a young village woman with a ruptured uterus to the chapel used temporarily as a mortuary. She had never before seen a corpse. Orderly Starr was deeply distressed, and almost overwhelmed, by the sights and sounds of men in agony. She was saved from breakdown by the understanding and sympathy of senior staff. Proctor felt being young was the important thing and this helped her to cope. Summerhayes 'took it perhaps for granted and knew that was what one had gone out for'.

Few described their deeper and more intimate feelings – a reflection perhaps of the stiff upper lip ethos of the time. Summerhayes came nearest to it. She was 98 years old when she recorded this memory:

> I'll always remember the wonderful Easter there [at Villers-Cotterets in 1918] ... We had a train that came into our camp with the wounded, and we spent the whole night unloading the train and dealing with them in the theatre and so on [she was theatre orderly] ... and then in the morning – suddenly – we had gone through this *bloody* night – and it was a beautiful morning – very calm – lovely sunshine – and the service ... I remember walking down the main floorway (duckboards between the wards) to the little chapel where the Canadian chaplain had arrived for the communion service. I always remember the lovely sort of – why did it give me such a good feeling? I don't know, because I suppose we'd achieved all this in the night.[13]

With their new-found freedom they discovered smoking. How many of them smoked, or how many of the doctors did, we do not know. Miss Ivens did not, though the founder, Dr Elsie Inglis, did. Proctor replied: 'we all smoke and it doesn't matter what one does'. She asks for cigarettes to be sent out, 'any-

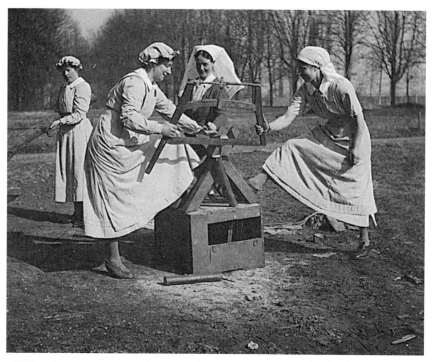

Villers-Cotterets, Autumn 1917 or early spring 1918. Preparing fuel. Orderly Violet Inglis on left. A sister, in veil, and a 'white-cap', auxiliary nurse. (By courtesy of Miss Helen Lowe).

thing as long as it is not Virginian'.[14] Simms felt unjustly treated when she was 'required to pay 67 francs on a present of cigarettes. Hardly worth it, is it? – It is so absurd, if this hospital contained Belgian, English, Portuguese or in fact any other nationality but French I could have had them for nothing'.[15] Summerhayes as usual had a robust answer. 'Damn it all, I thought, I'm not going to do this horrible thing just because others are doing it.' (She had tried it for six weeks.)[16]

Keeping pets was one area where authority was flouted – or perhaps authority turned a blind eye. The story of Jimmy the canary and his escape from Villers-Cotterets has already been told (Chapter 7), but he was only one of a number of other birds bred by Sister Everingham. Dinkie was another – and Dinkie was put in a little wooden cage on top of the pulpit in the chapel 'and how he sang! I think he felt he was in the right place to sing'.[17] Birks ('Binkie') had a guinea pig, and Barclay kept birds. One of these, Louis, died 'when everything was frozen hard and so had to be burned in the incinerator. I can recall her pretty tear-stained face as she rushed through the passages with the dead bird in her hand'.[18] 'Everyone knew La Colonelle's efforts to suppress surreptitious livestock that *would* find its way into the wards but they suffered a severe setback when Butler's condemned bitch was not only living long after the date of her supposed execution but had brought up a flourishing family – one of whom rode in her lap driving up to Villers-Cotterets'.[19]

Spot, the mongrel, left behind at Villers-Cotterets by retreating British troops, became the hospital mascot and so held almost an official position. A study of Royaumont photographs reveals other items of livestock: Jack the rabbit, Tranche the cat, and Peter and Dimitri, the dogs. The pets that were not approved of were 'two dirty little pups running around the kitchen, also a big dog, and none of them are trained, so you can imagine what it's like. The kitchen people are always complaining, but the pups are the chef's [Michelet's] and everyone is afraid of offending him in case he should leave'.[20] It would seem that there was some justification for Summerhayes' opinion that though the surgery and medical treatment were very good, the hygiene did leave something to be desired.

There was some slight shortening of the skirts as the years rolled on, but Miss Ivens was adamant about the hair. Short hair would seem to be a sensible rationalisation when water for washing was always in short supply ('I don't think we washed much', said Summerhayes when she thought about it later), and there were probably others besides Rolt whose hair fell down in moments of crisis. Simms rebelled at Villers-Cotterets where she was not under the eagle eye of Miss Ivens. 'I had to have my hair cut off again yesterday, it was getting so untidy. A Frenchwoman sat watching the operation with her mouth open. There are three others here with cropped heads, one a sister, so I'm not lonely.'[21]

Two orderlies, apart from Mary Peter (Chapter 5), found their future husbands at Royaumont. In 1914 Percival came over with her car, and, in case the authorities would not allow her to drive it, she brought along her brother for a short period. But this was long enough for him to fall in love, and later marry, her fellow-orderly, Allan. Towards the end a relative of Mary Anderson, who was ill, asked a young French officer to visit her. She became Madame Petitpierre and settled permanently in France.

For a few of the orderlies their experiences at Royaumont set the pattern of their future careers. Cranage, Stein and Summerhayes qualified in medicine, and Buckley and Almond completed their interrupted medical studies. Buckley made her career in radiology. She had been fortunate, unlike Berry, Collum, Butler and Large, to have escaped radiological injury at Royaumont. Almond (Mrs Johnson) sadly died in childbirth. A few, having gained considerable competence in nursing in the hospital, embarked on full training after the war. Miller, a close friend of Ruth Nicholson and much admired by Miss Ivens, became sister, later Sister Tutor in the Stanley Hospital in Liverpool; she later held the same position in the Edinburgh Royal Infirmary. She looked after Ruth Nicholson in Devonshire when she became disabled from arthritis. Agnes Anderson, 'Big Andy', trained in midwifery, worked in

India and Ceylon and had a distinguished nursing service in World War Two with the British Red Cross. Merrilees was a 'masseuse' in St Bartholemew's Hospital for 20 years, and Middleton became an almoner at St Thomas's Hospital.

There was a wide scattering over the globe after the end of the war. Some followed their husbands, but a considerable number who remained unmarried seem to have sought more experience and adventure abroad. Simms was one of these. Her letters home indicate the extent of her travels. She always intended to settle down, but never quite achieved it. The Gamwell twins ran a coffee farm in Northern Rhodesia. Armstrong farmed in Australia, and Figgis finally settled down in Melbourne. Alison Nicholson ('Nicky', Ruth Nicholson's sister) worked in Bucharest and Daunt went to Leningrad. Carter (later Lady Hills) became an economics don at Cambridge. Davidson went back to teaching, and Freeman and Martin were both, in turn, headmistress of Westonbirt School for Girls.

For others the return from a life of adventure and achievement was less exciting. Some went back to the traditional role of caring for the family. Chapman brought up her motherless nephews and nieces; other cared for aging parents. Many did useful work in World War Two. They kept up their wartime friendships to a remarkable degree.

Looking back, Bruce found it was 'an amazing and unforgettable experience – that widened one's outlook and enriched one's life',[22] and for Minchin it was 'an enchanting memory'. When she visited Royaumont much later Mackay wrote:

> But isn't it curious today, twenty years after the war, that little and tragi-comic part of our lives which we spent at Royaumont should stand out so clearly amongst much that is blurred and half-remembered? Quite apart from the fact that many of us were then in what is called an impression-able age, none of the other war work some of us did before or after our time at Royaumont left the same clear-cut imprint on our memories. Yet those of us who have visited Royaumont and its surroundings find that few if any of the inhabitants remember the strange badly-dressed foreign ladies who worked there during the war.[23]

References

1. 'Skia' (V.C.C. Collum), *Blackwood's Magazine*, Nov. 1918, p. 620.
2. *John Masefield's Letters from the Front, 1915–1917*. Ed. Peter Vansittart. Constable 1984, pp. 57 and 84.
3. Interview with Miss Una Moffat (aged 98), 1.7.93, by courtesy of Dr Leah Leneman.
4. Antonia Marian Gamwell, IWM SR 502/11.
5. Interview with Dr Grace MacRae (née Summerhayes) 10.6.93, by courtesy of

Dr Leah Leneman.

6. Personal communication from Mrs Fairlie (niece).

7. NL 1973, p. 7.

8. IWM. E.H. Proctor, 'On landing in France'. An essay.

9. NL 1956, p. 5 and NL 1961, p. 5.

10. NL 1950, p. 1.

11. Personal communication from Mrs Mona Calder (daughter).

12. NL 1959, p. 2.

13. Interview Dr MacRae.

14. IWM. Proctor letters, 27.7.17.

15. F.B. Simms, letter to governess, 13.2.18, by kind permission of Miss M.P. Simms (niece).

16. Personal interview with Dr Grace MacRae, 12.7.93.

17. NL 1955, p.7.

18. NL 1957, p.7.

19. NL 1928, April, p. 9.

20. F.B. Simms, *loc. cit.*, 9.1.18.

21. F.B. Simms, *loc. cit.*, 27.3.18.

22. NL 1962, p. 4.

23. NL 1934, p. 1.

The Sisters

The work of nurses in World War One was a crucial milestone in the long evolution of the nursing profession. In the pre-Nightingale days the standards of so-called 'nurses' were abysmally low, but by the turn of the century the Nightingale reforms had already achieved great changes and standards were rising. The need for training was fully recognised but there was not as yet any agreement as to what that training should be. The Nightingale reforms required that 'ladies' of higher social class and education who were destined for positions of authority should undertake one year's training in hospital. 'Probationers', on the other hand, on whom the basic work of the hospital depended, and who were generally recruited from a lower and less well-educated class, were required to have three years' training. In the later decades of the nineteenth century and up to the beginning of the war the demand for nurses was increasing. More patients were being treated in hospitals; there were more patients in the workhouses and the demand for home nursing was rising – by the rich in their own homes and by the poor since the introduction of the District Nursing Service in 1900.

The new 'lady nurses' now leading the profession wanted to make a clear distinction between 'trained' and 'untrained', both to protect the public and to enhance the prestige of the profession. This was part of the wider feminist movement which became particularly powerful in the years preceding the war. On the outbreak of war the movement towards the registration of nurses, based on recognised standards of training, was gathering strength though

Washing. Chauffeur Young uses a bit of private enterprise.
(By courtesy of Miss Heather Mackay).

there was still considerable opposition both in the country at large and also among some leaders of the profession. How, they asked, could they ever, given the general state of girls' education at the time, provide the very large numbers required? This question was still unresolved when war broke out, and, as with so many issues, active campaigning died down and energies were directed towards the war effort. It was not until 1919 that the registration of nurses was finally introduced.

The war produced an enormous escalation in the demand for nurses. Nursing the wounded was a popular goal for many women, trained and experienced nurses as well as the members of Voluntary Aid Detachments. The popularity of the armed forces and the voluntary hospitals, particularly those serving abroad, in attracting nurses was unfortunate for the civilian population at home. Throughout the war it was the chronic sick, the sick in the workhouse infirmaries and mental institutions, as well as the 'ordinary' patient in the civilian hospitals, who suffered most from the shortages. By the final year of the war recruitment of nurses for the armed forces as well as voluntary hospitals such as Royaumont was becoming difficult.

In all, 184 nurses served at Royaumont. Of these, almost all completed their six-month contract: 37 extended their service, presumably an arrangement satisfactory for both sides; three returned for further service after a spell at home or elsewhere; 18 did not complete their contracted service of six months, but of these, 11 left because the war had come to an end and the hospital was closing. Three were dismissed: one for insubordination, one for 'bad behaviour' and one for a reason unspecified. Miss Ivens asked the Committee not to renew the contract of a fourth as she was the cause of much friction with the other sisters. It was only to be expected that there should be some variation in the quality of the sisters sent to Royaumont, some indifferent but others of top quality. The orderlies were well-placed to judge the quality and character of the sisters. One was known as 'God Almighty'; another was 'lazy' but obeyed her orderly when told it was time to make the beds! Starr provides clear evidence of the variable quality in her diary recording the 'rushes' of Autumn 1915:

> I have had the most trying sister to train me. Now I have another and
> what a difference – the other used to lose her head in a rush ... now it is
> heaven in comparison.[1]

This was probably Sister Lindsay from Glasgow Royal Infirmary – 'A first-rate surgical nurse – she gets all the difficult dressings to do'. She was a very popular member of the Unit, was later promoted to Matron and proved to be one of the most successful of the Royaumont appointments. An orderly remembered her: 'She had patience and understanding when dealing with inexperienced young women'.[2]

Miss Duncan, the second matron, had a difficult time with some of her staff as Starr noted when she was nursing her during a short illness. She was 'a nice old soul' but 'the sisters are always squabbling among themselves and tattling to her and she has to please them all and it is no joke as she hasn't the authority she should have'.[3] At other times the sisters showed solidarity and after the battles of the Somme clubbed together to send money out of their meagre salaries for the relief of the civilian refugees.

The sisters have left very little record of their own views and experiences of their time at Royaumont, but for those (38) who joined the Association after the war one can assume that it was a positive experience. This was certainly the case for Sister Douglas. She wrote from the Royal Naval Hospital in July and August 1917:

> I gave my name to the Navy a short time ago not expecting to be called
> up for a long time. Unfortunately they have called me up so soon. It was
> a terrible wrench to leave Royaumont. I would go straight back now if I
> could. I don't know why I ever thought of leaving it ... Haslar is very
> nice, and we have a very nice time, picnics, tennis, bathing, cycling etc.
> Yet I believe if it were possible I'd start back to Villers-Cotterets tomor-
> row ... The life in France suited me better than all the conventional
> civilisation here. Then the cases are less interesting, and the treatment –
> much the same as was done in the days of Nelson!!! – I keep wanting to

tell them how things were done at Royaumont, but of course it wouldn't do, and also like everything else the treatment must be carried out according to routine and as it has always been done. All the time is taken up with rules and regulations.[4]

Sister O'Rorke was another who regretted leaving Royaumont, but, unlike Sister Douglas, she did manage to return. This was fortunate for Royaumont, for the Scottish Women's Hospitals and for the children of Serbia. Writing from the enormous 4000-bedded Policlinico in Rome in May 1916, she wrote:

I am very lonely over leaving Royaumont but had to do so, having unhappily signed on for service in Italy during the early days of the war, however I do not like the work here as the patients are not at all nicely treated, so I am resigning and will write to 2 St Andrew Square [the HQ of the SWH Committee] to ask if they will put me on their list.[5]

The case of Sister O'Rorke illustrates the pragmatic attitude taken by Miss Ivens for which she had the support of the Committee. Technically Sister O'Rorke did not fulfil the War Office definition of 'trained' nurse because she had received her training from Nurse Edith Cavell* in the Belgian Institute of Nursing and not in a recognised British hospital. Nevertheless Miss Ivens promoted her to be 'sister-in-charge' to succeed Sister MacKnight who had been in the forefront of the campaign (Chapter 7) to bar 'not fully trained' nurses. She was now to take charge of Sister MacKnight's ward. Miss Ivens wrote:

Sister O'Rorke has taken on a very difficult post owing to the agitation created by Sister MacKnight ... she is doing extremely well and is one of the few nurses who is always prepared to do her utmost without argument and I think it would be treating her with base ingratitude not to appoint her.[6]

She stayed at Royaumont until the end, was awarded the Croix de Guerre and then transferred to the America Unit of the Scottish Women's Hospitals in Serbia to help with a typhus epidemic. In 1921 she joined the staff of the Anglo-Serbian Children's Hospital and remained in Serbia until her final illness in 1931. She was awarded the Order of St Sava, and on her death her obituary in *The Times* noted:

Her life was an example of rare devotion to others and of true charity, and her name will not soon be forgotten among the peasants of Serbia who entrusted their children to her care.[7]

---

* Executed by the Germans in 1915 for her part in assisting in the escape of Allied prisoners of war.

Other sisters served Royaumont well: Sister (later Matron) Winstanley, 'an excellent organiser' who was remembered for her 'quickness, brightness and willingness to take on any amount of work'; Sister Grey whose death so saddened the Unit and called forth the tribute of a *poilu* – 'our good friend Miss Grey who has always something gentle to do to us'; Sister Inkson, 'hardworking and efficient throughout those terrible months'; Sister Whitworth, 'one of our favourite and most efficient sisters'; Sister Rose Morris of Blanche de Castille Ward, loved by her orderlies; Sister MacGregor, admired by Dr Courtauld and her patients in 'Mary'; Sister Williams with her Senegalese and Arab patients who called forth the admiration of Mrs Robertson; Sister Everingham, chief theatre sister through the stresses of the evacuation of Villers-Cotterets and subsequently at Royaumont in 1918; and Sister Goodwin who was surgical nurse through the bombardments when, as she wrote to Miss Ivens:

> we stayed for hours in the darkness and that ammunition train was
> bombed, and we had so much work to do, and the shrapnel was flying in
> all directions. That indeed was a dreadful night but you were like the
> Rock of Gibraltar and inspired us all.[8]

Miss Ivens paid her tribute in turn to Sister Goodwin and recommended her successfully for the Croix de Guerre. After the war she went to Serbia with the Scottish Women's Hospitals, then to the American Red Cross and finally to the Belgrade Nursing Training School. Other sisters who continued to work for the Scottish Women's Hospitals were Houston (Lady Tew), Lawson and Wallace. For all of these the experience of working at Royaumont must have been very significant. What a loss it is that they said so little about it themselves.

References

1. IWM. Starr Diary, 27.9.15.
2. NL 1967, p. 3.
3. IWM. Starr Diary, 2.12.15.
4. ML. Tin 30, Douglas to Laurie, 28.7.17.
5. ML. Tin 36, O'Rorke to Laurie, 7.7.16.
6. ML. Tin 42, Ivens to May, 30.8.17.
7. *Times*, 13.1.32.
8. NL 1938, p. 14.

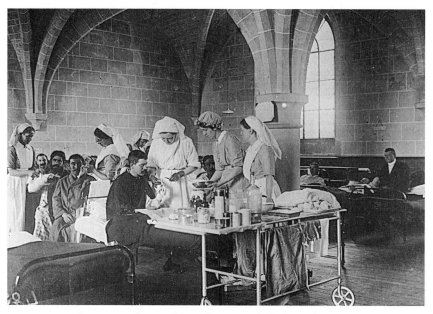

Sister in veil assisted by 'Blue cap' orderly doing dressings.

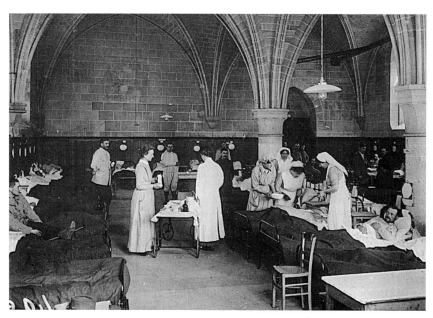

*Dressings in Blanche de Castille Ward. Sister in veil,
orderly in blue uniform with blue cap.
(By permission of the Imperial War Museum).*

PART THREE

Envoi

CHAPTER FIFTEEN

In Action Again: France 1940

The experience shared by the women who served in Royaumont and Villers-Cotterets during World War One inspired many of them with a wish to serve once more in France on the outbreak of World War Two. Throughout the inter-war years they had cherished a strong emotional attachment to the French *poilu*. They had admired his courage in the face of his devastating experiences, had suffered with him in the bad times, and shared the good.

Their emotional involvement extended from their personal and fondly remembered associations with the *blessés* to the whole French nation. Furthermore, through their Association they had kept in touch with each other, maintaining and strengthening old friendships. They saw now an opportunity to share once again a thirst for adventure and commitment that had led them to Royaumont in the first place.

They remembered the great need they had been able to fulfil in Soissons in 1917 by the provision of a canteen, and this seemed an appropriate area for their energies nearly a quarter-century later.

A small group met in December 1939, a committee was formed, and plans were set in hand to offer a canteen – a Scottish Women's Hospital Canteen – to the French authorities to operate behind the Maginot Line to provide refreshments and recreational facilities for the French Army. This was to be manned by Royaumont veterans, medically fit, and capable of supporting themselves to the tune of £1 per week. The offer was accepted, funds were collected, and by February 16th 1940 Etta Inglis and Dorothy Carey-Morgan left for Paris as joint managers.

They had both been at Royaumont for long periods. Etta (to distinguish her from her two Inglis sisters who were also at Royaumont) went out as an orderly (later promoted to Auxiliary Nurse) in January 1915 and remained almost continuously until the abbey closed in 1919. She had been in charge of the Soissons canteen in 1917, and in 1918 she took part in the final traumatic evacuation of Villers-Cotterets when, with the German Army already ensconced in the Forest and advancing rapidly, the hospital became quite untenable. She was decorated with the Croix de Guerre for her heroism, particularly under bombardment at Soissons.

Morgan served as an orderly for almost three years from June 1915 to February 1918, and was therefore involved in the Somme rushes. She served part of her time as storekeeper, earning her the title of 'Miss Magazin' by the men. In quieter spells she used her off-duty times to produce some very beautiful aquatints and etchings now in the Imperial War Museum.

In Paris they negotiated with Mme de Wendel of the Association des Dames de France (ADF) who informed them that they were welcome *but* the Royaumont committee would be expected to equip, staff and control the canteen; that the staff would be responsible to the ADF and any profits would go to the ADF. In return the ADF agreed to cover any losses.

With these arrangements made, they went to Metz and then proceeded east in the *zone des Armées*, through the *Zone interdite* and, 50 kms further on, to the Zone *fortifiée*. On the way they noted: 'everywhere there were soldiers, guns, horses, ammunition carts, but never a place for the men to go to write letters or to be at peace'. They would have liked to have a canteen in every village they passed: it seemed that the lack of canteens which had been so noticeable in World War One was still a problem.

They reached Mouzaia which had been selected for them by the ADF. This was only 1 km from the nearest Maginot fort which had been constructed within a coal mine built by the Germans as reparations after the war. It was to be the most advanced canteen in France.

(Before World War One the French Army had almost totally neglected the forts that had been built after the 1870 débâcle, deeming them unnecessary in modern warfare – a policy with disastrous results. Before the Second World War they swung to the other extreme and built what they deemed to be an impregnable wall. The deficiencies of the Maginot Line are now a matter of history.)

Other old Royaumontites arrived: Percival had been a clerk in the early days; MacPherson (now Mrs Bruce) came in May 1916 and stayed to the end. Like Morgan, she was an artist in civil life, and had been another 'Miss Magazin' at Royaumont. Their experiences of storekeeping must have been useful in their new work. Mrs Robinson had been an orderly for a year from 1917 to 1918 and Howard-Smith from April 1918 to January 1919. (Her performance as Widow Twanky in the 1918 Christmas pantomime was a fondly cherished Royaumont memory.) Macfie had been an orderly in 1915, and Prance was one of the early chauffeurs. The canteen staff as it was now constituted included some with experience of the early chaotic days in the Abbey and others who knew all about the tremendous rushes of work in the most stressful periods. Macfie brought her car – a roomy Vauxhall 14, and Prance her little two-seater Standard 9. These were welcomed as useful in running the canteens, but little did they know what a godsend they were to be in the future.

The canteen was to be set up in several rooms of an abandoned school. The Army undertook to furnish a house for their own use – and so they did, with 6 bedsteads, 2 spring mattresses, one feather bed, 4 pillows, a jumble of odd jugs and basins and dressing tables and an endless procession of 'tables de nuit'. Only three of the bedsteads actually fitted the frames. They also promised to instal water and electricity, both of which were absent (shades of the old days at the Abbey). These materialised only when they threatened to open on Easter Sunday with or without such facilities. The blackmail worked – their previous experience had served them well. Their own preparations went on apace: food and drink supplies laid on, a bar, a shop, bright furnishings, games etc. On the declaration of 'Foyer Ouvert', what seemed like the entire French Army descended on them with one gigantic thirst. After the initial rush the crowds moderated somewhat and they settled down to around 1000 a day. The canteen was a resounding success and they were asked to take over a second one at Créhanges nearby.

Everything was going smoothly until one night the order came through that all women, children and civilians (this did not apply to them) were to be evacuated forthwith, and the men were to be withdrawn into the Maginot Line fort. The Battle of France had begun. All the ADF canteens closed. They alone remained.

It seems strange that they had no idea of the tremendous events then unfolding: 'All English wireless news had been jammed and the French broadcasts told them practically nothing'.

They did not know that the Belgians had capitulated on 26th May. They did not know that a bridgehead had been established at Dunkirk on May 27th to evacuate British troops or that a quarter of a million had been evacuated between then and June 4th. They did not know that the Germans had entered Rouen on 7th June, that the French Government had left Paris for Tours on June 11th or that the French Army was rapidly disintegrating from June 12th.

It was only on the afternoon of June 13th that they received the order to evacuate – they must be gone by 7 p.m. Shortly after – another message. They must be away by 6 p.m.

They packed into two cars – five in the Vauxhall which was to be driven by Macfie, and three in Prance's little two-seater which she would drive herself. They were still unaware of the gravity of the situation. They planned a pleasant evening in Metz: they would have a hot bath, visit a hairdresser, and do some sightseeing. They only began to realise what a serious situation they were in when Howard-Smith met the British RTO who warned them the bridges were about to be blown and they should get out immediately. Then, over dinner, 'doubts changed to horror' as they heard Paul Reynaud's almost hysterical final appeal to America. By 11 p.m. they were on their way to Nancy, driving in dense traffic and arriving at 4 a.m. They got a short sleep, food and left at 10 a.m., heading for Neufchateau:

> The roads were again crowded with cars full of refugees, their luggage
> piled high, and always with a mattress tied on the roof. Every conceivable
> kind of vehicle was there, petrol-driven and horse-drawn, and the poorer

refugees trudged along pushing handcarts, prams, bicycles, all laden with household goods, pathetic *lares* and *penates*, mingled with dogs, cats, goats, birds in cages and hens in coops.

At noon they were in Neufchateau. The town was in turmoil. It had been heavily and systematically bombed during the night. They realised now they would have to get back to England and regroup. They intended to make for Le Havre, but, hearing that the Germans were already there, decided Bordeaux was their only hope.

They selected a route through Chaumont, Dijon and Périgueux. They were told that the road to Chaumont had been bombed out of existence, but as it was the only one they decided to attempt it:

It was in a terrible mess, with burning cars and buses lying in heaps and all angles, and the banks and both sides pitted with bomb craters. Still we always found just room to pass between the burning cars ... Always there were the unending streams of refugees. Sometimes their car had broken down; sometimes their horse lay dead in the ditch, the distracted family group around the laden cart, looking vainly for help. Every village we passed had houses that were still burning fiercely, and more bomb craters.

They had some pieces of luck. The warning that the bridge ahead was down proved to be incorrect and they got across, got a tankful of petrol (they were carrying army coupons), and 1½ kms from Langres they learned that the Germans were already in occupation. A 50 km detour kept them from driving straight into them. A long weary drive brought them to Dijon at 7 p.m., the same day the Germans entered Paris.

At Dijon the two cars separated. Percival, in Prance's little car, had a most ill-timed attack of malaria and had to spend the night in what appeared to be the only available bed in Dijon. The Vauxhall party went on again at 9 p.m. and drove till they could go no further. They spent a few hours, all five of them, huddled inside the car in the pouring rain. At 4.30 they set off again for Mâcon, Puy de Dome, Clermont-Ferrand, Rouanne, Cluny and Tulle into the Dordogne. The roads were now peaceful. Few refugees had managed to get as far. They slept, or failed to sleep, in a pinewood, and set off once more at 5 a.m. for Périgueux and Bordeaux.

Bordeaux was a 'seething mass of refugees'. The French Government had arrived there from Tours on the previous day, June 14th. Every British unit left in France was there, but fortunately for them the Consulate was still functioning. They got their names on the list for the next boat and reported hourly. They slept heavily and next morning, armed with two cooked chickens, 36 hard-boiled eggs, yards of bread and kilos of butter and cheese to keep them for the next five days, they boarded the collier *Rhineland*.

Just as they up-anchored, the French surrender was announced among scenes of great emotion: 'Many of the rough dockers were in tears, and so was our pilot. Our hearts were heavy as we steamed to the mouth of the Gironde'. Here they anchored and waited while a German plane, aiming at the oil tanks, hit and sank the ships just ahead of them. The *Rhineland* was carrying 150 refugees in addition to its normal crew of 26. There were now 20 ships straggling back to England, without protection of any kind and without either boats or lifebelts. With characteristic Royaumont efficiency they organised a casualty station in one of the cabins, offered treatment to the other refugees, and dressed the injuries of a wounded airman.

Five days later they landed at Falmouth. For them this was a most happy landfall as they were within a few miles of the home of Miss Ivens, their old Médecin-Chef. As yet they knew nothing of the fate of the other car.

They had left them at Neufchateau. Fortunately Percival had recovered sufficiently for them to be able to continue their journey, but the day had been serious. Prance wrote: 'Unhappily hundreds of cars had passed us in the night, congesting roads and devouring petrol. I only could make 40 miles in 6 hours closest driving'. In Autun they slept in the Grande Place, Prance on the ground, the other two in the car. They set off again at 6 a.m. on the 16th. Prance was sure the Germans would make for Bordeaux, and would therefore be likely to go through Chateaudun. She decided on a route more to the south. This was a wise decision. The Germans had entered Dijon just after they had left and were in Autun and Chateaudun later that day – the 16th.

They stopped at 'G' (unidentified), where there was a military petrol station. The officer persistently refused them in spite of their military petrol coupons – possibly he was suspicious of the non-military appearance of the little two-seater. All day long, from 9.30 a.m. to 6.30 p.m., they sat there, repeatedly asking for petrol. The officer was getting impatient. 'When are you going on?' 'As soon as we get some petrol.' Exasperated, he shouted at them to go to the wine merchant up the street. M. Vanier was charming and he was charmed by Prance. After five minutes' chat he let her have four gallons. The charm continued – if she could have just one more gallon, her tank would be full and that 'would halve my strain'. She got her petrol. It was now getting late and the tender-hearted M. Vanier could not bear the thought of their getting no rest and offered them a bed. They were in it at 10 p.m. but at 11 p.m. the message came that the Germans were one hour behind them and the Loire bridges, 25 miles away, were due to be blown in two hours' time. They were off again, got across safely, and were safe for the time being. The German advance was checked at the Loire as they had to prepare bridgeheads.

From 2.45 to 3.45 a.m. – 'the black hour' – Prance slept at the wheel on the grassy verge. At 9 a.m. she fell asleep at the wheel, stopped for half an hour and drove on again till 6.30 p.m. She woke up to find her little car on the left side of the road 'purring along as straight as a die'. It was now really time to stop. They found a friendly farm, supped on eggs and milk and slept soundly in the barn on golden straw.

During the day the French had requested an armistice.

Next day, the 18th, a long drive towards Bordeaux. They planned another blissful night on a farm, but no sooner had they made their arrangements than a message came through that the Germans would arrive that night. So it was into the car again. At 2 a.m. they were stopped by a sentry at 'M' (unidentified). By this time they were glad to be stopped. Next day, the 19th, the Chief of Police, who had steadily refused to give them permission to move, became fed up with these tiresome and persistent women: 'Oh, go on then, and be quick about it'.

They reached Bordeaux at midday. The port was closed, and so was the British Consulate. A notice on the door advised all British subjects to go to Bayonne. More driving for Prance. She found that running at 35 mph she could not keep awake. At 55 mph she could, just.

At last they were in Bayonne. It did not help that the hotel was very abusive. (There were those who felt that the British were deserting them in their hour of need.) So for two nights they had to sleep on the floor of a garage until they could board a Dutch boat. They zigzagged to Plymouth in 24 hours, arriving on June 22nd, one day before the Pétain government signed the armistice.

Reading this account of Prance and her car, it seems almost incredible that she was 65 years old at the time of this epic journey. She had been the first owner-driver to respond to the call of the Scottish Women's Hospitals for Foreign Service on the outbreak of war in 1914. She was almost 40 then. She did yeoman service as a chauffeur, and at lighter moments played her violin in ward concerts and parties. She also served for a time in Serbia.

It is not surprising that she felt the journey had taken quite a lot out of her – but it did not deter her from driving ambulances in London for the rest of the war, though she did admit the first couple of months 'were a bit of an effort'.

'Big Andy', Auxiliary Nurse Agnes Anderson, had served at Royaumont from April 1915 to August 1918. In World War Two she had an experience rather different from the story just told, which she described as 'An Inglorious Adventure' or 'The Canteen that Never Was'. With two friends, Lewis and Vereker (not Royaumontites), she left London on May 29th hoping to work in one of the canteens on the Belgian frontier run by the Association des Dames de France. At Waterloo station they were advised that the only route to Paris was via Jersey. At Southampton they were told that if they went there they would be there for the duration. (The Dunkirk evacuation was already in progress.) They were allowed on a troopship which got as far as Portsmouth where they anchored all night as the Germans were laying mines. Next morning they were back in Southampton again where they filled up with British Tommies and French sailors and set off for Cherbourg 'mines or no mines'. Fortunately it was 'no mines'. In Paris they were asked what they had come for – a question they found difficult to answer in the situation which was rapidly developing.

On June 3rd they reported to the ADF where they were met with 'astonished dismay'. 'On ne vous attend pas!' It was clear the ADF had no idea what to do with them. So they offered themselves to the Société des Services Sociales to help with refugees. This was welcomed and they were each given a vehicle to collect children from Rouen, bring them back to Paris and put them on a train for the South. The next task was for Anderson and Lewis to take a *camionette* stacked high with clothing, layettes, etc and work for the local organisation in La Rochelle in Brittany. Vereker was sent with another vehicle to Limoges. Or Périgueux. Or somewhere. (They never knew where she went.) On the way they met the same distressing crowds of refugees as the other party had done: cars crammed with luggage and passengers, mattresses piled on the roofs to deflect machine gun bullets, and pitiful groups on foot trudging along – going anywhere as long as it was to get away from the Germans.

In La Rochelle and in some of the outlying villages they did what they could, but in the general chaos felt they could do nothing effective in France and they had better get back to England if at all possible where they might be of some use.

The consul advised Bordeaux, but they preferred to try the nearer port of La Palisse. More work on the way with the never-ending streams of refugees, and then, at noon on June 17th, 'they heard the radio announcing that Pétain had asked for a *cesse-feu*. This was followed by the Marseillaise. A hush fell on the town for a moment or two. Then horrified men and women poured out of their houses, asking each other incredulously if it could be true. They looked in despair but were stunned and quiet'.

At La Palisse they were at first refused passage but a few hours later were allowed to join a convoy of lorries trundling towards the mole. 'Perhaps', wrote Anderson, 'the authorities were sick of the sight of us sitting there looking pathetic.' Here every car was abandoned. There was no time to dismantle anything, so the men smashed the petrol tanks with picks and slashed the tyres. 2000 men piled on board a half-empty collier, and lay in a heap anywhere they could find, exhausted. The boat sailed far out into the Atlantic to avoid submarines which were reported to be active nearby. Four days later, at 3.30 a.m. on June 21st, they landed in Newport, smothered in coal dust, but safe.

Looking back over 50 years, we cannot but admire the way they made themselves useful wherever they went in those terrible days of the collapse of France, always undertaking practical action where they saw the need and upholding the high standards of Royaumont.

There is one more story to tell, that of Rolt. Hers was a solitary journey, and the one that came closest to disaster.

At Royaumont she had been an auxiliary nurse from November 1915 to February 1919. Her long service had included the Somme rushes of 1916 and the stressful months of 1918. In addition in 1917, a quieter year for many of the unit, she had served with Inglis in the Soissons canteen which had been under bombardment for much of the time. She, like Inglis, had received the Croix de Guerre for this work. She was reckoned to be one of the most out-standingly useful members of the Unit. As one of her fellow-workers wrote: 'I wonder how many jobs she took on at Royaumont and made a success of them all'.

Her life between the wars must have been very quiet in comparison, running her own dressmaking and millinery business, but when the Royaumont canteens were planned she decided to volunteer.

However, her brother's illness detained her so that she only reached Paris on June 9th. She hoped to proceed to Metz the following day. The Rouge Croix offices were preparing to evacuate and had closed down. The Ministry which was responsible for issuing papers to allow her to enter the War Zone had already left for Tours. The Association des Dames de France was in confusion and could tell her nothing. She was unable to communicate with the canteens.

Paris was now declared an 'open city'. It was clear that her only hope of being of any use was to go south. No rail tickets were being issued that day. Nor the next, the 10th, nor on the 11th, nor the 12th. The Germans were expected to take over the city on the 13th (actually they arrived on June 14th). There was now nothing for it but to walk. Paris had emptied: cafes had closed; there were no taxis but the metro was still running. Shouldering her kitbag, she got as far as the Porte d'Orléans. Here she found herself among

> hundreds of thousands of people, all going South, pushing bicycles, hand-carts, wheelbarrows, boxes on wheels and even hospital trolleys, all piled high with bundles, yard-long loaves, cats in baskets, birds in cages, and with children and dogs trotting alongside, all jostling one another on the crowded road and completely holding up all motor traffic that tried to force a way through. It looked as though the whole population of Paris was moving out of the city. No panic, just grim determination to get away before the Germans came in. Their one clear aim was to reach the other side of the Loire.

It was hot, and progress was slow. Along with a number of children she got a lift on an army lorry travelling in convoy. 'At the top of a hill I looked forward and back to the solid mass of people, and began to picture the scene if German planes started machine-gunning as they had done in Belgium and Northern France.'

They crawled along so that by night time they had made only 15 kms. 'People camped by the roadside under improvised tents made from blankets or under their barrows.' She settled the children to sleep in the lorry and next morning the Army provided soup in bully-beef tins 'rather jagged round the edges'. She left the lorry to enquire about the situation, but when she got back it had gone, taking with it her kitbag containing her papers and nearly all her money. She found a message pinned to a tree, presumably for another straggler – 'se rendre à Malesherbes'. This was 45 kms further on. With the help of two short lifts she managed to get within 12 kms of Malesherbes. At 1 a.m. she burrowed into some hay and got a few hours' sleep. Then on again on foot – and to her joy she found her convoy, labelled with its white elephant badge, and finally her own lorry. The driver had been 'désolé' to leave her, but he had his orders as the Germans were now very close. The refugees were now a pitiable sight:

> Old people completely exhausted, young women pushing tiny children in broken-down prams piled high with bundles of their belongings. Cars were stranded, broken down or out of petrol. Several young mothers, seeing my uniform, knelt in the roadside at my feet and implored my help.

The convoy took on board 150 of the most needy 'but it was only a drop in the ocean'.

German planes were active that day, and for many days after. They had to stop frequently to put the old people under the lorry and throw the children into ditches or hedges. At Chateaudun 'the station was wrecked and the lines torn up and twisted, and there was not a soul in sight. Some of the people were glad that I was to continue with the convoy as by this time I had been adopted as their "infirmière" '.

Roads were now somewhat less crowded, but still refugees were everywhere. A deserted farm provided hens and rabbits and the women of the convoy were able to prepare a good meal.

On the evening of the fourth day they reached and crossed the Loire. The understanding had been 'If Paris falls, we hold the line of the Loire'. The refugees had been struggling to get that far. When they reached the Loire, the bridge was still intact, guarded by only one tired sentry, an inadequate barricade at one end and a few heaps of stones at the other 'that a child might have knocked over'.

Next day the Germans crossed the Loire. The bridges had never been blown. Armistice was declared. The people were absolutely stunned. Everyone thought the British would give in as well. Rolt told them she 'KNEW we would never surrender', and brought, she thought, 'a little comfort to those broken French people'.

It was clear that she would have to make every effort to get back to England. So she parted from her convoy, shouldering her kitbag, and again set off on foot. She left money to get comforts for the children and old people, and the driver presented her with a knife, a mug and a large hunk of bread, the most valuable gifts she could have had:

> It was now just a matter of keeping on – sleeping in barns or in woods or under haystacks, washing in streams, eating chunks of bread, and sometimes pâté or chocolate, with now and then some coffee or pinard or a mug of milk at a farm.

There was never a hope of a lift from civilian cars: they were all packed full. Her only hope was an army lorry, and she developed a technique:

> I would stand well out in the road, flap of coat turned back and chest thrown out displaying medals (with shame I confess it!) and hold up my hand authoritatively. It worked so well that French people whose presence had been ignored by driver after driver came and put themselves under my protection, and often I had to hand up whole families into the lorry before getting up myself.

She was immeasurably saddened to see French officers in their own cars leading the retreat and to see how readily they seemed to accept defeat. She compared this with the spirit she had witnessed in the First World War.

On the 12th day after leaving Paris (probably June 24th) she had got as far as Périgueux. A proper dinner at last, but she could only find a shakedown in a refugee centre for sleeping. She was very grateful for this, as it was

> pouring in torrents and I had been wet through already so many times in the last few days. It had not been much good changing because the contents of my kitbag were also soaked, and after I had spread my sopping garments out in the sun to dry during the hour's rest I allowed myself during the day, there had usually been another deluge which caught me on some unprotected road and the good work would be undone.

Next day a real bus took her 30 miles towards Bordeaux, but this was still 50 miles short. Lifts were becoming difficult. Army lorries were now under orders not to pick up civilians. Rolt, in uniform, was able to circumvent this to some extent by enlisting the help of a gendarme, though it could take as much as three hours. Possibly her Croix de Guerre medal was also helpful. In this way she finally reached Bordeaux.

In Bordeaux she made for the British Consulate. She was, of course, too late. They had all sailed for England, but a notice directed callers to the American Consulate. It had closed for the night. Here she found that the last boats for England had left some days previously. She was given accommodation in a hostel run by the Association des Dames de France. This,

Auxiliary nurse Rolt at the canteen at Soissons in 1917. Twenty-two years later, after the fall of France, and with the German army close behind her, she made her way alone from Paris to the Spanish border.
(By courtesy of Miss Heather Mackay).

she said, was the most uncomfortable night she had spent so far – none of the other occupants of the dormitory would allow any 'courants d'air' and she stifled.

Next day at the American Consulate she learned that Bordeaux was surrounded, and the Consul was very doubtful that he would be able to get her out:

> It was the worst moment of the whole 13 days. Up till then I had kept well ahead of the enemy – at least 15 to 20 kms – and here at the end of it all they had caught up! I began planning how to escape internment.

The Consul, however, finally found an uncovered iron tender used for hauling stone, and on this a few of them started off on the 200-km run to Bayonne mostly in pouring rain. Their hopes were dashed once more. Again, the last boats had sailed. The Spanish frontier was now closed and their only hope was the tiny port of St Jean de Luz. Here her luck finally turned. There on the quay stood two British sailors:

> Angels from Heaven. We knew we were now safe. We had no further doubts, but we dared not leave the quay in search of food or shelter from the rain and the howling gale that had now got up for fear of being left behind.

It was too rough to sail that night, but they managed to collect some bread and a bottle of wine, and by pooling resources got quite a good meal. Someone had some *confiture de marrons*, someone else sardines, and Rolt herself still had some Périgueux pâté. They were early on the quay next morning. All ports were to be closed by the French at noon.

The British began the boarding. Polish troops in their hundreds filled two of the three ships. The remainder went on the third boat:

> every kind of Ally, a most varied assortment of people claiming British nationality; foreign wives of British men, Palestinians, West Indians and people from all parts of the Empire. We were taken out in small boats and had to climb up a rope ladder, but the last man, woman, child and dog was on board with just twenty minutes to spare. Perhaps the less said about the journey the better. We were just a human cargo and the last one before us had been coal. The women slept in rows on the floor in the hold, the men in another part of the ship, and the troops in the stern; the Navy supplied us with bully-beef, biscuits and water. There were 800 of us ... There were two other Red Cross people on the boat and together we organised the distribution of food and water and did what was possible about sanitation and caring for the sick. Anyone who was ever night orderly in 'Millicent' will get a faint glimmering – but only a glimmering – of what things were like: but nothing seemed to matter since we had escaped.

With one alarm they were brought safely into harbour on the fourth day to a tremendous welcome:

> What chiefly struck me was the order and efficiency everywhere and the feeling of preparedness, so great a contrast to the awful chaos I had witnessed all the way from Paris to St Jean de Luz.

She concluded that if it had not been for the 'good old SWH uniform I do not think I could have made it in time to escape'.

Much of this account is in Rolt's own words and it is interesting to read what a friend said about her on her death in 1966. 'Although gentle and unassuming, she had a will of steel and possessed tremendous powers of endurance, never sparing of herself on behalf of others. It was her 'sheer guts' that got her through from Paris to the South of France, covering hundreds of miles by means of lifts and walking.'

Miss Ivens spoke for many when she said that 'Royaumont has not failed to hold out a helping hand to the sons of the generation whose comrades they were in the World War of 1914'.

Appendix One

Voluntary Hospitals serving in France (as listed in *Official History of the War. Medical Services*. HMSO 1923)

Under the British Red Cross

1. Duchess of Westminster's Hospital for Officers. 200–250 beds. September 1914 to 1918.
2. Officer's Hospital at Rouen. 200–250 beds. September 1914 to 1918.
3. Friends' Ambulance Unit, Abbeville. 50 beds. July 1915 to January 1916.
4. Sir Henry Norman's Hospital at Wimereux. 100 beds. November 1914 to December 1915.
5. Lady Hadfield's Anglo-American Hospital at Wimereux. 70 beds. December 1914 to 1918.
6. Liverpool Merchants' Hospital. 200 beds. Paris-Plage April 1915. Then 350 beds at Etaples November 1917 to June 1918. Then Trouville September to December 1918.
7. Lady Sarah Wilson's Allied Forces Base Hospital. 200 beds. Boulogne October 1914 to January 1915. Then Etaples August to November 1915.
8. Baltic and Corn Exchange Hospital. 105 beds. Calais October 1914. Later to Paris-Plage with 300 beds decreasing to 200. End of 1917 to January 1918 in Boulogne.
9. Millicent, Duchess of Sutherland's Hospital. In Belgium at outbreak of war, captured Namur August 1914. To Dunkirk with 100 beds November 1914. To Calais November 1915. To St Omer March 1918 – thereafter followed advance to victory.
10. Lady Murray's Hospital. 60 beds. Le Tréport November 1914 to June 1916.

Under St John's Ambulance

1. Etaples July 1915. 520 beds. Damaged with loss of life 19–31 May 1918. Opened Trouville October 1918. Closed March 1919.
2. Queen Alexandra's Hospital for Franco-Belgians. Dunkirk. 50 beds for British Sick.
3. Countess Dudley's Australian Voluntary hospital. 200 beds. September

1914 to Wimereux. Became a military hospital as it could not be maintained from voluntary sources.

Not listed in Official History

Women's Imperial Service League. In Claridge's Hotel, Paris, under predominantly female staff. Moved to Cherbourg and closed in March 1915. Subsequently Drs Flora Murray and Louisa Garrett Anderson (daughter of Elizabeth) were appointed by the War Office to run the military hospital in Endell Street, London. The staff were still predominantly female. This hospital closed only after the Armistice.

The Use of Voluntary Hospitals on the Outbreak of War

On September 9th, 1914 Surgeon-General Woodhouse wrote to Sir Arthur Slogget, Director-General of the Army Medical Services at the War Office:

> We have more unwieldy units at our disposal than we can use. We may send home, to be kept in reserve, three general and four stationary hospitals. We have nowhere to park them out here, and the billeting of hundreds of sisters causes a great nuisance. [He was, of course, referring to military hospitals but he went on:]
>
> The arrival, therefore, of voluntary units at that time would only have embarrassed and added difficulties to the medical administration.

In the light of these remarks could it be that Dr Elsie Inglis' rebuff from the War Office was not *entirely* anti-feminist, though it was an undoubted fact that the notion of an all-female staff held no appeal.

By 1915 it was becoming plain that the war was not going to end in the near future, and it was also plain that the supply of doctors was not unlimited. There was need to make full use of women to staff the two military hospitals in London, at Endell Street and in Fulham Road, and this need broke down many old prejudices. During the war there was an unprecedented increase in the number of women entering medical school, and many medical schools were opening their doors to women for the first time. Before the war there were approximately 1500 women medical students. In 1919 there were 3000. The battle was not won, however, as, with the exception of University College Hospital, all the other London hospitals closed their doors to women after the war. St George's Hospital closed in 1919; the London Hospital in 1924; and Charing Cross, Westminster and King's College Hospitals closed in 1928. Whatever the reasons put forward for restricting the entry of women to medicine, it could not be on the grounds of competence.

APPENDIX TWO

Gas Gangrene

Probably the most important contribution to the treatment of battle casualties made by the women doctors at Royaumont was in the field of gas gangrene. They showed how co-operation between physician, surgeon, bacteriologist and radiologist, combined with the use of specific anti-gas gangrene sera, could combat wound infection of this type with success. They could not have done this without the enthusiastic co-operation of Professor Weinberg of the Pasteur Institute in Paris who was widely recognised as the leading authority on the bacteriology of gas gangrene infections.

Michel Weinberg was a Russian by birth (see Chapter 9). After medical qualification he concentrated on laboratory work in the Pasteur Institute from 1900 till his death in 1940. On the outbreak of war he enlisted and devoted himself to the study of the anaerobic organisms of gas gangrene. His researches threw new light on the complicated bacteriology of these organisms. The next step was to prepare specific anti-gas gangrene sera appropriate to the different organisms and to evolve a suitable mixture for use in the field. This work occupied him for the next twenty years. He had great confidence in the ability of women doctors, a confidence which was fully justified. On their part they were alert to the fact that they were privileged to receive supplies of specific sera, and they recognised they had an obligation to record carefully the results of treatment. Miss Ivens herself published two papers in the medical press.[1,2]

Gas gangrene infections of wounds were particularly common in France, because the heavily manured soil of the battlefields contained high concentrations of the organisms responsible. In addition the nature of the injuries (from high-explosive shells and multiple injuries from machine-gun fire) resulted in soil and clothing, as well as metallic fragments, being driven deep into the tissues where they formed a nidus in which infection could readily develop.

Soon after the outbreak of hostilities the British GHQ issued a circular alerting the medical services to the condition, as it became clear that gas gangrene infection was going to be a serious problem, and one with which few medical officers would be familiar.[3]

The infection spreads rapidly after injury, with crepitation of the tissues indicating gas formation, discolouration of muscle, bronzing of the skin, oedema (swelling), and exudation of a foul-smelling fluid. Death of the tissues (gangrene) follows. The patient suffers vomiting, often severe, and collapse. Death follows rapidly once the infection is established. One of the most distressing features is that the mind remains perfectly clear until near the end. Dr Henry described this as 'often one of abnormal cheerfulness'.[4]

Writing in 1916, Dr Savill commented:

> The most terrible of all the horrors which come under the care of the surgeon in this war is undoubtedly gas gangrene. Dramatic in the suddenness of its onset, the rapidity of its advance, and the repulsiveness of its too frequently fatal outcome, it has reaped a cruel harvest of our young and vigorous manhood.[5]

From the early days a procedure was gradually developed at Royaumont whereby, on admission, cases were examined by one of the Assistant Medical Officers, case sheets were started with temperature and pulse recorded, clothes removed or cut off, and wounds cleaned. Cases were graded according to their apparent severity. Smears were taken from every wound and sent immediately to the laboratory for examination. The presence of gram-positive bacteria was reported back to the receiving ward as this indicated the presence of anaerobic, and possible gas gangrene, infection. Final identification of the organism took longer but treatment could not wait for a final identification. If gas gangrene was evident on admission but there was delay in getting the patient to the theatre, serum was administered in the receiving ward. Otherwise it was given in the theatre once the patient was anaesthetised. This was by intra-muscular or subcutaneous injection (into the axillae if possible) in saline. Cardiac stimulants were also given and sometimes rectal or intravenous saline. (Blood was not available.) The wounds were fully opened up, foreign bodies removed (shell fragments, pieces of cloth, loose pieces of bone, damaged muscle and blood clot) and drainage established using Carrell's tubes. Smears were taken from all the material removed and sent to the laboratory. Subsequently films and cultures were sent to the Pasteur Institute.

To reduce cross-infection as far as possible one theatre was reserved for the most severely infected cases, another for the less severe, and a third for those in whom gas gangrene was only a possibility.

The choice of serum depended partly on what was available at the time. The serum produced by Weinberg and his colleague Séguin (W and S) was active against *B. perfringens* (B. Welchii), *Vibrion septique* and *B. oedematiens*. The alternative serum, that of Leclanche and Vallée (L and V) was effective for the first two of these, but not for *B. oedematiens*. It had the advantage, however, of having some anti-streptococcal effect. Streptococcal infection was an extremely serious complication, and on occasions death was due to a streptococcal septicaemia after gas gangrene had been brought under control. Sometimes both sera were used. If a follow-up operation was necessary, it was always preceded by a repeat injection of serum, and repeat doses as long as necessary.

The x-ray appearances were described by the chief radiologist, Dr Agnes

Savill.[5] She analysed 100 plates of gas gangrene cases all taken during the summer of 1916 at Royaumont. By the end of July (the Somme rush having started on July 2nd) she was able to conclude that the presence of gas, its extent and situation as seen on the x-ray, was of great value to the surgeon. By September she was able to report on the probable variety of gas infection by x-ray appearances alone – information which could be of value before bacteriological examinations were complete. This was significant, as often at this stage the presence of gas was not detected clinically.

Miss Ivens published her first report, already mentioned, in 1916 when she analysed her cases from 1915 to October 1916, the end of the Great Push on the Somme. She described clearly the different types of gas infection she had observed and the operative and post-operative techniques she used, which must have been of great value to new doctors joining the forces. Anti-sera were then very scarce but she obtained sufficient to treat ten very seriously infected cases, all of whom might be expected to be fatal. Of these, five died, one from a septicaemia after the gas infection had subsided.

By 1918 the development of specific anti-sera had advanced and Miss Ivens was able to test her belief in the value of the preventive use of sera.[2] Between March 21st and September 6th, 1918, 3660 wounded were operated on, and 433 cases of gas infection, all severe, were treated. These 433 seriously infected cases were treated with different combinations of sera. There were 38 deaths, only seven of which were due to gas gangrene. Of these seven, three also had a streptococcal septicaemia, in itself a fatal condition.

One of the Assistant Surgeons, Dr L.M. Henry, wrote her MD thesis after the war[6] on the serum treatment of gas gangrene infections. She compared the period 1915 to 1917, when serum treatment was in its infancy, with 1918, by which time it had become much more developed. Comparing similar cases – fractured tibia and fibula – there were 40 cases in the earlier period with three deaths and 12 amputations. In 1918, out of 107 similar cases, there were five deaths, only one of which was due to gas gangrene; there were 10 amputations, six of which were due to gas gangrene.

A third series of patients from Royaumont were reported on by M. Delbet, to a French medical society in 1918.[7] Out of 1666 severely wounded patients admitted in June and July 1918, 155 were treated with anti-gas gangrene serum; 16 of these died, but not one of these was attributable to gas gangrene. During the same period there were eight deaths from gas infection, all of which occurred in patients who had not received serum owing to shortage of supplies.

The results of serum treatment reported from Royaumont compare favourably with others reported from French hospitals. For instance, G. Vitoux[8] reported a series of 81 cases with eight deaths due to gas gangrene although three of these died within four hours of admission. Sauquepée and de Lavergne[9] reported 136 cases treated with serum with a mortality of

16.9%. This they compared with a 75% mortality in cases receiving no serum. These papers do not provide details of other forms of treatment apart from the serum therapy, and it is possible that the superiority of Royaumont results may be due to the meticulous operative and post-operative care that was given.

At this distance in time it seems a reasonable conclusion.*

---

* Miss Ivens's 1918 paper includes a number of case histories which illustrate the nature of the problems with which they were dealing and the quality of their records. Case VI is one with a happy ending. 'M. was wounded at 9 a.m. on August 19th. There was a penetrating wound of the thigh with fracture of femur. At 10 p.m. on August 22nd excision of the wound, sequestrotomy with removal of the bullet was performed. A Thomas's splint was applied, and Leclanche and Vallée serum 30 c.cm was given. The following day there was a rise of temperature and pulse, and a bacteriologist report of *B. perfringens* was reported from the wound. The wound was freely opened up and Carrel tubes inserted. At night the condition of the patient was very grave. There was great swelling of the thigh (temperature 105.6, respirations 40), the pulse was uncountable and barely perceptible. A subcutaneous saline was given, with 30 c.cm of *mélange* (W and S) serum and 10 c.cm of camphorated oil. Early the following morning, though the thigh was enormously swollen, the patient was a little better. Amputation was performed above the seat of the fracture (circular with lateral incisions), while an intravenous saline was given; 30 c.cm of *mélange* were given subcutaneously and 10 c.cm of camphorated oil. The usual dressing of 5% salt and 2½% carbolic acid was applied. *B. perfringens* and a streptococcus were found in the wound. The following day there was decided improvement (pulse 120, temperature 100). A further dose of 30 c.cm *mélange* serum was given, and on August 29th 20 c.cm anti-*perfringens* serum. The patient made an excellent recovery.

Not every case, however, was successful. In Case VIII there were 'multiple infected shell wounds, with several fractures, and a wound of the left popliteal vein. The patient was wounded on July 25th at 3.30 a.m. and was admitted and operated on the same evening. Numerous projectiles were removed, including a large superficial one from the right thigh. Unfortunately no serum was given. The following morning the patient presented a blanched appearance. In the early afternoon the right thigh began to swell, crepitation extending on to the abdomen. A high amputation was performed, gas bubbling from the divided muscles; 30 ccs of *mélange* were given, with two pints of saline intravenously at the time of the operation, but had no effect on the ultimate issue, death taking place in a couple of hours. *B. perfringens* was isolated from the piece of shell and from the blood.' One might speculate that the outcome could have been different had blood transfusion been available.

References

1. Ivens, F.M. 'A Clinical Study of Anaerobic Wound Infection. Analysis of 107 Cases of Gas Gangrene', *Proc. Roy. Soc. Med. 1916—1917*, X Part 3, Surgical Section, 29—110.

2. Ivens, F.M., 'The Prevention and Curative Treatment of Gas Gangrene by Mixed Serums', *Brit. Med. J.* Oct 19, 1918, 425—427.

3. Bowlby, A.A. and Rowland, S., Field Laboratory GHQ, Nov 11th 1914.

4. Henry, L.M., 'The Treatment of War Wounds by Serum Therapy', MD Thesis, University of Sheffield, 1920.

5. Savill, A., *Archives of Radiology and Electrotherapy*, Vol XXI No. 7, December 1916.

6. Henry, L.M. *op. cit.*

7. Delbet P. *Presse Médicale*, Aug 29, 1918 (verbal communication).

8. Vitoux G., 'Results of Multi-serum Treatment', *Presse Médicale* 23, January 1919, 23.

9. Saquepée and de Lavergne, 'Treatment of Gas Gangrene by Specific Serums', *Presse Medicale*, 20 February, 1919, 85.

Bibliography

Brian Abel-Smith, *History of the Nursing Profession*. Heinemann 1960.

W. Alexander, *First Ladies of Medicine*. Wellcome Unit for the History of Medicine. University of Glasgow 1987.

Auntie Mabel's War: An account of her part in the hostilities, 1914–1918. Compiled by Marion Wengel and John Cornish. Allan Lane 1980.

Henri Barbusse, *Le Feu*. Flammarion 1965.

E. Moberly Bell, *Storming the Citadel. The Rise of the Woman Doctor*. Constable 1953.

Lawrence Binyon, *For Dauntless France. An Account of Britain's Aid to the Wounded and Victims of War*. Hodder and Stoughton 1918.

Catriona Blake, *The Charge of the Parasols. Women's Entry to the Medical Profession*. Women's Press 1990.

Gail Braybon, *Women Workers in the First World War. The British Experience*. Croom Helm 1981.

Roland Dorgeles, *Les Croix des Bois*. Albin Michel 1919.

Andrew Ducasse, Jaques Meyer, Gabriel Perieux. *Vie et Mort des Français, 1914–1918*. Hachette 1962.

Cicely Hamilton, *Life Errant*. Dent 1935.

B.H. Liddell Hart, *History of the First World War*. Cassell 1970.

Alastair Horne, *The Price of Glory: Verdun 1916*. Penguin Books 1964.

Alastair Horne, *Death of a Generation. Neuve Chapelle to Verdun and the Somme*. McDonald Library of the Twentieth Century 1970.

Isabel Hutton, *Memoirs of a Doctor in War and Peace*. Heinemann 1960.

M. Hutton-Neve, *This Mad Folly. The History of Australian Pioneer Women Doctors*. Library of Australian History 1980.

Imperial War Museum (Malcolm Brown), *The First World War* 1991.

Monica Krippner, *The Quality of Mercy*. David and Charles 1980.

Margot Lawrence, *Shadow of Swords. A Biography of Elsie Inglis*. Michael Joseph 1971.

Leah Leneman, *In the Service of Life: The Story of Dr Elsie Inglis and the Scottish Women's Hospitals*. Mercat Press 1994.

Leah Leneman, *The Guid Cause*. Mercat Press 1995.

Leah Leneman, 'Medical Women of the First World War – Ranking Nowhere.' 1993, *British Medical Journal, 307*, 1592–1594.

Leah Leneman, 'Medical Women at War, 1914–1918.' 1994, *Medical History, 38*, 160-177.

Andro Linklater, *An Unhusbanded Life. Charlotte Despard, Suffragette, Socialist and Sinn Feiner*. Hutchinson 1980.

Lyn Macdonald, *Roses of No Man's Land*. Michael Joseph 1980.

Lyn Macdonald, *Somme*. Michael Joseph 1983.

Lyn Macdonald, *They Called it Passchendaele*. Penguin 1993.

Lyn Macdonald, *1915: The Death of Innocence*. Headline 1993.

Eva Shaw McLaren, *A History of the Scottish Women's Hospitals*. Hodder and Stoughton 1918.

Redmond McLaughlan, *The RAMC*. Lee Cooper 1972.

Jessie Main, chapter on 'Nursing' in *Improving the Common Weal. Aspects of the Scottish Health Service, 1900 to 1984*, ed. Gordon McLaughlan. Edinburgh University Press 1987.

Louisa Martindale, *A Woman Surgeon*. Gollancz 1951.

Arthur Marwick. *The Deluge: British Society in the First World War*. Bodley Head 1965.

Arthur Marwick, *Women at War, 1914–18*. Croom Helm 1977.

John Masefield's Letters from the Front, 1915–1917, ed. Peter Vansittart. Constable 1984.

David Mitchell, *Women on the War Path: The Story of Women in the First World War*. Jonathan Cape 1966.

Flora Murray, *Women as Army Surgeons*. Hodder and Stoughton 1920.

Antonio de Navarro, *The Scottish Women's Hospital at the French Abbey of Royaumont*. Geo. Allan and Unwin 1917.

Official History of the War. Medical Services. 12 vols, ed. Major-General Sir W.G. Macpherson. HMSO 1923.

A.F. Savill, *Music, Health and Character*. John Lane 1923.

Denis Stuart, *Dear Duchess: Millicent, Duchess of Sutherland, 1867–1955*. Constable 1953.

John Terraine, *The Road to Passchendaele*. Leo Cooper 1984.

Liz Whitelaw, *The Life and Rebellious Times of Cicely Hamilton*. Women's Press 1990.

Leslie M. Williams, *No Easy Path: The Life and Times of Lilian Violet Cooper*. Brisbane 1991.

Index